encounters
with the
self second edition

encounters with the self
second edition

by
Don E. Hamachek
Michigan State University

Holt, Rinehart and Winston

New York Chicago San Francisco Dallas
Montreal Toronto London Sydney

Library of Congress Cataloging in Publication Data

Hamachek, Don E.
  Encounters with the self.

  Includes bibliographies.
  1. Self-perception. 2. Humanistic psychology.
I. Title.
BF697.H327   1978   155.2   77-19123
ISBN 0-03-019851-8

To Alice

You make a difference.
And it is good.

Preface

This is a book about self-concept. It is directed to that very private picture each of us has which reflects who we think we are, what we feel we can do, and how best we think we can do it. As in the first edition, this is a book about how this phenomenon called the self grows, changes, and expresses itself in behavior. Included in the book are discussions about what it means to understand one's self, a consideration of the perceptual theory and theorist undergirding some of the major ideas related to self-concepts, a look at some of the many ways in which we are self-consistent (sometimes without even knowing it), an examination of how self-concept is linked to physical growth, appearance, and development outcomes, and how it is related to family relationships and child-rearing practices, an overview of how self-concept is connected to school achievement and academic adjustment, along with some implications for teaching practices and some reflections concerning the encouragement and development of a healthy self-image.

The underlying philosophy of this book resides on a simple assumption, namely, the better we know ourselves the more able we will be to forget ourselves, for it is usually those things we do *not* know about ourselves, in terms of personal dynamics, that bog us down from time to time. I do not mean to suggest that this is in any sense a "self-help" or "self-analysis" type of book. I do hope, however, that it might be helpful in facilitating a bit more "self-awareness." With this in mind, I have attempted to write in a descriptive and explanatory manner as opposed to a style that might be viewed as prescriptive and theoretical. More specifically, I made a deliberate effort to present the content of this book in such a manner that it could be understood by readers who may be relatively unsophisticated in psychological jargon and terminology. I realize that not all people who read psychology books will end up in psychological work, and so a goal I had in mind as I planned and wrote this book was to reach a diverse audience with diverse interests, who, among other things, were curious about who they were as individuals and how they got to be the way they are.

It may be no great revelation for you to learn that the things I have chosen to study and include in this volume are things I have been curious about for a long time. My own search for an identity that fit, my own curiosities about self-consistency or lack of it, my own questions about the way my parents reared me and the impact they had (and have) on my behavior and self-attitudes, my queries about the connections between how well or how poorly I did in certain school subjects and the relation these had to my own self-concept of ability at different points in time—indeed, my own need to have some kind of unifying theme or framework that would facilitate a better understanding of my own and other persons' behavior—these questions and many others stimulated the ideas and content of the book and helped to make writing it generally more adventure-like than task-like.

The scope of this volume is broad, including as it does ideas about self-consistency, growth and development, child-rearing practices, academic achievement as related to self-concept, and so on, but the ideas all fit under the same theoretical umbrella, which, for me at least, provides the sort of unifying framework and "tying together" I find necessary to operate at some level of effectiveness as a teacher and therapist. The theoretical umbrella evolves from a frame of reference which has been variously called the "phenomenological," "perceptual," "existential," "interactional," or "humanistic-perceptual" approach. It is a point of view in psychological circles that is sometimes referred to as the "new look" as "third force," which simply means that this is another way of looking at behavior other than in strictly behavioristic or psychoanalytic terms. More succinctly, it is a point of view which looks at human behavior not only through the eyes of an outsider, but through the eyes of the person doing the behaving. It is a psychology searching to understand what goes on inside us—our needs, wants, desires, feelings, values, and unique ways of perceiving and understanding that cause us to behave the way we do. In an everyday sense, it is the psychology concerned friends use as they wonder why we're "looking so sad"; in a clinical sense; it is what therapists use as they probe for the deeper meanings behind what personal experiences mean to the client.

The book has an extensive base drawn from both empirical and clinical sources. A great many exciting research discoveries have occurred since the first edition of this book appeared, and I have made every effort to up-date and revise this volume so it reflects the advancements we have made in recent years. I really do not think that a book related to self-concept has to be just one kind of presentation, and in keeping with this notice I have made a deliberate effort to blend the hard data of empirical research with the "softer" findings of clinical discoveries. From time to time, I found it helpful to illustrate certain ideas with examples drawn from my own or others' clinical experiences, which I hope you will find clarifying and interesting.

I hope that this book can be a useful source in courses concerned with the preparation of teachers, counselors, mental hygienists, social workers, school psychologists, child development specialists, and researchers interested in understanding humans both as they view themselves and are acted on by forces outside themselves. If you have questions about who you are and how you arrived at being the sort of person you are at this point in time, I would hope that this volume might be one small step en route to answering those questions and stimulating you to read more widely and more deeply in developing insights into yourself and others. (The references of related interests at the end of each chapter are intended to help guide your further reading.)

I would like to extend a sincere thank-you to Professors Randy Isaacson (Indiana University, South Bend), Albert Noguchi (Contra Costa College), Melgola Ross (University of Cincinnati), Jeanne Wagenfeld (Western Michigan University), and to Joanne R. Whitmore (George Peabody College for Teachers) for their critical reviews of the manuscript and very helpful suggestions for its improvement.

D. E. H.

December 1977

Contents

Know thyself. A Yale undergraduate left on his door a placard for the janitor on which was written, "Call me at 7 o'clock; it is absolutely necessary that I get up at seven. Make no mistake. Keep knocking until I answer." Under this he had written: "Try again at ten."

William Lyon Phelps (1865–1945)

Toward Understanding
One's Self

PROLOGUE

We humans are interesting, paradoxical creatures. Think about it. It is
sometimes easier for us to be friendly to a person we don't like than it is
to be loving to a person we care for deeply. We look in the mirror hoping
for an image of what we want to be only to be disappointed when it simply
reflects what we are. We can characterize what we are against, but we frequently have trouble specifying what we are for. We love what we want,
but once we have it we do not necessarily love what we get. We can identify what we've done, but we're not always sure why we did it in the first
place. We can see where we are, but we're not always certain how we got
there. We can tell people our names, but have questions about our identities. We find it easier to explain what we do than to explain who we are.

Indeed, in each of our individual pursuits for answers, values, a personal life style that fits, we are inescapably confronted with the problem of meaning—with the question of what life is all about.

Ultimately, each of us is faced with three questions that must be answered to our satisfaction if we are to grow to greater personal maturity:

Who am I?
Where am I going?
What route shall I take?

These are important questions, dealing as they do with our goals, our values, our real and imagined strengths and weaknesses, and our particular life style. But mostly they are important because they deal with this personal inner etching we call our sense of self.

What is the self? What are its different components? How does it differ from the ego? How is the self related to different ego states? How does the self grow and how do we defend its integrity? Why should some persons want to resist personal growth? Let's turn our attention now to these other issues related to understanding one's self.

The Self and Its Related Components

Interest in the self, what it is and how it develops, is not a recent phenomenon. As a theoretical concept, the self has ebbed and flowed with the currents of philosophical and psychological pondering since the seventeenth century when the French mathematician and philosopher, René Descartes, first discussed the "cognito," or self, as a thinking substance. With Descartes pointing the way, the self was subjected to the vigorous philosophical examinations of such thinkers as Leibnitz, Locke, Hume, and Berkeley. As psychology evolved from philosophy as a separate entity, the self, as a related construct, moved along with it. However, as the tides of behaviorism swept the shores of psychological thinking during the first forty years of this century, the self all but disappeared as a theoretical or empirical construct of any stature. Study of the self was not something which could be easily investigated under rigidly controlled laboratory conditions. As a consequence, the subject was not considered an appropriate one for scientific pursuit. Nonetheless, the concept was kept alive during the early part of the twentieth century, by such men as Cooley,[1] Mead,[2] Dewey,[3] and James.[4] During the period since World War II, the concept of self has been revived and has exhibited remarkable vitality. For example, Allport writes:

> In very recent years the tide has turned. Perhaps without being fully aware of the historical situation, many psychologists have commenced to embrace what two decades ago would have been considered a heresy. They have re-introduced self and ego unashamedly and, as if to make up for lost time, have employed ancillary concepts such as self-image, self-actualization, self-affirmation, phenomenal ego, ego-

involvement, ego-striving, and many other hyphenated elaborations which to experimental positivism still have a slight flavor of scientific obscenity.[5]

The Self, Self-Concept, and Self-Esteem

Self, self-concept, and self-esteem are overlapping terms and each refers to a particular component of a person's total personality. The *self*, as we will use it here, is that part of each of us of which we are consciously aware. *Self-concept* refers to that particular cluster of ideas and attitudes we have about our awareness at any given moment in time. Or, another way of looking at it is to view our self-concept as the organized cognitive structure derived from experiences of our own self. Thus, out of our awareness of ourselves grow the ideas (concepts) of the kind of person we see ourselves as being. Whereas self-concept is the cognitive part of the self, we might view *self-esteem* as the affective portion of the self. That is, not only do we have certain ideas about who we are, but we have certain *feelings* about who we are. Our self-esteem, then, refers quite literally to the extent to which we admire or value the self. Out of all of this emerges what we commonly refer to as *personality*. You can begin to see why personalities differ so greatly among individuals. Different people have different levels of awareness of the self, different ideas about their awareness, and, as a consequence, different feelings about themselves as persons.

Acquiring a self-concept involves a slow process of differentiation as a person gradually emerges into focus out of his total world of awareness and defines progressively more clearly just who and what he is. Jersild is probably as clear as anyone about what the self is when he says:

> A person's self is the sum total of all he can call his. The self includes, among other things, a system of ideas, attitudes, values, and commitments. The self is a person's total subjective environment; it is the distinctive center of experience and significance. The self constitutes a person's inner world as distinguished from the outer world consisting of all other people and things.[6]

As the *self* has evolved in psychological literature, it has come to have two distinct meanings. From one point of view it is defined as a person's attitudes and feelings about himself, and from another it is regarded as a group of psychological processes which influence behavior and adjustment. The first meaning can be looked at as a *self-as-object* definition, as it conveys a person's attitudes, feelings, and perceptions of himself as an object. That is, it is as if one could stand outside of himself and evaluate what he sees from a more or less detached point of view. In this sense, the self is what a person thinks of himself. The second meaning may be called the *self-as-process* definition. In other words, the self is a doer, in the sense that it includes an active group of processes such as thinking, remembering, and perceiving.

It is through the door of the self that one's personality is expressed. How the self is expressed is a complex phenomena conveyed in different ways by different people. It is one person's brashness and another person's shyness; it is one person's loving nature and another person's vindictive attitude; it is one person's openness and another person's guardedness. An individual's image of himself is constructed from his conception of the "sort of person I am." All of us have beliefs about our relative value and our ultimate worth. We feel superior to some persons but inferior to others. We may or may not feel as worthy or as able as most other individuals, and much of our energy is spent trying to maintain or modify our beliefs about how adequate we are (or would like to be).

William James, a psychologist both of and beyond his time, has observed that how a person feels about himself depends entirely on what he *backs* himself to be and do. For example, in a famous passage James wrote:

> I am not often confronted by the necessity of standing by one of my empirical selves and relinquishing the rest. Not that I would not, if I could, be both handsome and fat and well-dressed, and a great athlete, and make a million a year, be a wit, a bon-vivant, and lady-killer, as well as a philosopher, a philanthropist, statesman, warrior, and African explorer, as well as a "tone-poet" and saint. But the thing is simply impossible. The millionaire's work would run counter to the saint's; the bon-vivant and the philanthropist would trip each other up; the philosopher and lady-killer could not keep house in the same tenement of clay . . . to make any one of them actual, the rest must more or less be suppressed . . . . So the seeker of his truest, strongest, deepest self must review the list carefully, and pick out the one on which to stake his salvation. All other selves thereupon become unreal, but the fortunes of this self are real. Its failures are real failures, its triumphs real triumphs, carrying shame and gladness with them . . . .
>
> I, who for the time have staked my all on being a psychologist, am mortified if others know more psychology than I. But I am contented to wallow in the grossest ignorance of Greek. My deficiencies there give me no sense of personal humiliation at all.[7]

I think it is clear from the above quotation that how James felt about himself depended, in large measure, on how he saw himself ranking in comparison to others *who also backed themselves to be psychologists.* In other words, we might generalize that our feelings of self-worth and self-esteem grow in part from our perceptions of where we see ourselves standing in relation to persons whose skills, abilities, talents, and aptitudes are similar to our own.

Psychologists David Mettee and John Riskin[8] found some interesting experimental evidence for this by pitting pairs of college women against each other in written tests. After revealing the results of the tests, they asked each woman whether she liked her partner. To their surprise they found that the woman who was decisively beaten by her partner tended to like that partner. But the woman who was only marginally defeated generally disliked her partner. The probable reason for this outcome is that the woman who was defeated by a wide margin didn't really compare herself to her competitor, because she saw the other person as too different from herself for comparison. But the woman who was defeated by only a slight margin perceived herself as worse than her competitor. This threatened her self-esteem, and in defense she developed a strong dislike for her competitor. Mettee and Riskin speculate that the most accurate and hence most potent comparison information is derived from people who are similar to us. When we perceive others as greatly dissimilar, they are perceived as incomparable. This comparable–incomparable distinction allows people to screen out much negative information about themselves, because the only information that really "counts" comes from comparable people. Thus, C students tend to compare themselves with other C students and A students compare themselves with other A students. The point is, most of us ''back'' ourselves to be at least as good as most others in one or two areas and the reference group we use for comparison purposes will tend to be more like us than unlike us. We might add, too, that this same comparable–incomparable defense system is used to protect us from the achievements of persons we may regard as inferior. For example, if an individual is outperformed by somebody he perceives as far inferior to himself, the performance can be dismissed as an isolated incident. Self-esteem is not apt to suffer much because of the tendency to consider the inferior person too far below us for comparison.

All in all, the groups we compare ourselves with play an important part in helping us sort through how we feel and think about ourselves. As high self-esteem usually comes from being able to do one or two things at least as good as, if not a trifle better than, most other people, it would be difficult to maintain, not to mention enhance, self-esteem if we compared ourselves with persons who were obviously either too superior or too inferior to ourselves in accomplishment. In the first case it's a losing battle, while in the second case it's a hollow victory.

What we set as our personal levels of aspirations are also important to our feelings of self-esteem because they help establish what we regard as either success or failure. What is a success or enhancing experience for one can be a failure or deflating experience for another. For example, I remember I received a C in an undergraduate course which I regarded as particularly difficult. That C, however, was quite consistent with my expectations and level of aspiration for performance, and I felt it was a minor, if not a major, success. On the other hand, a friend of mine who also received a C in that course viewed this as a total failure, because his expectations and level of aspiration were not lower than a B. In other words, by getting that C I maintained my self-esteem, because it was an even money return on my personal investment in the course. My friend lost a measure of self-esteem, *because the return was less than his personal investment.* By starting out with different amounts of personal investment, we had different expectations for a personal return in order to maintain our original investments. In a similar vein, both of us could have enhanced our self-esteem if we had received a grade which *exceeded* our original levels of aspiration.

Although each person's level of aspiration determines to a large extent what he interprets as failure or success, and hence what either adds to or takes from his self-esteem, another factor worth considering is one's history of successes and failures. For example, to fail at something is more tolerable and less apt to threaten our self-esteem if we have had a history of success in that particular endeavor. Some cases in point: a girl who has had many boyfriends is not likely to sour on boys if she loses one, but a girl with few boyfriends could; a team with a 10-0 record is not apt to give up after losing the eleventh game, but a 0-10 team might; a .350 baseball player is not particularly discouraged when he strikes out, but a .150 player is; a student with a long string of above average grades is not likely to quit school if he fails his first course, but a below average student who fails his tenth course might. In other words, the impact of falling short of one's personal aspirations stands to be a

If we set realistic levels of aspiration in the beginning, we are less likely to be disappointed in the end.

less self-deflating experience if one's list of successes in that endeavor exceeds one's tally of failures.

In summary, then, the self is what we *know* about ourselves, self-concept is what we *think* about ourselves, and self-esteem is how we *feel* about ourselves.

There is another aspect of the self we need to consider. It goes by a different name and is arrived at by a different process.

The Ego

Although there is no single, universally accepted definition of the self, most psychologists accept a distinction between two major facets of the self—one of which the person himself is aware and one inferred by an external observer. The *inferred self* is that dimension of the self commonly called the *ego,* a term borrowed from Freud, though not adhering exactly to the Freudian definition. When we talk about the ego we're referring to that portion of personality structure that embodies the core of decision-making, planning, and defensiveness. We call the ego the inferred self because it can be best understood by an external observer (who, in fact, may detect unconscious features of which the individual is unaware). Thus, the ego is a construction from behavior, a hypothetical construct that, though it cannot be directly observed, can be inferred from one's behavior. For example, we speak of a person as having a weak or a strong ego based on how we have observed that person behave under given conditions. The ego is the primary agent of personality which is inferred on the basis of certain observed effects. In a sense, our concept of ego is similar to our concept of electricity, that is, even though we cannot see electricity we can still know what it does by defining it in terms of its functions and effects. Just as we can assess electric current as weak or strong, in terms of its effects on fuses, gauges, or light bulbs, so we can estimate one's ego as being strong or weak in terms of certain behavioral expressions. Indeed, just as an electrical line can be overloaded to the point of blowing an electrical fuse, so, too, can a person's ego be overloaded to the point of blowing an emotional fuse. When this happens we usually hear about it in terms of an individual "exploding with anger" or even experiencing a nervous breakdown. Lingering depression, feelings of a slow but building anger, or even consistent fatigue are three of the more common symptoms a person is apt to feel when ego boundaries are being stretched to an emotional breaking point.

In the language of psychoanalytic psychology, personality is usually thought of as having three distinct components: the *id*, the *ego,* and the *superego.* The id is unconscious and is the source of basic urges and impulses. The id, according, to Freud, "has no organization and unified will, only an impulsion to obtain satisfaction for the instinctual needs in accordance with the pleasure principle . . . the id knows no value, no good and evil, no morality."[9] In a manner of speaking, it is that part of each of us that demands vengeance if we are hurt or immediate gratification if we want something. The superego is synonymous with conscience and is at the other extreme of what has been termed the id. Freud has defined the superego as "the representative of all moral restrictions, the advocate of the impulse toward perfection; in short, it is as much as we have been able to apprehend psychologically of what people call the 'higher' things in human life."[10] It is that part of each of us which may say, "No, you shouldn't," if vengeance is our goal or "No, you mustn't," if immediate gratification of a harmful impulse is our objective. This is where our ego comes into play. The ego is that part of personality which is in contact with external reality. It is responsible for perceiving inner and outer reality, for regulating behavior, and for controlling our impulses. Think of it this way: the ego is the personality's executive secretary whose job it is to screen and temper the demands and impulses of the id and superego before those demands and impulses are expressed in behavior. When we say that a person has a weak ego, we are also saying that he finds it difficult to check his impulses, or he has low frustration tolerance, or he has a hard time postponing gratification, or he can be easily hurt, or any combination of these possibilities. In other words, a strong ego can more successfully hold id–superego demands in check in order to achieve a healthy balance between what we want and what we can have. In short, the ego perceives, tests reality, selects, and rejects behavior patterns. It is responsible for learning and for the control and suppression of basic impulses.

This has been one way to understand the concept, ego, and its basic functions. It is primarily a psychoanalytic view and influenced heavily by Freudian tradition. There is still another way to understand ego functioning and this is through an examination of three different "ego states" that exist in all of us.

Ego States: Child, Parent, and Adult

The idea of the ego's being divided into three separate but related parts is an outgrowth of the work of the late Eric Berne, who started out as a traditional Freudian analyst and who ended up fathering a new creative approach to psychotherapy known as *Transactional Analysis*. This is an approach to psychotherapy, by the way, which focuses on an analysis of what people do and say to one another. An important part of Transactional Analysis is what Berne has called *Structural Analysis,* which is, quite literally, a study of the structure of personality. This sort of analysis is one way of answering the questions: Who am I? How did I get this way? Why do I act the way I do? More specifically, it is an approach to analyzing a person's thoughts, feelings, and behavior, based on the idea that each individual has three different ego states.[11]

As Berne conceptualized them, a person's Child, Parent, and Adult ego states are neither roles nor are they concepts like Superego, Ego, and Id. They are, rather, "phenomenological realities."[12] To say that they are phenomenological realities means that they can be directly observed in oneself and in others. Another way of looking at it is to view our three ego states as voices within us. When we pay attention and listen carefully we can usually tell which of the three ego states is dominant at any particular moment. Our Child ego state may say things like: "I want what I want when I want it," or "I hope I get a high grade on that test," or "Try and make me!". Our Parent ego state may say things like: "I should study tonight," or "I better not smoke so much," or "I ought to clean up my room." Our Adult ego state is still different and prefers to operate on facts, not feelings. It's likely to say things like: "How can I ask Bonnie for a date," or "Here is a formula for solving that problem," or "What is the best way for getting my work done so I can go to a movie?"

According to Berne's Structural Analysis, an individual's personality can be schematically drawn as in figure 1.1.

The three ego states can be defined as follows:

The *Child ego state* contains all the impulses and behaviors that come naturally to an infant. It also contains the recordings of early life experiences and how we responded to them. When you are feeling and acting as you did as a child, you are in your Child ego state. Indeed, when you feel yourself behaving in a child-like way, it very likely is your Child ego state kicking up its heels.

The *Adult ego state* operates as an information-gatherer and is not at all related to a person's age. It is that part of you which organizes and assimilates information in order to seek solutions and solve problems. It functions by testing reality, assessing consequences, and figuring out ways to get things done. When you are dealing with current reality, gathering information, and thinking objectively, you are in your Adult ego state.

The *Parent ego state* contains the attitudes, behaviors, and values incorporated from external sources, parents or parent-figures being the primary inputs. Outwardly, your Parent ego state is expressed when you are behaving in critical or nurturing ways. Inwardly, it is experienced as old Parental messages which continue

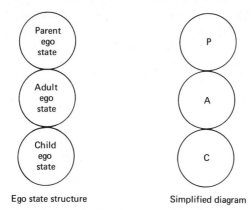

Ego state structure   Simplified diagram

to influence your inner Child. When you are behaving, thinking, and feeling as your parents did, you are in your Parent ego state.

These ego state definitions are consistent with Berne's more formal definition of ego state, which he described as: "A consistent pattern of feeling and experience directly related to a corresponding consistent pattern of behavior."[13] Each ego state is triggered by the playback of recorded past experiences, involving real people, real times, real places, and real feelings.

Brain Recordings As Related to Ego States

The idea for a person's ability to "play back," as it were, certain buried life experiences and past events was observed over forty years ago by neurosurgeon Wilder Penfield,[14] who found that electrode stimulation to different parts of the brain evoked long-forgotten memories and feelings. In order to more clearly define the boundaries where defective cortical tissue (the outer surface of the brain) was located, Penfield developed an electric-probe technique. This was done by removing the section of the skull covering the area where the defective tissue was suspected to be, restoring the patient to consciousness in the operating room, and then asking the patient to describe his sensations as electrodes were placed in various parts of the brain. (Since the brain contains no nerve endings to record pain, the patient suffers no discomfort in such tests.) What Penfield and other neurosurgeons have discovered is that cortical stimulation can evoke not only memories of past events but also the feelings that were associated with those events. In one case, for instance, a woman who was experiencing electrode stimulation just above her ear (an area associated with memory) suddenly reported that she felt transported back to her early childhood. In the operating room, she essentially relived an experience out of her remote and forgotten past, even feeling again the same fear that had accompanied the original event.[15]

It has further been noted that the electrically induced events always appear to be real even though the patient has not consciously been carrying them in his memory. The induced recollection can be stopped abruptly by turning off the electrode, and often restarted by turning it on again. When restarted, a fascinating feature is that the recalled event never continues where it left off, but, rather, starts again from the beginning, as though it were stored on a tape or film that automatically rewinds with each interruption. Berne has observed that ". . . in this respect the brain functions like a tape recorder to preserve complete experiences in serial sequence, in a form recognizable as 'ego states'—indicating that ego states comprise the natural way of experiencing and of recording experiences in this totality."[16]

Perhaps the most significant finding in Penfield's work is that not only are past events recorded in detail, but so, too, are the feelings associated with those events. Thus, an experience and the particular feeling associated with it are interwoven together in the brain so that one cannot be elicited without the other. As Penfield describes it:

> The subject feels again the emotion which the situation originally produced in him, and he is aware of the same interpretations, true or false, which he himself gave to the experience in the first place. Thus, evoked recollection is not the exact photographic or phonographic reproduction of past scenes or events. It is reproduction of what the patient saw and heard and felt and understood.[17]

The implications here are enormous because it means that what happens to a person is recorded and stored in his brain and nervous tissue. This includes our childhood experiences, all that we incorporate from parents and parent-figures, our perceptions of life events, and the feelings associated with those events. These experiences are stored as though they were recordings on a videotape. They can be replayed and experiences recalled and even relived. "Consciousness," to quote William James, "is never quite the same in successive moments of time. It is a stream forever flowing, forever changing."[18] The stream of changing states of mind that James captured so well does indeed flow through our waking hours until the time when we fall asleep to wake no more. But the stream, unlike a river, leaves a record in the living brain that serves as a seedbed for the growth, development, and ultimate expression of our ego states in everyday behavior.

Ego States Are Objective Realities

You can see why the three ego states we've been talking about are realities and not just abstract concepts. As Berne observed, "Parent, Adult, and Child represent real people who now exist or who once existed, who have legal names and civic identities."[19] Understanding our ego states is a way for understanding ourselves better because we can begin to see the link between past experience and current reality. An example of how this self-understanding can be used in a constructive way is nicely illustrated by a thirty-three-year-old client of mine who learned to control his temper tantrums by recognizing the ego state he was in while having them. The tantrums could be about anything and directed at almost anyone; wife and co-workers were favorite targets. He came to understand that he was still doing at age thirty-three what had been highly successful—in terms of getting his own way—when he was three. When things didn't go his way he would kick, scream, and throw things. Mother and father usually gave in to him. As an adult male he was still doing the same thing except now he was getting into more trouble because more people resisted that sort of behavior. The final straw came the day he accidently hit his wife with a pan while in the midst of one of his tantrums. Now when he feels like screaming and throwing things he recognizes that he is in his Child ego state, with the potential for feeling and doing all the things he used to do as a young child. It is at that point that he decides to be more adult and, quite literally, moves into his Adult ego state. This is, by the way, one of the nice benefits of self-understanding—you can *choose* to be different because you are aware of more options from which to choose. My client does not get any less angry, but he handles it differently. By deciding to be more adult about it he is now better able to state his feelings rather than screaming them. And everyone is happier.

To summarize and simplify, your Child is your feeling and intuitive side. It's that part of you that likes ice cream cones and fun at parties. Your Parent is made up of learned "tapes" in your head about what is right and wrong, good and bad, moral and immoral, and how you should or "ought" to act. It's that part of you that cares deeply for a loved one or admonishes a child for not looking both ways before crossing the street. And your Adult is the data-processing, decision-making, "computer" side. It's that side of you that balances the checkbook or figures out how to prepare for an exam.

Think of each of these ego states as connected by semi-permeable membranes through which psychic energy can flow freely from one to the other. These ego boundaries must be semi-permeable, otherwise psychic energy becomes contained in one ego state and unable to move spontaneously as situations change. When this happens a person finds himself giving up the emotional and cognitive flexibility so necessary for healthy day-to-day living. Some persons, for instance, use one particular ego state constantly and exclude the other two. The individual who operates primarily from the Child ego state may be fun-loving and even adventuresome, but he is also inclined to be irresponsible and undependable. The Constant Child looks for someone to take care of him. The man or woman who wants to be taken care of, babied, punished, rewarded, or applauded is likely to seek out a Constant Parent who will take care of those needs. Indeed, the person who does operate from a Constant Parent often treats others, even peers, as though they were children. One type of Constant Parent is a hardworker, has a strong sense of duty, and frequently seeks positions of power. This is the sort of person who may be critical of others, judgmental, and moralistic. He is the kind who usually has ready advice for how we "should" behave. Another type of Constant Parent is the perpetual nurturer or rescuer who seems to have a singular dedication to helping others. Either consciously or unconsciously the Constant Parent is inclined to collect people who are willing to be dependent upon or subordinate to him. The person who behaves mainly as a Constant Adult is quite different from the two we've looked at so far. Here we have a person who is consistently objective and concerned primarily with facts and information processing. He may come across to others as one who is essentially unfeeling and uncaring. As others are having fun at a party, he may be off to the side trying to figure out *why* they're having fun. The Constant Adult frequently has job-related problems if he is given a position supervising others. With little of the fun-loving Child or caring Parent, his relationships are likely to be overly professionalized or objective and, hence, sterile. As a high school principal expressed it to me in a moment of insight about his own Constant Adult behavior: "I think one of my problems is that I've been so busy trying to find answers to my staff's problems that I've neglected to understand their feelings."

Each of these ego-states, then, is a necessary and important aspect of healthy behavior. Indeed, in a healthy person there is a rational, decision-making Adult that seeks answers, a Parent whose teachings help us make judgments about good, bad, right, and wrong, and a Child that permits us to feel things and experience emotions and pleasure. These are all part of what we have defined as the self. Which leads us to ask an important question.

How Does the Self Become Known?

William James once described an infant's consciousness as a "big, blooming, buzzing confusion." Although the accuracy of this description may never be determined, it nonetheless seems pretty certain that the young infant's consciousness includes no awareness of himself as an individual. It also seems pretty clear from contemporary research that an infant's consciousness in terms of his personality development and educational potential begins at a very tender age. Burton White, Harvard psychologist, concluded seventeen years of research on the behavior and development of infants between birth and three years of age with an important book titled, *The First Three Years of Life*. One of his major conclusions: ". . . our studies show that the period that starts at eight months and ends at three years is a period of primary importance in the development of a human being."[20] An infant or young child surely cannot know himself very well, but he can express himself, which is the beginning basis for how others respond to him. Since we cannot directly assess the nature of a child's growing awareness, we must appraise the stages through which a child becomes aware of himself largely through an inferential process.

Beginnings of Awareness

Self-awareness develops slowly as the child recognizes the distinction between self and not-self, between his body and the remainder of his visible environment. Only gradually does he learn to recognize and sort out his body parts, name, feelings, and behavior as integral parts of a single *me* and build a cluster of beliefs about himself.

His serendipitous discoveries of the various parts of his body and the recognition of his own voice are the beginnings of his growing awareness of personal properties and resources. It seems likely that a child's body-awareness furnishes a common core around which self-reference becomes organized, although later he does learn to distinguish self from the physical body. From his behavior we can reasonably infer that soon after he is born he is flooded with a wave of sensory impressions—sensations that exist in his body when he's hungry, sensations from the surface of his body when it is hot or cold, sensations that reach him through his eyes and ears, and probably also sensations of taste and smell. As near as can be judged from a child's earliest reactions, he is not at first able to make a clear distinction between his early sensory experiences and the stimuli which elicit them. For example, if you touch a hot stove you know what is causing the pain. When something hot touches an infant he probably doesn't know where the pain comes from. The birth of self-awareness very likely occurs when a child begins to make a distinction between his sensations and the conditions which produce them.

As a growing child's experiences broaden, his sense of personhood gradually extends to include things outside of himself with which he feels personal involvement. When we think of *me* or *my*, we may include such things as our home, possessions we own, groups we are loyal to, the values we subscribe to, and, most particularly, the people we love. The process of identification is an important part of coming to know and expand one's definition of self. Allport describes this process more fully:

> A child . . . who identifies with his parent is definitely extending his sense of self, as he does likewise through his love for pets, dolls, or other possessions, animate or inanimate . . . .

> As we grow older we identify with groups, neighbors, and nation as well as with possessions, clothes, and home. They become matters of importance to us in a sense that other people's families, nations, or possessions are not. Later in life the process of extension may go to great lengths, through the development of loyalties and interests focused on abstractions and on moral and religious values.[21]

Influence of Social Roles and Others' Expectations

To some extent, our sense of identity is influenced by other peoples' appraisal of the social roles we happen to be in. For example, if the group regards us as a leader, a solid Joe, a follower, a good athlete, or a social rum-dum, we are likely to regard ourselves in the same way. In other words, we tend to adopt the values and attitudes that are expected of one in our position. In so doing, we begin to get a certain kind of feedback; this in turn reinforces how we feel about ourselves. I recall a student I had some years ago who was elected chairman of a group of about fifteen students whose assignment it was to work as a total group on a research paper which the chairman would present to the whole class. The lad chosen was a shy, quiet sort of person, I thought, but he did such a remarkable job of presenting the paper that the entire class broke into spontaneous applause when he concluded. (I think it may be that most students are so prepared to be bored by dull presentations made by their peers that violations of their expectations are welcome reliefs indeed.) After class I expressed to the young man what a great job I thought he had done and he responded with something like this: "You know, I was scared to death. I didn't think I could do it! But then I got to thinking about it and I figured that if they wanted me to be a chairman, I'd *act* like a chairman—even if I had to fake it. And you know, that's what I did—faked it. From our first meeeting on I just took charge like I had all the confidence in the world. And you know, a strange thing happened. The other kids in the group began to treat me as if I really *was* confident. They seemed to expect me to have answers and be able to organize and pretty soon I didn't know if I was faking it or if that's the way I really felt." Not only did this student learn that he had potential leadership abilities, which was an important discovery in itself, but *he also learned that how he behaved influenced how others behaved toward him.* Although, in this boy's words, he had to "fake" the initial leadership behavior, it may be important for us to remember that all the faking in the world would not have helped his cause if he did not have leadership potential to begin with. By "faking it" he discovered in himself latent qualities which had always been there.

The idea of a person responding in terms of what he thinks another person expects of him is not a new one, but it has been receiving increasing attention as a phenomenon in psychological research. For example, Rosenthal[22] and Friedman,[23] have demonstrated that at least one very important variable which has not been controlled in past psychological experimentation is the variable of *what the experimenter expects to happen.* In other words, the result the scientist *expects* to get is more likely to occur than any other. Haimowitz has extended the "expectation for behavior" idea to an examination of how criminals are "made" and writes:

> Gradually, over the years, if he (the Criminal) comes to expect of himself what his neighbors expect of him, he becomes a professional criminal. . . . As a professional criminal, he has standards to live up to, friends who will help him when in trouble, . . . tell him where the police are lax and where strict . . . At twelve, fourteen, sixteen, or eighteen he has come to a conclusion about his career that ordinary boys may not make until they are twenty or even forty. And he could not have drifted into his career without the help of his family and neighbors who sought a scapegoat and unwittingly suggested to him that he become an outlaw.[24]

The basic unit of interaction that concerns us here is a simple one. One person acts and in so doing intentionally or unintentionally expresses a part of his self, something of what he is, or thinks he is, or hopes he is. A second person responds to the first person's behavior. Very frequently the second person's reactions convey approval or disapproval, acceptance or rejection. The effects of these different responses to behavior soon become quite apparent. Behavior that results in attention or approval or affection tends to be repeated more and more frequently. Behavior that leads to withdrawal or indifference or rejection occurs less and less frequently. There are, of course, exceptions to this general tendency as, for example, when a person behaves in such a way so as to obtain a response, any response, in order to bring attention to himself or take it away from someone else.

However, because of the human capacity for self-consciousness the process of developing a sense of self is not a matter of simple reinforcement. That is, an individual's behavior patterns arouse responses within himself leading to perceptions of himself which become stable. As an illustration, if a student has had reasonably good success in school and has high personal expectations for maintaining a high achievement level, he is not likely to respond to the expectations that his less achievement-oriented buddies may have for him to study less often. On the other hand, if it is more important for a student to be socially accepted than it is to get high grades, then that student may, in fact, be more susceptible to the shifting whims of others' expectations. Riesman[25] has described these different modes of responding to either internal or external expectations an *inner-directedness or other-directedness*. Julian Rotter[26,27] has extended this idea into a theoretical "locus of control" model to describe those who are "internals" and those who are "externals" when it comes to responding to the world around them.

Both Riesman's and Rotter's research suggests that an important first step along the road of self-understanding is the ability to be able to discriminate between those expectations which come from inside the self and those which come from outside the self. Rogers,[28] for example, speaking from his many years as a psychotherapist, has noted that when people move away from compulsively "meeting others' " expectations, they become freer to listen to their own expectations and to become the person they *feel* they want to be.

Just as it is likely that a certain behavior can arouse certain expectations in the minds of others for future behavior of a similar sort, it is also possible that perceived expectations may trigger behavior which may not have been produced if those expectations had not been there in the first place. Let's untangle this with a few examples. A ninth-grade girl I counseled some years ago told me of an incident with her mother which may help make this idea of expectations clearer. She brought home her first ninth-grade report card with three C's and a D in math. Her mother looked at it and said something like, "The way you think when numbers are involved it's no wonder you got a D. Besides, I was never any good in math so I'm not surprised you're not either. You'll probably be lucky to pass." The girl received a somewhat similar response from her father and the matter was dropped. As a consequence of this feedback (and other feedback like it), the girl nurtured the impression that she was expected to do poorly. That is, her mother and father did not expect her to do well in math. In other words, her behavior (a D in math) evoked certain expectations ("You'll be lucky to pass.") for this girl's future behavior, which she began to believe as being true.

This anecdotal account is not merely an isolated example of how expectations can influence behavior. There is a growing and convincing body of research literature to suggest that expectations or "self-fulfilling prophecies," as they are called, work with significant potency both in schools and in homes. Braun's[29] monumental review of over 85 studies related to the impact of teacher expectations on student behavior and achievement indicates strongly that student imput variables such as name, ethnic background, sex, cumulative folder, physical characteristics, and intelligence test results all tend to influence a teacher's expectations significantly. What happens in turn is that these expectations affect, for good or bad, teacher behaviors such as grouping, tone of voice, and general quality and quantity of interaction.

Other support for the influence of expectancies on behavior comes from research done with parents who raise children with high self-esteem. For example, Coopersmith[30] found that families that produced high self-esteem children were not only high in warmth, but they also had high expectations for academic performance and excellence. That is, parents who *expected* their children to live up to the high standards they established were more likely to facilitate a positive self-concept than those who did *not* have those expectancies.

As another illustration of the expectancy idea, I remember an interview I had with a seventeen-year-old delinquent boy who had just been returned to the reformatory. I asked him why he had gotten into so much trouble while he was back home for three weeks. He screwed up his face and replied, "Man, what did you expect. The whole neighborhood knew I was at this place for nine months. Man, I wanted to do good—I tried, but even my grandfather wouldn't hardly talk to me. Some of the parents in the neighborhood—some with kids in more trouble than me—wouldn't even let their kids talk to me. They would say something like there goes that kid from the vocational school; watch out for him. They had their minds made up before they even looked to see if I had changed. Hell with them. They want me to be bad—I'll *be* bad." In other words, it was clear to this boy that people in his neighborhood *expected* him to play the role of the delinquent boy and he ended up behaving in terms of what he perceived their expectations to be for him. True, his delinquency history determined their expectations, but their expectations facilitated the very behavior they were opposed to in the first place. This doesn't excuse the boy's behavior, but it does help us understand it. Expectations for behavior have a strong influence of what kind of behavior is expressed. Since this is one of the themes basic to this book, more will be said about this in subsequent chapters.

Influence of Social Interaction

The self grows within a social framework. If, for example, you were to make a list of as many personality characteristics as you could think of, you would find that each is influenced in some way or other by social interaction. Some, like friendliness or shyness are social by definition; that is, one cannot be friendly or shy except in relation to other people. Other characteristics, like creativeness or independence, are less social by definition. Although one can be creative or independent in solitude, it is difficult to see how one could nurture such traits apart from social interaction.

Mead, in describing the social interaction processes involved in the development of the self writes: "The self arises in conduct, when the individual becomes a social object in experience to himself. This takes place when the individual assumes the attitude or uses the gesture which another individual would use and responds to it himself or tends to so respond. . . . The child gradually becomes a social being in his own experience, and he acts toward himself in a manner analogous to that in which he acts toward others.''[31]

This description may be made clear by a single example. Let's say that a child play-acts being mother or father. In her play, she talks to herself as her mother and father have talked to her, and she responds to this imaginary talk of her mother and father. Eventually, the end result of speaking to herself as others have spoken to her is that she comes to perceive herself as a person to whom other people respond. She learns to conceive of herself as having characteristics which are perceived and encouraged by others. For example, as a young child grows, she learns that words such as cute, good, bad, intelligent, dumb, heavy, lazy, shy, and so on, are attributed to her as a person; it is through her long immersion in an interpersonal stream of continual reflected appraisals from other people (particularly people who *matter* to her) that she gradually develops a picture of herself which she then strives to maintain.

Perhaps we can appreciate the importance of social interaction if we look at an example in which there was virtually no interaction at all. Davis[32] reported the case of Anna, a five-year-old child, who was found tied to a chair in a secluded room. She had apparently been kept there for several years by her grandfather who found her unbearable because she was a second illegitimate child. When found she was unable to move or talk. Her leg muscles had atrophied to the point that her flaccid feet fell forward. She was malnourished and showed no response to sound or sight. Within three days of being taken out of this isolated environment she was able to sit up if placed in a sitting position and could move her arms and hands. She was massaged, placed on a high vitamin diet, and given lots of attention. At first she neither smiled nor cried and was almost expressionless, although later she began to smile if coaxed and showed signs of temper if physically restrained. Ten days after the first visit, the examiners found the child more alert and able to fix her attention. She showed taste and visual discrimination, smiled more often, and began to display ritualistic motions with her hands and a series of tricks that any infant performs. Two months after being found, Anna ceased to improve. In nine months she had learned little. She could not chew or drink from a glass or control her bodily processes, and she could barely stand even when holding on to some support.

At this time Anna was placed in a foster home in the keeping of a warm, supporting foster mother. Within a month of this placement she had learned to eat, hold a glass, and feed herself. Improvement continued until she understood many instructions and babbled, although she could not use words. Motor ability increased, but her initiative was low. Again she seemed to hit a plateau and was placed in a home for retarded children. In several years she was speaking at about the level of a two-year-old. She reflected signs of being socialized, used a spoon, conformed to toilet habits, loved her dolls, and spoke a few simple sentences. She died shortly thereafter at an estimated age of ten and a half.

Records revealed that as a baby she had appeared normal, indeed attractive. The matter of hereditary endowment is open to speculation, for the mother was dull mentally, and there was doubt as to her father's identity. Nonetheless, there is little doubt but that Anna's lack of social interaction and environmental stimulation contributed heavily to her retarded growth as a total human being.

Social interaction is the medium of exchange through which we hone our perceptions of the outside world, develop our interpersonal skills, extend intelligence, and acquire attitudes about ourselves. Tenenbaum[33] and Deutsch and Brown,[34] among others, have demonstrated in their research that impoverished children who grow up with restricted cultural and social opportunities suffer both intellectually and emotionally. After an extensive review of research evidence, Bloom[35] estimates that exposure to extreme environments—that is, either a very good environment or a poor one—during the first four years of life may affect the development of intelligence by about 2.5 IQ points per year. Not much when looked at on a yearly basis, but over a four-year period this adds up to as much as 10 points. Suffice it to say, interaction with others is an important social vitamin in one's daily nourishment of a growing, expanding self.

For some, however, the self does not grow and expand easily and fluidly. To them, personal growth seems more scary than exciting. Why? Let's turn to some speculations about why this may be.

Reasons for Resisting Personal Growth

Fear of Maturity

Some individuals avoid finding out more about themselves for fear of having to give up a self with which they have grown comfortable or "satisfied." Most people have an initial inclination to resist personal change anyway, but this resistance is even stronger for a person who refuses to try new or changed behavior into his current concept of self. For example, a shy, timid, submissive person may not want to see his strengths and assets for fear that he might have to be more assertive and socially aggressive. If shyness has become a way of life designed to protect one from the risks of social disapproval (in this case, nothing ventured, nothing lost—in terms of self-esteem), then it may be difficult indeed for a shy person to give up his timidity. Other individuals are reluctant to find out more about themselves because of the threat of having to change in the direction of being more personally mature. Maturity implies many things, among which are a certain degree of independence and autonomy, capacity for self-discipline, certainty about goals and values, and motivation toward some level of personal achievement. Most of all, greater maturity means greater responsibility, and for some this is a frightening possibility.

Fear of Success

Success has many meanings—it may mean getting an A grade in a particular course, or winning a tennis match, or changing a psychological "tape," or getting married,

Sometimes a person may fear maturity because it may mean giving up certain comforting dependencies.

or losing weight, or making a million dollars, and on and on. What is a success for one person may not be to another, and in this sense success is a highly individualistic matter. The fears and penalties associated with achieving success, however we define it, appear to be an age-old phenomenon which few entirely escape.

Why should some people fear success more than others? There are probably many reasons, but it is likely that success establishes a precedent, a standard to be lived up to, a performance level to be maintained, and this is frightening to individuals who have basic doubts about their ability to sustain a high level of personal performance. For example, I have known students who will invest only a given amount of time to preparation for an exam and then stop. One student expressed it to me somewhat like this: "You see, if I study too hard—I mean really study—then I might get a high grade on the test. But it really wouldn't be because I was smart that I got the high grade; it would be because I studied so hard. Other students in the class might think I was smarter than I really was and what would happen to me the first time I *didn't* do real well? They would probably think I was dumb or something." This particular student persisted in getting C's and an occasional B here and there and in so doing avoided both the stigma of failure and the risk of success.

Success may also mean, "I am my brother's keeper," That is, success could be interpreted as having to take care of those less successful, which could be felt as something of a burden. I recall a salesman client of mine some years ago who deliberately made less money (and in that sense was less successful) than he was capable of making to avoid the possibility of taking care of his parents in their later years. As he expressed it, "Look, I've never felt too close to my parents anyway and if I made more money I'd feel guilty if I didn't look out for them. This way I make enough but not so much that I have to worry about that."

Fear of success or more mature behavior is expressed in many different ways. One of my colleagues told me of a twenty-year-old woman he had worked with for over five months in therapy. Among the many conflicts this young lady had to work through were her ambivalent feelings about men. She liked men; yet she didn't. She wanted to be more successful with men; yet she didn't. Basically she was afraid of a possible close relationship with a man, because she dreaded the possibility of not being liked, of being disappointed, let down, and hurt. She was fearful of establishing a close relationship because *she questioned her ability to maintain a close relationship*. Compounding the problem was the fact that she was perhaps thirty pounds overweight. Her therapist discussed the possibility of dieting and exercise, but she resisted both. The dawn of insight broke through during one session when she discovered that being overweight, and hence being less attractive, was one way of assuring that she would *not* be too successful with men. Being overweight reduced the risk of being hurt, because fewer men would be attracted to her in the first place.

Back to our original point. Some persons are fearful of success, fearful of moving on to higher levels of personal realization and personal performance primarily because they doubt their ability to maintain a high standard of performance if they do achieve it. In this sense, fear of success and fear of greater maturity are very much related. The more successful one is in, let's say, performance, skills, knowledge, sense of perspective, leadership ability, and so on, the more people expect of that person. And the more people expect of a person the more opportunities or possibilities there are for failing. For some individuals there is just too great a risk in establishing a reputation of competency; too much is then expected. Some persons find refuge and safety in being neither too far behind the pack nor too far ahead of it.

As a final note, we might add here that the somewhat popular idea that women are more fearful of success than men and therefore not as successful is an idea not borne out by research.[36] In fact, recent research suggests that women may be more likely than men to fear rejection, but not more likely to fear success.[37]

Fear of One's Best

Maslow[38] has noted that although we all have an impulse to improve ourselves, to actualize more of our potentialities, and move further in the direction of human fulfillment, many of us stop short of becoming what we could become because of what he calls a "fear of one's own greatness" or the "evasion of one's destiny" or the "running away from one's best talents." He goes on to observe:

> Not only are we ambivalent about our own highest possibilities, we are also in perpetual . . . conflict and ambivalence over these same possibilities in other people, and in

human nature in general. Certainly we love and admire good men, saints—honest, virtuous, clean men. But could anybody who has looked into the depths of human nature fail to be aware of our mixed and often hostile feelings toward saintly men? Or toward our intellectual geniuses? . . . We surely love and admire all the persons who have incarnated the true, the good, the beautiful, the just, the perfect, the ultimately successful. And yet they also make us uneasy, anxious, confused, perhaps a little jealous or envious, a little inferior, clumsy. They usually make us lose our aplomb, our self-possession and self regard.[39]

Why should this be? Why is it that our self-composure frequently takes leave in the face of another person's eminence, or greatness, or intellect, or beauty, or whatever? One reason may be that people who are superior in one way or other make us momentarily more aware of our lesser abilities or skills, without even intending to do so. What usually happens is that we are not conscious of why we feel stupid or ugly or inferior, and we sometimes end up being defensive and resentful. That is, we respond as if the person we regard as superior were deliberately trying to make us feel inferior. Hostility, anger, resentment, even jealousy or envy are then understandable consequences.

Understandable as they may be, feelings of this sort are ultimately self-defeating. In the process of being resentful or envious of another person's accomplishments, we sometimes deny that that person attained them in any honorable way. So what frequently happens is that we invent excuses for why people who are superior to us happen to be more important or successful or skilled than we see ourselves as being. For example, how many times have you heard comments like: "If I brown-nosed like he did, I'd get A's, too"; or "Sure she dates lots of men, but look at how aggressive she is"; or "Big deal—I'd have high grades, too, if all I did was study"; or "Well, who wouldn't be beautiful if they could afford to have their hair done once a week like she does!" And so it goes. These are self-defeating feelings because in the process of denying that another person is bright or skilled or accomplished or good-looking, we are also denying the possibility of these qualities existing in ourselves. For example, the student who says, "I'd have high grades, too, if all I did was study," could be making an assertion which is, in fact, true or he could be trying to make it seem as if anyone (including himself, of course) was capable of getting high grades if he studied hard. In either case, the net effect is an effort to make nonattainment of high grades seem less important and less threatening than what actually may be the case. (If high grades were really *not* important to a person, then he wouldn't have to *act* as if they were unimportant by reducing another individual's accomplishments.) Or, as another example, a woman who constantly finds faults in other women's appearances may be doing so because she sees other women looking better than she does and is threatened by the possibility that this could be true. One way of reducing the threat of another woman being more attractive is to exaggerate her flaws and in that way distort the beauty that is there in the first place (or at least detract from it).

We are back to our original point. When we stop responding to people who are in some way superior to us as if they were trying to make us feel inferior, then we are closer to appreciating not only what they have, but what we could be. That is, if we are willing to be very self-aware and self-critical of our own inclinations to be defensively reactive, that is, our own fears or hatreds or tendencies to be threatened by truly good, or beautiful, or ingenious people, we may very likely be less hostile, resentful, and negative to them. We may also find that, as we learn to accept more completely the highest values and qualities in others, we may be able to accept our own high qualities and values in a less frightened way. Of course it can work the other way, too. As we learn to accept our own accomplishments or talents without embarrassment, discomfort, defensiveness, or false humility, we may be better able to accept them in others as well.

Fear of Knowing

This is a tricky phenomenon. Although "knowing" or having knowledge can be one of the quickest ways to enhance self-esteem and to feel personally competent, it can also be felt as among the most scary, and threatening ways for doing these things. So long as the *fear* of knowing is felt more intensely than the *challenge* of knowing, then this can, indeed, be another roadblock to personal growth. Why should this fear exist in the first place? An observation by Maslow may help in understanding the deeper roots to this question:

> . . . we can seek knowledge in order to reduce anxiety and we can also avoid knowing in order to reduce anxiety. Knowledge and action are very closely bound together (and) this close relation between knowing and doing can help us to interpret one cause of the fear of knowing as deeply a fear of doing, a fear of the consequences that flow from knowing, a fear of its dangerous responsibilities. Often it is better not to know, because if you *did* know, then you would *have* to stick your neck out.[40]

What Maslow is talking about is not unlike the wife who fears her husband is being unfaithful, but prefers not to know it. If she did, she would have to do something about it and perhaps lose him in the process. Better not to know. Or the pedestrians who continue hurridly by a fallen man clutching his chest and asking for help as if they were suddenly deaf and blind to the sights and sounds around them. Safer not to know. For if they knew, they would either have to do something about it or else feel guilty about being cowards. Or the frustrated and lonely person who seeks neither people that may help him or books that could enlighten him because he may discover that *he* is responsible for his suffering and not the world out there he blames. Better not to know.

"Knowing" more or having more knowledge may cause three separate, but related events to happen, any one of which may intensify the fear of knowing.

One, it heightens expectations from others for what we can do. Two, knowing makes it more difficult to remain in a safe, subordinate position to those a person regards as superior to himself. When we think of the number of times that children are taught that "knowing" more than their parents is wrong ("Who do you think you are, young lady!" "You're acting pretty big for your britches, aren't you fella!"), it is not difficult to understand why knowing more than someone in authority can be scary. And three, knowing makes us more personally responsible for our own behavior; we can not as easily claim either innocence or ignorance as our excuses. A friend of mine, an avid heavy smoker, deliberately goes out of his way to avoid either discussions or reading material that may enlighten him regarding possible causal ties between cancer and smoking. As he says with his usual candor: "I don't *want* to know, dammit. I want to smoke!"

Mechanisms for Defending the Self

Whether we are always aware of it or not, each of us uses certain "defense" mechanisms to help us "preserve" or "protect" our self-systems. Indeed, our effectiveness in using certain defenses has a lot to do with how successful we are in meeting the daily stresses and strains of living. Although defense mechanisms are necessary, they can prove debilitating, if one uses them, however consciously or unconsciously, to avoid assuming responsibility, to abstain from taking risks now and then, or to manufacture excuses for persisting in behavior which may be immature and self-defeating.

As each person's self is the integrating core of his personality, threats to its worth or adequacy are quickly viewed as potential intimidations to that individual's very center of existence. Defense mechanisms help us preserve our integrity and sense of personal worth when we find ourselves in ego-involved stress situations. For example, the fan who proudly announces, "my team won today," may find some measure of importance by "identifying" himself with a successful team. (Have you ever noted how an entire student body exhibits a kind of "collective chest puffing" after their team wins a big one?); the student who flunks an exam may "project" the blame for his performance onto the instructor's lack of fairness or the poor construction of the test; the student who cheats on an exam may "rationalize" that everyone else cheats and he might as well, too. The protection of self from possible devaluation and thus from anxiety is the very essence of the defensive functions of these mechanisms.

The use of defense mechanisms is a normal human reaction, unless they are used to such an extreme that they begin to interfere with the maintenance of self-esteem rather than aiding it. In a sense, the self, like a soldier busy defending himself against an enemy's charge, may break down under the very weight of its defensive activities. In addition, these mechanisms, necessary as they are, have certain drawbacks. They are not usually adaptive in the sense of realistically coping with problems. For example, a person who continually rationalizes away his blunders is not likely to profit from his mistakes on subsequent occasions. Defense mechanisms involve a fair degree of self-deception and reality distortion. Furthermore, they function on relatively unconscious levels and therefore are not subject to the usual checks and balances of more conscious processes. In fact, we usually resent having someone call our attention to them because once they become conscious they do not serve their purposes as well.

Defense mechanisms can be best understood in view of the *objective* they serve, which is to safeguard the integrity and worth of the self. Thus, it is only as we conceive of an active, dynamic self which struggles to maintain a certain stability that they make sense. Once we view the "self" in this framework, we may be better able to understand our ability to protect the self by utilizing defense mechanisms to change the so-called "facts" so that they fit our personal needs.

With this small introduction, let us now turn to a consideration of the more important of these defense mechanisms along with a brief discussion of how each functions.

Denial of Reality

Sometimes we manage to avoid disagreeable realities by ignoring or refusing to acknowledge them. This inclination is exemplified in a great many of our everyday behaviors. We turn away from unpleasant sights; we refuse to discuss unpleasant topics; we ignore or disclaim criticism; and sometimes we refuse to face our real problems. A vain woman may deny a vision problem in order to avoid wearing glasses; an insecure middle-aged man may deny his years by pursuing younger girls; or a low self-esteem student may deny his competency by attributing a high grade on a test to "luck." Parents, for example, are notoriously blind when it comes to the defects of their offspring. I recall one mother, whose ten-year-old boy had been diagnosed as brain-damaged by a team of experts, who asserted that his "head was just developing slower than the rest of him, that's all." The common adages, "None is so blind as he who will not see," and "Love is blind," perhaps illustrate even more clearly our tendency to look away from those things which are incompatible with our wishes, desires, and needs. This mechanism does, indeed, guard us from painful experiences. However, like the proverbial ostrich who buries his head in the sand, denial may also get in the way of our "seeing" things which might otherwise facilitate progress toward more effective living and greater maturity of self.

Fantasy

Not only do we frequently deny unpleasant reality, but we are also inclined to "embellish" our perceptions so that the world is seen more as we would like it to be. Fantasy is stimulated by frustrated desires and grows primarily out of mental images associated with need gratification. It can be productive or nonproductive. Productive fantasy can be used constructively in solving problems, as in creative imagination, or it can be a kind of nonproductive wish-fulfilling activity which compensates for a *lack* of achievement rather than stimulating or promoting achievement. James Thurber's *The Secret Life of Walter Mitty* is a classic example of how one can achieve wished-for status by imagining that he is rich, powerful, and respected. Einstein, on the other hand, had mental pictures or "fantasies" which led to productive hypotheses, formulas, and solutions.

Many of our fantasies are ready-made for us in the form of magazines, books, movies, and soap operas. Not infrequently we escape from our own life problems by identifying ourselves, fantasy fashion, with the hero or heroine, bravely facing and surmounting their problems with them, and sharing in their adventures and triumphs. Soap operas might be a good example of this sort of fantasy identification.

The capacity to remove ourselves temporarily from unpleasant reality into a more affable world of fantasy has considerable therapeutic value. Fantasy may, for example, add the dash of excitement and interest we need to motivate us to greater efforts toward our goals in real life. However, the individual who *consistently* turns to fantasy as his solution to a troublesome reality is in danger psychologically. It is particularly under conditions of extreme frustration and deprivation that our fantasies are likely to get out of hand and during times of this sort we should be wary of solutions conjured by the mind's eye. For example, Bettelheim[41] found that at the concentration camps of Dachau and Buchenwald, ''the longer the time a prisoner had spent in camp, the less true to reality were his daydreams; so much so that the hopes and expectations of the old prisoners often took the form of eschatological and messianic hopes.''

Nonetheless, there is substantial evidence to suggest that fantasizing and daydreaming is not only normal, but an almost universal activity among people of both sexes.[42] It is when we use it as a permanent and not a temporary escape that we are apt to get ourselves into trouble. It is one thing to build a castle in the sky; it is quite another to try to live in it.

A little fantasy now and then can help add a bit of zest to otherwise dreary days.

Compensation

Compensation is an attempt to disguise the existence of a weak or undesirable characteristic by emphasizing a more positive one. This defensive reaction takes many forms. For example, a physically handicapped individual may attempt to overcome his handicap directly through increased effort and persistence. The heroic and successful efforts of the fine actress, Patricia Neal, following her stroke is an example of what sheer effort and persistence can accomplish. Tom Demsey, whose genetically deformed foot set a National Football League field goal record of 63 yards, is another example. Usually, however, compensatory reactions are more indirect. That is, there is an effort to either substitute for the defect or to draw attention away from it. As illustrations, the girl who regards herself as unattractive may develop an exceptionally winning personality; the uncoordinated boy may turn from athletics to scholastics; the mediocre, insecure nobody may become the Chief Imperial Wizard of the Ku Klux Klan. Indeed, a whole science of cosmetics and dress has developed which seems to have as its major objectives the modification or alteration of the human anatomy, its features, expressions, and protrusions. The short man is made to look tall, the fat girl thin, the colorless one glamorous, the flat one curvaceous, and so on.

Not all compensatory behaviors are desirable or useful. For example, a person who feels unloved may become sexually promiscuous; the boy who feels inferior may become the neighborhood bully; the person who feels insecure may eat or drink too much; the individual who feels inadequate may brag too much.

We constantly compare ourselves with others and frequently gauge our worth in terms of how we see ourselves in relation to other people's status, achievements, and possessions. This can lead to strong motivation toward at least average, and if possible, superior achievement. In meeting these conditions, compensating behaviors may help, but where they become exaggerated or take antisocial forms, they hinder rather than assist a person express his potential.

Introjection (Internalization)

Introjection is a process in which a person internalizes threatening situations. That is, he incorporates into his own personality structure the achievements or qualities of those who threaten him. We can see examples of this in the behavior of a young child as he gradually learns and accepts as his own the various social boundaries and value attitudes of his parents. By becoming like his parents, it is then possible for him to regulate his own behavior in terms of internalized values and protect himself from possible infractions of rules, thus avoiding social retaliation and punishment. The saying, "If you can't beat them, join them," reflects the use of this mechanism in everyday life. This "identification with the aggressor" behavior is primarily a defense mechanism of the weak against the strong. Prisoners, for example, often attempt to reduce the threat to their existence by becoming "informers" or otherwise cultivating the favor of guards whom they hate and fear. The dynamics behind a threatened prisoner's frantic efforts to win a guard's favor are basically no different than those of a frightened, intimidated college student who goes out of his way to be friendly to a professor who terrifies him. Fundamentally the thinking is, "If I'm on his side maybe he won't be harsh on me. Or better still, maybe he won't give me a low grade." Whether it is the frightened prisoner or the intimidated student the dynamics are the same, namely, a total effort to incorporate, to "introject," those characteristics of that person who is seen as most threatening.

Projection

Projection is a means by which we (1) relegate the blame for our own shortcomings, mistakes, and transgressions to others, and (2) attribute to others our own unacceptable impulses, thoughts, and desires. It is perhaps most commonly apparent in our tendency to blame others for our own mistakes. The athlete who fails to make the team may feel sure the coach was unfair; an exwife may conclude: "It's all his fault"; a bruised seven-year-old may exclaim, "It wasn't my fault, he hit me first"; the baseball player called out on strikes may suggest that the umpire not delay in consulting an ophthalmologist, and so it goes. Fate and bad luck are particularly overworked targets of projection. Even inanimate objects are not exempt from blame. The golfer who whiffs his tee shot may examine his driver as if expecting to find a hole in it, or the three-year-old who tumbles from his hobby horse may accuse it or someone of deliberately throwing him off. Sometimes a person may ascribe ethically unacceptable desires and impulses to others while remaining blithely unaware of their internal origins within himself. For example, the individual with suppressed homosexual leanings may be the first to spot a wide assortment of homosexual tendencies or characteristics in other males. Or the girl who is frightened by her own very strong sexual urges may accuse men of "always being on the make."

Such projections help maintain our feelings of adequacy and self-esteem in the face of failure, and probably develop from the early realization that placing the blame on others for our own mistakes helps us to avoid social rejection and disapproval. This can, however, be carried to extremes. Some individuals are so busy looking for faults and shortcomings in other people that they never get around to examining their own, which ultimately deprives them of growing to higher levels of maturity.

Rationalization

Rationalization has two primary defensive objectives: (1) it helps us invent excuses for doing what we don't think we should do but want to do anyway, and (2) it aids us in softening the disappointment connected to not reaching a goal we had set for ourselves. Typically, it involves thinking up logical, socially acceptable reasons for our past, present, or future behavior. With not too much effort we can soon think of a reason for not getting up for an eight o'clock class ("It'll probably be a dull lecture anyway."), for going to a movie instead of studying ("There really isn't *that* much to do.''), for smoking heavily (''The lung cancer and smoking relationship isn't conclusive and besides they'll soon have a cancer cure anyway.'').

We have endless ways for justifying our behavior and protecting our adequacy and self-esteem. How many parents, for example, are honest enough to admit that the child they just spanked got spanked because they (the parents) were angry, without having to mask it with ''It was for his own good,'' or ''It hurt me more than it did him.'' Or how many students are honest enough to admit they cheated because they didn't know the material rather than cover it with ''Everyone else does, so I *have* to in order to pass.'' If a parent had to face his anger or if a student had to face his lack of savvy, each would probably feel ashamed and guilty. Hence, the rationalizations, the excuses.

Sometimes, of course, it is difficult to know where an objective consideration of facts leaves off and rationalization begins. Two good behavioral symptoms of excessive rationalization are: (1) hunting for reasons to justify behavior and beliefs and (2) getting emotional (angry, guarded, ''up-tight'') when someone questions the reasons we offer. Should these reactions occur, it is usually a good time to take pause and examine how factual our reasons really are. The price of excessive rationalization, of course, is self-deception, for if we accept reasons for our behavior which are not true ones, we are less likely to profit from our errors. Carried to extremes this could lead eventually to the development of false beliefs or delusions sustained in the face of contradictory evidence.

© 1972 United Feature Syndicate, Inc.

For some people, if one rationalization doesn't work, another will.

Repression

Repression is a defensive reaction through which painful or dangerous thoughts and desires are excluded from consciousness. It has often been labeled as selective forgetting, but it is more in the nature of selective remembering. It is a way of protecting one's personal equilibrium by forgetting experiences which are upsetting. Repression is by no means always complete. Vague feelings of unworthiness, insecurity, and guilt often are signs of incomplete repression. Along this line I recall a client of mine who struggled for several months working through the nagging guilt feelings he always experienced whenever he felt sexually attracted to a woman. He knew it was in some way related to his childhood and his mother's attitudes, but he didn't know exactly how. During one of our sessions, as he was sorting through his buried file of memories, he recalled a time when he was eight years old when his mother caught him and a seven-year-old neighbor girl in the basement, both with pants down, exploring each other. He was spanked, admonished for being a terrible, nasty boy, and sent directly to bed. So painful was that experience that he soon "forgot" it, but it served nonetheless as an unconscious hatchery from which guilt was spawned whenever he had any kind of sexual feeling about a woman. It was the key to insight, and once he had unlocked that memory and was able to look at it in connection with a mother who had neurotic fears about sex, he was in a better position to examine his own fears.

The repression of undesirable impulses and experiences not only demands considerable energy, but it also hinders healthy personality integration. A more realistic confrontation of problems is always more conducive to good mental health and positive self-development.

Reaction Formation

Reaction formation refers to the development of conscious attitudes and behavior patterns which are opposite to what one really feels and would like to do. It is a way of suppressing impulses and desires which we think might get us into trouble, if we actually carried them out. Reaction formation can be recognized by its extreme and intolerant attitudes, which are usually far out of proportion to the importance of the situation. For example, self-appointed guardians of the public's morals who voluntarily devote their time to reading "dirty" books and magazines, investigating burlesque shows, and who are generally obsessed with censoring all things related to sex, alcohol, and other alleged vices are frequently found to have unusually high impulses in the same direction themselves. Indeed, the most aggressive crusaders are very often fighting their own suppressed impulses as well as condemning the expression of such impulses in others.

In everyday behavior, reaction formation may take the form of being excessively kind to a person we do not like, or of developing a "who cares how other people feel" attitude to conceal feelings of loneliness and a craving for acceptance, or of assuming an air of bravado when our adequacy is threatened, for example, "That test tomorrow doesn't frighten me . . . much."

Reaction formation has adjustive value insofar as it helps us to maintain socially approved behavior and to control unacceptable impulses. On the other hand, this mechanism, too, is self-deceptive and can lead to exaggerated and rigid fears or beliefs which could lead to excessive harshness or severity in dealing with the values of others and ourselves.

Displacement

Displacement refers to the shift of emotion or fantasy away from the person or object toward which it was originally directed to a more neutral or less dangerous person or object. For example, the man upbraided by his boss may suppress the anger he feels toward the boss because he knows he would be in deep trouble if he expressed his feelings. So what does he do? He comes home and hollers at his wife for not having dinner ready and yells at the children for being too noisy. Not infrequently the smallest incident may serve as the trigger which releases pent-up emotional feelings in a torrent of displaced anger and abuse. A young housewife had been admonished by her husband for not being more efficient and later in the same day lost her purse while shopping. On her way home she was halted by a patrolman for speeding. That was the final straw. She exploded with a volley of abuse on the startled officer with questions ranging all the way from ''Haven't you anything better to do than chase women?'' to blaming him generally for the city's traffic condition which he should have been working on rather than harassing busy, civic-minded citizens for barely exceeding the speed limit.

Through a process of symbolic association, displacement can be extremely indirect and complex. For example, ''beating'' a disliked rival at a game or in an athletic match may symbolically represent his destruction. Under the guise of ''I just want to help'' many a next-door neighbor has indulged in destructive and vindictive gossip as a means of expressing anger, resentment, and hostility.

Displacement is a valuable mechanism because it enables one to vent dangerous emotional impulses without risking loss of love and possible retaliation, and without the necessity of even recognizing the person for whom such feelings were originally intended. By displacing his bottled-up anger on his wife and children, the man maintains his feelings of respect and cordiality toward his domineering boss. The wife who released her rage on the patrolman can more easily avoid ambivalent feelings toward a husband who demands that she be more tidy.

Unfortunately, displacements can become too deviant and can result in continual avoidance of situations which could be more efficiently handled by a more direct approach. On the whole, we are psychologically better off when we learn to express and discuss our feelings with the person at whom the feelings are intended in the first place, rather than aim them at someone who does not even know what they're all about.

Emotional Insulation

In emotional insulation, the individual attempts to reduce his needs and fears by withdrawing into a sort of shell of passivity. As a consequence of prior hurts and disappointments, we sometimes learn to garrison ourselves not only by lowering our level of aspiration but by curbing the extent of our emotional involvement in the achievement of our goals. For example, the woman disappointed in her first real love may be extremely cautious about allowing herself to get emotionally involved on subsequent occasions. She may experience difficulty in "letting herself go" in the sense of entering into a close emotional relationship. Sometimes persons who have been badly bruised in the school of hard knocks develop a kind of emotional scar tissue and are often unable to either give or receive affection. Although persons of this kind may appear to be unusually self-sufficient, they are frequently victims of intense feelings of loneliness and anxiety.

Another way of emotionally insulating ourselves is to avoid competitive activities in which we may not rate favorably with others. For example, some persons will not engage in sports such as golf, bowling, or tennis, or card games such as bridge or poker unless they excel in them. In this way it is possible to minimize the possible "loss of face" that might result from doing less well than others.

Getting emotionally involved in the business of living does, indeed, involve certain "calculated risks." For example, there is always the possibility that the person we give our affection to may reject us or be taken from us by death. Healthy people operate on the assumption that the rewards of emotional involvement are worth the risks, even though they also know that they shall inevitably experience pain and disappointments in life, too.

Used in mild dosages, emotional insulation is an important defense against too much hurt and disappointment. However, when used to the extent that a person becomes "an island onto himself," it can curtail a person's healthy and active participation in life and lead to eventual shallowness and blunting of emotional involvement. When we "dare not to hope" we cease to grow.

Regression

Regression is behavior involving a retreat, in the face of stress, to the use of behavioral patterns appropriate at earlier levels of development. It usually involves modification of behavior in the direction of more primitive, infantile expressions. For example, when a new addition to the family is brought home from the hospital, it is not uncommon for the older child, who may feel that his status is threatened, to regress or "go back" to bedwetting, baby-talk, thumb-sucking, demands for mother's attention, and other infantile behaviors. As other examples the frustrated adult may return to the temper tantrums or sulkings which got him his way when growing up, a wife may run home to mother whenever there is discord, or a person may "cry like a baby" when experiencing great emotional pain.

Regression can perhaps be better understood if we remember a child's gradual shift from a position of helplessness and dependency on parents to one which demands increasing independent behavior and responsibility. This developmental process from dependency to independency is an arduous task, and it is common for all of us, confronting a harsher and more demanding adult world, to yearn now and then for the carefree and sheltered days of infancy and childhood. Consequently it is not surprising that in the face of severe stress we may retreat periodically from our adult status to an earlier level of growth and adjustment.

Regression is, however, more comprehensive than merely resorting to earlier behavior patterns when new ones have failed. In regression a person retreats to a less demanding personal status—one which involves lower personal goals and expectations and more readily accomplished satisfaction. For example, a wife who runs home to mother after an argument with her husband could be substituting her "little girl" need for mother's support for the more mature behavior involved in working the problem through with her husband. That is, behaving like a hurt little girl, less is expected of her, and the satisfactions are in the immediate reduction of anxiety.

Regression has its useful purposes, but, like other defensive mechanisms, when used as a primary mode of adjustment, it can serve as a giant roadblock in one's route to more mature behavior.

Sublimation

Sublimation involves the acceptance of a socially approved substitute goal for a drive whose normal channel of expression is blocked. There are many ways in which motives can be sublimated. As an illustration, curiosity about people, which can express itself in undesirable ways (voyeurism, sexual conversation, gossip, nosiness about the affairs of others) and lead to feelings of guilt, can be sublimated into art and medicine, where the human body can be viewed without conflict or reprisal, or it can be sublimated into counseling or psychology, where behavior and motives can be discussed at will. As another example, a young man with strong aggressive impulses may find suitable expression for those impulses in being a very assertive basketball player or maybe in being a hardnosed linebacker.

The defensive functions of sublimation are somewhat different from those of compensation because the motivation is different. Whereas compensation is founded on some kind of inadequacy, sublimation is directed more towards the reduction of guilt feelings associated with such motives as aggression, sex, curiosity, cruelty, and the paternal or maternal. A classic illustration of sublimation is the redirection of the maternal drive through teaching, social work, recreation work, or pediatric medicine, all of which provide opportunities for a wholesome expression of the desire for and love of children.

Defense Mechanisms in Retrospect

Understanding one's self involves, among other things, an awareness of the mechanisms we use to preserve the self. It is worth remembering that defense mechanisms are learned adjustive behaviors, that they function on relatively unconscious levels, and that they involve a certain amount of reality distortion and self-deception. Defense mechanisms serve the aims of adjustment by reducing conflict and frustration, and particularly because they stand in guard of the self, they function as a bulwark against more serious disturbances. Consequently they can be considered quite normal and desirable except when they are used to an excessive degree and operate at the expense of a person's ultimate adaptive efficiency and continued personal progress toward greater maturity.

In Perspective

This chapter has introduced you to the nature of the self, ideas about how it becomes known, influences of self-awareness and social interaction on the growth of self, reasons for resisting personal growth and the functions and purpose of the defense mechanisms we use to preserve and protect the self.

One's concept of oneself is a very personal possession. How we view ourselves is determined partially by how we perceive ourselves as really being, partially through how we view ourselves as ideally wanting to be, and partially through the expectations we perceive that others have for us. These are complex interrelated perceptual processes, no one of which is more important than the other. Depending on the individual, each of these three perceptions contributes more or less to our feelings of selfhood. For some, expressing their real self, whatever it may be, is most important and they struggle to stay as close in tune with the harmony of that inner self as is possible. For others, striving to become that ideal self is the guiding star which gives them their sense of purpose and direction. For still otheers, looking to and obeying the expectations of the word around them is their most satisfying mode of self-expression.

Social interaction is the primary medium through which we come to know ourselves. Self-awareness develops as we compare and contrast our physical bodies, skills, attitudes, and achievements to those of other people. Some persons are concerned primarily with physical qualities, and so this becomes their measuring stick for self-esteem (I am stronger, handsomer, more beautiful, or more agile; therefore I am adequate.) Others focus primarily on spiritual qualities and so this is their barometer of self-esteem (I am a faithful believer and worship regularly; therefore I am doing the best I can.) Still others are concerned essentially with matters of the mind, and this is their measure of self-esteem (I know more answers, or I can solve more problems, or I am more creative; therefore I am OK).

Although complete knowledge about one's self is probably neither necessary nor possible, it is, nonetheless, possible to come closer to an understanding of our upper and lower limits, our private fears and guarded hopes, our secret dreams and wildest ambitions if we remain open to who we think we are, where we would like to go, and why we are headed in that direction to begin with.

Notes

1. C. H. Cooley, *Human Native and Social Order*. New York: Charles Scribner's Sons, 1902.
2. G. H. Mead, *Mind, Self and Society*. Chicago: University of Chicago Press, 1934.
3. J. Dewey, *Democracy & Education*. New York: The Macmillan Co., 1916.
4. W. James, *Principles of Psychology, I*. New York: Henry Holt & Co., 1890.
5. G. Allport, *Becoming*. New Haven: Yale University Press, 1955, pp. 104–105.
6. A. T. Jersild, *In Search of Self*. New York: Teachers College Press, Columbia University, 1952.
7. W. James, p. 91.
8. D. Mattee, and J. Riskin, "Size of Defeat and Liking for Superior Ability Competitors," *Journal of Experimental Social Psychology*. 1974, 10: 333–351.
9. S. Freud, *New Introductory Lectures on Psycho-Analysis*. W. J. H. Sprott, trans. New York: W. W. Norton & Company, Inc., 1933, pp. 104–105.
10. S. Freud, p. 95.
11. E. Berne, *Transactional Analysis in Psychotherapy*. New York: Grove Press, 1961, pp. 17–43.
12. E. Berne, p. 24.
13. E. Berne, *Principles of Group Treatment*. New York: Oxford University Press, 1964, p. 364.
14. W. Penfield, *The Excitable Cortex in Conscious Man*. Springfield, Ill.: Charles C Thomas, 1958.
15. W. Penfield, "Memory Mechanisms," *Archives of Neurology and Psychiatry*. 1952, 67: 178–198.
16. E. Berne, *Principles of Group Treatment*, p. 281.
17. W. Penfield, "Memory Mechanisms," p. 187.
18. W. James, *Principles of Psychology, I*.
19. E. Berne, *Transactional Analysis in Psychotherapy*, p. 32.
20. B. White, *The First Three Years of Life*. Englewood Cliffs, N.J.: Prentice-Hall, Inc., 1975, p. 4.
21. G. W. Allport, p. 45.
22. R. Rosenthal, *Experimenter Effects in Psychological Research*. New York: Appleton-Century-Crofts, 1966.
23. N. Friedman, *The Social Nature of Psychological Research: The Psychological Experiment as a Social Interaction*. New York: Basic Books, Inc., 1967.
24. M. Haimowitz, "Criminals Are Made, Not Born," in M. L. Haimowitz & N. R. Haimowitz (Eds.) *Human Development: Selected Readings*. 2nd edition. New York: Thomas Y. Crowell Company, 1966, p. 399.
25. D. Riesman, *Faces in The Crowd*. New Haven: Yale University Press, 1952.
26. J. Rotter, "External Control and Internal Control," *Psychology Today*. June 1971: 37–42, 58–59.
27. J. Rotter, "Generalized Expectancies for Internal versus External Lows of Control of Reinforcement," *Psychological Monographs*. 1966, 80: (Whole No. 609).
28. C. R. Rogers, *On Becoming a Person*. Boston: Houghton Mifflin Company, 1961, pp. 163–198.
29. C. Braun, "Teacher Expectation: Socio-psychological Dynamics," *Review of Educational Research*. Spring 1976, 46: pp. 185–213.

30. S. Coopersmith, *The Antecedents of Self-Esteem*. San Francisco: W. H. Freeman, 1967.
31. Mead, p. 48.
32. K. Davis, "Extreme Social Isolation of a Child," *American Journal of Sociology*. 1940, 45: 554–565.
33. S. Tenenbaum, "The Teacher, The Middle Class, The Lower Class," *Phi Delta Kappan*. 1963, 45: 82–86.
34. M. Deutsch, and B. Brown, "Social Influences in Negro-White Intelligence Differences," *Journal of Social Issues*. 1964, 20: pp. 24–35.
35. B. S. Bloom, *Stability and Change in Human Characteristics*. New York: John Wiley & Sons, Inc., 1964.
36. D. Tresemer, "Fear of Success: Popular But Unproven," *Psychology Today,* March 1974: 82–85.
37. R. Curtis, Mark Zanna, and Woodrow Campbell, Jr., "Sex, Fear of Success, and The Perceptions & Performance of Law School Students," *American Education Research Journal*. Summer 1975, 12: 287–297.
38. A. H. Maslow, "Neurosis as a Failure of Personal Growth," *Humanitas*. 1967, 2: 153–159.
39. Maslow, p. 164.
40. A. H. Maslow, *Toward a Psychology of Being*. New York: Van Nostrand Reinhold Co., 1968, p. 66.
41. B. Bettelheim, "Individual & Mass Behavior in Extreme Situations," *Journal of Abnormal & Social Psychology*. 1943, 38: 443.
42. J. L. Singer, "Fantasy: The Foundation of Serenity," *Psychology Today*. July 1976: 32–37.

References of Related Interest

Bennis, W. A., D. E. Berlew, E. H. Schein, and F. I. Steele (Eds.) *Interpersonal Dynamics: Essays and Readings on Human Interaction* (3rd ed.). Homewood, Ill.: The Dorsey Press, 1973.

Berne, E., *Games People Play*. New York: Grove Press, 1964.

Borgatta, E. F., and W. W. Lambert (Eds.), *Handbook of Personality Theory and Research*. Chicago: Rand McNally, 1968.

Grebstein, L. C., (Ed.), *Toward Self-Understanding*. Glenview, Ill.: Scott, Foresman and Company, 1969.

Hall, C. S., and G. Lindzey, *Theories of Personality* (2nd ed.). New York: John Wiley and Sons, Inc., 1970, Chap. 13.

Hamachek, D. E. (Ed.), *Human Dynamics in Psychology and Education*. Boston: Allyn and Bacon, Inc., 1977, Part V.

Harris, T. A., *I'm OK—You're OK: A Practical Guide to Transactional Analysis*. New York: Harper & Row, Publishers, 1967.

Jourard, S., *The Transparent Self* (Rev.). New York: Van Nostrand Reinhold Company, 1971.

Levy, R. B., *Self-Revelation through Relationships*. Englewood Cliffs, N.J.: Prentice-Hall, Inc., 1972.

Major, J. (Ed.), *The Search for Self*. New York: The Macmillan Co., 1968.

Maslow, A. H., *Motivation and Personality* (2nd ed.). New York: Harper & Row, Publishers, 1970.

May, R., *Man's Search for Himself*. New York: W. W. Norton & Company, Inc., 1953.

Symonds, P. M., *The Ego and the Self*. New York: Appleton-Century-Crofts, Inc., 1951.

Wells, L. E., and G. Marwell, *Self-Esteem: Its Conceptualization and Measurement*. Beverly Hills, Calif.: Sage Publications, 1976.

Wylie, R. C., *The Self-Concept* (Rev.), vol. 1. Lincoln, Neb.: University of Nebraska Press, 1974.

Wyne, M. D., K. P. White, and R. H. Coop, *The Black Self*. Englewood Cliffs, N.J.: Prentice-Hall, Inc., 1974.

Young, P. T., *Understanding Your Feelings and Emotions*. Englewood Cliffs, N.J.: Prentice-Hall, Inc., 1975.

The Self and
Perceptual Processes:
Theory and Theorists

PROLOGUE

The ideas undergirding this volume grow from a frame of reference in psychology which has variously been called the "phenomenological," "perceptual," "existential," "interactional," or "humanistic" approach. More specifically, it is a point of view that seeks to understand people in terms of how they see themselves. It tries to understand behavior from the point of view of the person doing the behaving. It is a psychology searching to understand what goes on inside people in terms of how their needs, feelings, values, and unique ways of perceiving influence them to behave as they do. In a personal sense, it is the psychology a concerned friend uses as he or she wonders why we're "feeling so sad;" in a clinical sense, it is what a therapist uses while probing for the deeper meanings in a client's personal experiences.

A thesis fundamental to this point of view is that behavior is influenced not only by the accumulation of our past and current experiences, but even more importantly it is influenced by the *personal meanings we attach to our perceptions of those experiences.* In other words, how we behave is more than simply a result of what happens to us from the outside; it is also a function of how we feel about it on the inside, how we interpret it. There seems little question but that our experiences can have a vast influence on our current behavior. Although we cannot change what happened to us yesterday, we *can* change how we *feel* about it today. We cannot change the event, but we can modify our perceptions *about* the event. Therapy, for example, does not "cure" a person in the sense of removing problems, but it does assist an individual towards *new perceptions* of the problems so they can be coped with effectively.

Perception, defined, refers to a process by which we select, organize, and interpret sensory stimulation into a meaningful and coherent picture of the world. Which brings us logically to our first topic for consideration.

The Nature of Perceptual Processes

Combs *et al.*[1] have developed the idea that each person behaves in a manner consistent with his "perceptual field," which is a more or less fluid organization of personal meanings existing for every individual at any given instant in time. Perceptual field has also been called one's private or personal world, one's psychological field or life-space, or one's phenomenal field. The last term, which is appearing more frequently in psychological circles these days, is derived from the Greek, *phainesthai,* which means "to appear," or "to appear so," or "as it appears." In its original usage, a phenomenon was "that which is known through the senses and immediate experience" rather than through deductions. This is still the case. That is, to a phenomenologist, reality lies not in the event but in the phenomenon, which is to say, in a person's *perception* of the event. The idea of how perception can influence behavior is nicely illustrated in the following example cited by Combs:

> Several years ago a friend of mine was driving in a car at dusk along a Western road. A globular mass, about two feet in diameter, suddenly appeared directly in the path of the car. A passenger screamed and grasped the wheel attempting to steer the car around the object. The driver, however, tightened his grip on the wheel and drove directly into the object. The behavior of both the driver and the passenger was determined by his own (perceptions). The passenger, an Easterner, saw the object in the highway as a boulder and fought desperately to steer the car around it. The driver, a native Westerner, saw it as a tumbleweed and devoted his efforts to keeping his passenger from overturning the car.[2]

Each person in the car behaved according to what he "saw." The behavior of each was determined not by what the "objective" facts were, but by their "subjective" interpretations of the facts. It turned out that the driver was correct: it wasn't a boulder, but the passenger, at the instant of behaving, responded in terms of what he *thought* the facts were and not what they *actually* were. When the passenger grabbed the wheel, *he* was right, and he behaved accordingly. Our perceptions usually have the feeling of "being right" at the instant of behaving. This may not be true in retrospect as we look back over things we did yesterday, or last week, or five years ago, but at the time we acted it very likely seemed to us that the things we did, the thoughts we had, and the feelings we felt were legitimate, valid, and rational. For example, consider the following incident reported by Shlien about a twenty-eight-year-old sociology graduate student who was wearily on his way home by bus after midterm examinations. In the graduate student's own words, this is what happened:

> After an hour or so, the bus stopped in a small town, and a few passengers got on. One of them was a blonde girl, very good looking in a fresh but sort of sleazy way. I thought that she was probably a farm girl, and I wished she'd sit by me. By God, she did. She was really comely, if you know what I mean, and she smiled a bit so I felt sure she'd be approachable. Oh boy, what luck. I didn't want to be too eager, and I was still exhausted so we just smiled then sort of dozed off for a little while, hoping to recuperate by the time the driver turned out the lights and meanwhile enjoying my fantasies about the prospectus for the rest of the trip. The last thing I remember was smiling at her and noticing that when her skirt slipped up on her knee as she reached up to the back of the seat, she didn't pull it down. Wow! About four hours later we were pounding along the road in complete darkness when I opened my eyes. Her leg, the outside of it, was against mine, and the way it pressed and moved with the motion of the bus woke me up. This was more than I'd dreamed of. I was terribly excited, and when I stirred a little the steady pressure of leg didn't move away. By this time, I had a terrific erection, and the more I thought about this cute little babe pressing against me, the worse it got. I was just about to reach out and touch her when we pulled into a gas station for a stop, and when the light came through the window, *she* wasn't there at all! She must have left while I was asleep. A fat man with a growth of beard and a dead cigar dropping ash on his vest was sprawled next to me, sound asleep. It was *his* leg pressing against me, and he was so fat and slovenly that even when I drew myself away, his sloppy flesh stayed against me. I was so dumfounded—disappointed too, and the funny thing—I lost that erection almost immediately, got up and moved to another seat. What a letdown.[3]

We organize, we "see" our environment in such a way so that it has personal meaning for us. The perceptual world of each of us is organized in ways that are dictated not only by our central nervous system physiology, but also in accordance with the needs, values, beliefs and self-concepts that each of us brings to our perception of "reality." Let's turn our attention to how this works.

Needs and Values Affect Perception

Each of us is continually motivated to maintain and enhance how we feel about ourselves. Our perceptions enable us to be aware of the world around us and to behave in ways that result in the satisfaction of our fundamental needs for personal adequacy. We might expect, then, that an individual's needs for personal adequacy would strongly influence his or her perceptions. This is exactly what proves to be so.

Out of all the phenomena we might perceive, we usually select what is meaningful to us and consistent with the needs we feel at the moment. For example, experiments on food deprivation in which participants were kept off food for varying periods of time have shown repeatedly that as hunger increases, so, too, do erroneous perceptions of food. As lunch hour approaches, have you noted how your mind sometimes flashes more and more food images across your mental screen? Osgood[4] describes this nicely from his own personal experience as follows: "An office that I pass each day is numbered 400D; inevitably, when the hour is near mealtime, I perceive this as FOOD. The car I used to drive had the euphemistic label SILVER STREAK on its dashboard; inevitably when the hour was near mealtime, I would read this as SILVER STEAK." And of course we're all familiar with the common desert scene of the parched, dehydrated man pulling himself across the hot sands toward some watery illusion created in answer to a desperate need for body fluid.

The influence of needs on perceptions has also been demonstrated under more rigorous laboratory conditions. For example, Levine and others,[5] presented food-deprived subjects with pictures of various objects distorted behind a ground-glass screen and found that those who had gone three to nine hours without eating saw more food objects than did those who had eaten forty-five minutes to two hours before the experiment. McClelland and Atkinson[6] deprived Navy men of food for periods ranging from one to sixteen hours. The investigators then pretended to flash food pictures on a screen, but actually projected nothing. All of the subjects were unaware of the relation between their hunger and the perceptual test they were taking. Under the general set to see objects, the hungrier men had a greater frequency of food perceptions than the less hungry ones. The differences in the number of food responses were particularly large between the one-hour and sixteen-hour groups. The experimenters also found that as the hours of food deprivation increased so, too, did the apparent *size* of the perceived food objects.

Even psychologists, who should know about such things, are not immune to the effect of needs on perception. In a study of the evaluations of other people by clinical psychologists, Weingarten[7] found that psychotherapists saw more problems in their clients in those areas in which the clinicians themselves had problems. Even when the purpose of the investigation was brought to their attention, they persisted in seeing in the clients they examined the problems they wrestled with themselves!

Similarly, values are determinants of our perceptions and behavior. We more readily perceive those things, experiences, and people we value, prize, and esteem. For example, have you ever realized how quickly you are able to spot the person you care for in a crowd of people, or how fast you find your name on an entire page of names. Or have you noticed your inclination to buy more food than you really need when exceptionally hungry? The need for something, in this case, food, seems to have the effect of increasing its value potential.

The influence of one's values on perceptions has also been demonstrated in research. A case in point is Vroom's[8] findings which suggest that an individual tends to perceive his own values and attitudes in persons for whom he has a negative attitude. Apparently we do not like to see characteristics we value in ourselves as being part of a disliked individual's personality. Could it be that if we see certain of our own values reflected in a person we do not like, that these same values seem to us less important or less good in ourselves?

Postman and others[9] have been able to demonstrate that personal values are determinants of an individual's perceptual selectivity. First they measured the value orientation of twenty-five students with a value scale. Then they flashed words representing the six values one at a time on a screen with increasingly longer exposures until they were recognized by each student. Their general finding was that the more closely a given work reflected a value already held by the student, the more rapidly he was able to recognize it. For example, subjects with dominant religious values would recognize on very brief exposure such words as "priest" or "minister" while taking longer to perceive economic words such as "cost," "price," or "bonds." In other words, there seemed to be a predisposition, or readiness, to see more quickly words reflecting one's personal values. In another study, Bruner and Goodman[10] found that values exert other kinds of influence on perception. They asked ten- and eleven-year-old boys from wealthy and poor families to guess the size of various denominations of coins (1, 5, 10, 25, 50 cents) by having them vary the diameter of a circle of light to the size of a specified coin. When asked to adjust the light to the size of a remembered nickel or dime or half dollar, all the children tended to overestimate the size of the coins, with the overestimation increasing with the increased value of the coin. The poorer boys, however, overestimated to a greater extent than boys from more prosperous families. The hunch here is that perhaps because perceived size is related to perceived value, the personal value of the coins was greater for the poorer boys.

It may be no surprise to you to learn that Majasan's[11] research, which was designed to examine the similarity and differences between college students' and their professors' values, found that students who get higher grades tend to have values similar to the values of their instructors. Students whose values were different than their instructors tended to get lower grades. These grades, by the way, were derived solely from textbook-based objective exams. Could it be that the closer your values are to your instructor's the more you are likely to "hear" and therefore learn from that person?

A very lifelike example of how social values influence perception was reported by Hastorf and Cantril[12] and dealt with the perceptions of Princeton and Dartmouth students to a rough and tense football game between the two schools. Each group of students was asked questions about which side was responsible for the "roughness" or "dirtiness" of the game. When asked which team "started it," 64 percent of the Dartmouth students said Princeton did, while 86 percent of the Princeton students blamed Dartmouth. When later shown the complete movie for the game, Princeton players "saw," on the average, about 10 rule infractions by Dartmouth players. On the other hand, Dartmouth players "saw" less than half that much foul play on the part of their own team. (Alas, the report failed to mention who won.)

Beliefs Can Influence Perceptions

By and large, people tend to behave in a manner which is consistent with what they believe to be true. In this sense, seeing is not only believing; seeing is behaving! A fact is not what is; a fact is what one believes it to be. When people believed that the earth was flat they avoided its edges; when they believed that blood-letting would drain out the evil spirits and cure a patient, they persisted in this practice despite the fact that people died before their very eyes. When people believed that phrenology could help them, they had their heads examined (literally). There is even evidence to suggest that when researchers believe that their hypothesis is true, they are more apt to find evidence supporting that hypothesis than if they didn't believe it was true.[13] And so it goes.

Kelley[14] conducted an experiment which very clearly shows the influence of beliefs on behavior. Students in a college class were presented with brief written descriptions of a guest lecturer prior to his appearance in class. The descriptions were almost the same except for one phrase, which in one case described him as a "rather cold" person and in the other case as a "very warm" person. Some students received the "warm" and some the "cold" description. They did not know that two different descriptions had been distributed.

After hearing his lecture the students who had received the "warm" descriptions rated the lecturer as more considerate of others, more sociable, more popular, better natured, more humorous, and more humane than did students who had received the "cold" description. The findings directly reflect how implicit beliefs regarding what traits go with warmth and coldness can influence what one "sees" in another person.

Kelley also found that the warm-cold variable affected the amount of interactions that the students engaged in with the guest lecturer. Fifty-six percent of the students who received the "warm" description participated in class discussion, but only thirty-two percent of the students who received the "cold" description did so. This was the case even though the students were sitting in the same room hearing the same lecture. Thus do our beliefs about people sway our reactions to them and influence the course of interpersonal behavior.

Bills and McGehee[15] found that the students who learned and retained the most in a psychology experiment were inclined to believe things such as, "Psychology experiments are useful and will eventually help us to completely understand people," and "Psychology, in general, is a valuable, quantitative science with many practical aspects." On the other hand, students who quickly forgot the material were those who held beliefs such as "Psychological experiments are a total waste of time," and "Psychology, in general, is nothing but a witch hunt." Along somewhat similar lines, research has also shown that persons who believe in ESP tend to score higher on tests designed to assess this capacity in themselves.[16] It seems that whether it be psychology or ESP, one's beliefs can, indeed, affect one's performance.

Beliefs can also influence what we think we see. This point was illustrated several years ago when one of the Minneapolis papers ran a photograph of a pair of beautiful breasts with the caption, "Can you identify this famous movie star?" For three days letters were printed from indignant citizens who felt that rampant free sex had taken over a formerly responsible "family" newspaper. Then, on the fourth day, they showed a picture of the entire head and torso and it turned out to be none other than Johnny Weissmuller of Tarzan fame (and a first class swimmer, hence the over-developed pectoral muscles). Another example of how our beliefs can lead us to erroneous perceptions. What we believe to be true does not always correspond to reality.

Our beliefs influence our perceptions, nurture our assumptions, and to a large extent determine our behavior. We do not easily give up that which we believe to be true. The church of our youth and the first political party to which we gave our allegiance usually continue to be our choices. Perceptions of one person by another person can be as varied as the assumptions on which the perceptions are based. An interesting example of how different beliefs can influence different perceptions was reported by Stachnik and Ulrich[17] in a paper in which they described the divergent perceptions of Barry Goldwater by psychiatrists after he received the 1964 Republican nomination for President. *Fact* magazine sent a questionnaire to all 12,356 psychiatrists registered in the American Medical Association asking, "Do you believe Barry Goldwater is psychologically fit to serve as President of the United States?" Not all answered, but of the 2,417 who did reply, 571 said they did not know enough about him to answer, 657 said they thought him psychologically fit, and 1,189 said he was not. Consider some examples of how dramatically the perceptions of Goldwater differed. One psychiatrist said, "I not only believe Barry Goldwater is psychologically fit to serve as President, but I believe he is a very mature person." On the same subject, however, another psychiatrist observed, "I believe Mr. Goldwater is basically immature . . . He has little understanding of himself or why he does the things he does." It is also interesting to note that diametrically opposing views regarding Goldwater's fitness were defended with rock-like conviction. For example, a Connecticut psychiatrist concluded:

> I believe Goldwater is grossly psychotic . . . he is a mass murderer at heart and a suicide. He is amoral and immoral, a dangerous lunatic. Any psychiatrist who does not agree with the above is himself psychologically unfit to be a psychiatrist.

A Georgia psychiatrist was just as adamant, but had a different belief about Goldwater:

> I value my reputation as a psychiatrist, but I am willing to stake it on the opinion that Barry Goldwater is eminently qualified—psychologically and in every other way—to serve as President of the United States.

The authors suggested, tongue-in-cheek(?), that among other things "A Republican seeking psychiatric counsel should be sure to see a Republican psychiatrist since this apparently enhances the probability of receiving a favorable diagnosis. . . ."

Beliefs are difficult to change. Research has shown that this is especially true for persons who have strong prejudices,[18, 19] which, after all, are nothing more than beliefs which have become so fixed as to become permanent props in one's personality structure. Perhaps the point that beliefs change slowly can be illustrated by the yarn about the man who believed he was dead. His psychiatrist, after hearing his story, suggested that during the next week he repeat thrice daily, "Dead men don't bleed." When the man returned the next week the psychiatrist asked the man if he had followed his advice. Assured that he had, the psychiatrist took a needle and pricked the man's finger and squeezed out a drop of blood. "Well," said the psychiatrist, "What do you think about that?" The man regarded his finger with some care, looked up at the psychiatrist with a puzzled expression and answered, "I'll be darned. Dead men *do* bleed!"

Self-Concept Affects Perceptions

Perception is a selective process and the picture that we have of ourselves is a vital factor in determining the richness and variety of perceptions selected. It makes a great deal of difference how one perceives, let's say, the Pope if one sees oneself as a Jew, Protestant, or Catholic. Depending on one's concept of self, an exam is perceived as either something to avoid failing or something to pass with as high a grade as possible; a class discussion is viewed as either something to actively engage in or something to sit quietly through for fear of saying the wrong thing; front seats of classrooms are seen as either vantage points for better seeing and

© 1964 United Feature Syndicate, Inc.

Once a belief is firmly established, it can influence behavior in strange ways.

hearing or as potentially dangerous spots where one could be more easily seen and, heaven forbid, called on! It all depends on how we perceive ourselves.

There is another consideration related to the impact of self-concept on perception and that is connected to its possible boomerang effect. For example, a student who views himself as poor in math not only internalizes that perception, but he is also likely to *project* it in his behavior. That is, he "projects" the "I can't do math" perception outside of himself by either, (1) avoiding math courses, and/or (2) by being so tense in the math courses he does take that he trips over his own anxiety trying to work problems he doesn't think he can solve in the first place. Through either course of action it is possible to perpetuate a negative self-image. By avoiding math, the student is in effect saying, "I'm too dumb to take math," which serves to reinforce the negative attitude with which he started. By taking math with the "I can't do it," feeling he is apt to increase the likelihood of overstimulating his anxiety to the point of not being able to think clearly when it counts. Naturally enough this usually leads to poor performance and ultimately leads to further evidence to support his negative self-concept. That is what is meant by the boomerang effect. The very process of *beginning* with a negative attitude usually guarantees that it will be projected in behavior in such a way as to 'bring back' to the person evidence that he really cannot do what he thought he couldn't do in the first place. It ends up being a self-fulfilling prophecy. Of course, the boomerang effect can also work in the other direction. It is possible to start with a more positive attitude and accumulate evidence to support and maintain a more favorable self-perception.

I am not for a moment suggesting that how one performs or behaves is a simple matter of saying "I can" or "I can't," and therefore it will be true. Behavior is far more complex than that. Each of us has certain aptitudes and skills which equip us to do a few things a little better than some and some things a little better than most. The task before any person desiring to grow more competent is to keep himself as open as possible to experiences and opportunities which could broaden and expand his perception of self. By sampling new experiences and by testing one's self is as wide a variety of ways as possible, one not only increases the possibility of discovering those things which one does a little better than most, but one also decreases the possibility of being deflated by things one is not particularly good at. Most of us are better than we give ourselves credit for being and taking on new challenges now and then is one good way to find that out.

How We Perceive Others

Ralph Waldo Emerson once observed, "What we are, that only can we see." As both common sense and research have shown, this simple aphorism stands as the cornerstone upon which our most important principles of people perception are built. As the famous psychiatrist Harry Stack Sullivan has expressed it: "It is not as ye judge that ye shall be judged, but as you judge yourself so shall you judge others."[20]

Psychologist Frank Barron offers some striking evidence for the deep truth in Sullivan's and Emerson's observations. While doing research related to the nature and meaning of psychological health, Dr. Barron and his colleagues first of all had to develop some working ideas about what a healthy person would probably be like. They then studied subjects chosen for their general effectiveness as persons and had each staff member describe each subject on an adjective checklist. The intention was to derive from these checklists a composite staff description of each subject's so-called "Soundness as a Person." The results of this endeavor were quite surprising. As it turned out, individual staff members used quite different adjectives to describe the same person. The revealing aspect of this was the great consistency with which staff members described highly effective people with exactly the adjectives that in private moments of good will toward themselves they could use to characterize *themselves*. Barron went on to add:

> Moreover, they tended to describe clearly *ineffective* persons as possessing traits which in themselves they most strongly denied . . . Thus, one staff member noted for his simple and clear thought processes most frequently described an ineffective person as *confused;* another staff member who is especially well-behaved in matters of duty checked the adjectives *conscientious* and *responsible* most frequently in describing highly rated subjects. . . . another staff member who has subsequently been interested professionally in independence of judgment saw effective subjects as *independent* and *fairminded. Each of us, in brief, saw his own image in what he judged to be good.*[21]

The inclination to see in others what is in oneself is true as early as adolescence. Rosenberg,[22] for example, found that adolescents who thought poorly of themselves tended to think poorly of others and to feel that others thought poorly of them. Those high in self-regard, on the other hand, thought well of others and believed others thought well of them.

It will be no great surprise to you to learn that self-esteem plays an important part in how we perceive others. Research by Penny Baron[23] and Walster[24] indicates that not only do high self-esteem people expect more acceptance and less rejection than low self-esteem people, but they are also inclined to view others in a more favorable light. You can do some interesting (and perhaps revealing) research with yourself on this point. Pay particular attention to your feelings about yourself for the next three or four days and note how they influence your behavior toward others. It may be that it is not our friend or our loved one or our children we are mad at; it is ourselves. What we feel toward ourselves gets aimed at others, and we sometimes treat others not as persons, but as targets.

Although we may not be at all aware of it, research indicates that an individual's judgments of others are drawn largely from what that person develops as his or her "implicit theory of personality."[25, 26, 27] That is, most people seem to have certain conceptions of other peoples' personality based upon certain preconceived ideas or stereotypes.

For better or for worse, we have endless ways for stereotyping others. We do it on the basis of ethnic background,[28, 29] first names[30] (a stereotyping that may begin as early as grade school[31]), voice,[32] clothes and manner of dressing,[33, 34] body build,[35, 36] and physical attractiveness.[37, 38, 39]

All in all, research shows that we are more affected by physically attractive people than by physically unattractive people, and unless we are specifically abused by them, we tend to like them better. In addition, the evidence suggests that, as a general rule, attractive people—young and old—tend to receive more favorable treatment than less attractive people. Apparently, then, despite repeated warnings to the contrary, we seem to operate under the basic assumption that beauty is, after all, more than "skin deep." (More about this idea in chapter four.)

The disquieting aspect of this evidence is that there is a strong possibility that such preferential treatment could be the beginning of a cycle of a self-fulfilling prophecy. That is, if people are treated poorly (or well, as the case may be), it affects how they perceive themselves and how they feel about their personal qualities. Thus, unattractive children may come to perceive themselves as unlovable, or at least as undesirable, if they are continually treated in negative, rejecting ways. Ultimately, they may begin to behave in a style that is consistent with this self-concept, a way that is in keeping with how they were treated in the first place. As professional persons or parents, we need to keep an eye on our preferences for this individual or that one so that we aren't caught in the trap of believing, either consciously or unconsciously, that only that which is beautiful is good.

It would appear that one of the best ways to find out what a person is really like is to pay close attention to what he thinks other people are like, what he thinks the world is like. Frequently, the way we perceive others is primarily a projection of our own ambitions, needs and fears. This sort of projection may serve several functions—one, it may tend to make others seem more like us than they really are and therefore more compatible; and two, it may help perpetuate the feeling that the way we are is really the "right" way.

The man who tells us that people are basically trustworthy and kind—ignoring the plain fact that they can also be devious and cruel—may be saying more about himself than about the world. Oscar Wilde's observation that "all criticism is a form of autobiography" is perhaps more true than we ever thought. When we think we are looking out a window, it could be that we are merely gazing into a looking-glass.

Perceptions Can Be Modified

As difficult as it is to change perceptions once they are acquired and incorporated into one's self-system, there nonetheless is abundant evidence to suggest that perceptions toward one's self and others can be modified. For example, studies in psychotherapy have shown us that if a therapist is genuine, accepting, and empathically understanding of a client's private world, then the client is better able to alter his self-perceptions in the direction of becoming more confident and self-directing, more mature and socialized, more healthy and integrated.[40]

On the other hand, clinical studies of "brainwashing" techniques used by the Chinese communists on American prisoners during the Korean conflict have shown that it is possible to break down a man's confidence, destroy the concept he has of himself, and, in general, disintegrate his personality structure to the point of apathetic resignation.[41]

As another illustration, research has demonstrated that some members of a group will report perceptions which are contrary to the evidence of their senses. They will, for example, report that Figure A covers a larger area than Figure B, when their visual perceptions *plainly indicate that this is not true.* Experiments by Asch;[42] later refined and improved by Crutchfield,[43] have shown that when a person is *led to believe* that other members in a group see B as larger than A, then he is inclined to go along with this judgment. More than that, he frequently does so with a real belief in his false perception.

Perception can be dramatically altered by setting up conditions which produce vivid hallucinations and other abnormal reactions in a thoroughly normal, awake individual. For example, in sensory deprivation experiments at McGill University[44] it was discovered that if all sensory input was cut off or reduced, abnormal perceptions resulted. If healthy subjects lie relatively motionless, to reduce kinesthetic stimuli, with eyes covered to eliminate light, with hearing muffled by foam-rubber pillows as well as being in a quiet cubicle, and with tactile sensations reduced by cuffs over the hands, then within forty-eight hours many subjects experience weird perceptual processes and hallucinations resembling that of a psychotic individual.

The ingestion of various drugs is another way of modifying perceptions, alcohol being the drug of choice for many people. Alcohol alters your psychological state in an odd manner. In small doses it is a depressant that reduces the effective expression of your impulses, needs, and anxieties. It relaxes the guards that watch your behavior, but after that point it scrambles your sensations and perceptions. For example, research indicates that when an individual has had a given amount to drink, he is inclined to distort the subjective probability of success and begin to perceive various alternatives as less serious than they really are.[45] Several drinks in an hour's time on a relatively empty stomach is a quick way to distort reality and to take the sorts of risks we wouldn't think of taking in a more sober state. Perhaps this is one reason why up to 70 percent of all highway accident deaths can be attributed to alcohol.[46] It may also help to explain why 60 percent of those killed in alcohol-related accidents are teenagers,[47] whose natural inclination for accelerated living and high risk-taking is hardly modulated by booze.

How fast your perceptions get scrambled as a consequence of alcohol depends on many factors, some of which include how much you weigh, how much you move around when drinking, what kind of mood you are in, and what you had to eat before you started bending your elbow. Research shows that your personality and sex can make a difference, too. For example, extroverts show the effects of drinking sooner than introverts (that is, the extroverts blood alcohol level goes up at a faster rate), and women get tipsy more easily than men.[48] (The apparent reason for this is that a woman's body is made up of about 55 to 65 percent water, whereas a man's is about 65–75 percent water. A given amount of alcohol is therefore more diluted in man's body.)

Marijuana is another mind-altering drug capable of dramatically altering perceptions. As with alcohol, it acts on the central nervous system and the reaction often occurs in two stages: a period of stimulation and euphoria followed by a period of sedation and tranquility, and, with higher doses, sleep. Tart[49] interviewed 150 regular marijuana users and found that many sensory and perceptual changes were reported, including distortions of time and space, changes in social perception and experience, and a number of ''out-of-body'' experiences. Other research on the effects of marijuana indicate that:

> The user under the effect of the drug may appear normal to the casual observer. . . . but underneath the surface he may be experiencing a succession of augmented sensory impressions. Under stress he is likely to be unable (and/or unmotivated) to perform mental or motor functions with normal efficiency.[50]

Alcohol and marijuana are only two of many different kinds of drugs capable of altering a person's perceptions. If you're interested in further reading on this topic, a book by Matheson and Davison, *The Behavioral Effects of Drugs,*[51] is an excellent source.

Perceptions can be modified or changed by conditions both inside and outside the self. The changes can be for better or for worse and they can be either temporary or permanent. What we see may be real or imagined and whether we perceive when we are drunk or sober, manic or depressed, anxious or tranquil, we persist in behaving in a manner which, at the moment of behaving, is consistent with what we perceive to be true.

Things Are Not Always What They Seem

When we look at things from our own point of view they don't always square with how they may be perceived by another person. For example, I recall an incident involving a youthful art teacher who admonished one of her first-grade pupils for drawing a cow the way he did because, after all, ''Cows just don't look like that.'' The little boy frowned a bit, examined his cow closely, looked up at the teacher and said, ''Maybe they don't, but I bet if you were down here with me they would.''

Schlien[52] has reported a story about a psychologist which perhaps best illustrates some of the things about perception we have been talking about: influence of needs, impact of self-concept, behavior which is consistent with perceptions, the possibility of misinterpreting behavior if we examine it only from our own point of view, etc. It goes like this.

The parents of a small boy were worried. He was quiet, sensitive, lonely, and acted afraid of other children. The parents wanted some professional advice before the child entered school and so invited a psychologist friend of theirs to the house for an afternoon and dinner so he could observe the boy under more natural conditions. Upon arriving, the psychologist asked all the appropriate questions about history and behavior and then took a spot on the balcony where he watched, unseen, the boy play in a garden by himself. The boy sat pensively in the sun, listening to the neighborhood children shout. He frowned, rolled over on his stomach, kicked the toes of his white shoes in the grass, sat up and looked at the stains. Then he saw an earthworm. He stretched it out on a flat stone, found a sharp edged chip, and proceeded to saw the worm in half. Many impressions were taking shape in the psychologist's mind, and he made some tentative notes to the effect: "Seems isolated and angry, perhaps over-aggressive, or sadistic, should be watched carefully when playing with other children, not have knives or pets." Then he heard the boy talking to himself. He leaned forward and strained to catch the words. The boy finished his separation of the worm, his frown disappeared, and he said, "There. Now you have a friend."

Reality Is a Shifting Image

In Figures 2.1 and 2.2 are two famous drawings that Gestalt psychologists like to show to their students. One is a picture of an old witch-like woman and the other is a picture of a goblet. At least that is what most people see the first time around. But if you look at the old woman long enough, she turns into a pretty young woman wearing a boa; and if you look at the goblet long enough, it turns into two faces peering at each other. And if you look at them even longer, they reverse themselves again.

The point is that we cannot see the old woman and the young girl at the same time; nor the goblet and the two faces. Each is a composite of both and what we see depends upon our shifting idea of what is reality.

What is the "reality" of these drawings? It depends upon who's looking at them and for how long and at what moment. There is no "single" reality, for the drawings have been so cleverly composed that the same composition seems different to us at different times, and when we see one image we cannot see the other.

This show of Gestalt trickery may be an important lesson for us. It indicates that what we may call our view of life is a shifting image rather than a continuous reality. It can probably be safely said that our lives—like the two pictures—are ambiguous patterns, and although at different times we choose to look at one pattern rather than another, this does not make one more real than the other. Indeed, maintaining our sense of sanity and personal balance very likely depends in part upon the acceptance of a certain level of ambiguity in our lives. What we see may not be what others see and what others see may not be what we want to see. Life, for the most part, is not either or, but both.

Whether it is in our work, our friendships, or love relationships, we are ready to be perplexed and even angry when the picture turns into the opposite. On Monday, everything seems fine; on Friday it is barely tolerable. Which is the true picture—the witch-like woman or the pretty girl? We can go a bit crazy trying to decide, until we realize that no one's life situation is so good that he sees the pretty girl all the time, or so bad that he views the witch all the time.

Reality is not one picture, but two. We cannot see them at the same time, but they are both there. Perhaps if we can accept this idea, we can more easily and graciously bear with life's inevitable shades of gray before jumping to hasty conclusions about what is black and what is white, about what is right and what is wrong.

Figure 2.1
An ambiguous drawing than can be seen as an attractive young lady or as an ugly witch-like woman.

Figure 2.2
Another ambiguous drawing that can be seen as a goblet or as two faces peering at each other.

Sometimes our inner feelings trick us into seeing a "reality" that doesn't even make sense.

Humanistic Social Psychological Theory

The theoretical orientation or position we will examine in the remainder of this chapter is one which focuses on humans as social beings who are influenced and guided by the personal meanings they attach to their experiences. In its most simple terms, it is an orientation which seeks to understand humans by studying humans. We can understand astronomy only by being an astronomer; we can understand entomology only by being an entomologist (or perhaps an insect); but we can understand a great deal about psychology merely by being a person, *by being the object of our own study.* This may seem to be a self-evident point of view, an obvious direction for psychology to take, but alas, this has not always been the case. Why? Perhaps the following observation by a clinical psychologist may help us understand:

> Because of our need to compete with the physical sciences, behavioral sciences have skipped over, by and large, the naturalistic stage from which other disciplines developed. We have not been people-watchers as biologists were bird- and bug-watchers. We have moved too quickly into the laboratory and looked only at special populations of people under special circumstances; we have thought we could derive generalizations about human behavior without first gaining the kind of understanding that could come only from years of performing normal tasks. Very few of us make any attempt to use our scientific training to investigate what people are really like when

they are being themselves. When one examines the literature in the behavioral sciences, one seldom has the feeling, "that's what it's like to be me." The *person* is usually missing and the findings have no reality or meaning for us because we cannot find *ourselves*.[53]

As if in answer to the need to put the person back into the behavioral sciences, humanistic psychology has emerged as a major orientation toward the study of human behavior. The humanistic orientation represents "the third force" in psychology, insofar as it endeavors to go beyond the points of view of behaviorism and psychoanalysis, the two most dominant perspectives within the broad arena of psychology. The humanistic point of view does not see itself as competitive with the other two systems; rather it attempts to supplement their observations and to introduce further perceptions and insights.

Since humanistic psychology, phenomenology, and existential psychology are frequently used in the same breath by those who identify with any frame of reference that discusses a psychology of the self, it might be well if we take a look at the meaning of each of these terms, their relationships to each other and to perceptual psychology.

Let's begin with existentialism. This is basically a twentieth-century philosophy which stresses an individual's responsibility for making himself what he is. It is an introspective theory which expresses a person's intense awareness of his or her own existence and freedom to choose among alternatives for behaving. A main tenet of existentialism is the idea that people struggle to transcend themselves, to reach beyond themselves. In this sense, the idea of transcendence boils down to our capacity for "dynamic self-consciousness."[54] Not only can we think, but we can also think about (criticize and correct) our thinking. Not only can we feel, but we can have feeling about our feelings. We are not only *conscious,* but we are *self-conscious*.

We have already noted that to a phenomenologist, reality lies not in the event but in the phenomenon, that is to say, the person's *perception* of the event. This is not so different from the existential point of view which suggests that humans are the determiners of their own natures and definers of their own values. For the phenomenologist, one's perceptions grow out of one's experiences; for the existentialist, one's "essence" or "being" grows out of one's capacity to make choices. Both of these points of view regard humans to be the measure of all things and that the reality they respond to is their own. This is in opposition to the more deterministic points of view (psychoanalytic or behavioristic) that maintain a person's "being" is shaped primarily by outside forces.

Humanistic psychology fits comfortably in the company of phenomenology and existentialism inasmuch as it is an orientation which centers on human interests and values. It is concerned with the sort of human experiences and expressions that psychology has long neglected, for example, love, creativity, sense of self, higher values, becoming, spontaneity, warmth, meaning, fair-play, transcendental experiences, psychological health, and related concepts. It is, in the best sense of the word, an expression of what psychology still means to the average, intelligent layman, that is, the functioning and experience of a total human being.

Bugental[55] has suggested five basic postulates for humanistic psychology that outline the scope of this frame of reference for understanding human behavior.

1. *Man, as man, supersedes the sum of his parts.* In other words, man is more than the accumulative product of various part-functions. I suppose that this is something like saying that Beethoven's *Fifth Symphony* is more than the summation of individual musical notes that went into composing it.

2. *Man has his being in a human context.* The unique nature of man is expressed through his relationship to his fellows and, in this sense, humanistic psychology is always concerned with man in his interpersonal potential.

3. *Man is aware.* This suggests that whatever the degree of consciousness, man is aware of himself and his existence. He does not move from one experience to the next as if they were discrete and independent episodes unrelated to each other. How a man behaves in the present is related to what happened in his past and connected to his hopes for the future.

4. *Man has choice.* Phenomenologically, choice is a given of experience. When man is aware, he can choose and thereby become not a bystander but a participant in experience.

5. *Man is intentional.* Through his choice of this or that, of going here or there, man demonstrates his intent. He "intends" through having purpose, through valuing, and through seeking meaning in his life. Man's intentionality, his "conscious deliberateness," is the basis on which he builds his identity and distinguishes himself from other species.

Bugental[56] has also articulated five basic characteristics of the humanistic orientation in psychology, which are as follows:

1. Humanistic psychology cares about people.
2. Humanistic psychology values meaning more than procedure.
3. Humanistic psychology looks for human rather than nonhuman validation.
4. Humanistic psychology accepts the relativism of all knowledge.
5. Humanistic psychology relies heavily upon the phenomenological orientation.

Humanistic Social Psychological Contributors

Many great names in psychology are either directly or indirectly related to a humanistic social-psychological orientation toward the study of human behavior. Contributors such as Alfred Adler, Gordon Allport, Eric Berne, Hadley Cantril, Charles H. Cooley, Arthur Combs, Erik Erikson, Erich Fromm, Karen Horney, William James, Kurt Lewin, Abraham Maslow, George H. Mead, Gardner Murphy, Henry Murray, Otto Rank, C. Rogers, Harry S. Sullivan, and Donald Syngg, among many others have made significant contributions to the point of view we're considering. (Basic references to each of these contributors are suggested at the end of this chapter.)

Since there is neither sufficient space nor a necessity to detail the contributions of each contributor, we will consider a cross-section of their theoretical points of view to get some idea of the variety of interpretations possible within a humanistic social psychological framework.

C. H. Cooley (The Looking-Glass Self)

C. H. Cooley was one of the earliest social psychologists to explore the idea of self. He recognized that the social milieu from which a person comes contributes heavily to how a person views himself. With this idea in mind, he developed a theory of the self that was concerned primarily with how the self grows as a consequence of interpersonal interactions. From this he posited the concept of "the looking-glass self" that is perhaps best expressed in his own words:

> In a very large and interesting class of cases the social reference takes the form of a somewhat definite imagination of how one's self . . . appears in a particular mind, and the kind of self-feeling one has is determined by the attitude toward this attributed to that other mind. A social self might be called the reflected or looking-glass self.
>
> Each to each a looking glass
Reflects the other that doth pass.
>
> The self that is most important is a reflection, largely, from the minds of others. . . . We live on, cheerful, self-confident . . . until in some rude hour we learn that we do not stand as well as we thought we did, that the image of us is tarnished. Perhaps we do something, quite naturally, that we find the social order is set against, or perhaps it is the ordinary course of our life that is not so well regarded as we supposed. At any rate, we find with a chill of terror that . . . our self-esteem, self confidence, and hope, being chiefly founded upon the opinions of others, go down in a crash . . .[57]

We can see here, in the process of self-appraisal by an individual, the importance of his accurate perception and interpretation of the reaction of the other person to him.

George H. Mead (Socially Formed Self)

A somewhat more sophisticated view of the self was developed by G. H. Mead,[58] who, as Cooley did, felt it necessary to root the self in the social conditions relevant to the individual and to derive the content of the self from the interaction between the individual and his social world. Mead's self is an *object of awareness,* rather than a system of processes. That is, we come to know ourselves and respond to ourselves as we see others responding to us. Mead's self is a *socially* formed self which grows in a *social* setting where there is *social* communication. He further suggests that a person can have as many selves as there are numbers of social groups in which he participates. For instance, a person may have a family self that reflects the values and attitudes expressed by his family, a school self which represents the expectations and attitudes expressed by his teachers and fellow students, and many other selves.

Harry Stack Sullivan (Reflected Appraisals)

Closely related to the social interaction ideas of Mead and Cooley is the theoretical position of Sullivan,[59] a psychiatrist who developed what has been called an interpersonal theory of personality development. As Sullivan sees it, from the first day of life, the infant is immersed in a continual stream of interpersonal situations in which he is the recipient of a never-ending flow of "reflected appraisals." It is through his assimilation of these reflected appraisals that the child comes to develop expectations and attitudes toward himself as an individual. If these appraisals have been mainly derogatory, then the self-image is apt to be disparaging and hostile. If, on the other hand, the reflected appraisals have been chiefly positive and constructive, then one's feelings about oneself are more inclined to be positive and approving.

Alfred Adler (Life Plan or Life Style)

The essential pillar of Adlerian psychology,[60] in terms of which the rest of it takes on meaning, is his conception of a "life plan" of the individual, or the purpose, the goal, the "end in view" which determines behavior. Adler's self is a highly personalized, subjective system through which a person interprets and gives meaning to his experiences. Unlike Freud, who made the unconscious the center of personality, Adler (who, by the way, was one of Freud's earliest pupils) stressed *consciousness* as the center of personality. He viewed each person as a conscious being ordinarily aware of his reasons for behavior. More than that, each person is a self-conscious individual, who is capable of planning and guiding his actions with full awareness of their meaning for his own self-realization.

Adler saw every person as having the same goal, namely that of superiority, but he also saw that there were countless different "life styles" for achieving that goal. For example, one person may try to become superior through developing her intellect, another may strive to be a Don Juan, and still another bends all his efforts to achieving the body beautiful. The intellectual, the lady-killer, the muscleman each has an individual life style. The intellectual seeks knowledge, the Don Juan women, the muscleman strength. Each arranges his life in such a way as to achieve the end of being more or less superior to those seeking similar goals.

From Adler's point of view, the person's life style is determined largely by the specific inferiorities, either fancied or real, that a person has. An individual who is, let's say, small, physically inferior, and feels unnoticed may shape his whole life in terms of this characteristic. (It is not uncommon, for example, to find that many "musclemen" did, in fact, start out in the "90-lb. weakling" category.) Or it may be a voice defect, a facial blemish, a physical handicap, or some other characteristic which is the primary feature determining a person's total reaction to his or her environment. The important matter is that the individual sets up a certain "life plan" that is directed in such a way as either to overcome the defect or compensate for it. It is this setting up of a goal or direction in life that gives meaning to events which might not otherwise make sense. Adler's conception of the nature of personality coincides nicely with the humanistic idea that a person can be the master, and not the victim, of his fate.

Karen Horney (Moving Toward, Against, and Away from People)

Like Sullivan and Adler, Karen Horney was another psychiatrist who reacted critically to Freud's instinctivistic and genetic psychology. Horney's ideas spring from
her primary concept of basic anxiety, which she defined as:

> . . . the feeling a child has of being isolated and helpless in a potentially hostile world.
> A wide range of adverse factors in the environment can produce this insecurity in a
> child; direct or indirect domination, indifference, erratic behavior, lack of respect for
> the child's individual needs, lack of real guidance, disparaging attitudes, too much
> admiration or the absence of it, lack of reliable warmth, having to take sides in parental
> disagreements, too much or too little responsibility, overprotection, isolation from
> other children, injustice, discrimination, unkept promises, hostile atmosphere, so on
> and so on.[61]

Any one or a combination of these experiences could predispose an individual to
adopt certain strategies of adjustment in order to satisfy a neurotic need or needs
growing from disturbed human relationships. Horney developed a list of ten needs,
any one of which could be acquired as a consequence of trying to deal with the
problem of disturbed human relationships. She calls these needs "neurotic" because they are irrational solutions to the basic problem:[62]

    1. *The neurotic need for affection and approval.* This need is highlighted by
an indiscriminate need to please others and to do what others want. This sort of
person wants the good will of others and is extremely sensitive to signs of rejection
and unfriendliness. "If I am rejected I am unworthy."

    2. *The neurotic need for a "partner" who will take over one's life.* This
individual has a dread of being deserted or left alone and tends to "overvalue" love
in the sense of seeing love as the magic potion to solve all problems. "If I am loved
I am worthwhile."

    3. *The neurotic need to restrict one's life within narrow borders.* Such a
person is more inclined to save than to spend, fears making demands on others, and
feels a strong necessity for remaining inconspicuous and in the background as much
as possible. "If I am cautious I will not be hurt or disappointed."

    4. *The neurotic need for power.* This need expresses itself in craving power
for its own sake, in an essential disrespect for the feelings and individuality of
others, and in a basic fear of uncontrollable situations. There is also a strong belief
in the omnipotence of intelligence and reason along with a denial of powers of
emotional forces and even contempt for expressions of emotion. Such persons dread
"stupidity" and bad judgment and believe that most anything is possible through
the sheer exertion of will power. "I rely primarily on my ability to think and reason;
emotional people are weak people."

    5. *The neurotic need to exploit others.* This person evaluates others primarily
in terms of whether or not they can be exploited or used. "Do they have power,
position, or authority to do something for me?"

    6. *The neurotic need for prestige.* This sort of person's self-evaluation is
dependent on the amount of public recognition he receives. "If I am recognized by
many people, I feel worthwhile."

7. *The neurotic need for personal admiration.* Here we have a person with an inflated image of himself, a need to be admired not for what he possesses or presents in the public eye but for the imagined self. Self-evaluation is dependent on living up to his image and on admiration of it by others. "Even though it is difficult being something I am not, it is worth it for the admiration I receive. Besides, what would happen if people saw me as I really am?"

8. *The neurotic ambition for personal achievement.* In this case there is usually a relentless driving of one's self to higher and higher levels of achievement, usually accompanied by an intense fear of failure. Self-esteem is dependent on being the very best, particularly in one's own mind. "If I fail I could never accept myself and neither would others; I had better fight for the number one spot."

9. *The neurotic need for self-sufficiency and independence.* Having experienced personal pain in attempts to find warm, satisfying relationships with people, this person turns to distance and separateness as his major source of security. Usually there is a fear of being hurt and so the person acts as though other people were not needed. "If I don't get close to people no one can hurt me."

10. *The neurotic need for perfection and unassailability.* This sort of person usually has a deep fear of making mistakes and being criticized and so tries to make himself impregnable and infallible. He is constantly in search of flaws in himself so that they can be covered up before they become too obvious to others. "If I am perfect, who can criticize me?"

From Horney's point of view, these ten needs are the sources from which inner conflicts develop. The neurotic's need for power, for example, is insatiable: the more he acquires the more he wants. He's never satisfied. In a similar vein, the need for independence can never be fully satisfied because another part of the personality cries out to be loved and accepted. The search for perfection is a lost cause from the beginning. In one way or another, all of the above needs are unrealistic and self-defeating.

Horney later classified these ten neurotic needs under three headings: (1) moving toward people, (2) moving away from people, and (3) moving against people.[63] Each of these interpersonal response traits represents a basic orientation toward others and oneself. Consider some examples of each of these three types.

A person whose predominant interpersonal trait is one of *moving toward people:*

> . . . shows a marked need for affection and approval and an especial need for a "partner"—that is, a friend, lover, husband or wife who is to fulfill all expectations of life and take responsibility for good and evil. . . . (He) needs to be liked, wanted, desired, loved; to feel accepted, welcome, approved of, appreciated; to be needed, to be of importance to others, especially to one particular person.

A person whose predominant interpersonal response trait is one of *moving against people* perceives:

> . . . that the world is an arena where, in the Darwinian sense, only the fittest survive and the strong annihilate the weak . . . a callous pursuit of self-interest is the paramount law. . . . He needs to excel, to achieve success, prestige or recognition in any form.

From the person whose interpersonal response trait is *moving away from people:*

> The underlying principle . . . is never to become so attached to anybody or anything that he or it becomes indispensable. . . . Another pronounced need is for privacy. He is like a person in a hotel room who rarely removes the "Do Not Disturb" sign from his door. . . . His independence, like the whole phenomenon of detachment of which it is a part, has a negative orientation; it is aimed at *not* being influenced, coerced, tied, obligated.

The three types could be summarized as follows: The *compliant* type worries about how he can make people like him so they won't hurt him. The *aggressive* type considers the best defense to be the best offense. The *detached* person has the philosophy that if he doesn't get close to people then he won't get hurt too badly.

Horney suggests that the essential difference between a normal and a neurotic conflict is one of degree. For example, she states, ". . . the disparity between the conflicting issues is much less great for the normal person than for the neurotic."[64] In other words, everyone has these conflicts to some degree, but some people, usually because of early experiences with rejection, neglect, overprotection and other expressions of unfortunate parental treatment, possess theirs in exaggerated form.

Carl Rogers (The Fully Functioning Person)

Rogers[65] self-theory and ideas about the fully functioning individual represents a synthesis of phenomenology as developed by Combs and Snygg, social interaction theory as represented in the writings of Mead and Cooley, and of Sullivan's interpersonal theory.

The principle conceptual ingredients of Rogers' self-theory are the following: (1) the *organism,* which is the total person, (2) the *phenomenal* field, which is the totality of experience, and (3) the *self* which is a differentiated portion of the phenomenal field and consists of conscious perceptions and values of the "I" or "me."

The self, which is the nuclear concept in Rogers' theory, has numerous features, the most important of which are these: (a) the self strives for consistency, (b) a person behaves in ways which are consistent with the self, (c) experiences that are not consistent with the self are perceived as threats and are either distorted or denied, (d) the self may change as a result of maturation and learning.

The nature of these concepts and their interrelationships are discussed in a series of nineteen propositions formulated by Rogers in his book, *Client-Centered Therapy*. To give you a feeling for how these propositions are related to Rogers' ideas about the self and how it functions, consider seven of the most basic propositions:[66]

1. Every individual exists in a continually changing world of experience of which he is the center. In this sense, each person is the best source of information about himself.

2. Each individual reacts to his perceptual field as it is perceived and experienced. Consequently, knowledge of a person's experiences is not sufficient for

predicting behavior; one must know how the person perceives the experiences and what it *means* to him.

3. Each individual has a basic tendency to strive, to actualize, maintain, and enhance the experiencing organism.

4. As a result of interaction with the environment, and particularly as a result of interactions with others, one's picture of one-self is formed—an organized, fluid, but consistent conceptual pattern of perceptions of characteristics and relationships of the "I" or the "me."

5. Perception is selective, and the primary criterion for selection is whether the experience is consistent with how one views oneself at the moment.

6. Most ways of behaving which are adopted by the individual are those that are consistent with his concept of self.

7. When a person perceives and accepts into one integrated system all his sensory and visceral experiences, then he is in a position to be more accepting and understanding of others as separate and *different* individuals. For example, a person who feels threatened by his own hostile or sexual feelings may tend to criticize or move away from others whom he perceives as behaving in sexual or hostile ways. On the other hand, if he can accept his own sexual or hostile feelings he is likely to be more tolerant of their expression by others.

Out of this self theory and from his many years as a practicing psychotherapist, Rogers developed some ideas of what it means to be a "fully functioning person." For the most part, his ideas evolved from his very personal experiences with his clients as he was able to observe them developing a "self" which was uniquely their own. According to Rogers, a person en route to becoming "fully functioning" usually exhibits characteristics such as the following:[67]

1. He tends to move away from facades. That is, he moves away from a self that he is *not* and moves towards the self that he really *is*.
2. He tends to move away from "oughts." In other words, he ceases to guide his conduct in terms of what he "ought" to be or "ought" to become.
3. He tends to move away from meeting others' expectations and moves more toward meeting his *own* expectations.
4. He tends to move away from pleasing others and begins to be more self-directing.
5. He tends to be more accepting of himself and able to view himself as a person in the process of "becoming." That is, he is not upset by the fact that he does not always hold the same feelings toward a given experience or person, or that he is not always consistent. The striving for conclusions or end states seems to decrease.
6. He tends to move toward being more open to his experiences in the sense of not having to always blot out thoughts, feelings, perceptions, and memories which might be unpleasant.
7. He tends to move in the direction of greater acceptance of others. That is, as he is more able to accept the experiences of others.

A. H. Maslow (Self-Actualization)

Maslow's[68] unique contribution to the humanistic social psychological viewpoint lies in his preoccupation with healthy people rather than sick ones, and his feeling that studies of these two groups generate different types of theory. He feels that psychology has focused too intently on man's frailties and not enough on his strengths, that in the process of exploring man's sins it has neglected his virtues. Where is the psychology, Maslow asks, that takes into account such experiences as love, compassion, gaiety, exhilaration, and well-being to the same extent that it deals with hate, pain, misery, guilt, and conflict? Maslow has undertaken to supply the other half of the picture, the brighter, better half, and to round out a portrait of the whole man.

Maslow offers a theory of human motivation which assumes that needs are ordered along a hierarchy of priority of prepotency. That is, when the more basic needs are satisfied, the next need in the hierarchy emerges and presses for satisfaction. He assumes that each person has five basic needs, which are arranged in hierarchical order of relative prepotency:[69]

1. The physiological needs, that is, hunger and thirst
2. The safety needs
3. The love and belongingness needs
4. The esteem needs
5. The self-actualization needs, that is, the desire for self-fulfillment, for becoming what one has the potential to become.

In order to study what makes healthy people healthy, or great people great, or extraordinary people extraordinary, Maslow has made intensive clinical investigations of people who are, or were, in the truest sense of the word, self-actualizing, in the sense of moving in the direction of achieving and reaching their highest potentials. People of this sort are rare, indeed, as Maslow discovered when he was selecting his group. Some were historical figures, such as Lincoln, Jefferson, Walt Whitman, Beethoven, William James, F. D. Roosevelt, while others were living at the time they were studied, like Einstein, Eleanor Roosevelt, Albert Schweitzer, along with some personal acquaintances of the investigator. Upon studying healthy, self-actualizing individuals, Maslow was able to sort out fifteen basic personality characteristics which distinguished them from, how shall we say, "ordinary" people. This is not to suggest that each person he studied reflected all fifteen self-actualizing characteristics, but each did, however, exhibit a greater number of these characteristics and in more different ways than might be expected in a less "self-actualized" person. Maslow describes the features as follows:[70]

1. They are realistically oriented.
2. They accept themselves, other people, and the natural world for what they are.
3. They are spontaneous in thought, emotions, and behavior.
4. They are problem-centered rather than self-centered in the sense of being able to devote their attention to a task, duty, or mission that seemed peculiarly cut out for them.
5. They have a need for privacy and even seek it out on occasion, needing it for periods of intense concentration on subjects of interest to them.
6. They are autonomous, independent, and able to remain true to themselves in the face of rejection or unpopularity.
7. They have a continuous freshness of appreciation and capacity to stand in awe

again and again of the basic goods of life, a sunset, a flower, a baby, a melody, a person.

8. They have frequent "mystic" or "oceanic" experiences, although not necessarily religious in character.

9. They feel a sense of identification with mankind as a whole in the sense of being concerned not only with the lot of their own immediate families, but with the welfare of the world as a whole.

10. Their intimate relationships with a few specifically loved people tend to be profound and deeply emotional rather than superficial.

11. They have democratic character structures in the sense of judging people and being friendly not on the basis of race, status, religion, but rather on the basis of who other people are as individuals.

12. They have a highly developed sense of ethics and are inclined to choose their behavior with reference to its ethical implications.

13. They have unhostile senses of humor, which are expressed in their capacity to make common human foibles, pretensions, and foolishness the subject of laughter, rather than sadism, smut, or hatred of authority.

14. They have a great fund of creativeness.

15. They resist total conformity to culture.

An impressive list to be sure, and one of the most detailed conceptions of self-actualization yet developed.

© 1970 United Feature Syndicate, Inc.

Lucy may not agree, but the fact is all of us have a chance to be
self-actualizing if we work at it.

In Perspective

This chapter has introduced you to the nature of perceptual processes and how needs, values, beliefs, and self-concept can influence perception. In addition, we have looked at some of the crucial factors which affect how we perceive others; we have examined how perceptions can be modified, and we have seen how reality, being the shifting image it is, can distort our perceptions of what we believe to be true, what we think to be right.

How we perceive the world determines how we behave in it and feel about ourselves. There is a large body of research to suggest that we humans will go to great lengths in adjusting our perceptions to fit our preconceptions. Consider, for example, the observations of Berelson and Steiner, who, at the conclusion of their monumental review of research related to human behavior, had this to say about our knowledge about the nature of man:

> In his quest for satisfaction, man is not just a seeker of truth, but of deceptions, of himself as well as others. . . . Thus, he adjusts his social perceptions to fit not only the objective reality but also what suits his wishes and needs; he tends to remember what fits his needs and expectations, or what he thinks others will want to hear; . . . in the mass media he tends to hear and see not simply what is there but what he prefers to be told, and he will misinterpret rather than face up to an opposing set of facts or point of view; he avoids the conflicts of issues and ideals whenever he can by changing the people around him rather than his mind, and when he cannot, private fantasies can lighten the load and carry him through; he thinks . . . that his own group agrees with him more fully than it really does; and if it does not, he finds a way to escape to a less uncongenial world. . . . For the truth is, apparently, that no matter how successful man becomes in dealing with his problems, he still finds it hard to live in the real world, undiluted: to see what one really is, to hear what others really think of one, to face the conflicts and threats really present, or, for that matter, the bare human feelings. . . . In short, man lives not only with the reality that confronts him but with the reality he makes.[71]

Each of the contributors who have discussed in relation to this humanistic social psychological orientation tends to espouse a ''dynamic'' view of human behavior in the sense of seeing man as an active, choosing, conscious organism whose behavior is shaped by both internal and external forces. Moreover, they represent points of view that give people credit for not only assigning personal meaning to their perceptions and experiences, but for adjusting their behavior so it is consistent with their personal meanings. This is not to suggest that one's perceptions and, hence, one's personal meanings are always correct. Hardly. Most of our personal and interpersonal problems arise not from disagreements about reality, but from distortions and misperceptions of reality. In order to be as accurate as possible in our perceptions, we must develop as much insight as we can into ourselves as individuals and the ways in which our needs, values, and beliefs influence how we perceive the world in which we live.

Thus, if we are to behave effectively and appropriately, our perceptions of reality must be fairly accurate. When our perceptions of ourselves and/or others are inaccurate, we are more likely to undertake actions which have little chance of success. Indeed, we seriously reduce our opportunities for engaging in many things we might otherwise do and enjoy if it were not for our misperceptions.

The need for knowing one's self is basic and universal in human experience, not confined to a heroic few or to the giants among men. The need which has been variously labeled "self-acceptance," "self-love," "self-understanding," and the like is neither innate nor indistinct in function and origin. It is basically a need for an image of one's self that is accurate enough to be workable and acceptable so a person can enjoy experiencing and expressing it.

Notes

1. A. C. Combs, X. Richards, and X. Richards, *Perceptual Psychology*. New York: Harper & Row, Publishers, 1976, p. 22.
2. A. Combs, et al., p. 17.
3. J. M. Shlien, "Phenomenology and Personality," in S. M. Wepman & R. W. Heine (Eds.), *Concepts of Personality*. Chicago: Aldine Publishing Co., 1963, p. 295.
4. C. E. Osgood, *Method & Theory in Experimental Psychology*. New York: Oxford University Press, 1953, p. 286.
5. R. Levine, I. Chein, and G. Murphy, "The Relation of the Intensity of the Need to the Amount of Perceptual Distortion, a Preliminary Report," *Journal of Psychology*. 1942, 13: 283–293.
6. D. C. McClelland, and J. W. Atkinson, "The Projective Expression of Needs: I. The Effect of Different Intensities of the Hunger Drive on Perception," *Journal of Psychology*. 1948, 25: 205–222.
7. E. M. Weingarten, "A Study of Selective Perception in Clinical Judgment," *Journal of Personality*. 1949, 17: p. 369–406.
8. V. H. Vroom, "Projection, Negation, and the Self-Concept," *Human Relations*. 1959, 12: 335–344.
9. L. Postman, J. S. Bruner and E. McGinnis, "Personal Values as Selective Factors in Perception," *Psychological Review*. 1948, 55: 314–324.
10. J. S. Bruner, and C. C. Goodman, "Value and Need as Organizing Factors in Perception," *Journal of Abnormal and Social Psychology*. 1947, 42: 33–44.
11. J. K. Majasan, *College Students' Achievement As a Function of the Congruence between Their Beliefs and Their Instructor's Beliefs*. Unpublished doctoral dissertation, Stanford Univ., 1972.
12. A. Hastorf, and H. Cantril, "They Saw a Game: A Case Study," *Journal of Abnormal & Social Psychology*. 1954, 49: 129–234.
13. R. Rosenthal, *Experiments Effects in Behavioral Research*. New York: Appleton-Century-Crofts, 1966.
14. H. H. Kelley, "The Warm–Cold Variable in First Impressions of Persons," *Journal of Personality*. 1950, 18: 431–439.

15. R. E. Bills, and G. R. McGehee, "The Effect of Attitude toward Psychology in an Learning Experiment," *Journal of Personality.* 1955, 23: 499–500.
16. J. Palmer, "Scoring in ESP Tests as a Function of Belief in ESP. Part I: The Sheep-Goat Effect," *Journal of the American Society for Physical Research.* 1971, 65: 373–408.
17. T. J. Stachaik, and R. Ulrich, "Psychiatric Diagnosis: Some Cracks in the Crystal Ball," *Psychological Reports.* 1965, 17: 989–990.
18. M. Rokeach, *The Open and Closed Mind.* New York: Basic Books, Inc., Publishers, 1960.
19. G. Allport, *The Nature of Prejudice.* Addison-Wesley Publishing Company, Inc., Reading, Mass., 1954.
20. H. S. Sullivan, *Conceptions of Modern Psychiatry.* Washington, D.C.: William Alanson White Psychiatric Foundations, 1947, p. 17.
21. F. Baron, *Creativity and Personal Freedom.* New York: Van Nostrand Reinhold Company, 1968, p. 12.
22. M. Rosenberg, *Society and the Adolescent Self-Image.* Princeton, N.J.: Princeton University Press, 1965.
23. P. Barron, "Self-Esteem, Ingratiation, and Evaluation of Unknown Others," *Journal of Personality and Social Psychology.* 1974, 30: 104–109.
24. E. Walster, "The Effect of Self-Esteem on Romantic Liking," *Journal of Experimental & Social Psychology.* 1965, 1: 184–197.
25. J. H. Cantor, "Individual Needs and Salient Constructs in Interpersonal Perception," *Journal of Personality and Social Psychology.* 1976, 34: 519–525.
26. D. J. Schneider, "Implicit Personality Theory: A Review," *Psychological Bulletin.* 1973, 79: 294–309.
27. S. Rosenberg, and R. A. Jones, "A Method for Investigating and Representing a Person's Implicit Theory of Personality: Theodore Drieser's View of People," *Journal of Personality and Social Psychology.* 1972, 22: 372–376.
28. G. Razran, "Ethnic Dislikes and Stereotypes," *Journal of Abnormal and Social Psychology.* 1950, 45: 7–27.
29. M. Anisfeld, N. Bogo, and W. E. Lambert, "Evaluational Reactions to Accential English Speech," *Journal of Abnormal & Social Psychology.* 1962, 65: 223–231.
30. M. G. Marcus, "The Power of a Name," *Psychology Today.* October 1976: 75–76, 108.
31. J. W. McDavid, and H. Harari, "Stereotyping of Names and Popularity in Grade School Children," *Child Development.* 1966, 37: 453–459.
32. D. Scherer, "Attribution of Personality from Voice: A Cross-Cultural Study of Interpersonal Perception," *Proceedings of the 79th Annual Convention of the American Psychological Association.* 1971, 6: 351–352.
33. K. Gibbins, "Communication Aspects of Women's Clothes & Their Relation to Fashion Ability," *British Journal of Social & Clinical Psychology.* 1969, 8; 301–312.
34. P. Zimbardo, *Freaks, Hippies, and Voters: The Effects of Deviant Dress and Appearance on Political Persuasion Processes.* Symposium presented at meeting of the Eastern Psychological Association, New York City, April, 1971.
35. C. M. Brodsky, *A Study of Norms for Body Form-Behavior Relationships.* Washington, D.C.: The Catholic University of America Press, 1954.
36. J. Staffieri, "A Study of Social Stereotype of Body Image in Children," *Journal of Personality and Social Psychology.* 1957, 7: 101–104.
37. K. Dion, "Physical Attractiveness and Evaluation of Children's Transgressions," *Journal of Personality and Social Psychology.* 1972, 24: 207–213.

38. K. Dion, E. Berseheid, and E. Walster, "What is Beautiful is Good," *Journal of Personality and Social Psychology.* 1972, 24: 285–290.

39. D. Landy, and H. Sigall, "Beauty is Talent: Task Evaluation as a Function of the Performer's Physical Attractiveness," *Journal of Personality and Social Psychology.* 1974, 29: 299–304.

40. C. R. Rogers, and R. F. Dymond (Eds.), *Psychotherapy & Personality Change.* Chicago: University of Chicago Press., 1954.

41. E. H. Schein, "Reaction Patterns to Severe Chronic Stress in American Army Prisoners of War of the Chinese," *Journal of Social Issues.* 1957, 13: 21–30.

42. S. E. Asch, *Social Psychology.* Englewood Cliffs, N.J.: Prentice-Hall. Inc., 1952, pp. 450–483.

43. Richard S. Crutchfield, "Conformity and Character," *American Psychologist.* 1955, 10: 191–198.

44. W. H. Beston, H. Woodburn, and T. H. Scott, "Effects of Decreased Variation in the Sensory Environment," *Canadian Journal of Psychology.* 1954, 8: 70–76.

45. A. I. Teger, S. Katkin, and D. G. Pruitt, "Effects of Alcoholic Beverages and Their Congener Content on Level and Style of Risk Taking," *Journal of Personality and Social Psychology.* 1969, 11: 170–176.

46. J. F. Fort, *Alcohol: Our Biggest Drug Problem.* New York: McGraw-Hill, Inc. 1973, p. 107.

47. *Detroit Free Press,* January, 1975.

48. B. M. Jones, and O. A. Parsons, "Getting High, Coming Down." *Psychology Today.* January 1975: 53–58.

49. C. T. Tart, "Scientific Foundations for the Study of Altered States of Consciousness," *Journal of Transpersonal Psychology.* 1971, 3: 93–124.

50. R. W. Deisher, "Drug Abuse in Adolescence," *Pediatrics.* 1969, 44: 131–141.

51. D. W. Matheson, and M. A. Davison, *The Behavioral Effects of Drugs.* New York: Holt, Rinehart and Winston, 1972.

52. J. M. Schlien, "Phenomenology and Personality," in S. M. Wepman and R. W. Heine (Eds.), *Concepts of Personality.* Chicago: Aldine Publishing Co., 1963, pp. 324–325.

53. R. E. Farson, (Ed.), *Science and Human Affairs.* Palo Alto, Calif.: Science & Behavior Books, 1965, p. 13.

54. V. C. Morris, "Existentialism and Education," *Educational Theory.* 1954, 4: 252–253.

55. J. F. T. Bugental, "The Third Force in Psychology," *Journal of Humanistic Psychology.* 1964, Spring: 23–24.

56. Bugental, pp. 24–25.

57. C. H. Cooley, *Human Nature of the Social Order.* New York: Charles Scribner's Sons, 1902, pp. 20–21.

58. G. H. Mead, *Mind, Self and Society.* Chicago: University of Chicago Press, 1934.

59. H. S. Sullivan, *The Interpersonal Theory of Psychiatry.* New York: W. W. Norton & Company, Inc., 1953.

60. A. Adler, *Practice & Theory of Individual Psychology.* New York: Harcourt, Brace & World, Inc., 1927.

61. K. Horney, *Our Inner Conflicts.* New York: W. W. Norton & Company, Inc., 1945, p. 41.

62. K. Horney, *Self-Analysis.* New York: W. W. Norton & Company, Inc., 1942, pp. 54–60.

63. K. Horney, *Our Inner Conflicts,* pp. 48–95

64. K. Horney, *Our Inner Conflicts*, p. 31.
65. C. R. Rogers, *Client-Centered Therapy*. Boston: Houghton Mifflin Company, 1951.
66. Rogers, pp. 483–520.
67. C. R. Rogers, *On Becoming a Person*. Boston: Houghton Mifflin Company, 1961, pp. 163–198.
68. A. H. Maslow, *Motivation & Personality* (2nd ed.). New York: Harper & Row, Publishers, 1970.
69. Maslow, pp. 35–58.
70. Maslow, pp. 149–180.
71. B. Berelson, and G. A. Steiner, *Human Behavior: An Inventory of Scientific Findings*. New York: Harcourt, Brace & World, Inc., 1964, pp. 663–665.

References of Related Interest

Allport, G. W., *Pattern & Growth in Personality*. New York: Holt, Rinehart and Winston, 1961.

Berne, E., *Transactional Analysis in Psychotherapy*. New York: Grove Press, Inc., 1961.

Bischof, L. J., *Interpreting Personality Theories* (2nd ed.). New York: Harper & Row, Publishers, 1970.

Cartril, H., "The Place of Personality in Social Psychology," *Journal of Psychology*. 1947, 24: 19–56.

Carterette, E. C., and M. P. Freidman (Eds.), *Handbook of Perception, Vol. 7*, New York: Academic Press, Inc., 1976.

Erickson, E. H., *Childhood to Society* (2nd ed.). New York: W. W. Norton & Company, Inc., 1963.

Fieandt, Kai von, *The World of Perception*. Homewood, Ill: The Dorsey Press, 1966.

Fromm, E., *Escape from Freedom*. New York: Holt, Rinehart, & Winston, 1941.

Hall, C. S., and G. Lindzey, *Theories of Personality* (2nd ed.). New York: John Wiley & Sons, Inc., 1970.

James, W., *Psychology: The Briefer Course*. New York: Harper Torchbooks—The Academy Library, 1961.

Kleinke, C. L., *First Impressions*. Englewood Cliffs, N.J., Prentice-Hall, Inc., 1975.

Lewin, K., *Field Theory in Social Science*. New York: Harper & Row, Publishers, 1951.

Maddi, Salvatore R., *Personality Theories: A Comparative Analysis* (Rev.). Homewood, Ill.: The Dorsey Press, 1972.

May, R. (Ed.) *Existential Psychology*. New York: Random House, Inc., 1961.

Miller, G. A., and P. N. Johnson-Lairel, *Language and Perception*. Cambridge, Mass. Harvard University Press, 1976.

Murphy, G., *Personality*. New York: Harper & Row, Publishers, 1947.

Murray, H. A., *Explorations in Personality: A Clinical Experimental Study of Fifty College Age Men*. New York: Oxford University Press, 1938.

Patterson, C. H., "Phenomenological Psychology." *The Personnel & Guidance Journal*. 1965, XL11: 997-1005.

Rank, O., *Will Therapy and Truth and Reality*. New York: Alfred A. Knopf, Inc., 1945.

Snygg, D., "The Need for Phenomenological System of Psychology," *Psychological Review*. 1941, 48: 404–424.

Thevenaz, Pierre, *What Is Phenomenology?* Chicago: Quadrangle Books, 1962.

Tiryakian, Edward A., "The Existential Self and the Person," in C. Gordon and K. Gergen (Eds.), *The Self in Social Interaction*. New York: John Wiley & Sons, 1968, pp. 75–86.

Self-Consistency:
Its Nature
and Expressions

PROLOGUE

This phenomenon we refer to as our personality is a remarkable achievement. Although it is a complex network of interrelated ideas, attitudes, beliefs, experiences, and feelings seeking expression in a single source, it is more apt to function as a unified whole than as fragmented parts. The person we are today is probably pretty much like the person we were yesterday and rather similar to the person we will, in all probability, be tomorrow. You may or may not like your personality, but it is, nonetheless, you as you have come to know yourself as a person. Although we may wear other hats, assume different roles and behavior for short periods of time, each of us ultimately expresses that self which he or she truly is. *A person cannot help but be himself or herself.* Which is the whole point of this chapter.

What is self-consistency? Why is it important? How does it develop? How is it expressed? How consistent is behavior over time? Can behavior change once it is established? Let's turn our attention to these and related questions.

Why Is Behavioral Consistency Important?

Most of us have what seems to be a strong inclination to perceive, expect and assume personal consistency of behavior on the part of others in our social environment. There are several good reasons for this. In the first place, there is much less personal strain and anxiety if the social environment is not in a constant state of change. In the second place, the appropriateness of our behavior toward another person is in direct proportion to the correctness of our conception of him. "Correct" conceptions, of course, depend on the other person's behaving in a more or less consistent manner. Indeed, there is evidence to suggest that when a person behaves inconsistently, he is not as well-liked. For example, one study demonstrated that, over a variety of conditions, a predictable person comes to be liked and an unpredictable one produces a negative reaction.[1]

Behavioral consistency is also important because it serves as the foundation for stable, human relationships. We may love someone as much as we want; we may even respect that person a great deal, but if that individual proves to be too unreliable and too unpredictable then we usually find ourselves withdrawing our emotional investment in that relationship. Initial uncertainty and ultimate loss of trust, both of which serve to push people further apart, are natural but lamentable by-products of unstable and inconsistent relationships.

Actually, it is questionable whether total unity of personality is ever achieved in terms of an individual developing a completely consistent, unified self-image. Even though such unification of personality as exists seems to be only a matter of degree, psychological evidence suggests that each of us develops certain primary dispositions and response styles which we can be counted on to more or less consistently reflect in the general course of our behavior. We commonly detect more consistency in our own and other people's behavior than we can always put our finger on and have the lurking suspicion that there is more overall consistency than that which meets the eye. One author wryly observed, for example, that ". . . we not only see people as being all of one piece, but we treat them as if they are, and we often punish them if they are not."[2]

On the whole, the world of social perception tends to be fairly stable; it is through our abilities to conceptualize that the complex flux of interpersonal relationships is simplified and made comprehensible. For example, as we are exposed to facts and information about another, these perceptions are ordered, synthesized, and integrated into a mind's eye concept of the sort of individual we believe that other person to be. Noting a person's self-effacing manner and submissive behavior, for example, may lead us to conceptualize or picture this person as "shy." This concept is then used as the label for a cluster of observations which serve as the keystone for what we regard as "understanding" the other person. When conceptual judgements are made they tend to remain intact and unchanging. Once we label a person as shy, aggressive, deceptive, friendly, or whatever, we do not easily give up that perception. Even if later information grossly contradicts our perception of what we believe another person is like, it may be either distorted or misperceived so that it fits what we believe to be true. For example, research has shown that when persons receive contradictory information about another, they often misconstrue new information so that what they hear or see is internally consistent with what they already believe to be true about the other person.[3] In ways like this, persons tend to be seen as stable and consistent.

Not only is it important to be able to predict, to count on a certain consistency in others' behaviors, but it is crucial that we see threads of consistency in our own behavior as well. You will recall that in Chapter One we discussed the importance of being able to answer the "Who am I" question as the first step toward understanding one's self. The capacity to know who one is and what one stands for is the cornerstone on which behavioral consistency is built. Just as there is less personal strain and anxiety if others we relate to are not in a constant state of change, so, too, is it less taxing and anxiety-provoking if our own personality is not constantly shifting. Being able to predict one's self with reasonable accuracy is comforting because it serves to free a person from unnecessary fretting and worrying about how he might behave under certain conditions. It is when we cannot predict how we might behave or what we might say or be that we get most anxious. A young male client of mine expressed the problem in the following way during our initial interview:

> The thing that bothers me most is me. Isn't that stupid? I don't even know who me is. Every now and then I think I know, but I keep changing. My girlfriend—I should say, my ex-girlfriend—broke up with me because she says I was always breaking my promises. Couldn't trust me, she said. I think she's right, actually. I did break promises. The thing I don't know is how I can keep a promise if I can't even tell when I'm making it whether or not I can keep it. Isn't that stupid—I can't even tell that.

The young man was right, of course; it is difficult to carry out a promise (which is, after all, an explicit declaration that one will do or refrain from doing something which he himself specifies) if he doesn't know himself well enough to make that sort of declaration (prediction) in the first place.

The fact is, our everyday experiences have taught most of us that it is possible to make predictions about our own and others' behavior. Many times our soothsayings ring true, which suggests a certain unity of personality. This unity grows out of our need to be consistent with our "self" concept. Although consistency is more apt to be the rule than the exception, it is by no means a guaranteed outcome. Dr. Walter Mischel, who has done important research in the area of behavioral consistency, has observed that "Clinically, it seems remarkable how each of us generally manages to reconcile his seemingly diverse behaviors into one consistent whole."[4]

Behaving in predictably consistent ways is not always easy to do.

However, our predictions about our own and other's behavior is not always correct because, of all things, we are not always perfectly consistent. Indeed, some of our past behavior may so surprise us that we find ourselves looking back on it and saying things like, "I don't know how I could have done such a thing," or "I couldn't have been myself when I said that." A student cheats on an examination, a behavior that is contrary to his self-image and as he looks back on it, he may be genuinely baffled at how he could have done such a thing. The genial, warm, and somewhat self-effacing woman who lashes out in rage may have great difficulty understanding what happened or why she expressed herself in such a manner. However, the very rarity of such occurrances points to the personal need for unity and consistency of behavior.

Behavioral Consistency as Related to Self-Concept Theory

William James, one of our greatest psychologists, was among the first to speak about the importance of inner consistency. He distinguished between the essentially healthy person whose inner constitution is "harmonious and well balanced from the outset" and the "sick souls" whose "spirit wars with their flesh. They wish for incompatibles, wayward impulses interrupt their most deliberate plans, and their lives are one long drama of repentance and of effort to repair misdemeanors and mistakes.''[5] For James the only hope for these "divided selves" was in the "normal evolution of character," which involved the "straightening out and unifying of the inner self."

Prescott Lecky was one of the first psychologists to develop the idea that the "normally" functioning human being strives for consistency in all aspects of his life. He looked at personality as an organization of ideas which he felt were consistent with one another. Lecky suggested that one overpowering motivation in life is to sustain the unity of this system, a concept that is strongly reflected in the following quote:

> Behavior expresses the effort to maintain integrity and unity of the organization . . . In order to be immediately assimilated, the idea formed as the result of a new experience must be felt to be consistent with the ideas already present in the system. On the other hand, ideas whose inconsistency is recognized as the personality develops must be expelled from the system. There is thus a constant assimilation of new ideas and the expulsion of old ideas throughout life.[6]

Another psychologist, Carl Rogers, has observed that the integration of various aspects of an individual into a unified concept of self "is accompanied by feelings of comfort and freedom from tension."[7] He goes further to say that one major way of preserving the unity of the self-system is by filtering one's experiences so that they are either ". . . (a) symbolized, perceived and organized into some relationship to the self, (b) ignored because there is no perceived relationship to the self-structure, (c) denied symbolization or given a distorted symbolization because the experience is inconsistent with the structure of the self."[8] This proposition states, in effect, that perception is selective, and the primary criteria for selection is whether the experience is consistent with one's self-picture.

A somewhat related approach is found in the neo-Freudian concept of *identity*. For example, Erikson has made this concept the core of a modern version of psychoanalytic theory and has observed that it is especially during adolescence that one attempts to bring the sense of one's own identity into closer unity with one's social relationships. Erikson writes:

> The sense of ego identity is the accrued confidence that one's ability to maintain inner sameness and continuity . . . is matched by the sameness and continuity of one's meaning for others.[9]

Extending Erikson's idea a step further, Allport suggests that one's ability to maintain inner sameness and continuity is more likely to occur when one is ego- or "self"-involved in whatever the experience at hand happens to be. As Allport states it:

> . . . thoughts and behavior have greater consistency when they relate to what we consider to be warm, central, and important in our lives than they have when they are not so related.[10]

Research evidence tends to support this view. For example, public opinion polls show that people who feel strongly about an issue will be quite consistent in endorsing all the propositions that are related to the issue. If they feel less strongly involved (less "self"-involved) they are more likely to be variable and inconsistent.[11] They are, in a word, less predictable.

As you can see, the value of "inner sameness" has been stressed by many psychologists who have been curious about the relationships between self-concept and behavioral consistency. This line of thinking identifies a healthy personality with a reasonably unified self-image. We must remember that self-image includes not only a view of "What I am" but also "What I would like to be" and "What I ought to be." By bringing these three dimensions of the self together a person approaches a greater degree of unification and consistency of behavior. Indeed, Maslow[12] has clinically observed that the healthier people are, the more their capacities are interrelated. He further observed that certain behaviors tend to cluster together, a phenomenon that helps us to further understand why behavioral patterns within the same person tend to be related. For instance, conventionality, morality, modesty, and obedience seem to fall together or belong together very naturally, as do another cluster of qualities, such as self-confidence, poise, assertiveness, and social boldness. Maslow also noted that where there is a sudden change in a well-organized behavioral syndrome, there is a tendency—and it is just that, a tendency and not a certainty—for that behavior to reestablish itself. As Maslow has expressed it:

> It is a tribute to the ubiquity of this tendency (that normally healthy people) can recover from any shock at all if only given enough time. The death of a wife or a son, financial ruin, and any other such basic traumatic experiences may throw individuals badly off balance for a while, but they usually recover almost wholly. It is only a chronically bad external or interpersonal situation that is able to create permanent changes in the healthy character structure.[13]

In short, self-concept theory strongly suggests that we will "act like" the sort of person we perceive ourselves to be. As we encounter new experiences in everyday living, we tend to accept or reject them in terms of their compatibility with our present concept of self. In this way, we can reduce the inevitable conflicts we face while, at the same time, maintaining our individuality as persons.

How Primary Motives and Dominant Values Influence Behavioral Consistency

Each of us has certain primary motivations and dominant values around which our self-system is organized. It is through the process of being internally consistent with those motivations and values that we can see overt expressions of behavioral consistencies. (Sometimes we are not even aware of our more dominant values, which is something that the recent emphasis on value clarifications is seeking to change.[14, 15])

Early research by Hartshorne and May[16] presented findings that were in apparent contradiction to the idea of self-consistency when they reported data from their studies of deceit to show that a child who cheated in one situation did not always cheat in another, although an outside observer might have expected him to do so. They concluded that there is no general personality factor such as honesty,

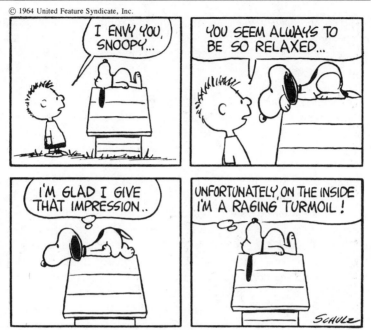

Sometimes the self we present to others on the outside is different than the self we feel on the inside.

but that honesty is specific and situational, a position which is contrary to the behavioral consistency idea postulated by self-concept theory. The key to the contradiction lies in the fact that it is only to the person doing the observing that the child's behavior is unpredictable. From the point of view of the person doing the behaving, behavior stems from and is determined by a set of dominant values distributed along a definite hierarchy of prepotency. For example, a person might keep money dropped on the sidewalk by a stranger but would never think of doing this if it were lost by a cherished friend. The explanation for the perceived inconsistency in behavior could be that loyalty is more a dominant value for the person in question than is honesty. Hence, he behaves in an honest fashion because he is loyal, not because he is honest.

Since most situations to which we react are complex events, they bring into play a multiplicity of motives and values. Usually, however, the dominant value system prevails and the resulting behavior is logical, if not always justifiable, from the standpoint of the person doing the behaving. For example, the student who cheats in one instance but not another may still be self-consistent. If his dominant values center around high achievement, he may feel he *has* to cheat if he suspects he is in serious grade trouble. If, on the other hand, he places honesty above high achievement in his hierarchy of values, he might sooner fail than cheat and even feel a bit self-righteous about passing up what he considers to be a golden opportunity to copy from someone else's paper during an exam. (Along this line, I am reminded of a student who approached me after an exam and complained bitterly about the rampant cheating he saw going on among three other members of the class, all of whom sat near him. He concluded with the time-honored observation that "They're just cheating themselves." As he turned to leave, heavily burdened with the cross he was bearing, he remarked, "I may fail this test, but at least I flunked on my own!") Of course, to pursue the example a step further, if a student's dominant value *is* honesty and he *does* cheat, then he would have to deny or rationalize his dishonesty in order to avoid the heavy weight of his guilt. In general, when a person continually behaves in a manner which is inconsistent with his primary motives and dominant values, he is usually in trouble from a psychological point of view. When an individual's behavior is inconsistent with the kind of person he either thinks he should be or wants to be, he may be in need of some kind of therapeutic assistance in integrating his system of values so as to reduce internal conflict.

The fact is, each of us projects a certain personality "style" which makes us more or less identifiable and predictable to others. The deeper people know us, the more predictable we may become to them, particularly if they understand our primary motivations and dominant values.

Sometimes we are wrong in our observations and predictions about another person, not necessarily because he behaved inconsistently, but because our perceptions of him were in error. For example, consider the story of G. B. Shaw's *Pygmalion* (most of us know it better as *My Fair Lady*) in which Eliza Doolittle, an ignorant little flower girl, is taken on by Professor Higgins for speech training. He not only teaches her to speak in an educated manner, but he finds that she unquestioningly obeys his every order. If he tells her to act like a servant, she does so; like a lady, and she does. On the surface, it seems that Eliza has no consistency at all in her personality. Underneath, however, there is one unifying explanation for her conduct: she is in love with the good professor. Her love is her primary motivation. When we view her behavior in this light we can see that her behavior lacked unity because of a misperception on our part and not because of her inconsistency. Although she was absurdly inconsistent in her manners of speech and behavior, she was highly consistent in her love for Professor Higgins. Once we know this, we are tapping a deep primary value which, from Eliza's point of view, unifies much of her behavior.

Another example of how behavioral consistency can be misconstrued by mistaken perceptions is cited by Allport:

> There is the case of a thirteen-year-old girl who was referred for counseling because she used excessive makeup on her face. This habit seemed sadly at variance with her scholarly nature. Her teacher felt something must be "wrong." The apparent split in the girl's personality was readily explained. She had a heavy crush on her teacher, who was herself scholarly and enjoyed a high natural complexion. The little girl was entirely (consistent) in her striving to be like her beloved teacher.[17]

In every personality there are primary motives of major significance and others of minor significance. Occasionally a primary motive is so outstanding in a person that it deserves to be called a *cardinal* motive. Allport has suggested that such a master quality could also be called ". . . the eminent trait, the ruling passion, the master-sentiment, the unity-thema, or the radix of life."[18] Tolstoy's passion for the "simplification of life," or Schweitzer's guiding ideal of "reverence for life," or Martin Luther King's struggle to make his "dream" a reality, of Gloria Steinem's fight for equal rights for women, might be examples of cardinal motives which brought a high degree of unity to behavior. Sometimes, however, we have to look hard for that one cardinal motive which might unify what otherwise seems like inconsistent behavior.

Take the case of Tom, a college senior, who has trouble sustaining long-term relationships with women. When he is on a date, he is warm, giving, and empathic, but during the week he is cold, rejecting, and nonfeeling to the same young ladies he dates. Does this contradiction in behavior mean that he lacks primary motives or dominant values? Not at all. He has two opposing primary motives, one which is warm and giving, and another which is cold and rejecting. Different situations arouse different primary motives. Pursuing the case further, the duality is at least partly explained by the fact Tom has *one* primary motive from which these contrasting behaviors proceed. The outstanding fact about his personality is that he is a self-centered egotist who is friendly, warm, and giving only when he thinks this behavior will serve his own best interest. This cardinal self-centeredness expresses itself in warm, congenial behavior when he wants something or in cold, distant behavior when he does not. Most of his dates were quick to sense the expediency of his motives and simply refused to be used by him in this selfish manner. Hence, his difficulty establishing long-term relationships.

The consistency of a motive is a matter of degree. As you can see in Tom's case, there must be some demonstrable relationship between separate behaviors before its existence can be inferred. The existence of contradictory behaviors does not necessarily mean that a person is behaving inconsistently; it may mean only that we have failed to spot correctly the deepest (most cardinal) motive that is operating.

Distinctions between Genotypical, Phenotypical, and Pseudo Motives

This last point brings us to a useful distinction suggested by Lewin[19] and elaborated further by Allport.[20] Descriptions of behavior in terms of the "here and now" are *phenotypical*. For instance, in the example above, Tom can either be warm and giving or cold and rejecting. These are phenotypical descriptions. Explanatory accounts, which seek deeper motives, are *genotypical*. To take Tom as a case in point again, he has both warm and cold ways of behaving (phenotypical), but these opposing responses are rooted in a more fundamental or primary motive (genotypical) that has been diagnosed as self-centeredness.

It would not be accurate to conclude that phenotypical or primary motives are not true motives. Although they may not reflect the nucleus of a person's basic personality structure, they at least show some consistency in behavior. For example, whether we know that Tom's primary motive was self-centeredness or not, we might still be able to detect that at certain times he was consistently warm and accepting and at other times cold and distant. Getting to the genotypical motive helps us understand the otherwise contradictory and opposing phenotypical motives.

Sometimes our judgements about another person can be totally erroneous. We may, for example, regard a father who buys many gifts for his children as being a *caring* and *generous* person. But what if he is merely trying to buy their favor and affection? In this instance we are not even dealing with a phenotypical motives, for the father has no inclination at all for generosity or caring. The phenotypical or secondary motive is bribery (not generosity or caring) and the underlying genotype (primary motive), for all we know, may contain as its core a feeling of insecurity about whether people generally, and his children specifically, could ever love him if he didn't first bring them gifts. This is an example of pseudo motives, errors of inference, misjudgments that result from drawing conclusions about another person based solely on appearances.

A quite common error of inference many parents make, for example, is in regard to what seems to be the contradictory behavior of their children when the children are in school as opposed to when they are home. As a case in point, a mother approached me after a meeting recently and wondered what was wrong with her nine-year-old boy. She went on to explain that at school he was "a reasonably quiet, well-mannered little boy who behaved pretty well," but that at home he was "unruly, noisy, and frequently sasses both his mother and father." He was, the

© 1965 United Feature Syndicate, Inc.

Sometimes a person's psuedo motives are difficult to spot. Other times, however. . . .

mother concluded "two different boys." And she wanted to know, "Why?" The boy was, unquestioningly, showing phenotypically contrary behaviors. That is, at school his primary motive seemed to be to behave well; at home it was to behave poorly. Was there a deeper, more genotypical motive? Later, after several counseling sessions with both the mother and the father it turned out that there was indeed. The boy was starved for attention and he found that one way to get is was to be good at school and bad at home. Although his surface behavior seemed inconsistent (good at school, bad at home), both behaviors were quite consistent with the underlying genotypical or primary motive of getting attention. (The parents discovered, by the way, that the reason he misbehaved at home was that they never showed much attention to him when he was good—a heavy price to pay for good manners. Needless to say, they set out to change their behavior that very evening.)

It is only through being careful, disciplined, critical, yet sensitive observers of behavior that we can begin to see behavior for what it really is.

Personality Style and Expressions of Consistency

Although we are not always aware of it, each of us projects a certain personality "style" that makes us more or less "knowable" to others. When we talk about personality style, we are referring to the sum total of all that one is and does, to a person's *characteristic patterns of perceiving and responding*. Each painter and composer has a style all his or her own; so, too, each surgeon, secretary, ball player, teacher, novelist, housewife, and mechanic. From style alone it is possible to recognize the stories by Hemingway, the mysteries of Agatha Christie, the musicals of Rogers and Hammerstein, the paintings of Picasso, the comedy of Carol Burnett, the quarterbacking of Fran Tarkington, or the cooking of one's wife (or husband, as the case may be). Each of these activities carries its own unique mark. Although another person's art may resemble that of Picasso's, no one but Picasso can paint exactly like Picasso. An artist, it is said, is not a special type of person, but every person is a special type of artist. You might say that each person's artistry is projected more or less consistently in his characteristic ways of behaving. With this as a working concept, let's turn our attention now to some of the evidence that indicates how various perceptual styles and response styles are ultimately linked to the organized unity of the individual personality.

Expressive Versus Coping Behavior

Before we examine how different people express different kinds of consistency, it may be helpful to first consider the distinction between *expressive* and *coping* behavior. Allport[21] has suggested that one way of distinguishing between the two is to think of coping behavior as the *predicate* of action (what we are doing), and expressive behavior as the *adverb* of action (how we are doing it).

There are at least three important differences between coping and expressive behavior. (1) Coping behavior is typically conscious, even though it may employ automatic skills, and expressive behavior generally springs from our unconscious. (2) Since coping behavior is more conscious than expressive behavior, it is more readily controlled. Expressive behavior, because it is unconsciously motivated, is more difficult to change and often uncontrollable. (For example, changing our style of walking, speaking, or handwriting, which are expressive behaviors, can be kept up for only a short time.) (3) Coping behavior is more apt to be determined by the demands of the situation, while expressive behavior reflects deeper personal motives.

As an example, take handwriting, which is an expression of both coping and expressive behavior. We deliberately set out to convey our thoughts, we use some of the conventions of writing we learned in school, and we adapt to the pen and paper available to us. These are coping behaviors. At the same time, we project our personal style in the slant of our writing, the size of our margins and letter, the way we cross our t's, and so on. These are all expressive behaviors in the sense that our own unique personality styles are unconsciously expressed in the particular way that we write. To take a specific example, I remember times when, as a student taking a tough essay exam, I would deliberately change my handwriting from my normal cursive style to a semi-printing approach. I did this as a way of handling my anxiety, which I knew could influence my legibility. Invariably, by the time I finished the exam I had usually evolved to my illegible script style. My semi-printing approach was coping behavior in the sense that it was situationally determined and consciously decided upon. However, by the time it was over, my more dominant and natural expressive behavior had usually taken over, and the last several paragraphs of the exam stood as glaring, illegible testimonials to the real state of my inner feelings. I didn't try to do it that way, but that is surely how it ended up.

Expressive behavior, then, is most likely to occur in those things we do spontaneously and unconsciously. That is, most people develop highly characteristic and consistent styles of talking, writing, sitting, walking, gesturing, laughing, and relating to others. At a distance we spot a friend by her gait. We recognize the presence of a friend in a crowded theater by his laugh. We identify persons over the phone not so much by what they say, but from their voices and manner of speaking. Our expressive behavior is perhaps the most irrepressible part of our natures. Our coping behavior is variable, and it depends on *what* we have to do. But *how* we do it carries the mark of our particular and individual personality styles.

Different people have different ways for revealing the deeper levels of their personalities in expressive behaviors. For example, some people have faces that are open books and some are "poker faces." For some people gestures are merely conventional, whereas for others they are highly spontaneous and individual. Sometimes the color or style of dress or perhaps the handwriting seems "just like" the person, and in other cases they seem entirely nonexpressive. One person reveals himself consistently and primarily through the way he talks, another, through his posture and gait, and a third through his style of dress or ornamentation. Allport has suggested that "every person has one or two leading expressive features which reveal his true nature."[22] If this is so, and there is evidence to support that it is, then what we first have to do is to become as aware as possible of the various ways in which people reveal themselves in expressive behaviors.

At the same time, we need to keep in mind that any expressive behavior may have some compensatory deception built into it. In other words, it is not enough to rely on the obvious interpretation (the face-validity) of an expressive behavior. Self-defensiveness and other countercurrents may be seriously affecting how the other person behaves. We can never be totally certain what the expressive aspect of an act signifies because the unity of expression is a question of degree, just as the unity of personality is a matter of degree. There are few uncomplicated one-to-one relationships. We might hunch, for example, that an "introverted" (quiet, shy, withdrawn) person would "logically" express his doodling in small, or tight, or constricted lines. What does research say about this? Consider the following:

> Two psychologists asked a group of subjects to draw doodles and then measured the area covered in their doodlings. As you might suspect, the introverted subjects, on the average, drew small and tight doodles. But there were marked exceptions. Some drew expansively large ones. Also, as you might suspect, extroverted (out-going, confident) subjects tended to draw large doodles, but some of them scribbled in a remarkably small and tidy manner. The explanation for these confusing results is that the deviants were found to be, by other measurements, highly *anxious* people. Their *expressive* behavior was an effort to compensate for the underlying feeling. For example, the anxious introvert *compensated* for his anxiety by exaggerated drawings; the anxious extrovert *compensated* in the opposite way.[23]

These findings help us understand that what we see is not always what is there. We all know persons, for example, who are skilled at portraying a rough, tough, even authoritarian posture, which they hope will mask their more basic feelings of inferiority or insecurity. Their behavior may be very specific to certain situations, or it may become a daily expression of personality style. Whatever the case, we need to remain alert to the possibility of compensating deception existing in expressive behaviors.

Perceptual Style as Related to Personality and Consistency

As we discussed in Chapter Two, what we "see" and what we "hear" depend in large measure on who we are and how we feel about ourselves. As William James long ago pointed out, if four men go to Europe—a politician, an artist, a businessman, and a playboy—they will see, hear, note, and remember entirely different scenes and events.

George Klein[24] was among the first to demonstrate that people develop characteristic ways, which he called "perceptual attitudes," of dealing with how they see things, irrespective of content and sensory modality. A person's "perceptual style" is an important source of unity and consistency within the personality. Consequently, one's perceptual style is a factor making for a characteristic way of

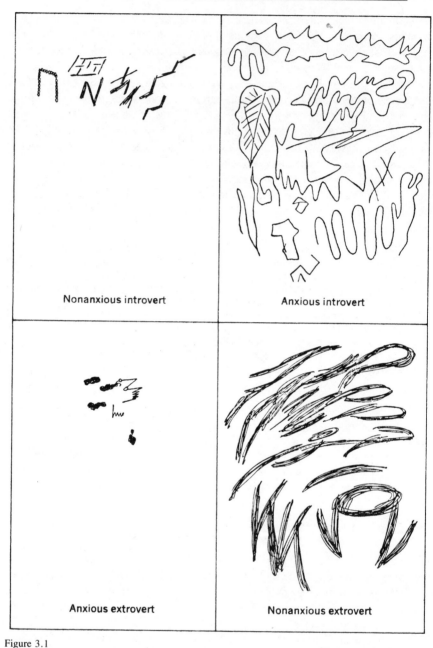

Figure 3.1

Illustrative expressive doodles. (From M. A. Wallach and R. C. Gahm, "Personality Functions of Graphic Restriction and Expansiveness." *Journal of Personality,* Copyright 1960 by Duke University Press, 28, 73–88, by permission.)

dealing with the environment which eventually comes to be an identifying feature of the unique personality. How do personality and perceptual style interact? Consider the following experiment by Holzman and Klein:

> A group of subjects were presented with square designs and asked to judge each for size. At first only squares 2 and 5 inches on a side were presented. Later the 2-inch square was omitted and a 7-inch square substituted. Eventually, the 3-inch square was replaced by an 8-inch one, the 4-inch square by a 9-inch one, and so on. Thus without their knowledge, the subjects were required to deal with gradually changing sizes. The results were surprising. Some subjects were realistic and accurate and held closely to the actual sizes presented, while others apparently fell into a rut and continued to repeat a judgment when it was no longer appropriate. The extent of this lag is made even more dramatic by the fact that toward the end of the experiment some subjects were judging a 13-inch square to be only 4 inches on a side.[25]

Holzman and Gardner[26] have proposed a "leveling-sharpening" continuum of perceptual functioning to describe this difference among individuals. *Leveling* refers to the inclinations to overlook or "level" perceptual differences among objects; that is, this sort of person tends to see things in terms of their sameness or similarity rather than in terms of distinctions between them. In contrast, *sharpening* is a way of looking at things in terms of their differences. A sharpener, for example, would have less trouble than a leveler in picking out the embedded figure in figure 3.2. (Can you find it?) Levelers also have more trouble finding hidden faces in puzzle pictures, and they reported less contrast in pictures of differing brightness. Thus there seems to be some evidence to suggest that different people have different perceptual styles that characterize them in many different situations. Personality studies have found that "levelers" tend to avoid competition (perhaps as a way of avoiding sharp distinctions in performance?), to be the dependent one in relation-

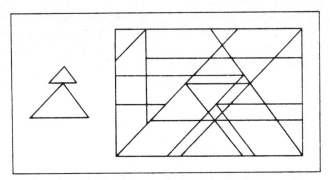

Figure 3.2
The embedded figures task. This task, devised by Gottschaldt, requires that the person locate the simple figure at left in the complex figure at right. A test using many of these has been employed in studies of perceptual style. (From K. Gottschaldt, "ueber den Einfluss der Ehrfahrung auf die Wahrnehmung von Figuren." *Psychologische Forschung*, 1926, 8: 261–317).

ships, to be self-oriented, and passive. "Sharpeners" are inclined to be more competitive, exhibitionistic, and to have high achievement needs. You might say that sharpeners look for ways to emphasize the differences in themselves and others, while levelers seek to smooth the differences out.

From different approaches different investigators, including Klein, have made a single central discovery. To put it simply, some people are unable to change their mental "set" (their minds, judgments, perceptions, first conclusions) even when confronted with new information or changing conditions. For example, Witkin[27] and his co-workers identified what he called *field-dependent* and *field-independent* persons. He found that the field-independent mode of perceiving focuses on the figure or "central object of perception" and resists the influence of the background. Field-dependent perceiving is markedly influenced by variations in the background. Tested individuals vary in their tendency to be field-dependent or field-independent, but—and this is important for us—a given individual's perceptual style tends to remain constant over a variety of test situations. For example, in one experiment the subject sat in a tilted chair and was asked to adjust a movable rod so it would be vertical. The field-dependent person tended to keep the rod parallel to his own body and line of sight. He could not abstract the "true vertical" from his own position and line of sight. The field-independent person was better able to correct for his own position and handle the pointer as the external conditions changed. Another task called for a similar judgement of the vertical in a small room tilted off the horizontal. Still another involved finding an embedded figure buried in a complex figure (See Figure 3.2). The "field-independent" persons were not disturbed by the tilted framework and could find the embedded figure easily, whereas the "field-dependent" subjects had great difficulty with both tasks.

Now let us look at the personalities of the field-dependent—those who are strongly influenced and controlled by the situation in which they find themselves. Witkin and his associates found that adults who were field-dependent were inclined to be passive and submissive to authority, to be afraid of their sexual and aggressive impulses, and to have low self-esteem and self-acceptance. In general, they are people who are very dependent on environmental supports. Field-independent people, on the other hand, tended to be independent in their social behavior, rather accepting of their hostile and sexual impulses, and better able to control them. They were generally less anxious, more self-confident, and more accepting. Other research reviewed by Elliot[28] indicated that field-dependent people tend to rate high on gregariousness and conventionality, whereas field-independent people tend to rate high on measures of interpersonal hostility, creativeness, and originality.

Our everyday experiences have taught us that some people are inclined to see everything as black or white, or all good or all bad. Some people have a high need for two-plus-two-equals-four type answer to their questions, while others are more tolerant of ambiguity and uncertainty. Frenkel-Brunswik[29] tested for tolerance of ambiguity in a strictly perceptual sense by presenting pictures in a series which gradually changed from one percept to another (for example, cat to dog). The subjects who were judged as being "intolerant of ambiguity" were those who held onto the original percept for a considerable time, then switched to the other, but were unable to admit that the picture might be either object. It *had* to be one or the other. Frenkel-Brunswik found that these individuals tended toward extremes in their emotional reactions as well as in their perceptual style.

Particularly interesting in this connection is the discovery that people who are rigid (who are "levelers," field-dependent) in their perceptual style and thinking tend to be prejudiced against Blacks, Jews, Catholics and other groups.[30] It is as if they cannot tolerate ambiguity or something different from what they know of any sort: neither in their perceptions, in their ways of thinking, nor in "taking chances" with ethnic or religious groups other than their own.

Our perceptual style does, indeed, seem to be related to our total personality. It affects our perceptions of ourselves, our view of others, and our adjustment to the day-to-day demands of living. For example, a person who is insecure, feels inadequate, self-distrustful, and who feels threatened by life generally tends to have a congruent perceptual style which is rigid, field-bound, concrete, and passive. In contrast, the more active, confident, secure, relaxed individual is better able to perceive and think across a broader range of ideas and circumstances and is on the whole, better adapted to the objective demands of the situation in which he finds himself.

How does it happen that people develop such differing perceptual styles? To a large extent it depends on how they were raised. For example, working with ten-year-olds, to whom perceptual tests similar to Witkin's had been given, it was found that the background and training of the field-dependent (less secure) and field-independent (more secure) children differed markedly. Field-dependent children were found to have mothers who were more restrictive, more concerned with dominating their children, and inclined to discourage curiosity and to encourage conformity. The mothers of field-independent children tended to encourage individuality, responsibility, exploring behavior, and independence.[31]

When considering the relationships between personality and perceptual preferences, Barron[32] has suggested that we are dealing with two types of perceptual preferences. One of them is a perceptual style which chooses that which is stable, regular, balanced, predictable, clear-cut, traditional, and follows some general abstract principle, which in human affairs is personified as authority. The other perceptual style is that which chooses what is complex, which is to say unstable, asymmetrical, unbalanced, whimsical, rebellious against tradition, and even at times irrational, disordered, and chaotic. To see things predominantly one way or the other is a sort of perceptual decision related to one's total personality style. For example, in our private world of experience, we may attend primarily to its ordered aspects, to regular sequences of events, to a stable center of the universe (God, the church, the state, the home, the parent, and so on.) or we may attend primarily to its complex aspects, to the eccentric, the relative, and the arbitrary aspects of the world (briefness of individual life, hypocrisy of the "system," accidents of circumstances of fate, the impossibility of total freedom, and so on).

A perceptual style which enables a person to see the world as primarily orderly and predictable can have two kinds of consequences. At its best, the decision to see things in an orderly and predictable way could reflect personal stability and balance, a sort of easygoing optimism combined with religious faith, a friendliness towards tradition, custom, and ceremony, and a respect for authority. We might expect people to be this way who are open, trusting, and independent.

At its worst, a perceptual decision in favor of order and predictableness could reflect a need to reject all that threatens the order, a fear of anything that might "rock the boat." Such a decision is associated with stereotyped thinking, rigid and compulsive morality, and a distrust of angry feelings and sexual impulses. Personal stability depends essentially upon exclusion of impulses and experiences that do not fit easily into some preconceived system. We might expect people to be this way who are somewhat closed-minded, suspicious, and dependent.

A perceptual style in which a person tends to see the world in its various shades of complexity can also have two consequences. At its best, an inclination to see the complexities of daily living could reflect an inclination for originality and creativeness, a greater tolerance of the unusual and the different, and a willingness to work at a reasonable balance between the inner and outer complexity in a higher order synthesis. The goal is to attain the psychological analog of mathematical elegance, to allow one's self to absorb the greatest possible richness of experience, while searching for some unifying pattern or theme. We might expect people to be this way who were creative, sensitive, even flighty.

At its worst, a perceptual style in favor of complexity could lead to grossly disorganized behavior, nihilism, despair, disintegration, and surrender to chaos. One's personal life becomes a simple acting out of the meaninglessness of the universe and the apparent insolubility of the problem. We might expect people to be this way who have a sense of futility, who seem aimless, and who feel little sense of responsibility.

As you can see, how a person behaves depends in large measure on how that person perceives his world. There is a certain consistency between the perceptions and the behaviors. We also find that there is a certain consistency between what one establishes as his or her "locus of control" and behavior, an idea we turn to next.

Locus of Control as Related to Personality and Consistency

Before reading any further, you may find it interesting to take a moment to respond to the short 10-item internal-external control test in figure 3.3. There are no right or wrong answers as such. An answer is "right" if it feels right to you. Check off your responses and then we will discuss what they may mean.

If most of your responses to the little test in figure 3.3 were in the A column, this may suggest that your locus of control is more *internal* than *external*. If, on the other hand, you find more of your responses in column B, then perhaps you are

A	**B**
I more strongly believe that:	**OR**

1.	Promotions are earned through hard work and persistence.	Making a lot of money is largely a matter of getting the right breaks.
2.	In my experience I have noticed that there is usually a direct connection between how hard I study and the grades I get.	Many times the reactions of teachers seem haphazard to me.
3.	The number of divorces indicates that more and more people are not trying to make their marriages work.	Marriage is largely a gamble.
4.	When I am right I can convince others.	It is silly to think that one can really change another person's basic attitudes.
5.	In our society a man's future earning power is dependent upon his ability.	Getting promoted is really a matter of being a little luckier than the next guy.
6.	If one knows how to deal with people they are really quite easily led.	I have little influence over the way other people behave.
7.	In my case the grades I make are the results of my own efforts; luck has little or nothing to do with it.	Sometimes I feel that I have little to do with the grades I get.
8.	People like me can change the course of world affairs if we make ourselves heard.	It is only wishful thinking to believe that one can really influence what happens in society at large.
9.	I am the master of my fate.	A great deal that happens to me is probably a matter of chance.
10.	Getting along with people is a skill that must be practiced.	It is almost impossible to figure out how to please some people.

Figure 3.3

Test of Internal-External Control. Julian Rotter is the developer of a 29-item scale for measuring an individual's degree of internal or external control. Above sample items taken from an earlier version of the test, but not used in the final version. There are ten statements here. In each instance, choose the one you agree with the most. Is your locus of control internal or external? (The original and longer version of this test is presented and discussed in the following source: J. B. Rotter, "Generalized Expectancies for Internal Versus External Control of Reinforcement," *Psychological Monographs,* 1966, 80: whole No. 609.)

more of an external than an internal. The fact that we are talking about locus of control as being either external or internal is not meant to imply that there are only two personality types and that everyone can be classified as either one or the other. Research does suggest, however, that there is a continuum, and that persons have varying degrees of internality and externality.

What do we mean by locus of control? Quite simply, "locus of control" is a personality characteristic that represents the extent to which an individual believes that events in his life are under his personal control. Rotter's[33] creative efforts in developing the Internal-External Scale have shown us that an internally controlled individual is one who has a generalized belief that life's outcomes are predominantly the consequences of his own actions. The externally controlled individual, on the other hand, believes that his outcomes are mainly determined by external forces such as fate, chance, luck, or more powerful others. We have seen how persons with different perceptual styles tend to perceive the world in different ways. The same is true for people with different locuses of control. Except in this case, they tend to *behave* in characteristically consistent ways. In order for behavior to be consistent, it has to be consistent *with* something. In this instance, the consistency can be measured against the degree to which a person feels he is in control of the environment (internal) or the environment is in control of him (external). Research points to some interesting consistencies between locus of control and behavior that may help us more fully understand how and why beliefs and behavior tend to go together. Perhaps if we review a sample of that research, you will have a better idea of how it is that a variety of behaviors can be more or less consistent with a single, but dominant, personality characteristic such as externality or internality.

Insofar as the internal-external locus of control continuum refers to a generalized expectancy for control of one's life, then we might reasonably predict that internals will be more assertive in their attempts to control, master, manipulate, or otherwise cope with their environment in an effective way. Research shows that this is, in fact, the case.

Seeman and Evans[34] found that internally-oriented hospital patients had acquired more information about their physical condition than had externals. In addition, internals had more information about the hospital, asked more questions of the doctors and nurses, and desired more information. Interestingly, similar results were found among internals who were prison inmates.[35] In this instance, internals knew more about how the institution was operated, about parole, and other information relevant to their future. In both of these studies, internals were shown to be better able to influence the course of their lives through their active attempts to understand their environment better.

Do you prefer games of chance or skill? Would you rather engage in an activity where your final ranking depended on your luck or your savvy? Research[36, 37] indicates that internals prefer activities involving skill and strategy, while externals are more inclined to choose activities involving luck and chance. The preference is quite consistent with the locus of control orientation. Internals want the control that comes from within (the use of skill), while externals give control to outside factors (luck, chance).

When you fail or do poorly on a task, is it your inclination to blame yourself or outside factors? When you do well on a task, are you able to take pride in your work and feel good about your effort, or are you inclined to categorize it as something "anyone could have done?" Again, your response to these questions will probably be consistent with your locus of control. Research by Phares, Wilson and Klyver[38] and Hochreich[39] found that internals are less likely to blame outside factors for failure than are externals. In fact, Hochreich found that the more defensive (uptight, guarded) the externals were, the more they were apt to project the blame for their failure on the outside environment. In another source, Phares[40] has further noted that an internal belief system lends itself more easily to taking pride in one's work because with this kind of belief one is, after all, in a position to take credit for the success. An external is less able to pat himself on the back for a job well-done because if success is due to outside forces, how *can* one take credit for it?

If you're a smoker, have you ever tried to quit? As it turns out, smoking is another behavior that can be related to the external-internal continuum. And again we find evidence of consistency between the personality type and the behavior. For example, research[41] shows that nonsmokers are more apt to be internals than smokers. (How many times have we heard smokers say they wish they weren't *controlled* by their smoking? And that's the issue—control. Externals are more apt to give in to it: "I just can't help myself," and internals are less likely: "I can control this if I choose.") Further research by James, et al[42] confirms this finding and in addition found that male smokers who had quit smoking following the Surgeon General's report and did not return to smoking were more internal than those who said they believed the report but went on smoking anyway. The difference was not significant for females, who apparently were motivated by other factors including, for example, one's tendency to gain weight after quitting. Speaking of gaining weight, have you ever tried to lose pounds by tempering your eating habits? Even eating behavior is related to the internal-external continuum and the weight of the evidence (no pun intended) strongly suggests that the person who overdoes it at the dinner table is apt to have an external locus of control. Research[43, 44, 45] shows that there are marked differences between obese (from 14 to 75 percent overweight) and normal weight individuals not only in the amount they eat, but also in the cues that trigger eating. In general, obese persons are more responsive to external food cues such as the sight, smell, and taste of food than they are to internal physiological hunger signals. In other words, if you are in the obese range, the condition of your stomach has little to do with your eating behavior.

Goldman, Jaffa, and Schacter summed up the results of a series of eating studies in the following way:

> The eating behavior of the obese is under external, rather than internal, control. In effect, the obese seem stimulus-bound. When a food-relevant cue is present, the obese are more likely to eat and to eat a great deal than are normals. When such a cue is absent, the obese are less likely to eat or to complain of hunger.[46]

The practical implications of these findings seems clear: if you're overweight and have a difficult time resisting food while it's around, then the best thing to do is not to have it available. A friend of mine, who wages a kind of on-going but friendly battle of the bulge, is fond of saying, "If I don't see it, I can't eat it. If I can't smell it, I don't want it."

Understanding the idea of locus of control, then, is another way to understand behavioral consistency. Like currents in a river, different behaviors in the same individual have a tendency to flow in somewhat similar directions. For internals, the behavioral flow is one of trying to master their environments by trying to find out as much information as they can about it, by relying on their personal skills, and by paying attention to their own inner feelings. Externals are more easily manipulated, rely more on chance and luck, and seem generally more responsive to what happens outside the self than to what is going on inside the self.

Response Styles as Related to Personality and Consistency

Just as it is true that each of us reflects a certain locus of control and perceptual style which contributes to our unique and unified personality, so, too, does each of us reflect certain characteristic "response styles" that indicate something of the nature of our feelings about ourselves and others. Response styles have many outlets and can be expressed in one's general tension level, handwriting, facial expressions, voice and speech, posture, gesturing habits, and even by the way one walks. None of these behaviors are random and unrelated to the personality of the behaving person, and in the discussion to follow we will try to indicate how even somatic, visceral or motor expressions are more or less consistent with an individual's personality and feeling.

Visceral or Somatic Response Styles There is evidence to suggest that a person's visceral or somatic responses are related to and consistent with certain emotional states. For example, Malmo and others,[47] found that headache-prone patients were not only more tense people, but also developed more tension in their neck muscles than other patients. In another study, they found that certain feelings may elicit corresponding tension in various muscle groups. For example, a divorced woman was being interviewed about her problems, while electrical action potentials were recorded from different muscle groups. When she was talking mainly about her anger and hostility toward her ex-husband (and other people), the major electrical activity was in her arm muscles; when she was discussing her sexual problems, the major activity was localized in her leg muscles.[48] In other words, as she experienced different feelings about different situations and people, she also experienced different muscle tensions related to the feelings she was having.

Though we are quite unaware of it, even the way we gesture is consistent with the feelings we may be having at the moment. Consider an interesting study by Rosenfeld.[49] He instructed nine female students to seek approval and nine to avoid approval in a social interchange with another individual. They did this one at a time and, unbeknownst to them, were observed to see what gestures they used. *Approval seekers* used a far greater number of gestures (smiles and gesticulations, such as any noticeable movement of arm, hand, or finger, indicating attention and involvement) than did *approval avoiders*, who were much less expressive with their bodies. Apparently, then, a person who is seeking approval may be inclined to use more expressive body movements than a person who is not seeking approval. Be conscious of your own behavior in this regard—watch others—see for yourself if such a relationship exists. Research is showing us that there is usually a rather striking congruency between what the mind is feeling and what the body is doing.[50, 51, 52] Even handwriting is more or less congruent with a person's personality, an idea we turn to next.

Graphic Response Styles Each person's style of handwriting is unique. Proponents argue that handwriting is not merely handwriting, but "brainwriting," influenced by a complex circuitry of neural impulses which gives an individual flavor to how one writes. Critics who claim that there is "nothing to graphology" are probably as wrong as graphology enthusiasts who claim too much. Studies have indicated that graphologists are in fact able to relate handwriting to an individual's personality characteristics significantly more often than one might expect by chance.[53, 54, 55] It is not only the professionals who have the skill to detect consistencies between handwriting and personality characteristics. We may all have this ability to some extent. For example, it has been found that a randomly selected group of people can tell the sex of writers correctly from script alone in about 70 percent of the cases.[56] In another experiment, college students, faculty members, and graphologists were given samples of handwriting from ten subjects. By chance alone, the judges would be expected to be correct one out of ten times. The college students averaged 1.77; the faculty group 1.80; and the graphologists, 2.41. The fact that all groups exceeded chance, even to these small degrees, suggests that personality is at least to some extent revealed in handwriting.[57]

In an effort to be more precise in the measurement of relationships between graphic responses and personality, Mira[58] developed a standardized series of graphic tasks which he calls "myokinetic psychodiagnosis." For example, a subject starts to copy a simple design like, say, a staircase. As soon as he gets underway, a shield is placed in front of his eyes so he can no longer see what he is doing, but he continues copying. In this way the copying behavior is reduced and the expressive component becomes more prominent. Mira believes he can identify certain deep tendencies in the personality by observing his expressive graphic behavior. For instance, a marked drift *away* from the body, in the case of lines drawn to and from the body, was related to aggressive attitudes towards others, while an *inward* drift was related to self-directed aggression. In addition, he found that elated people exaggerate upward movements, while depressed people tend to overdo movements toward the body.

Although it is only a matter of degree, there does seem to be a relationship between a person's graphic response style and his personality. Consider, for example, the musical scores in Figure 3.4. One is by Beethoven, another by Mozart, and a third by Bach. If you know anything about the music of these three men, which score do you think was written by whom? Most people quickly see the unities: the tempestuousness of Beethoven (No. I), the spritely fastidiousness of Mozart (No.

Figure 3.4

Musical manuscript of Bach, Beethoven, and Mozart. (From W. Wolff, The *Expression of Personality*. New York: Harper & Row, 1943, pp. 20ff., by permission.)

II), and the ordered and steady flow of Bach (No. III). These qualities were reflected not only in their music and graphic style but in their personal lives as well.

The three samples in figure 3.5 of Richard Nixon's handwriting over a five year period are visual examples of the congruency that may exist between a person's inner feelings and something as simple as the way he signs his name.

Nixon Handwriting Reflects Pressure

New York [Aug. 14, 1974]—(AP)—Former President Nixon's signature tells it all, according to a handwriting analyst.

Felix Lehmann studied three examples of Nixon's signature—the first from shortly after Nixon took office in 1969, the second several months ago and the third shortly before he resigned from office.

"Tremendous capitals show pride, but the long thread at the end of his name shows he wants to leave room to maneuver," Lehmann said of the first signature. "The striving for recognition and ambition are overpowering in his handwriting."

The second example:

"He goes from an appearance of clarity to being wishy-washy . . . But in this signature there is still hope."

And Lehmann's analysis of the third signature:

"There's nothing left. Only a shadow. His ambitions are over. A shapeless stroke, ambiguity. A disintegration of personality, a person sinking within himself."

Examples of Richard Nixon's signature. Three examples were studied by handwriting analyst.

Figure 3.5

(From *Denver Post*, August 14, 1974. Reprinted by permission of AP.)

Voice and Speech Response Styles Our voices are highly expressive aspects of our personalities. Voice inflection, intonation, rhythm, accent, and pitch vary widely among individuals and research has shown that there are relationships between voice and personality. For example, using a matching method where the unanalyzed voice is compared with known expressions and facts about the person doing the speaking, Cantril and Allport discovered that:

1. Untrained voices are more expressive (more often correctly matched than trained voices).
2. Age can usually be told within ten years.
3. Deeper traits—whether the speaker is dominant, extroverted, esthetic, or religious in his interests, and so on—are judged with fair success.
4. Complete sketches of personality are matched with voice with still greater success. (This finding is important. It suggests that voice-as-an-expressive-pattern is consistent with personality-as-a-whole, which further suggests that too fine an analysis may lose the diagnostic revelation of the voice as an expressive response.)[59]

There is also evidence to suggest that there are relationships between speech and personality. For instance, Doob[60] found that people who used many adjective and adverb modifiers also used more active verbs. Furthermore, they were able to give more "field-independent" judgments such as being able to pick out hidden or embedded figures in a complex visual field. This particular study shows well the consistency of different expressions. That is, people who are active, analytic, and discriminating in handling their environment show this same tendency in their speech habits. They are neither passive in relating to their environment nor passive in their use of speech. In a sense, their active lives are reflected in their active use of the language.

Interrelatedness of Different Response Styles In a classic study to find out whether people expressed themselves in similar ways across many different kinds of activities, Allport and Vernon[61] conducted an extensive study on a group of subjects who were required to carry out several dozen different tasks and then measured for their performance. The response styles they measured included such things as reading and counting aloud, walking indoors and outdoors, appraisals of distances, drawing of circles to estimate the size of certain objects, estimates of angles and weights, and so on. The investigators found a marked tendency for each person to perform the same task in the same manner on two different occasions. They also found a strong consistency of expressive movement when the same task was performed with different muscle groups. For example, there were strong similarities and consistencies between a person's footwriting style and his handwriting style.

When the experimenters examined all their measures for the presence of general expressive traits, they found that there were indeed tendencies for the individual's expressive movements to be similar across many different kinds of activities. They reported, for instance, that there were significant relationships among variables such as the following: voice intensity ratings; ratings on movement during speech; writing pressure; tapping pressure; overestimation of weights; underestimation of distance between hands; verbal slowness; pressure of resting hand, and others.

The investigators considered this group of interrelated measures and ratings as constituting an expressive factor of *emphasis*. For example, the confident, take-charge, aggressive individual is likely to express these charactersitics across many tasks. In addition, we are apt to find this sort of person having a louder voice than most, exhibiting heavier (more aggressive) writing and tapping pressure, showing more restlessness during his talking periods, and probably more inclined to overestimate (like he may "over" do many other things?) the weight of various objects. On the other hand, a shyer, more withdrawn person might be expected to have a quieter (more passive) voice, exhibit lighter (less aggressive) writing and tapping pressure, show less body movement during his talking periods, and probably more inclined to underestimate the weight of various objects. Along this same line, Bills[62] found that people who have low acceptance of themselves underestimate their performances more than people with higher acceptance of themselves. As another indication to show the consistencies between feelings and behavior, there is also evidence to suggest that people who have low acceptance of themselves report on the average, twice as many physical complaints as people who are high in their acceptance of themselves.[63]

There is evidence to suggest that the way we cross the street may also reveal something about our individual approaches to life and our proclivity to risk. Psychologists Kastenbaum and Briscoe[64] staked out a busy street in a major city and ranked 125 men and women according to the amount of risk they took in getting across the street. They were rated on the basis of such factors as whether or not they watched traffic lights, kept an eye out for oncoming cars and stayed within the crosswalk or scurried from behind parked cars and other indications of recklessness or caution. After observing and rating each subject, they interviewed him or her to find out something about the subject's personality and attitudes. Although there were all types of people in all categories, generally the young and single took greater risks than those older and married. The safest street crossers were more aware of their actions and considered themselves generally safer, more self-protecting people. The less cautious reported they had been barely aware of even crossing the street. One thing to be said for the risky crossers is that they were not deluding themselves. They neither wanted nor expected to live as long as did the cautious pedestrians. The researchers concluded: "Seeing how a person crosses the street, we can make a number of 'good guesses' about his marital status, mental contents, driving habits, suicidal history, etc." By no coincidence, it seems we each cross the street much as we make our way through life, a finding unlikely to curb interest in such matters.

In still other research showing the interrelatedness of different response styles, Maslow[65] found that high-dominance women (strong, self-confident, self-assertive characters) reflect their dominant assertive characters in a variety of ways. For example, they choose foods that are saltier, stronger tasting, sharper, and more bitter, for example, strong cheeses rather than milder ones; foods that taste good even though ugly and unattractive, for example, clams; foods that are novel and different, for example, snails or fried squirrel. They are less picky, less easily nauseated, less fussy about unattractive or sloppily prepared food, and yet more sensuous and lusty about good food than low-dominance (passive, shy, retreating) women. These same qualities are apparent in other areas, too. For example, the language of high-dominance women is tougher, stronger, harder; the men they choose are tougher, stronger, harder, and their reaction to people who try to take advantage of them is tougher, stronger, and harder. In still other research, Maslow[66] found that the high-dominance woman is more apt to be pagan, permissive, and accepting in all sexual realms. She is less apt to be a virgin, more apt to have masturbated, and more apt to have done more sexual experimentation. In other words, her sexual behavior is consistent with what seems to be a general personality characteristic, for here, too, she is apt to be dominant in terms of being more forward and less inhibited.

This, then, is some of the evidence that supports the idea of the personality having a unitary organization. In its simplest terms it suggests that an individual's "personality style" reflects a degree of unity and congruency across many different expressive behaviors. Consider a simple example of behavioral congruency: Jimmy Carter titles his autobiography *Why Not the Best?* and Richard Nixon calls his book *Six Crises*. What do these titles suggest about the world view of each of these men and how they approach life?

However forceful the evidence may be, we must be cautious in our judgments of others for two reasons: (1) behavioral consistency is never perfect; (2) we can too easily misinterpret the inner state underlying a person's mask if we are insensitive to that person's primary motives, or if the person tries to conceal his real feelings with masquerading behavior. For example, people frequently misinterpret shyness for snobbishness, and self-confidence for conceit. A ready smile and a firm handshake do not provide valid indicators of honesty and integrity; indeed, the confidence man and the shyster are adept at providing such cues. It is only through remaining sensitive and alert to the total complex of perceptual, bodily, and graphic response styles that we can begin to see their overall interrelatedness in behavior.

Cognitive Dissonance and the Need for Consistency

In a musical sense, dissonance is the result of a mingling of dissonant sounds, while in a psychological sense, it is the result of a mingling of discordant ideas and behaviors. Festinger's[67] model of cognitive dissonance is a good case in point inasmuch as the entire theory rests on the premise that a person continuously strives for consistency among his thoughts and behavior. Although not all of the evidence is unequivocal, over 500 experimental investigations suggest strongly that such a tendency does indeed exist.[68] The kind of inconsistency or disagreement with which Festinger is chiefly concerned is that which occurs after a decision has been made so that there is an inconsistency between what one does and what one believes. In other words, if a person has two ideas or views which are "dissonant" or mutually inconsistent, he will take steps to reduce the conflict. For example, if you are a regular smoker and read some startling new evidence linking smoking to lung cancer, your smoking and your new information will be dissonant. If you continue to smoke as much as ever, you can reduce the dissonance in two ways: (1) act as if the medical report isn't really as serious as it sounds, or (2) disbelieve the report. On the other hand, if you are already a nonsmoker, or if you smoke but make a decision either to give it up or drastically cut it down, the information linking lung cancer and smoking can be stoutly defended.

Take another example. Let's say a man who happens to have very firm negative views about *Penthouse* magazine finds himself in a circumstance where he has to wait for an extended period with nothing to do, no one to talk to, and nothing to read except several *Penthouse* magazines which happen to be on a table. A short while later, an acquaintance walks by and catches him looking at a *Penthouse*. There he is, indulging in an activity which allegedly is against his principles. The friend says, "Do my eyes deceive me? Do I see you reading *Penthouse?*" How does the man handle the dissonance? He may reply: "Thought I'd find out why so many men are attracted to these things." (In other words, "I'm not really reading it, I'm doing research.") Or, "In desperation, I'd even read *Sunshine and Health.*" (In other words, "This is an emergency, and it doesn't really count.")

Cognitive dissonance and the need for consistency between what one believes and what is actually happening was nicely illustrated by Festinger and his co-workers[69] when they studied a religious group who predicted the earth's destruction. This group believed that they were receiving communications from the gods stating that a catastrophic flood would overwhelm the world and that only members of this particular group would be saved when flying saucers would come to whisk them off to safety. On the day of the predicted flood, the chosen few were waiting at the proper places for the saucers to rescue them. When the saucers did not arrive at the time first predicted, this development naturally enough produced dissonance. What they believed and what was happening were inconsistent events and, in order to reduce the anxiety, the development was interpreted as a test set up by the gods to see if true believers could withstand uncertainty. Subsequent word was received that flying saucers would come at a later time. Then, when they did not come as predicted and when several other predictions about their arrival were also proved wrong, and when grave doubt began to surface concerning the coming of the catastrophic flood, the really true believers had a problem. Indeed, they were in a state of dejected puzzlement until they came by the happy construction, conveyed to them as if it were a message from the gods, that, because of the faith and steadfastness of the followers, the gods had decided to spare the world and to rearrange the divine plan for the true believers. Thus the dissonance was relieved, and the events, as they were happening, were consistent with a new belief or idea. However, to keep it effective in relieving the dissonance, it had to be built up to more credible proportions. Consequently, the true believers exerted strong efforts, through news releases and missionary work, to publicize the great turn of events that had occurred and to win more converts to the cause. Through investing additional efforts in support of the interpretation of what had happened, they made the new interpretation seem even more believable.

The steps people take to reduce dissonance have also been demonstrated in experimental settings. For example, Buss and Brock[70] asked a number of men and women who had previously said they were opposed to the use of electric shock in scientific research to participate in an experiment in which they believed they were administering electric shock to induce learning. Just before the experiment began, they were asked to read a statement purporting to emanate from medical authorities. One version stated that electric shocks were extremely harmful and the other stated that they were, in fact, beneficial. After the experiment, subjects were asked to recall the content of the communication. Consistent with cognitive dissonance theory, there was significantly less recall of the medical statement which said that shocks were harmful. In other words, forgetting the negative material made it easier to accept the fact that they had, in fact, administered an electric shock to other persons and thus enabled them to reduce the dissonance between what they believed and what they had done. It is also an excellent example of how people selectively remember experiences and events so as to protect their self-concepts.

The point should be clear. Dissonant ideas and behavior produce conflict and tension. In the quest for an overall unity of personality, changing one's behavior to make it consistent with what one has already done is a course through which most people seek to reduce the dissonance and insure some degree of "sameness" on a day-to-day basis.

Consistency of Behavior over Time

To what extent does behavior remain consistent, and how much does it change over time? Although we would not expect to find perfect consistency of behavior between a person's childhood behavior and adult behavior, we might expect to find some resemblance. What does research have to say about this?

Early Reflections of Unique Personality Characteristics

In observations of twenty-five babies during the first two years of life, Shirley[71] found that the children showed a high degree of consistency in the general pattern of their behavior from month to month. Developmental characteristics (locomotor ability, manipulative skills, and general development) evidence the greatest constancy at the various age levels. Each baby tended to maintain its relative position in the group with respect to these. Shirley noted that their behavior changed as they matured but there were always "identifying earmarks." A given expression of behavior "would lapse only to be supplemented by another that apparently was its consistent outgrowth." For example, one baby was distinctive at an early age for his "timorous crying." As time went on, the crying waned, but then he exhibited "apprehensive watching" and, at a later age, showed similar fearful behavior by hiding behind his mother and by his reluctance to play and talk in the presence of a stranger. As you can see, even though the specific responses are different (timorous crying, apprehensive watching, hiding behind his mother), each is motivated by a basic feeling of fear. If we try to compare specific responses, we miss the boat by failing to see that the underlying consistency can express itself in different ways and at different times.

Shirley goes a step further and suggests that certain aspects of personality are inborn and persist from age level to age level. For example, he states that:

> Both constancy and change characterize the personality of the baby. Traits are constant enough to make it plausible that a nucleus of personality exists at birth and that this nucleus persists and grows and determines to a certain degree the relative importance of the various traits. Some change is doubtless wrought by environmental factors, but this change is limited by the limitations of the original personality nucleus.[72]

A study by Martin[73] revealed a high degree of constancy in social behavior patterns of nursery school children. On the basis of observational records, fifty-three middle-class children during each of four semesters of nursery school were scored in terms of seven response categories, which included dependency, nurturance, aggression, control-dominance, autonomous achievement, avoidance-withdrawal, and friendship affiliation. The findings revealed profile instability over the two-year period in only nine of the fifty-three children. Martin concludes that:

> . . . during a period in the life span when instrumental behavior is demonstrably changing, in response to modifications in individual capabilities and social expectations, and—more specifically in the nursery school setting, a pattern of individual social behavior that is strikingly unchanging emerged. It is as if each child has his own *behavioral economy* which persists through time.[74]

In other research, Escalona and Heider[75] made predictions based on observations of the behavior of thirty-one infants, then tested these predictions against behavioral data gathered about five years later. Predictions were made for many different aspects of behavior and the outcomes were similarly focused. For example:

> Prediction, item 35: I expect Janice to understand and use language with perfectly good competence. I would be surprised if her verbal abilities as measured by tests exceeded average standards for her age. Outcome: Achieved superior scores on vocabulary and verbal comprehension items.[76]

This was, as you can see, a predictive failure. In fact, most of the predictions for Janice were failures. A successful prediction is illustrated by the following protocols for Terry:

> Prediction, item 41: Have thought that he will be very vocal in the sense of talking with a great deal of eagerness and intensity. Outcome: He talked freely, usually with enjoyment and often with a sort of urgency.[77]

Predictions were, in general, more successful with certain children than with others. With one child they were 92 percent successful, while at the other extreme there was a child for whom only 33 percent of the outcomes agreed with the predictions. Some aspects of behavior were more accurately predicted than others, particularly those having to do with life style and adaptation to sex roles. Predictions which dealt with characteristics such as competitiveness or shyness were less accurate.

Studies dealing with the consistency of personality traits beyond the pre-school or early school periods are relatively few in number, the major reason being that it is difficult to keep track of the same individuals over a long period of time. There are some, however, and we will now take a look at the major studies related to long-term behavioral consistency to see if we can assess the relationships between childhood and adulthood behaviors in the same individuals.

Consistency of Behavior from Childhood to Adulthood

The adult we are today is quite related to the child we once were. It's not a matter of absolute consistency, but there is general similarity between who we are today and who we have been in all of the yesterdays of our lives. There are at least three good reasons why we are not exactly the same as we may have started out to be: (1) the human personality is too complex to remain absolutely the same from start to finish; (2) new and different experiences have the power to re-shape and even replace original attitudes and life styles; (3) different developmental stages and maturation demand that we make new adjustments and develop new perceptions of ourselves, others, and even the environment we live in. How strong is the relationship between the behavior of childhood and adulthood? Consider some of the evidence.

Cited often among studies of long-term consistency and change is the effort by Neilon,[78] who, after a fifteen-year interval, followed up the individuals who had been studied by Shirley from birth to age two. Neilon collected extensive autobiographical sketches of fifteen of the original nineteen children at the age of seventeen—ten boys and five girls. Descriptive sketches of the infant personality and of the adolescent personality were prepared independently, and presented to psychologists who knew none of the children. The judges were asked to match the infant sketch with what they believed to be the corresponding adolescent personality. (It should be noted here that although Neilon and her associates knew the names of the children who had participated in the original study, they did not know which child was represented in each of Shirley's published biographies because of the use of pseudonyms in publication.) After the psychologists finished matching, Shirley's original data were then consulted to find out the real names of the children associated with each infant sketch so that the accuracy of the matching could be measured. The judges succeeded in matching the girls so successfully that their results could be obtained by chance less than once in a million times. With the boys they were correct to an extent that could occur by chance only once in 4000 tries. Although great individual differences existed among individual children, one girl being matched correctly by all ten judges and another by none, it was evident that there was considerable consistency in personality over a period of time. In other words, *many characteristics which were evident in early childhood persisted into late adolescence.*

In another study related to long-term behavioral consistency, McKinnon[79] observed eight boys and eight girls over a five-year period beginning at an average age of around four years. A fourfold classification of types was employed: conformity, invasiveness, caution, and withdrawal, according to the child's dominant pattern. Five children were rated as predominately conformist types at the earliest age level, and three of these were similarly rated at the age of eight to nine years. Of five initially characterized as invasive (forcible use of materials, active approach, physical and/or verbal attack) two were also seen that way at the upper age level. Three characterized by withdrawal persisted in this trait throughout the period. Three were first rated as cautious and two of these were still perceived this way at the end of the period. Thus, although changes in characterization occurred in some cases, consistency predominated.

A high degree of persistence in "ascendance-submission" was found in an investigation by Stott,[80] who studied over a hundred youngsters during a period of about twelve years. The first assessment was made while children were in nursery school, and later the children were observed in the recreational clubs they attended. They were rated on a scale of ascendance-submission ranging from extreme bossiness to "dependent ineffective submissiveness," Stott found that "persistence of pattern was more frequent than change during the period covered" and that 82 percent of the children ". . . showed no consistent direction of change." When changes did occur, they were temporary in most instances with a subsequent return to the earlier pattern.

Even more impressive is the material from investigations tracing the same individuals from childhood to maturity. Birren,[81] for example, reported on thirty-eight children who were examined in a child guidance clinic and who later became psychotic. He found that their symptoms corresponded closely to the pattern of traits observed in childhood. "Personality characteristics of psychotic patients," he concludes, "are stable and evidence continuous development from childhood."

Birren's findings correspond closely to a more recent study by Robins,[82] who analyzed the emotional status of over 500 persons seen thirty years earlier in a child guidance clinic. A major finding in this study was that there tends to be a continuity of levels of antisocial behavior between childhood and adulthood. For example, 61 percent of those who were seriously antisocial as children were exhibiting equally serious antisocial behavior as adults. Robins also found that the level of childhood antisocial behavior not only predicted sociopathy, but also predicted which schizophrenics and alcoholics would be combative and acting out, and which would be relatively quiet and retiring.

Arkin[83] used case-history material to compare the personality traits of individuals five to eight years of age with their personality traits when twenty-five to forty years old. Forty cases were studied altogether. It was reported that 100 percent of the men were equally "emotional" at both age levels, but only 67 percent of the women were judged to be as emotional between twenty-five and forty as between five and eight years. Intellect, special endowment, social attitude, and initiative were judged to be consistent in 67 to 100 percent of the cases.

These results are consistent with those of Tuddenham,[84] who, following up individuals studied as adolescents nineteen years earlier, observed a significant stability in more than one-third of the traits studied. He found, however, that aggression was the most stable of thirty-four variables for men, which supports Robins' finding that combative behavior was predictable from childhood. It also supports one of the findings of the Kagan and Moss research, coming up next.

One of the most extensive studies of consistency over time was undertaken by Kagan and Moss.[85] They studied the stability from infancy to adulthood of such aspects of behavior as passivity, aggression, striving for achievement, and sexuality. Assessments were made over four childhood periods and again when some of the subjects were from nineteen to twenty-nine years old. Infant ratings for the eighty-nine subjects were compared with self-ratings and scores on various personality tests, and the results of interviews in adulthood. One characteristic which proved to be relatively stable was passivity. This generally became evident during the second year, and it was expressed in various ways during the school years, for example, timid behavior in social situations, avoidance of dangerous activities, and conformity to parents. The authors believe that they have reasonable grounds for the hypothesis that the foundations for "extreme degrees of passivity, or its derivatives, in late childhood, adolescence and adulthood are established during the first six years of life."[86] Males were more stable when it came to aggressive behavior and females more stable in terms of dependency. Both males and females reflected stability from the standpoint of achievement behavior and the evidence suggests that the period from six to ten years of age is important in establishing this form of motivation. Indeed, it is claimed that the first four or five years of school provide "critical situations and experiences" that are necessary to crystallize this and related forms of motivation. Psychiatrist William Glasser has made the same point in his important book, *Schools without Failure*.[87] Regarding the overall study, Kagan and Moss concluded that:

> Many of the behaviors exhibited by the child aged six to ten, and a few during the age period three to six, were moderately good predictors of theoretically related behaviors during early adulthood. Passive withdrawal from stressful situations, dependency on family, ease-of-anger arousal, involvement in intellectual mastery, social interaction anxiety, sex-role identification, and pattern of sexual behavior in adulthood were each related to reasonably analogous behavioral dispositions during the early school years. . . . These results offer strong support for the generalization that aspects of adult personality begin to take form during early childhood.[88]

Popular beliefs that aging causes massive changes in psychological functioning and restriction in ways of living find no support in a unique longitudinal study by Maas and Kuypers.[89] For this study, in-depth interviews were conducted with ninety-five women and forty-seven men (average age seventy) in order to gather information about the kind of persons they had become, their health conditions, and how they were living their lives. This information was then compared with survey data from the University of California (Berkeley) Institute of Human Development that had been gathered from the same persons for a project started in 1929. Some of the major findings emerging from this study are the following:

1. ''Pathology'' in old age has more visible roots in early adulthood than does ''strength.'' However, early adulthood pathology does *not* lead unchangingly to pathology in old age.
2. There was strong evidence that many of the persons interviewed, found to lead a similar life style or having a similar personality in their later years, were also alike in their young adulthood.
3. Old age does not usher in problems which are necessarily new, but tends, if anything, to highlight or underscore problems that have long-term antecedents.
4. Health problems among elderly persons are likely to be clearly foreshadowed in the early adult years. For example, where the investigators found life styles marked by social withdrawal, they also found strong indications of various expressions of illness and disability. At all stages of life between thirty and seventy, it was noted that there was a strong relationship between physical well-being and psychological health. Anxious, fearful persons, for example, are apt to have more health problems than assertive, autonomous persons, and this tends to be true no matter how old or young they are.
5. A general conclusion from this study is that if you're squared away emotionally and psychologically at age thirty, you're likely to stay that way into your seventies. The reverse is also true. Young adults who are depressed, fearful, rigid, and sickly are still troubled in life's last years. Whether one is healthy and glad or sickly and sad, it appears that old age merely continues for them what the earlier years have launched.

All in all, research indicates that there tends to be a consistency of behavior over time. In his analysis of nineteen personality and attitudinal factors abstracted from long-term studies with participants ranging in age from twenty-two to eighty-four years, psychologist K. Warner Schaie concluded that ''. . . stability of personality traits is the rule rather than the exception.''[90]

This, then, is some of the empirical evidence that lends even greater credibility to a clinical observation made by Maslow:

> Thus we find some tendency to hang on to the life style in the healthy as well as in the unhealthy person. The person who tends to believe that all people are essentially good will show the same resistance to change of this belief as will the person who believes all people are essentially bad.[91]

A Note of Caution Regarding Stability of Behavior over Time

Impressive as the evidence for the early determination of personality and stability of behavior over time may seem, there are also reasons for believing that personality ordinarily remains open to change over extended periods. In the first place, the findings do *not* indicate that personality characteristics are *completely* formed during childhood. Also, even though a general personality trend may be established quite early, the manner in which it is expressed, indeed whether it is expressed directly at all, may continue to be quite susceptible to change. Clinical and psychotherapeutic literature, for example, abounds with evidence suggesting that adults can change not only their general life styles, but specific behaviors as well.[92]

Although much of the forty-year longitudinal data cited earlier from the Berkeley study indicates that our personalities appear to be relatively stable throughout life, another Institute psychologist, Norma Haan,[93] found that many healthy individuals do adjust their personalities and values to reflect changes throughout the life cycle. It might be worth noting that two basic personality characteristics were prized by successful persons at all ages. Both young and old stressed the importance of being a dependable, productive person. These two characteristics, reliability and capability, may be the very essence of stable and well-functioning personality. For all the criticism against it, the Puritan Ethic may not be such a bad idea after all.

One of the most striking—and gratifying—features of studies of consistency and change in personality development is the evidence that has been unearthed regarding the tremendous adaptability of human beings. For example, MacFarlane[94] speaks of the ". . . almost incredible capacity" of the individual to process the ". . . welter of inner-outer stimulation." Many of the most outstandingly mature adults in the group MacFarlane and her associates studied had by-passed or overcome difficult situations, even though ". . . their characteristic responses during childhood or adolescence seemed to us to compound their problems."[95] MacFarlane went on to note that she and her associates had failed to appreciate the maturing utility of many painful, strain-producing and confusing experiences. On the other hand, many subjects who ". . . early had had easy and confidence-inducing lives," and who had been free from severe strains and had exhibited very promising abilities and talents were ". . . brittle, discontented, and puzzled adults."[96]

MacFarlane's observations are well taken. The fact that a person has certain personality characteristics in childhood is no guarantee that he will have those same characteristics in adulthood. There is little question but that a child's personality "style" begins in infancy. However, psychologists are pretty much in agreement that although the influence of the preschool years are important, the experiences of childhood and later years are also important in either reinforcing or changing the character structure tentatively formed during the early years. For example, after a thorough review of the empirical literature, one psychologist concluded that ". . . events subsequent to the first year or two of life have the power to "confirm or deny" the personality of the growing infant, to perpetuate or remake it, depending upon whether the circumstances of later childhood perpetuate or alter the situation in which the child was reared."[97]

On the whole, a child's personality continues to develop in the direction it started. Whether it be a shy, withdrawn four-year-old girl or an aggressive, demanding seven-year-old boy, these characteristics are likely to persist into adulthood if the primary people and basic life experiences remain essentially the same.

Learning to be consistent with new and healthier ways of behaving is an important
step toward developing a positive self-image.

In Perspective

A person cannot help but be himself. Each of us behaves more or less consistently with the sort of person we conceive ourselves to be. If we are poor at sports we are not likely to participate in activities which call for physical coordination; if good at orally expressing ourselves, we may seek out public speaking opportunities. We behave in ways that are congruent with our self-concept: a beautiful woman, upon entering a new room, gazes into the mirror; a less attractive one studies pictures on the wall. Maltz[98] has suggested that just as the "success-type personality" finds some way to succeed, so, too, does the "failure-type personality" find some way to fail, in spite of his good intentions *not* to fail. The unity in one's behavior is related to one's concept of self and to that cluster of primary motives and dominant values upon which one's self-concept is built. The closer we come to truly understanding another person's primary motives and dominant values (not to mention our own), the better able we are to see the consistency in his behavior and the unity of his personality. Expressions of consistency can change with time, even though the primary motives may remain the same. For example, the fearful child at age one screams a great deal; at age five he is less vocal but runs away from threatening situations; at age fifteen he is quiet and somewhat of a loner; at age twenty-five he is shy, introverted and perhaps busy at some job where people contact is minimal. The consistency of behavior is not always in the overt action, but in the perception. Once we understand, for example, that the boy's primary motive is to avoid the threat he feels when too close to people, then we can see that there is much unity in his behavior over time even though its expression has been modified.

Practically everything one does is related to that central core which marks one as an unique individual unlike any other. Our perceptual style, in terms of how we "see" things, is related to how we view ourselves and our own particular personality "style." No matter how we respond, whether it be with our handwriting, our viscera, our voice, or our choice of an occupation, we reflect something of the nature of our feelings about ourselves and others in a more or less unified and predictable way.

Probably no individual can be counted on to behave in a completely consistent manner day in and day out. Indeed, what a bore such a person would be. Nonetheless, the evidence does suggest that people do strive for and exhibit some measure of personal consistency and unity in their every-day lives. If we work hard at being sensitive, patient observers of what is going on below the surface of behavior, we can see many outer signs of inner consistencies both within ourselves and others.

The purpose for understanding something about the nature and ex-pressions of self-consistency and stability of behavior over time is not merely an academic one. The evidence suggests that basic personality styles begin early in life, which means that whether we are teachers or other professional people or parents we can be alert to early signs indicat-ing the possible direction of a child's growth. Too often we wait for a child to "grow out of" his shyness, or aggressiveness, or lack of motiva-tion, or speech problem, or whatever without realizing that we are confus-ing the symptom of a possible personality defect for what is frequently called "just a stage he's going through." Behavior which is established early and reinforced while the child is young is likely to remain stable over time and serve as the seedbed in which one's primary motives and domi-nant values are nurtured. The fact that a child's basic personality structure is established early and tends to remain stable over time would suggest that, if we are to modify and induce positive change in warped values and distorted primary motives, then we must do this while children are going through their formative years. Sensitive parents and psychologically tuned elementary school teachers working in conjunction with extended guidance and counseling programs in the elementary grades would be a sound step in the right direction.

Notes

1. K. J. Gergen and E. E. Jones, "Mental Illness, Predictability, and Affective Consequences as Stimulus Factors in Person Perception," *Journal of Abnormal and Social Psychology*. 1963, 67: 95–104.
2. K. J. Gergen, "Personal Consistency and the Presentation of Self," in G. Gordon and K. J. Gergen (Eds.), *The Self in Social Interaction*. New York: John Wiley & Sons, Inc., 1968, p. 300.
3. E. S. Gollin, "Forming Impressions of Personality," *Journal of Personality*. 1954, 23: 65–76.
4. W. Mischel, "Continuity and Change in Personality," *American Psychologist*. 1969, 24: 1012–1018.
5. W. James, *The Varieties of Religious Experience*. New York: Modern Library Inc., 1929, pp. 77–162.
6. P. Lecky, *Self-Consistency: A Theory of Personality*. New York: Island Press, 1945, p. 135.
7. C. R. Rogers, "Some Observations on the Organization of Personality," *American Psychologist*. 1947, 2: 358–368.
8. C. R. Rogers, *Client-Centered Therapy; Its Current Practice, Implications, and Theory*. Boston: Houghton-Mifflin Company, 1951, p. 503.
9. E. H. Erikson, *Identity and the Life Cycle: Selected Papers*. New York: International Universities Press, 1959, p. 89.
10. G. W. Allport, *Pattern and Growth in Personality*. New York: Holt, Rinehart and Winston, 1961, p. 384.
11. H. Cantril, *Gauging Public Opinion*. Princeton, N.J.: Princeton University Press, 1943, Chapter 5.
12. A. H. Maslow, *Motivation and Personality* (2nd ed.). New York: Harper & Row, Publishers, 1970, pp. 283–315.
13. Maslow, p. 310.
14. S. B. Simon, L. W. Howe, and H. Kirschenbaum, *Values Clarification: A Handbook of Practical Strategies for Teacher and Students,* New York: Hart Publishing Co., 1972.
15. J. S. Stewart, *Toward a Theory of Values Development Education*. Unpublished doctoral dissertation, Michigan State University, 1974.
16. H. Hartshorne and M. A. May, *I: Studies in Deceit*. New York: Crowell-Collier and Macmillan, Inc., 1928.
17. Allport, p. 385.
18. Allport, p. 365.
19. K. Lewin, "Formalization and Progress in Psychology," in D. Cartwright (Ed.) *Field Theory in Social Psychology*. New York: Harper & Row, Publishers, 1951, pp. 1–29.
20. Allport, pp. 364–365.
21. Allport, pp. 462–464.
22. Allport, p. 369.
23. M. A. Wallach and R. C. Gahm, "Personality Functions of Graphic Constriction and Expansiveness," *Journal of Personality*. 1960, 28: 73–88.
24. G. Klein, "The Personal World through Perception," in R. R. Blake and G. V. Ramsen

(Eds.), *Perception: An Approach to Personality*. New York: Ronald Press, 1951, pp. 328–355.

25. P. S. Holzman and G. S. Klein, "Motive and Style in Reality Contact," *Bulletin of the Menninger Clinic*. 1956, 20: 181–191.

26. P. A. Holzman and R. W. Gardner, "Leveling and Repression," *Journal of Abnormal and Social Psychology*. 1959, 59: 151–155.

27. H. A. Witkin, H. B. Lewis, K. Machover, P. B. Meissner, and S. Wapner. *Personality through Perception*. New York: Harper & Row, Publishers, 1954.

28. R. Elliot, "Interrelationships among Measures of Field Dependence, Ability, and Personality Traits," *Journal of Abnormal and Social Psychology*. 1961: 63, 27–36.

29. Else Frenkel-Brunswik, "Intolerance of Ambiguity as an Emotional and Perceptual Personality Variable," *Journal of Personality*. 1949, 18: 108–143.

30. G. W. Allport, *The Nature of Prejudice*. Boston: Addison-Wesley Publishing Company, Inc., 1954, chap. 25.

31. J. Shaffer, S. Mednick, and J. Seder, "Some Developmental Factors Related to Field-Independence in Children," *American Psychologist*. 1957, 12: 399.

32. F. Barron, "Personality Style and Perceptual Choice," *Journal of Personality*. 1952, 20: 385–401.

33. J. B. Rotter, "Generalized Expectancies for Internal Versus External Control of Reinforcement," *Psychological Monographs*. 1966, 80 (whole no. 609).

34. M. Seeman and J. W. Evans, "Alienation and Learning in a Hospital Setting." *American Sociological Reviews*. 1962, 27: 772–783.

35. M. Seeman, "Alienation and Social Learning in a Reformatory," *American Journal of Sociology*. 1963, 69: 270–284.

36. J. B. Rotter and R. C. Mulry, "Internal versus External Control of Reinforcement and Decision Time," *Journal of Personality and Social Psychology*. 1965, 2: 598–604.

37. J. M. Schneider, "Relationship between Locus of Control and Activity Preferences: Effects of Masculinity, Activity, and Skill," *Journal of Consulting and Clinical Psychology*. 1972, 38: 225–230.

38. E. J. Phares, K. G. Wilson, and N. W. Klyver, "Internal-External Control and Attribution of Blame under Neutral and Distractive Conditions," *Journal of Personality and Social Psychology*. 1971, 18: 285–288.

39. D. J. Hochreich, "Defensive Externality and Blame Projection Following Failure," *Journal of Personality and Social Psychology*. 1975, 32: 540–546.

40. E. J. Phares, *Locus of Control: A Personality Determinant of Behavior*. Morristown, N.J.: General Learning Press, 1973, pp. 13–14.

41. B. C. Straits and L. Sechrest, "Further Support of Some Findings about Characteristics of Smokers and Non-Smokers," *Journal of Consulting Psychology*. 1963, 27: 282.

42. W. H. James, A. B. Woodruff, and W. Werner, "Effect of Internal and External Control upon Changes in Smoking Behavior," *Journal of Consulting Psychology*. 1965, 29: 127–129.

43. S. Schacter and J. Rodin, *Obese Humans and Rats*. Washington, D.C.: Erlbaum/ Halsted, 1974.

44. G. Tom and M. Rucker, "Fat, Full and Happy: Effects of Food Deprivation, External Cues, and Obesity on Preference Ratings, Consumption, and Buying Intentions," *Journal of Personality and Social Psychology*. 1975, 32: 761–766.

45. J. Rodin and J. Slochower, "Externality in the Obese: Effects of Environmental Re-

sponsiveness on Weight," *Journal of Personality and Social Psychology.* 1976, 33: 338–344.

46. R. Goldman, M. Jaffa, and S. Schacter, "Yom Kippur, Air France, Dormitory Food, and the Eating Behavior of Obese and Normal Persons," *Journal of Personality and Social Psychology.* 1968, 10: 133.

47. R. B. Malmo and C. Shagass, "Headache Proneness and Mechanisms of Motor Conflict in Psychiatric Patients," *Journal of Personality.* 1953, 22: 163–187.

48. R. B. Malmo, A. A. Smith, and W. A. Kohlmeyers, "Motor Manifestations of Conflict in Interview: A Case Study," *Journal of Abnormal and Social Psychology.* 1956, 52: 268–271.

49. N. M. Rosenfeld, "Instrumental Affiliative Functions of Facial and Gestural Expressions," *Journal of Personality and Social Psychology.* 1966, 4: 65–72.

50. J. Fast, *Body Language.* New York: Pocket Books, 1971.

51. A. E. Scheflen, *Body Language and Social Order.* Englewood Cliffs, N.J.: Prentice-Hall Inc., 1972.

52. S. Weitz, (Ed.), *Nonverbal Communication.* New York: Oxford University Press, 1974.

53. D. S. Anthony, "Is Graphology Valid?," *Psychology Today.* August, 1967: 38–39.

54. H. Cantril, G. W. Allport, and H. A. Rand, "The Determination of Personal Interests by Psychological and Graphological Methods," *Character and Personality.* 1933, 2: 134–151.

55. H. J. Eysenck, "Graphological Analysis and Psychiatry: An Experimental Study," *British Journal of Psychology.* 1945, 35: 70–80.

56. P. Eisenberg, "Judging Expressive Movement: I. Judgements of Sex and Dominance-Feeling from Handwriting Samples of Dominant and Non-Dominant Men and Women," *Journal of Applied Psychology.* 1938, 22: 480–486.

57. E. Powers, *Graphic Factors in Relation to Personality.* Hanover, N.H.: Dartmouth College Library, 1930.

58. E. Mira, *M. K. P.—Myokinetic Diagnosis.* New York: Logos, 1958.

59. H. Cantril and G. W. Allport, *The Psychology of Radio.* New York: Harper & Row, Publishers, 1935.

60. L. W. Doob, "Behavior and Grammatical Style," *Journal of Abnormal and Social Psychology.* 1958, 56: 398–401.

61. G. W. Allport and P. E. Vernon, *Studies in Expressive Movement.* New York: The Macmillan Company, 1933.

62. R. E. Bills, "A Comparison of Scores on the Index of Adjustment and Values with Behavior in Level of Aspiration Tasks," *Journal of Consulting Psychology.* 1953, 17: 206–212.

63. R. E. Bills, "About People and Teaching," *Bulletin of the Bureau of School Service.* Lexington: University Press of Kentucky, Dec. 1955, 28: no. 18.

64. R. Kastenbaum and L. Briscoe, "The Street Corner: A Laboratory for the Study of Life-Threatening Behavior," *Omega.* 1975, 6: 33–44.

65. A. H. Maslow, "Dominance-feeling, Personality, and Social Behavior in Women," *Journal of Social Psychology.* 1939, 10: 3–39.

66. A. H. Maslow, "Self-Esteem (dominance-feeling) and Sexuality in Women," *Journal of Social Psychology.* 1942, 16: 259–294.

67. L. Festinger, *A Theory of Cognitive Dissonance.* Evanston, Ill.: Row, Peterson & Company, 1957.

68. J. W. Brehm and A. R. Cohen, *Explorations in Cognitive Dissonance.* New York: John Wiley & Sons, Inc., 1962.

69. L. Festinger, H. W. Riecken, and S. Schacter, *When Prophecy Fails: A Social and Psychological Study of a Modern Group That Predicted the Destruction of the World.* New York: Harper & Row, Publishers, 1956.

70. A. H. Rhbuss and T. C. Brock, "Repression and Guilt in Relation to Aggression," *Journal of Abnormal and Social Psychology.* 1963, 66: 345–350.

71. M. M. Shirley, *The First Two Years: A Study of Twenty-Five Babies, Vol. III, Personality Manifestations.* Institute of Child Welfare Monograph Series, No. 8. Minneapolis: University of Minnesota Press, 1933.

72. Shirley, p. 56.

73. W. E. Martin, "Singularity and Stability of Profiles of Social Behavior," in C. B. Stendler (Ed.), *Readings in Child Behavior and Development.* New York: Harcourt, Brace & World, Inc., 1964, pp. 448–466.

74. Martin, p. 465.

75. S. Escalona, and G. M. Heider, *Prediction and Outcome: A Study in Child Development.* New York: Basic Books, Inc., 1959.

76. Escalona and Heider, p. 175.

77. Escalona and Heider, pp. 205–206.

78. P. Neilon, "Shirley's Babies after Fifteen Years: A Personality Study," *Journal of Genetic Psychology.* 1948, 73: 175–186.

79. K. M. McKinnon, "Consistency and Change in Behavior Manifestation," *Child Development Monographs.* 1942, No. 30. New York: Teachers College Press, Columbia University.

80. L. H. Stott, "Persistency Effects of Early Family Experiences Upon Personality Development," *Merrill-Palmer School Quarterly.* 1957, Spring, 3 (Special Issue, Seminar on Child Development) p. 12.

81. J. E. Birren, "Psychological Examinations of Children Who Later Became Psychotic," *Journal of Abnormal and Social Psychology.* 1944, 39: 84–95.

82. L. N. Robins, *Deviant Children Grown Up: Summation and Interpretation of Results.* Baltimore: The Williams & Wilkens Co., 1966.

83. Arkin, E., "The Problem of the Stability of the Human Organism," *Journal of Genetic Psychology.* 42: 228–236.

84. R. D. Tuddenham, "The Constancy of Personality Ratings Over Two Decades," *Genetic Psychology Monographs.* 1958, 60: 3-29.

85. J. Kagan and H. A. Moss, *From Birth to Maturity: A Study in Psychological Development.* New York: John Wiley & Sons, Inc., 1962.

86. Kagan and Moss, p. 83.

87. W. Glasser, *Schools without Failure.* New York: Harper & Row, Publishers, 1969, pp. 25–30.

88. Kagan and Moss, pp. 266–268.

89. H. S. Maas and J. A. Kuypers, *From Thirty to Seventy.* San Francisco: Jossey-Bass, 1974.

90. K. W. Schaie and I. A. Parhaum, "Stability of Adult Personality Traits: Fact of Fable?" *Journal of Personality and Social Psychology.* 1976, 34: 157.

91. A. H. Maslow, *Motivation and Personality (Rev.),* p. 309.

92. W. B. Reddy, D. B. Colson, and C. B. Keys, "The Group Psychotherapy Literature: 1975," *International Journal of Group Psychotherapy.* 1976, 26: 487–545.

93. N. Haan, "Personality Development from Adolescence to Adulthood in the Oakland Growth and Guidance Studies," *Seminars in Psychiatry*. 1972, 4: 399–414.
94. J. L. Macfarlane, "Perspectives on Personality Consistency and Change from the Guidance Study," *Vita Humana*. 1974, 7: 115–126.
95. Macfarlane, p. 121.
96. Macfarlane, p. 122.
97. H. Orlansky, "Infant Care and Personality." *Psychological Bulletin*. 1949, 46: 35.
98. M. Maltz, *Psycho-Cybernetics*. Englewood Cliffs, N.J.: Prentice-Hall Inc., 1960.

References of Related Interest

Block, J., and N. Haan, *Lives through Time*. Berkeley, Calif.: Bancroft Books, 1971.

Bloom, B. S., *Stability and Change in Human Characteristics*. New York: John Wiley & Sons, Inc., 1964.

Chapanis, N. P., and A. Chapanis, "Cognitive Dissonance: Five Years Later," *Psychological Bulletin*. 1964, 61: 1–22.

Emmerich, W., "Stability and Change in Early Personality Development," in W. W. Hartup and H. L. Smothergill (Eds.), *The Young Child*. Washington, D.C.: National Association for the Education of Young Children, 1967, pp. 248–261.

Epstein, W. (Ed.), *Stability and Constancy in Visual Perception*. New York: John Wiley & Sons, Inc., 1976.

Glass, D. C., "Theories of Consistency and the Study of Personality," in E. F. Borgatta and W. W. Lambert (Eds.), *Handbook of Personality Theory and Research*. Skokie, Ill.: Rand McNally & Company, 1968, pp. 788–854.

Goffman, E., *The Presentation of Self in Everyday Life*. New York: Doubleday & Company, 1959.

Kelly, E. L., "Consistency of the Adult Personality," *American Psychologist*. 1955, 10: 659–681.

Lowenthal, M. F., M. Thurnher, and D. Chiriboga, *Four Stages of Life: A Comparative Study of Women and Men Facing Transitions*. San Francisco: Jossey-Bass, 1976.

Nesselroade, J. R., and H. W. Reese (Eds.), *Life-Span Developmental Psychology: Methodological Issues*. New York: Academic Press, Inc., 1973.

Secord, P. F., and C. W. Blackman, "Personality Theory and the Problem of Stability and Change in Individual Behavior," *Psychological Review*. 1961, 68: 21–32.

Stagner, R., "Homeostasis as a Unifying Concept in Personality Theory," *Psychological Review*. 1951, 58: 5–17.

Williams, R. H., and C. G. Wirths, *Lives through the Years*. Chicago: Aldine-Atherton, 1965.

Wylie, R. C., *The Self-Concept* (Rev. vol. I). Lincoln, Neb.: University of Nebraska Press, 1974.

Self-Concept as Related to Physical Growth, Appearance, and Developmental Outcomes

PROLOGUE

How we feel about ourselves is related to how we feel about our bodies. The self-image is first and foremost a body image. Among a child's first discoveries are his hands and feet and among his first sensations are the assorted pleasures and pains of his own body. In fact, it is very likely that a child's first distinction between "me" and "you," between "I am running" and "she is running" is formed on the basis of his sensitivity to his own muscular reactions, his own viscera, his own bumps and falls. An endless stream of sensory inputs may provide the nucleus for an emerging self.

A central theme which will be underscored in the pages to follow is that our experiences with our body, as a psychological object, are infused widely into our lives. Our height, weight, girth, eye color, hair color, complexion, and general body proportions are very much related to our feelings of personal adequacy. Our bodies, for better or for worse, are perceptual realities from which we cannot escape. Whether we think we have grown up too fast or not fast enough, or whether we are too tall or too short, too fat or too thin, attractive or not attractive enough, can make a difference in our feelings about ourselves and, indeed, in the feelings others have toward us. In this chapter, then, our attention turns to an examination of the relationship between self-concept and physical growth, appearance, and developmental outcomes.

Physical Typologies and Personality

For thousands of years, philosophers and physicians and, more recently, anthropologists and psychologists have speculated about and researched the relationships between physical factors and personality. In their review of the literature dealing with physical factors and personality, Sheldon and his colleagues state: "It is a curious and perhaps significant fact that 2500 years ago Hippocrates said that there are two roots of human beings, the long thins and the short thicks. Almost all simple classifications of type since that time have nearly the same basis, despite variety of nomenclature and detail of description."[1] During the 1920s, Kretschmer[2] used a somewhat similar classification of body type in his controversial but influential hypotheses about the relationship of body build to temperament and mental illness. For example, he said that any given body can be typed as *asthenic* (thin and frail), *pyknik* (short, soft, rounded), *athletic* (muscular), or *dysplastic* (one type in one segment and another type somewhere else). An elaborate theory, but, like many theories, it fell to the wayside for lack of consistent research findings to support it.

Among the more recent attempts to develop a method of classifying personality on the basis of physical characteristics, Sheldon's[3] work during the 1950s stirred the attention of many developmental psychologists. Rejecting the idea that individuals can be divided into distinct physical types, he devised a method of classifying them according to three basic components. The terms used to describe the components are analogous to the names of the cell layers in the embryo from which different body tissues originate. The first or *endomorphic* component refers to the prominence of the intestines and other visceral organs. Obese individuals typically fit this category. The second or *mesomorphic* component refers to bone and muscle. The wide-shouldered, narrow-hipped, muscular athlete fits this category. The third or *ectomorphic* component is based on delicacy of skin, fine hair, and sensitive nervous system. Tall thin, stoop-shouldered individuals fit this category. Figure 4.1 may help give you a visual idea of these three physical types and their variations.

In rating a person's physical characteristics, Sheldon's system assigns one digit between 1 and 7 for each component in the order of endomorph, mesomorph,

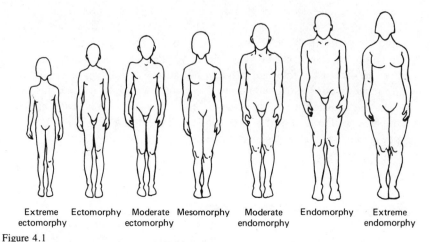

| Extreme ectomorphy | Ectomorphy | Moderate ectomorphy | Mesomorphy | Moderate endomorphy | Endomorphy | Extreme endomorphy |

Figure 4.1

Examples of Differences in Body Build.

and ectomorph with high numbers indicating more of a particular component. For example, a rating of 5-4-2 would describe a rounded but relatively muscular and sturdy individual.

Sheldon's rating system was accepted easily enough, but where he got in trouble was in assigning certain pyschological characteristics to particular physical components. According to Sheldon, the predominantly short, chubby endomorphic person is one who loves to eat, seeks bodily comforts, and is sociable and outgoing. The predominantly athletic mesomorphic person is described as energetic and direct in manner. The tall, thin ectomorph is classified as sensitive, given to worrying, fearing groups, and needing solitude.

This system of "somatotizing" individuals has been far from universally accepted and, in fact, strongly criticized.[4, 5] The fact is, endomorphs (obese, heavy) are *not all* large eaters, outgoing, and sociable. Mesomorphs (athletic, muscular) are *not all* energetic and athletically inclined. Ectomorphs (tall, thin) are *not all* sensitive, introverted, and fearful. (Indeed, some ectomorphs are aggressive, fearless basketball players whose sensitivity, if that's what you could call it, is apparent only by the pained expression on their faces when caught on the tailend of an opposing team's fast break.) As we shall see, there *are* relationships between physical factors and personality, although it is doubtful that these relationships can be packaged as easily as Sheldon suggests.

In considering the notion that certain personality characteristics are related to certain body types, we are, of course, going beyond the mere descriptions of behaviors associated with different body structures and are touching upon possible cause and effect relationships. Would it be accurate to conclude that certain body types, or structures or proportions or whatever you care to call them, *cause* certain personality effects? Probably not. At the moment, the best we can do is speculate that the components of one's body structure help determine not only what a person can do, *but what he and those close to him expect that he should be able to do.* This should not be so surprising. After all, the most obvious and observable part of our entire being is the body shell in which we house our private world and personal existence. Whether we like it or not, the fact is we have a strong tendency to stereotype and categorize each other according to the cues available to us. And one of the most prominent cues is body structure.

Let us turn our attention now to what research says about how different body structures are perceived and the possible relationships between body type and personality.

Body Build and Personality Stereotypes

Most of us don't have to go any further than our own personal experiences to know that different body proportions in men and women (and even children) elicit different feelings, attitudes, and responses from us. There is a substantial body of research[6, 7, 8] to show that the less well we know another person the more likely we are to judge that person in terms of certain preconceived attitudes related to physical features and proportions. How do people stereotype? What conclusions do they reach? Consider some of the evidence.

An ingenious study by Brodsky[9] has demonstrated very nicely that there are indeed different social reactions to different body builds. He prepared five fifteen-inch silhouettes of males, representing: (1) endomorph (obese); (2) endomesomorph (muscular, but short and heavy); (3) mesomorph (athletic, muscular); (4) ectomesomorph (muscular, but tall and thin); (5) ectomorph (thin and tall). He also constructed a questionnaire containing such questions as the following: Which one of this group of five men is most aggressive? Which one is least aggressive?

Brodsky's research sample consisted of 150 male college students, half of whom were black and half of whom were white. One of the interesting things he discovered was that there were no important differences in the way the two groups responded, which lends weight to the idea of a "cultural stereotype" when it comes to aligning certain personality characteristics to certain body types.

Personality characteristics were usually assigned by the respondents in Brodsky's study to the "pure" silhouettes: the endomorph, mesomorph, and ectomorph. Those characteristics assigned to a given silhouette by a third or more of the respondents are discussed in the extracts following.

> More than one-third of the respondents labeled the *endomorph* (short, chubby) silhouette as representing the man who probably eats the most, would make the worst soldier, the poorest athlete, would be the poorest professor of philosophy, can endure pain the least well, would make the least successful military leader, would be least likely to be chosen leader, would make the poorest university president, would be the least aggressive, would drink the most, be least preferred as a personal friend (but, ironically, would have many friends), would make the poorest doctor, and would probably put his own interests before those of others.[10]

As you can see, the picture which emerged was an almost consistently negative one. If there is any truth to the idea that a person behaves as he or she is expected to behave, a dismal picture of the direction of personality growth of the endomorph is presented by this study.

> The *mesomorph* (muscular, athletic) fared as favorably as the endomorph did unfavorably. The respondents said that he would make the best athlete, the most successful military leader, and the best soldier. They chose him as the man who would assume leadership, as well as the man who would be elected as leader. He was judged to be nonsmoker, and to be self-sufficient, in the sense of needing friends the least. However, he was most preferred as a friend, and was judged to have many friends. Respondents also said that he would be the most aggressive, would endure pain the best, would be least likely to have a nervous breakdown, and would probably drink the least.

> The stereotype of the *ectomorph* (tall, thin) is far less socially desirable than that of the mesomorph, but in general more favorable than that of the endomorph. The ectomorph was judged to be the most likely to have a nervous breakdown before the age of thirty, to eat the least and the least often, to be a heavy smoker, to be least self-sufficient, in the sense of needing friends the most (but, unfortunately, was judged to have the fewest friends), to hold his liquor the worst, to make a poor father, and, as a military leader, to be likely to sacrifice his men with the greatest emotional distress.[11]

This study suggests that there may be characteristic stereotyped ways of reacting to different types of male physiques, and the trend of this reaction is such as to favor the mesomorph. More recent research[12, 13] tends to support Brodsky's findings with the conclusion that three different male body builds are frequently characterized by the following traits:

1. *soft, fat, round*—old-fashioned, physically weak, talkative, warmhearted, sympathetic, good-natured, agreeable, trusting, needy, people-oriented, loving physical comfort, loving eating.
2. *muscular, athletic*—strong, masculine, adventurous, self-reliant, energetic, competitive, liking exercise, bold.
3. *tall, thin, fragile*—ambitious, tense, nervous, stubborn, quiet, liking privacy, sensitive to pain.

Other research supports these findings. For example, in studies of high school boys and a sample of college girls, Cortés and Gatti[14, 15] found endomorphs rated *themselves* significantly more often as kind, relaxed, warm, and softhearted. Mesomorphs were found to reflect a higher need for achievement than the other two body types.

The stereotypes of the happy-go-lucky plump person, the lanky bookworm, and the aggressive mesomorph may not be very scientific descriptions, but they do establish certain expectations of behavior for both young and old with these body types. For example, parents are probably less apt to encourage a thin ectomorphic offspring than a more muscular mesomorphic youngster to participate in athletic activities.

Cultural stereotypes associated with different body structures begin early. A case in point is the research of Staffieri,[16] who found that boys as young as six to ten years of age are already in close agreement when it comes to assigning certain personality characteristics to particular body types. For example, he found a remarkably similar tendency for the endomorphic silhouettes to be described as socially offensive and delinquent, the mesomorphic silhouettes as aggressive, outgoing, active, having leadership skills, and the ectomorphic silhouettes as retiring, nervous, shy, and introverted. He also found that ectomorphs and mesomorphs were chosen as the most popular by their peers, leading to the tentative conclusion that endomorphs are less popular, know that they are unpopular, and are inclined to reject their body image. Other research with five- and six-year-olds also supports this finding.[17]

We can begin to see the influence of body structure on behavior even among preschoolers. In an extensive study designed to look at the relationship between body build and behavior, Walker[18] had 125 preschool children rated by their teachers on sixty-four behavioral items. What he found was that there were more significant relationships between body build and behavior for boys than for girls. That is, on the basis of body build data, one could more accurately predict how boys might behave, which suggests that physical factors may be more important in affecting the behavior of boys. Despite the popular concern about female measurements, our cultural stereotypes and expectations concerning physique and behavior do seem more firmly established for males. Consistent with the research we've already looked at, the mesomorphic (athletic) body build, particularly among preschool boys, showed the strongest relationship to the behavioral ratings. You may be interested in knowing that subsequent research involving mothers' ratings of these same children tended to confirm the observations made by the teachers.[19] That is, both teachers and mothers are inclined to perceive the same general behavior in children of certain body types.

Body Build and Personality—What Are the Implications?

Body build and personality do seem to be related. These relationships are more definite for boys probably because we are clearer about what the physical criteria are for what a male should look like than we are for females. When it comes to being judged on the basis of physical appearance, the latitude allowed girls is apparently wider than is the case for boys. Be that as it may, the evidence does suggest that the broad-shouldered, muscular, narrow-hipped boy and the well-proportioned girls are more likely to win social approval and acceptance on the basis of pure physique than boys or men and girls or women who are either too heavy or too thin, too tall or too short. High self-confidence and self-esteem are personality correlates frequently associated with mesomorphic physiques in males and females. Although things like, say, leadership qualities, social approval, or high self-esteem are not *caused* by having a nice build or a well-proportioned figure, they may, in fact, be among the positive gains which *result from* a more mesomorphic appearance. Considering the feedback that a person both gives and receives on the basis of purely physical appearances, it is not difficult to see how an individual's physical proportions can influence his feelings about himself simply by affecting how other people react toward him. The overweight person who grows up in the face of assorted descriptive monikers like "Tubby," "Chubby," "Fatso," or "Lard," or the thin individual who is variously addressed as "Bony Ben," "Skinny Al," "Beanpole Sally," is hardly encouraged to develop self-confidence and self-esteem in the same way as is a person who is not markedly overweight, underweight, too tall, or too short. If used for a long enough period of time, the names that were originally meant to describe a person's physique can also have the effect of describing and defining, to some extent, his personality. Thus, the ectomorphic little boy or girl who frequently hears adjectives like "delicate" and "fragile" ascribed to him or her may in fact grow up to be that kind of person—delicate and fragile with a low threshold for pain, stress, or frustation.

In short, one's body build has a powerful potential for eliciting specific social responses. These can be positive or negative. How we feel about ourselves depends, to some degree, on how we feel about the basic body structure and physical boundaries of the body shell in which we reside. How we feel about that depends, to some extent, on the feedback we get from the mirror on the wall and from others in our social world. It would be wrong, however, to conclude that it is only one's physical size and proportions that influence feedback from others. There is a more subtle nuance about each of us that is more difficult to define, and it has to do with general appearance and "attractiveness." Both of these variables can have a powerful influence on one's self-concept, for better or for worse. Let us turn our attention to why this may be.

Appearance and Physical Attractiveness Influence Self-Other Perceptions

At a conscious level there seems to be a strong innate resistance to the idea that our judgments of others may be influenced by a pretty face or an ugly one, a handsome profile or a distorted one, a winsome smile or a twisted one, or such factors as height and manner of dressing. It is as though we would like to be free of what we view as primarily surface considerations in order that we might more clearly see the "real" person who resides at a deeper level. For example, if you ask a random sample of your male friends what it is in a woman that attracts them and a sampling of your female friends what it is in a man that attracts them, you will usually find that they are quick to list qualities such as "personality," "intelligence," "character," "sincerity," and the like ahead of "looks" or "physical attractiveness." Research[20, 21] is rather clear in showing us that if you ask people to rank what they are attracted to or find desirable in another person, they will place appearance or physical attractiveness somewhere in the middle.

Apparently, however, there is a difference between what people say they *value* in a person and what they *respond* to in a person. We may say physical

Although physical attractiveness is important, some people have a tendency to overdo it.

attractiveness isn't so important, but it turns out to be more crucial than we care to admit or even know about. For example, when a group of college students were asked how much they liked their date and whether they would date the same person again, both men and women gave significantly more preference to dates who had previously been rated (unknown to the students) by the researchers as physically attractive.[22] The more physically attractive the date, the more he or she was liked. We might also note that the investigators in this study made every effort to find other factors which might possibly predict attraction, but could find none. Students with exceptional social skills and intelligence levels, for example, were no better liked than those less fortunately endowed.

Two subsequent studies[23, 24], each with different college age populations, found that the partner's *perception* of the physical attractiveness of the date correlated higher with the "desire to date again" response than did any of the other perceived characteristics of the partner, including perception of "similar interests," "character," "personality," and so on.

As you can see, appearance and physical attractiveness play an important part in influencing how we feel about ourselves and how others respond to us. At this point you may be wondering: what factors influence our perceptions of who is physically attractive and who isn't? A good question for us to look at for a moment.

Factors Influencing Perceptions of Physical Attractiveness

Personal appearance is important in virtually all aspects of our lives, and people generally agree on standards of beauty. In their monumental review of research related to physical attractiveness, Berscheid and Walster[25] observed that although there is ". . . . no compendium of physical characteristics. . . . which people find attractive in others, (it) appears that the culture transmits effectively, and fairly uniformly, criteria for labeling others physically 'attractive' or 'unattractive.' "

Descriptions of "handsome" or "beautiful" aren't good enough for researchers, and so, in 1883, Sir Francis Galton set out to find what it takes to make a pretty face. Using a technique called composite portraiture, he superimposed a large number of faces on a single photographic plate, using very brief exposure times. The finished product is a face that averages the features of all of the faces, thus eliminating individual differences and peculiarities. He did this for both men and women. As reported in an interesting volume by Wilson and Nias[26], the result was a quite striking face, artistic and singularly beautiful. His experiment showed that a good-looking face is one with regular, typical features. A less attractive face is one with surprises.

When it comes to sex appeal, attractiveness tends to be based largely on differences in appearance between male and female. The more exaggerated these differences, up to a certain point, the more attractive a person is to the opposite sex. Cosmetics, for instance, do little more than accentuate these differences. Lipstick emphasizes the fuller lips of women and many women pluck perfectly good eyebrows to avoid the bushy brows sported by some men. And, while a beard may enhance a man's appearance, facial hair on a woman is regarded as quite distasteful. In general, then, men are attractive if their physical features look unlike women, and women are attractive if their physical features look unlike men. There is more latitude for men and women *dressing* more or less alike (within limits, of course) than there is for *looking* alike.

Beards Make a Difference If you're a man and wear a beard, you may be happy to know that women are inclined to perceive men with beards as masculine, sophisticated, and mature.[27] In a more controlled study, eight men between twenty-two and twenty-five had their beards shaved off and photographs taken at four different stages: full beard, goatee, moustache, clean-shaven. College students giving their impressions of the men in the photographs consistently gave higher ratings to men with the most facial hair. Full-bearded men were judged as more masculine, mature, self-confident, and liberal than clean-shaven men. Men with moustaches and goatees fell in between. Perhaps only college students are that favorable toward men with beards, but it was suggested by the investigator (a man, by the way) that inside many men "there is a beard screaming to be let out."[28]

Being Tall Helps Height is another factor that affects our perceptions of an individual's personal attractiveness. For example, in a study that required 140 corporate recruiters to choose between two hypothetical job applicants having the same qualifications and differing only in height (one man was six feet, one inch, the other five feet, five inches), the shorter man was favored by only one percent of the recruiters. Twenty-seven percent had no preference, and seventy-two percent would hire the tall man.[29]

A fascinating study by Wilson[30] illustrates nicely our unconscious inclination to assign greater heights to persons with greater social status. What Wilson did was to introduce a "Mr. England" to five similar groups of college students. To one group he was introduced as "a student from Cambridge"; to a second, he was "a demonstrator in psychology from Cambridge"; to the third group, "lecturer in psychology from Cambridge"; to another, "a senior lecturer from Cambridge"; and finally, as "Professor England from Cambridge."

After England had gone, students were asked to estimate his height to the nearest one-half inch, presumably for use in a statistics exercise. The results? As Mr. England climbed the ladder of success, he gained a full five inches in the eyes of the students. It is interesting to note that the course instructor, whose height was also estimated, remained the same in perceived height.

Perhaps it is not surprising that from 1900 to 1968, the man elected U.S. President was always the taller of the two candidates. It is worth noting that Nixon, Ford, and Carter are all above average in height for American males. Social scientist Conrad Hassel[31] has pointed out the interesting fact that, of the eight presidential assassins since 1835, only John Wilkes Booth could claim average stature.

Height, it seems, does make a difference in how we are inclined to perceive others, particularly men. Not only is there an inclination to ascribe more positive attributes to tall men, but there is even an inclination to see men of high social status as taller, bigger, if you will, than they really are. Why do we do this? There are probably many reasons, but one may have to do with the natural tendency to equate greater size with greater power and strength. When you consider that we spend the first fourteen to eighteen years of our lives surrounded by bigger and usually stronger adults, who can exercise their power and authority in benign and hostile ways, it is not so surprising that we may unconsciously equate status with height or height with status. If you happen to be a male and a bit shorter than you would like to be, it may be well to keep in mind that you don't have to be tall to be *perceived* as tall. Ultimately, whether we be male or female, it is the height of our accomplishments and not the height of our bodies that make the final difference.

Weight Weighs Heavily   Our earlier discussion of characteristics others associate with endomorphic body types would strongly suggest that excessive weight is more than a physical burden. Just as there is the tendency to perceive taller, lankier persons as stronger and more in control, there is also the inclination to perceive shorter, fatter persons as weaker and less in control. Whereas other kinds of physical problems people suffer are generally attributed to misfortune and elicit a certain amount of sympathy and understanding, obesity is often associated with laziness or lack of will power. Not only are obese persons perceived in a more negative light by others, but they also see themselves more negatively. For example, from a body image survey that included a sample of 1000 men and 1000 women, it was found that half of the women and about one-third of the men said that they are unhappy with their weight. And twice as many women are *very* dissatisfied.[32]

There is no simple answer for the problem of obesity. Some suggest that overweight people are "biologically determined" to be pudgy because their bodies contain more than the average number of fat cells,[33] while others suggest that overweight persons are "externals," whose eating is determined by outside cues such as sight, smell, and the taste of food.[34]

One fact seems clear: It is easy enough to put on extra pounds, but more difficult to take them off. As most seasoned weightwatchers know, 3,500 calories equals about one pound of fat. In terms of exercise, it takes about 15 hours to work off that pound of fat. Or, we can think of it another way: To walk off the 209 calories of a Hershey bar, a person would have to walk 40 minutes, or jog 21 minutes, or swim 25 minutes.

Suffice it to say, weight makes a difference in how we see ourselves and others, and also how others see us. Based on my clinical experiences with overweight persons in therapy, I am inclined to think that gaining weight is less a matter of lack of will power or heredity influences and more a matter of not enough motivation, and, sometimes, not enough love. Could it be that our weight, like the clothes we wear, is really a matter of choice? Speaking of clothes. . . .

What We Wear Matters   The way we adorn the body shell we live in can significantly affect both our self-perceptions and how others perceive us. My considerable hitch-hiking experiences during my college days taught me early that a neat appearing young man (looking appropriately hopeful, by the way) was more apt to be offered rides than one with a more unkempt look. You may have noted from your own personal experiences that what you wear can significantly alter your feelings about yourself on a particular day. Bright, cheery colors tend to elicit positive comments, which, in turn, help us feel good about ourselves.

Consider some examples of how clothes influence the behavior of others. One enterprising researcher arranged to have a thirty-one year old male model approach an intersection crowded with other pedestrians and either obey or violate the traffic signal. An interesting thing happened. When he walked against the red light while dressed neatly in a coat and tie, significantly more people would follow his example in disobeying the stop signal than was the case when he was dressed in plain everyday work clothes.[35]

Somewhat similar results were obtained in a novel experiment that involved placing a dime in pay phone return slots and then having men and women in two kinds of dress approach persons using these phones with the following request: "Excuse me, I think I might have left a dime in this phone booth a few minutes ago. Did you find it? " Half the time the men wore suits and ties and the women wore neat dresses and a dress coat. The other half of the time the men wore work clothes and the women appeared in generally unkempt-looking skirts and blouses. Significantly, more people returned the dime when they were approached by the well-dressed men and women.[36]

What we wear does matter. We may want others to love us and accept us for who we really are, but who we are is perceived by the beholder as a total package, and clothes, it appears, are the wrappings.

These, then, are some of the factors that may influence perceptions of who is and who isn't physically attractive. The next thing we need to do is to take a look at how people's behavior is affected by appearance and physical attractiveness or unattractiveness.

The Effect of Appearance and Physical Attraction Variables on Others' Expectations

This is an important consideration because, in the final analysis, others' expectations can have a powerful effect on a person's self-concept. We may conclude that beauty is only skin deep, but its effects run considerably deeper. Research by Berscheid and Walster[37] confirms that men and women generally like attractive

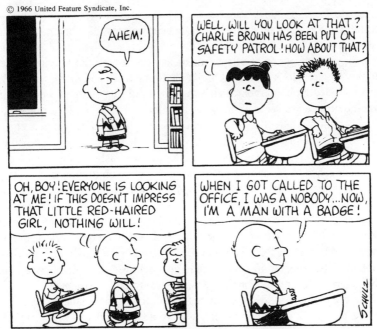

© 1966 United Feature Syndicate, Inc.

Whether we like it or not, how others respond to us is determined to some extent by what we wear.

people more, expect them to do better work, and rate their work more highly after it's done.

Psychologists Landy and Sigall[38] decided to see which was cause and which was effect in the relationship between a woman's attractiveness and the way others rate her work. What they did was to prepare two essays, one well written, the other disorganized and simplistic in its ideas. They made 30 copies of each essay and attached pictures, supposedly of the author, to 20 of them: an attractive woman in ten cases, an unattractive one in the other ten. Ten essays in each group had no picture. The essays were then graded by 60 male college students. The results? Attractive writers swept the ratings across the board, and they most surpassed the unattractive writers when the poor essay was judged. In other words, the same essay tended to get higher marks when it was accompanied by a photograph of an attractive woman than when presumed the author was plain.

There is evidence that physical attractiveness may even influence which students make the honor roll.[39] Four hundred fifth-grade teachers all received the same report card to evaluate. Each card itemized the student's grades in eight subject areas over six grading periods along with a report of his performance in personal development and work and study habits. Posted in the corner was a picture of a child, one of an attractive boy or girl, or one of an unattractive boy or girl. The results clearly indicated that when a child was good-looking, the teachers were more apt to guess that he had a higher IQ, had parents who were interested in his education, and go along better with his or her peers than did the less attractive children.

Karen Dion[40] came up with even more alarming results when it comes to the expectations people have of others based on appearance. She gave two hundred women written descriptions of alleged misbehaviors committed by either a seven-year-old boy or girl, along with the child's photograph clipped to the corner. When the report included a photograph of an attractive child, the students were inclined to excuse the misdeed or see it as an isolated incident. For example, a misbehaving, but attractive, child might elicit a comment such as: ''She appears to be a charming little girl . . . . . she plays well with everyone, but like anyone else, a bad day can occur. Her cruelty . . . . . . need not be taken too seriously.'' But when the same report came attached to the photograph of an unattractive child, the raters were more inclined to assume that the naughtiness was a typical incident and a reflection of generally bad behavior. While the attractive little girl was still seen as ''charming,'' in spite of misbehaving, an unattractive girl, with the same misbehavior attributed to her received comments such as: ''I think the child would be quite bratty and would be a problem to teachers . . . . . would probably try to pick fights . . . . all in all, a real problem.'' The women in Dion's study also believed that unattractive children were characteristically more dishonest than their attractive classmates.

If we are inclined to disclaim the results of any of these studies because they seem to be based on first impressions, we would do well to keep in mind that although first impressions are not necessarily *lasting* perceptions that can never change, there is strong evidence[41, 42] to suggest that they tend to influence our subsequent expectations and interactions with a particular person. Once a first impression is formed, it is difficult to change, which is a good enough reason for us to work on keeping our impressions of others tentative and open to new information.

As you can see, appearance and physical attraction variables have a great deal to do with how others perceive us and what they expect from us. It also has a lot to do with how we feel about ourselves. Which brings us to our next topic for discussion.

Body Images as Related to Self-Concept

Like all other aspects of the self-concept, the image we have of our body is subjective. We may have a generally positive body image—we like the way we look, or we may have a negative body image—how we look falls short of our expectations for ourselves.

The fact is, the most tangible and visible part of the self is our physical body. Our physical appearance is the one personal characteristic which is accessible to others in almost all social interactions. Occupying as it does a substantial portion of our visual and auditory fields, we see and hear a lot of ourselves. And so do others. To a very large extent our self-concept develops out of the reflected appraisals others have of us. People respond not only to what we say and do, but also to our appearance—clothes, grooming, physical attributes. We form opinions of our emotional states, personal abilities, and attractiveness largely from the feedback we get from others. In a very important way our bodies come to occupy a central role in our perceptions.

The particular *way* a person perceives his physical body—whether distorted or not—may have important psychological consequences for him. An adolescent boy, for example, may be so concerned about his awkward coordination that he refuses to try out for the team or even attend dances; a woman may be so sensitive to what she feels is inadequate breast development that she is hesitant to date or appear in a bathing suit; a young man could have such a narcissistic love for his own body development that he neglects doing anything about his social or intellectual growth. Perception of the body relates intimately to larger conceptions of the self. It is not surprising, then, that research[43] rather consistently points to a clear parallel between the way people appraise themselves as persons and the way they tend to evaluate their bodies. This certainly squares with my experiences with certain clients in therapy. I recall one thirty-five-year-old salesman in particular, who had just lost forty pounds through exercise and careful eating over a four-month period. As he put it:

> It's hard to explain how I feel, but one thing I do know is that I don't mind looking in the mirror anymore. I used to hate mirrors. I didn't even look at myself in store window reflections. But I like what I see now—well, except for this stomach that's still pretty flabby. What I mean is, I seem to like me—me as a person—better. I've also

noticed an interesting thing happening in my work. My sales record has gotten increasingly better the past three months. I'm not conscious of doing anything particularly different, but *I do know I feel less, what should I say, ashamed around people and more confident in myself.*

This man is saying what many people say after an improvement in their body image. It is not just a change in an external body shell that happens, but a change in their more internal and deeper sense of self. This feeling of shame that the salesman in the example above mentioned is something that can easily develop if one hears enough times that he or she is too fat or too skinny or too plain-looking or whatever. Feeling ashamed grows out of failing to meet another person's standards, while confidence grows out of successfully meeting our own standards. Our salesman friend spent most of his life taking in too much food, but neglected to take in the responsibility for its inevitable consequences. Not coincidentally, when he stopped blaming others for how he looked and felt, he was in a position to do something about a problem that was basically his own. And that gave him control over it. By moving the responsibility from "out there" to "in here", he was able to begin work on changing his body image so that he could experience a healthier self-image.

Another client of mine, a woman in her late twenties, experienced a dramatic change for the better in her self-concept after a visit to a cosmetologist, who taught her how to use make-up to best effect, and a hair stylist, who showed her several ways she might do her hair to take advantage of her particular facial structure. Like many women—and men, too, for that matter—she had never been taught how to present herself in more appealing ways. Her mother was a rather plain woman who believed in neither make-up nor hairstyling, and my client was embarked on a similar course, but unhappily so. But, through modifying her outer appearance, she changed her inner feelings, and her therapy progressed at a rapid rate. You may be interested to know that within three weeks of learning how to use make-up and having her hair styled, she had a portrait of herself taken—the first ever in her life. As she put it:

> You know, I didn't even have my picture in my high school yearbook. I used to hate to have my picture taken. I felt that a camera would make me see myself too clearly or something. I think I always wanted the camera to take a picture of the person I wanted to be, but all it did was take a picture of the person I was. But, you know, I kind of like the person I see now.

I do not mean to suggest that all it ever takes to change the psychological self is a modification of the physical self. I do mean to suggest, however, that sometimes a person's personal and interpersonal difficulties spring from body-image problems and not self-image problems per se. When this is the case, we need to do as much as we can to encourage changes in the body image so the owner of that image can be more at peace with himself or herself. Changes in self-image will then usually occur quite naturally. (The sorts of changes that are possible in self-concept following modifications in physical features are detailed in a fascinating book, *Psychocybernetics*, by the emminent plastic surgeon, Maxwell Maltz,[44] which you might find interesting and informative reading.)

Ordinarily, the body is experienced as a part or aspect of the self, often constituting its outer boundary. But there are some instances in which the body and self are not mutually inclusive. For example, we have probably all had the feeling of waking up in the morning with our arm so sound asleep that it seemed as if it were not even a part of us. Even amputations of parts of the body may not be perceived as resections of the self, although there are instances in which the loss of a highly valued part may really be experienced as a partial destruction of self. For example, some years ago a psychology professor friend of mine had an unfortunate power-saw accident in which he lost a portion of two fingers on his left hand. He viewed it as a dumb, careless mistake on his part, but persisted in going about the business of maintaining and enhancing his self-esteem and self-regard through being a professor of psychology. Another acquaintance of mine had a similar accident not long ago involving the loss of a portion of his left forefinger and its effect on him was great depression. The difference was that he was a skilled guitarist who earned part of his livelihood by being an entertainer. My psychology friend lost but a part of his fingers; my guitar-player friend lost not only part of a finger, but also means of self-expression and self-support. When we look at it from that point of view, it is easier to see why the loss of part of his finger should be experienced more as a partial lost of self.

If you were to ask a person to specify *where* he feels the center of self to be, he almost always locates it somewhere inside his body. Most often he points it out

How we appear to others can substantially influence how others respond to us.

as somewhere "in the head" or "in back of the eyes." This is not surprising, particularly in light of the fact that we are basically "visually oriented," having our most important commerce with the world around us through our eyes.

There is also evidence to suggest that different people assume different perspectives for the self in relation to the body. Relevant to this, consider the following experiment:

> In one demonstration the experimenter traced a script capital E on the subject's forehead. This symbol was deliberately chosen because its mirror image is 3. Logically, then, it can be identified as an E or a 3. If he "viewed" the symbol as though he were "looking out" at it from inside his head, he would have perceived it as a 3. If he "viewed" the symbol as though he were looking at his own forehead from the outside, as the experimenter was, he would have reported it to be an E . . . there are pronounced individual differences in readiness to perceive from the "inside" or the "outside" when no prior set is given. For example, in one demonstration 76 percent of a group of 202 student subjects reported the symbol as a 3 (i.e., in accord with an "inside" perspective), whereas 24 percent reported it as an E. Moreover, the tendency to see the symbol in the latter way (that is, according to an "outside" perspective) was clearly more pronounced in the male than in the female students. Perhaps here is confirmation of the common notion that females (at least in our culture) tend to be more "subjective" in their outlook than do males![45]

Self-Esteem as Related to Body Image

There is a considerable amount of research evidence to suggest that one's appearance is an important determiner of self-esteem, both among men and women.[46, 47, 48]

One possible reason for this relationship between self-acceptance and body-acceptance may be in the fact that the self-ideal includes attitudes related to the appearance of the body, or the so-called body-ideal. Each of us has a more or less clear idea of how we would *like* to look. If our actual body proportions come close to conforming to the dimensions and appearance of our ideal body image, we are more likely to think better of both our physical and nonphysical self. If, on the other hand, our body deviates too far from our body-ideal, then we are more likely to have lower self-esteem. It is not uncommon for a person with a poor body image to compensate for this deficit by becoming proficient in other ways, such as, for example, developing an intellectual skill, or musical aptitude, or some other special talent or ability. In this way, the emphasis on the body image is reduced or at least made less important through his ability to "know more" or "perform better" in specific areas than most other people. Of course another, but certainly a less healthy, way of handling a poor body image is by denying the idea that appearance or body image is important in the first place. "Looks and appearance aren't important—what I am and how I behave is what really counts." This is a praiseworthy attitude—one that most of us probably share to some extent. However, some persons proclaim this attitude as if it were some kind of Magna Charta releasing them from any sort of personal responsibility to themselves and use it to satisfy their needs to avoid the self-discipline involved in say, eating less, or drinking less or, in some instances, bathing more.

Usually, a person's body-ideal comforms more or less to the prevailing cultural standards of what a pleasant appearance is and what it is not. Margaret Mead[49], in her studies of various cultures, has observed that each society has its own idiosyncratic attitudes and standards of personal beauty. The Kalihari desert Bushman, for example, places a high premium on having oversized hips and buttocks, while in America the desired hip-buttock measurements are much smaller. The American glamor queens of days gone by were considerably heftier than our contemporary *Playmate* foldouts. The cultural concept of an ideal body has consequences for personality hygiene, since the cultural ideal helps shape one's personal body-ideal which, in turn, influences for better or for worse an individual's overall self-esteem.

Physical appearance is important to one's development of self-esteem because it plays a part in determining the nature of the responses a person receives from other people. However, we should keep in mind that it is only one of *many* determiners of self-esteem. Healthy, balanced people will build their feelings of self-regard on a variety of grounds, among which would include achievement, creativeness, social status, moral and ethical behavior, interpersonal relationships, and the like. While a certain degree of concern about one's total body image is compatible with developing a healthy personality, too much concern may be a signal that the individual's self-esteem is standing on *too limited a foundation*. For example, the woman whose entire self is wrapped up in being beautiful or sexy is left with very little, once the beauty and sex appeal are gone. The body-builder whose entire self rests on having large biceps and photographic muscle differentiation runs the risk of emotional bankruptcy when he gets older and discovers that there is more to life than big muscles and high protein diets. Body image and appearance are only parts of our total feelings about ourselves. When body image and/or physical concerns begin to dominate one's self-perception, this may be symptomatic of deeper personality disturbances, a possibility to which we now turn our attention.

Physical Expressions of Body Image Insecurity

We are using the term "body image" in its broadest sense to include one's perceptions of his total physical being. When our body image is secure we are relatively free from anxiety growing from physical concerns. Insecurity, as related to body image at least, typically manifests itself as worry and anxiety about expected pains and catastrophes. Indeed, some people seem to delight in expressing a kind of morbid preoccupation with their physical conditions and general body states. Hypochondriasis and neurasthenia are two common, but neurotic, expressions of unhealthy preoccupations with physical concerns. Let's look at the hypochondriac first.

Hypochondriasis In the first place, *hypochondria* has several meanings. It is used to refer to intense fear or anxiety regarding the state of one's health, and to a nonanxious but intense *preoccupation* with illness and symptoms. The term is usually used in the latter sense. The hypochondriac, like most neurotics, exhibits distinct personality characteristics. In the first place, his flight to illness is usually for purposes of protection. He typically is an individual continually preoccupied with his health, who complains about all manner of vague or specific aches and pains, and who may make frequent trips to the doctor's office, dose himself regularly with pills, vitamins, sedatives, and other medicines. The primary symptoms are, of course, expressions of discomfort, illness, or suffering, which, when read for their psychological meaning, are usually pleas for attention, sympathy, affection, or help.

It is generally found that hypochondriacal anxiety with respect to physical health is a substitute for, or displacement of, anxiety that springs from other sources, as, for example, repressed hostility, sexual difficulties, or achievement problems. At other times, a hypochondriac's "illness" may also be an expression of self-aggression or self-punishment for strong guilt feelings or hostility toward others.

Not infrequently, the hypochondriac is a product of an overprotecting home in which the parents repeatedly overreacted to pain and illness. Several things can happen as a consequence of overreacting parents. One, the child grows up with the uneasy feeling that his physical discomforts, no matter what they are, may be worse than he thinks. And two, he learns that one quick way to get attention, sympathy, or help is to have a physical problem. As he grows older, he may also discover that being "ill" is a convenient way to avoid responsibilities. Unfortunately, the hypochondriac launches himself into a perpetually self-defeating cycle. Since a lack of sufficient self-esteem is usually one of the major reasons for seeking a temporary respite in some form of illness in the face of a new responsibility or challenge, he is seldom in a position to assume the very challenge which might contribute to his having greater self-esteem if he assumed it and was successful. On the whole, the hypochondriac finds it less threatening to think about other problems. Health preoccupation takes his mind off more basic problems, as it were. A hypochondriac is tough to change because he gets so much satisfaction out of his assorted aches and pains and illnesses. And even if his family and friends won't give him attention and sympathy, he can at least call on doctors. Yes, tough to change indeed: You may recall the tale of the deceased, but formerly dedicated, hypochondriac whose tombstone bore the epitaph admonishing all who read it:

"See, I told you I was sick."

Neurasthenia *Neurasthenia* is another neurotic disorder that reflects anxiety and undue body-image insecurity. Its primary symptom and characteristic is chronic fatigue, but other psychosomatic disturbances are usually present, including headaches, insomnia, digestive ailments, constipation, and assorted aches and pains. Like the hypochondriac, the neurasthenic needs to be wanted and cared for, and the flight into illness is his expression of those needs. Also like the hypochondriac, the history of this sort of individual is likely to include being coddled and overprotected as he was growing up.

We don't have to be a hypochondriac or a neurasthenic in order for our anxieties and insecurities to seek some physical expression. For example, how many times have you had the feeling of suddenly feeling very tired and rundown when faced with a very important assignment like a paper due or an exam the next hour? This is a typical, normal neurasthenic reaction and usually reflects psychological tension associated with doing an unpleasant task. How many mothers hear something like "Mom, my stomach aches. I just *can't* go to school today." (Of course, it just "happens" to be report card day.) College and university health services are typically jammed with students suddenly concerned with their physical well-being during finals week. One coed explained her trip to the health service during finals week this way:

> "I went over there, you see, but I didn't know if there was really anything wrong. Actually it was that time of the month and I had cramps and I thought I'd better see if that's all it was. You never know about these things. It could've been intestinal flu or something." I questioned her further about her motivation for going and after some probing she finally said, "Actually, I really knew there was nothing wrong, but I think I hoped there would be, so I could have a good excuse for postponing some of my finals. But (a big sigh here), there wasn't."

Persons who reduce their insecurities and anxieties by converting their shaky feelings into physical symptoms may find temporary relief, but by responding only to the physical symptoms the cause of the basic anxiety is likely to remain the same. In the case of the girl described above, even if she had found something to be ill about, the exams which were causing her anxiety would *still* be there upon her recovery.

In sum, body image, appearance, and self-esteem do seem to be related, although it is perfectly possible to establish one's self-esteem on other grounds if one's body image falls short of what he would like. Indeed, research has shown that how we feel about ourselves is related not only to our total appearance, but also to the rate and pace of our growth as we were moving through our developmental years. Whether a person experienced accelerated or slow growth can make a difference—a consideration to which we now turn our attention.

Variations in Physical Growth: Social and Psychological Effect

It is a well-documented fact the the timing of puberty and the marked physical changes which herald its onset are subject to wide individual differences. Figure 4.2 will give you a quick overview of percentage of boys and girls who can be expected to reach puberty and physical maturity between nine-and-a-half and seventeen-and-a-half years of age.

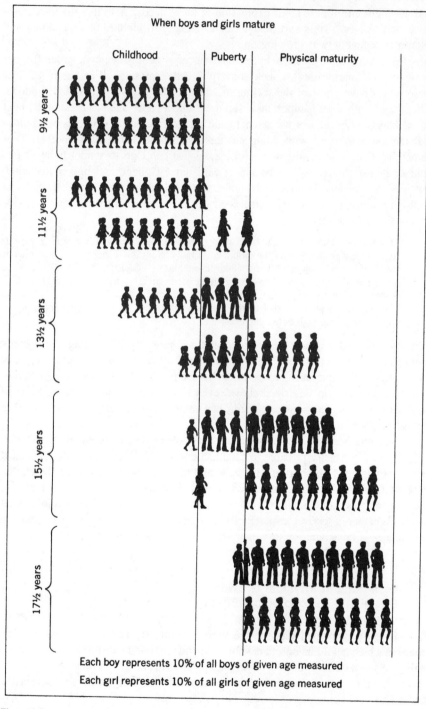

Figure 4.2

Individual differences in physical growth have been found to affect personal and social adjustment not only during the developmental years, but beyond that time as well. Since the effects of early or late growth are different for boys than for girls, perhaps we can more clearly see these differences, if we separate the sexes and examine them one at a time. Let's take the boys first.

Effect of Early Versus Late Maturation in Boys

Highly significant and classic growth studies have emerged from the Institute of Human Development at the University of California. One of these studies, conducted by Jones and Bayley[50] focused on a group of boys who were the sixteen most accelerated growers and the sixteen who were the most consistently slow growers for a four-and-one-half year period between the ages of twelve and seventeen. Figure 4.3 will give you an idea of typical growth differences between an early- and a late-maturing boy.

Many significant differences were found between the two groups. For example, when rated by adults, the slower-growing boys were judged as lower in physical attractiveness, less masculine, less well groomed, more animated, more affected, and more tense. They did not, however, differ from the more advanced boys in ratings of popularity, leadership, prestige, or social effect on the group. They were considered, though, to be less mature in heterosexual social relations.

When rated by their peers, the slower growers were judged to be more restless, talkative, and bossy. In addition, peer ratings showed them to be less popular, less likely to be leaders, more attention-seeking, less confident in class situations, and significantly, perhaps, shorter on a sense of humor about themselves.

In contrast, physically accelerated boys were more popular and treated by adults and peers as more mature. It was from their ranks that the outstanding student body leaders were chosen. The researchers concluded by stating that "The findings give clear evidence of the effect of physical maturing on behavior. Perhaps of greater importance, however, is the repeated demonstration of the multiplicity of factors, psychological and cultural, as well as physical, which contribute to the formation of personality patterns."[51] We might mention here that other research[52] has found that boys who mature at an average age have about as many relative advantages as those who mature early.

Further research by Mussen and Jones[53] has noted that high drives for social acceptance and for aggression are more characteristic of the slower-growing than the faster-growing boys. This may suggest that the late-maturer's need for recognition stems from feeling somewhat more insecure and inadequate than his faster-growing peers. It is as if these boys are saying in many different ways, "Hey, look at me!"

Looking at the total picture, we can begin to see that rate of physical maturation can affect personality and self-concept development in crucially important ways. Adult and peer attitudes toward adolescents, as well as their treatment and acceptance of them are related to some extent to their perceived physical status. This suggests that the socio-psychological environment in which late-maturers grow may be significantly less rewarding and more detrimental to positive self-feelings than that of their early-maturing peers.

Overall, late maturing during adolescence is more of a handicap than anything else. Early maturity, on the other hand, is a two-sided coin. On the positive side it

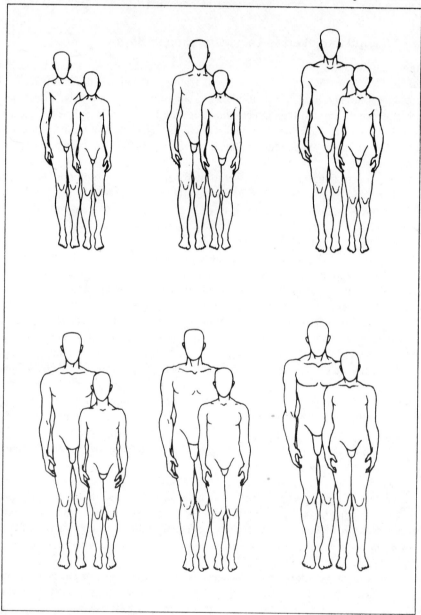

Figure 4.3

Differential growth of an earlier-maturing and a late-maturing boy. Drawings represent the boys' statuses at yearly intervals from 11½ through 16½ years of age. (From F. K. Shuttleworth, "The Adolescent Period: A Pictorial Atlas") *Monographs for the Society of Research and Child Development,* 1949, 14 (Ser. No. 50). By permission of the Society for Research and Child Development, Inc.

can lend itself to certain competitive and social advantages. On the negative side it sometimes puts the adolescent boy in the unfair position of having to respond to unrealistic expectations that may be determined too much by size and appearance and too little by ability and motivation. All in all, however, the early-maturing boy is likely to have a better time of it both in terms of certain physical advantages and more positive self-concept outcomes as he moves through his adolescent years than the late maturers.

Let us not forget to note that in any particular case the effects of early or late maturing may be significantly modified by the individual's psychological history and present circumstances. As was mentioned earlier, some very late-maturing boys are so talented in some specific areas (music, math, athletics, and so on) that their stature is hardly noticed. On the other hand, being a fast grower is no guarantee of instant social status and popularity. Some boys' physical growth spurts ahead of their coordination, and they end up stumbling all over themselves. Other fast-growing boys may be unmotivated, or unimaginative, or simply lack the social finesse to be popular or accepted at any height or weight. Being an average or fast grower may give a boy the initial edge, but unless he has other personal qualities to accompany his bulk he is as likely as anyone to flounder around in his interpersonal relationships.

The Long-Term Effect on Boys of Early or Late Maturation

It is clear that the pace of growth can have a considerable impact upon the social life and personal adjustment of some boys during adolescence. The question we need to ask is, how lasting is this impact?

In order to answer this question, Jones[54] studied boys who were fast or slow growers during adolescence and compared them again when they were thirty-three-year-old adults. One of the first things found was that the marked physical differences noted for these boys during adolescence tended to disappear in adulthood. Late maturers eventually caught up with their early-maturing peers as far as physical development was concerned, although there was a tendency for the fast grower to remain, on the average, slightly taller, heavier, and more mesomorphic than the slow grower. The physical differences that did remain were not, however, as striking as they were during adolescence.

Personality characteristics continued to show some continuing differences between the two groups. Early-maturing boys tended to achieve higher scores on such personality indices such as socialization, self-control, responsibility, ability to create good impressions, and dominance. These findings are also consistent with the descriptions of the early-maturing group when they were seventeen-years-old and noted to be more confident, more aggressive, and more socially poised. They were also consistent with the slower growing group when they were seventeen, who were found to be less aggressive, more affected, and more tense. On the whole, *when personality differences were found, they tended to describe the young adults much as they had been described in adolescence.*

No differences were found between the two groups in terms of marital status, family size, or educational level. A few of the early-maturers had made exceptionally rapid professional progress and a few of the late-maturers were still searching for their vocational "niche." Again, we should remind ourselves that there are vast individual differences within each group which result from the complex interplay of many factors. With regard to the overall impact of early and late maturity on boys and its lastingness over time, Dr. Jones has expressed it best:

> During the adolescent period late-maturing is a handicap for many boys and can rarely be found to offer special advantages. Early-maturing carries both advantages and disadvantages. In our culture it frequently gives competitive status, but sometimes also involves handicaps in the necessity for rapid readjustments and in requiring the adolescent to meet adult expectations which are more appropriate to size and appearance than to other aspects of maturing. The adolescent handicaps and advantages associated with late- or early-maturing appears to carry over into adulthood to some extent, and perhaps to a greater extent in psychological than in physical characteristics.[55]

Effect of Early Versus Late Maturation in Girls

Although the outcome of early maturation has fairly consistent advantages for boys, the picture for girls is more complex. On the whole, research suggests that the differences between early- and late-maturing girls may not be so dramatic as is the case for boys. In addition, the advantages or disadvantages of fast or slow growth may vary over time. Whereas early-maturing boys have physical advantages over other boys and are more likely to be socially in step with girls, the girl who "grows up" too fast, particularly during the junior high school years, may feel isolated to some extent. While she is physiologically a year or two out of step with the girls in her class, she is three or four years out of step with the boys—a vast developmental difference.

Considering that junior high school is, for the most part, full of little boys and young women, it is no wonder that a buxom seventh-grade girl experiences a certain amount of social isolation. It is also no wonder that she tends to date and seek social contact with older adolescents. Figure 4.4 may help to give you a clearer mental picture of the anatomical differences that exist between early- and late-maturing girls at different ages. As you can see, the early-maturing girl is inclined toward a stockier, broader physique, while the late-maturer tends toward a slimmer, slighter build, more in keeping with the feminine ideal in our society.

Does the impact of a girl's early or late growth persist into later adolescence? Jones and Mussen[56] addressed themselves to this question by studying the self-conceptions, motivations, and interpersonal attitudes of thiry-four seventeen-year-old girls—sixteen who had been consistently fast growers and eighteen who had been consistently slow growers. They began with the hunch that since the early-maturing girls had more social problems during junior high and early high school, they would have less favorable self-concepts as seventeen-year-olds. This was not, however, the case. Early-maturing girls had more favorable self-concepts, which is consistent with the conclusion of Faust,[57] who found that precocious physical development tends to become a decided asset as the girl moves into later adolescence.

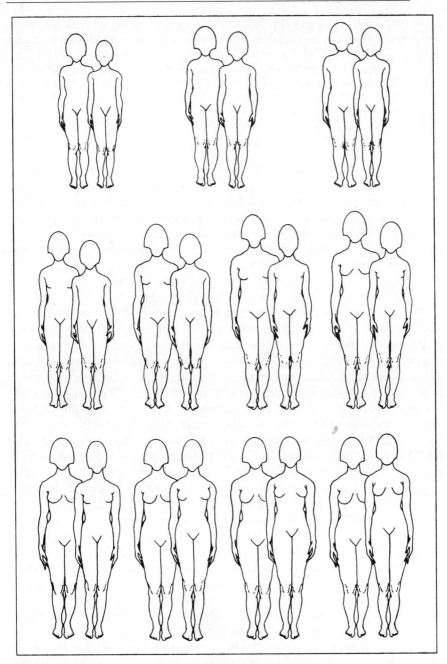

Figure 4.4
Differential growth of an early- and a late-maturing girl. The first four pairings are drawn at yearly birthdays from 8 through 11 years. Other pairings are at half-year intervals from 11½ years through 14½ years of age. (From F. K. Shuttleworth, "The Adolescent Period: A Pictorial Atlas." *Monographs of the Society for Research in Child Development*, 1949, 14 (Ser. No. 50). By permission of The Society for Research in Child Development, Inc.

All in all, it appears that late physical maturation has adverse affects on personal adjustment in *both* sexes in late adolescence. Jones and Mussen conclude:

> When the differences between early- and late-maturing girls are compared with the differences between early- and late-maturing boys, they are found to be in the same direction more often than in the opposite. These findings are interpreted to indicate that late-maturing adolescents of both sexes are characterized by less adequate self-concepts, slightly poorer parent-child relationships, and some tendency for stronger dependency needs.[58]

It seems apparent that the relationship between physical maturation and personality variables is much less definite for girls than for boys. Why should this be? One possible reason may be related to the fact that our cultural sex-role prescription for males is relatively clear and is one that places a high value upon attributes often associated with physical strength, coordination, and athletic deftness, especially in the adolescent and young adolescent years. For girls, however, the feminine sex-role prescription is less definite and stereotyped and is, therefore, not as likely to be connected to any specific pattern of physical attributes. In addition, whereas people seem to respond more to a boy's or a man's total physical make-up, the response to a girl's or a woman's physical make-up is apt to be more specific. That is, the physical qualities of a young woman capable of eliciting a favorable response include her face, bosom, hips, legs, and total proportion (although not necessarily in that order). For example, one woman might have a pretty face and very little else, but this could be sufficient to win her many signs of approval. Another woman may have an extremely attractive figure and only very plain facial features, but her nice legs or substantial bosom may be quite enough to win her some feeling of social approval. In other words, it may be more possible for a female than for a male to elicit different responses to different parts of her body so that even though she may fall short in one area, she can make it up in another. Although this idea is slowly changing, women, to a large extent, are expected to do little else with their bodies except adorn them and make them as attractive as possible. Males, on the other hand, are expected to do something with their bodies and are judged more on that basis. Another way of stating it, I suppose, would be to suggest that, when it comes to the physical side of the self, women are judged more in terms of how they *look* and men more in terms of how they *perform*. If this is true, then a tentative speculation about why it is that the rate of physical maturation has less dramatic effect on girls than boys is that girls have greater flexibility for altering or changing their looks than boys do for altering or changing their performances.

We might add here that it is precisely this kind of attention to the female "outer person" that is becoming increasingly more upsetting to larger segments of younger and older women who wish to be perceived and evaluated more in terms of the competencies and abilities rather than their looks. There seems to be slow but steady progress in destereotyping what young girls and women are "supposed" to be. One of the healthy outgrowths of the Women's Liberation Movement is the gradual shift in social expectations away from the traditional, stereotyped views about what constitutes "masculine" and "feminine" behavior to a more realistic

The idea that girls and women are or should be passive and fragile is slowly changing.

stance that recognizes that a woman can be strong and assertive without being masculine and that a man can be warm and sensitive without being effeminate. Indeed, recent surveys[59] are showing that the macho male who is tough, strong, aggressive, and has many sexual conquests is not admired by either sex. As social expectations change, an adolescent boy or girl may feel freer to experience and develop more aspects of the total self that each can potentially become, rather than just certain culturally accepted aspects of it.

In Perspective

Our self-concept includes and is influenced in important ways by our body concept. How we feel about ourselves is related to how we feel about our bodies. Although having a nice figure or a well-proportioned body does not guarantee a healthy, positive self-concept, research evidence does suggest that the nature of feedback we receive from the world around us is determined, at least in part, by the physical shell that surrounds us. More than we may be aware, we seem inclined to put each other in certain personality categories based on physical structure.

There is hardly a thing about our physical appearance, whether it be height, weight, hair color, eyes, or the clothes we wear, that does not in some way influence how others see us. This is not so surprising. In the absence of knowing more about a person's inner feelings or family history or values or intellectual capacity, we make judgments based on what we see. Generally speaking, the less well a person knows us, the more likely that person is to judge us on the basis of external appearances. As relationships between people develop—if they develop at all—physical appearance becomes less crucial and personality variables play an increasingly larger part.

Not only is appearance important in eliciting either positive or negative feedback, but so, too, is the rate at which a person grows. Physical maturity at an early age is a distinct advantage for a boy and research suggests that these advantages are likely to persist into his adult years as well. True enough, his slower growing peers eventually catch up with him physically, but not necessarily as far as certain psychological gains are concerned. The outcomes of early or late maturation for girls is more difficult to predict, although the general weight of the evidence suggests that fast-growing girls, like fast-growing boys, have more advantages and are somewhat better off than their slower-growing counterparts.

The kind of body image we have depends less on what we're born with and more on what we do with what we have in the first place. If we don't like it, body image is something that we can change for the better. Sensible eating habits, daily exercise, and good grooming can work wonders in assisting any person toward a more positive self-concept. Appearance does not necessarily make a person, but it does, for better or for worse, tend to reflect the person who lives within.

In sum, body image is an important aspect of one's self-image. A person's physical self is the outer shell which houses all of his or her inner feelings and, as such, it deserves to be recognized and understood for whatever its potential is for eliciting social responses that contribute to an individual's overall concept of self.

Notes

1. W. H. Sheldon, S. S. Stevens, and W. B. Tucker, *The Varieties of Human Physique.* New York: Harper & Row, Publishers, 1940, p. 419.
2. E. Kretschmer, *Physique and Character* (2nd ed.). W. J. H. Spratt trans. New York: Harcourt, Brace & World, Inc. 1925.
3. W. H. Sheldon, *Atlas of Men: A Guide for Somatotyping the Adult Male at All Ages.* New York: Harper & Row, Publishers, 1954.
4. W. H. Hammond, "The Status of Physical Types," *Human Biology.* 1957, 29: 223–241.
5. Humphreys, L. G., "Characteristics of Type Concepts with Special Reference to Sheldon's Typology," *Psychological Bulletin.* 1957, 54: 218–228.

6. E. Aronson, *The Social Animal*. San Francisco: W. H. Freeman & Co., Publishers, 1972, pp. 203–234.

7. C. L. Kleinke, *First Impressions*. Englewood Cliffs, N.J.: Prentice-Hall, Inc., 1975.

8. A. G. Miller, "Role of Physical Attractiveness in Impression Formation," *Psychonomic Science*. 1970, 19: 241–243.

9. C. M. Brodsky, *A Study of Norms for Body Form-Behavior Relationships*. Washington, D.C.: The Catholic University of America Press, 1954.

10. Brodsky, pp. 15–21.

11. Brodsky, pp. 15–21.

12. K. T. Strongman and C. J. Hart, "Stereotyped Reactions to Body Guild," *Psychological Reports*. 1968, 23: 1175–1178.

13. W. Wells and B. Siegel, "Stereotyped Somatotypes," *Psychological Reports*. 1961, 8: 77–78.

14. J. Cortés and C. M. Gatti, "Physique and Self-Description of Temperament," *Journal of Consulting Psychology*. 1965, 29: 432–439.

15. J. Cortés and F. M. Gatti, "Physique and Motivation," *Journal of Consulting Psychology*. 1966, 30: 408–414.

16. J. Staffieri, "A Study of Social Stereotype of Body Image in Children," *Journal of Personality and Social Psychology*. 1967, 7: 101–104.

17. R. M. Lerner and E. Gillert, "Body Build Identification, Preference, and Aversion in Children," *Developmental Psychology*. 1969, 1: 456–463.

18. R. N. Walker, "Body Build and Behavior in Young Children: I. Body Build and

17. R. M. Lemer and E. Gillert, "Body Build Identification, Preference, and Aversion in *Child Development*. 1962, 27: No. 3.

19. R. N. Walker, "Body Build and Behavior in Young Children: II. Body Build and Parents' Ratings," *Child Development*. 1963, 34: 1–23.

20. F. A. C. Perrin, "Physical Attractiveness and Repulsiveness," *Journal of Experimental Psychology*. 1921, 4: 203–207.

21. J. W. Hudson and L. F. Henze, "Campus Values in Mate Selection: A Replication," *Journal of Marriage and the Family*. 1969, 31: 772–775.

22. E. Walster, E. Aronson, D. Abrahams, and L. Rottman, "Importance of Physical Attractiveness in Dating Behavior," *Journal of Personality and Social Psychology*. 1966, 4: 508–516.

23. R. W. Brislin and S. A. Lewis, "Dating and Physical Attractiveness: Replication," *Psychological Reports*. 1968, 22: 976.

24. A. Tesser and M. Brodie, "A Note on the Evaluation of a 'Computer Date,' " *Psychonomic Science*. 1971, 23: 300.

25. E. Berscheid and E. Walster, "Physical Attractiveness," in L. Berkowitz (Ed.), *Advances in Experimental Social Psychology*. (Vol. 7) New York: Academic Press, 1974, p. 186.

26. G. Wilson and D. Nias, *The Mystery of Love: The Hows and Whys of Sexual Attraction*. New York: Quadrangle/The New York Times Book Co., 1976.

27. D. G. Freeman, "The Survival Value of the Beard," *Psychology Today*. 1969, 3: 36–39.

28. R. J. Pellegrini, "Impressions of the Male Personality as a Function of Beardedness," *Psychology*. 1973, 10: 29–33.

29. M. L. Knapp, *Nonverbal Communication in Human Interaction*. New York: Holt, Rinehart and Winston, 1972, p. 73.

30. P. R. Wilson, "Perceptual Distortion of Height as a Function of Ascribed Academic Status," *Journal of Social Psychology.* 1968, 63: 361–365.
31. C. V. Hassel, "The Political Assassin," *Journal of Political Science and Administration.* 1974, 7, No. 4.
32. E. Berscheid, E. Walster, and G. Bohrnstedt, "The Happy American Body: A Survey Report," *Psychology Today.* November, 1973: 121.
33. R. E. Nisbett, "Determinants of Food Intake in Human Obesity," *Science.* 1968, 159: 1254–1255.
34. R. Goldman, M. Jaffa, and S. Schachter, "Yom Kippur, Air France, Dormitory Food, and the Eating Behavior of Obese and Normal Persons," *Journal of Personality and Social Psychology.* 1968, 10: 117–123.
35. M. Lefkowitz, R. Blake, and J. Mouton, "Status Factors in Pedestrian Violation of Traffic Signals," *Journal of Abnormal and Social Psychology.* 1955, 51: 704–706.
36. L. Bickman, "The Effect of Social Status on the Honesty of Others," *Journal of Social Psychology.* 1971, 85: 87–92.
37. E. Berscheid and E. Walster, "Beauty and the Best," *Psychology Today.* March, 1972: 43–46, 74.
38. D. Landy and H. Sigall, "Beauty is Talent: Task Evaluation as a Function of the Performer's Physical Attractiveness," *Journal of Personality and Social Psychology.* 1974, 29: 299–304.
39. M. M. Clifford and E. Walster, "Effect of Physical Attractiveness on Teacher Expectations," *Sociology of Education.* 1973, 46: 248–258.
40. K. K. Dion, "Physical Attractiveness and Evaluation of Children's Transgressions," *Journal of Personality and Social Psychology.* 1972, 24: 207–213.
41. T. M. Newcomb, "Autistic Hostility and Social Reality," *Human Relations.* 1947, 1: 69–86.
42. C. A. Dailey, "The Effects of Premature Conclusion upon the Acquisition of Understanding of a Person," *Journal of Psychology.* 1952, 33: 133–152.
43. S. Fisher, *Body Experience in Fantasy and Behavior.* New York: Appleton-Century-Crofts, 1970, pp. 18–21.
44. M. Maltz, *Psychocybernetics.* Englewood Cliffs, N.J.: Prentice-Hall, Inc., 1960.
45. D. Krech and R. S. Crutchfield, *Elements of Psychology.* New York: A. A. Knopf, Inc., 1959, p. 203.
46. S. M. Jourard and I. F. Secord, "Body-Size and Body-Cathexis," *Journal of Consulting Psychology.* 1954, 18: 184.
47. G. M. Rosen and A. O. Ross, "Relationship of Body Image to Self-Concept," *Journal of Consulting and Clinical Psychology.* 1968, 32: 100.
48. L. C. Zion, "Body Concept as it Relates to Self-Concept," *Research Quarterly.* 1965, 36: 490–495.
49. M. Mead, *Male and Female.* New York: William Morrow and Company, Inc., 1949, pp. 138–142.
50. M. C. Jones and N. Bayley, "Physical Maturing Among Boys as Related to Behavior," *Journal of Educational Psychology.* 1950, 41: 129–148.
51. Jones and Bayley, p. 146.
52. D. Weatherly, "Self-Perceived Rate of Physical Maturation and Personality in Late Adolescence," *Child Development.* 1964, 35: 1197–1210.
53. P. H. Mussen and M. C. Jones, "The Behavior-Inferred Motivation of Late- and Early-Maturing Boys," *Child Development.* 1958, 29: 61–67.

54. M. C. Jones, "The Later Careers of Boys Who Were Early- or Late-Maturing," *Child Development*. 1957 28: 113–128.
55. Jones, p. 127.
56. M. C. Jones and P. H. Mussen, "Self-Conceptions, Motivations, and Interpersonal Attitudes of Early- and Later-Muturing Girls," *Child Development*. 1958, 29: 491–501.
57. S. F. Faust, "Developmental Maturity as a Determiner in Prestige of Adolescent Girls," *Child Development*. 1960, 31: 173–184.
58. Jones and Mussen, p. 500.
59. C. Tavris, "Men and Women Report Their Views on Masculinity," *Psychology Today*. January, 1977: 35–37, 42, 82.

References of Related Interest

Barocas, R., and F. L. Vance, "Physical Appearance and Personal Adjustment Counseling," *Journal of Counseling Psychology*. 1974, 21: 96–100.

Dermer, M., and D. L. Thiel, "When Beauty May Fail," *Journal of Personality and Social Psychology*. 1975, 31: 1168–1170.

Dion, K., E. Berscheid, and E. Walster, "What is Beautiful is Good," *Journal of Personality and Social Psychology*. 1972, 24: 285–290.

Ekman, P., and W. V. Friesen, *Unmasking the Face*. Englewood Cliffs, N.J.: Prentice-Hall, Inc., 1975.

Feldman, S. S., *Mannerisms of Speech and Gestures in Everyday Life*. New York: International Universities Press, Inc., 1959.

Fisher, S., and S. E. Cleveland, *Body Image and Personality* (Rev.). New York: Dover Publications, 1968.

Fisher, S., *Body Consciousness: You Are What You Feel*. Englewood Cliffs, N.J.: Prentice-Hall, Inc., 1973.

Flugel, J. C., *The Psychology of Clothes*. New York: International Universities Press, Inc., 1969.

Garn, S. M., "Body Size and Its Implications," in L. W. Hoffman and M. L. Hoffman (Eds.), *Review of Child Development Research, Vol. II*. New York: Russell Sage Foundation, 1966, pp. 529–562.

Kurtz, R., and H. Prestera, *The Body Reveals: An Illustrated Guide to the Psychology of the Body*. New York: Harper & Row, Publishers, 1976.

Lester, D., *A Physiological Basis for Personality Traits*. Springfield, Ill.: Charles C Thomas, Publisher, 1974.

Scheflen, A. E., *Body Language and Social Order*. Englewood Cliffs, N.J.: Prentice-Hall, Inc. 1972.

Thompson, W. R., "Development and the Biophysical Bases of Personality," in E. F. Borgatta and W. W. Lambert (Eds.), *Handbook of Personality Theory and Research*. Skokie, Ill.: Rand McNally and Co., 1968, pp. 149–214.

Wietz, S., (Ed.), *Nonverbal Communication*. New York: Oxford University Press, 1974.

Self-Concept as Related to Family Relationships and Childrearing Practices

PROLOGUE

Probably no relationship is more powerful or impactful than that which exists between parent and child. How a child ends up depends in large measure on how he or she starts out, and the starting point is always with parents. Whether the parents are Robert's actual biological parents or Sally's foster parent, the effect is the same. Those adults who have the primary caretaker responsibility will have the greatest influence, for better or for worse. When things go wrong, it seems a natural parental response to want to blame the schools or grandparents or television or even the kids next door. Nevertheless, the primary shaping of a child's personality belongs to the adult or adults who are raising that child.

It is within the emotional context of some kind of family unit that a growing youngster feels either loved or unloved, wanted or unwanted, capable or incapable, worthy or unworthy. Eight-year-old Tommy is not only subjected to inconsistent discipline, but he's uncertain about whether his parents even care for him. So he develops a guarded and suspicious attitude toward others as a way of protecting himself. Eleven-year-old Mary is overindulged and develops an exaggerated sense of her own importance. Fourteen-year-old Billy lives with parental expectations too great for his ability and develops a "what's the use of trying" attitude. Sixteen-year-old Pam has firm but flexible rules to follow, she feels loved by her parents, and she develops a healthy sense of responsibility toward herself and others.

How children are raised, whether by natural parents or someone else, *does* make a difference in terms of how they feel about themselves and other people. In this chapter we will take a look at what research is teaching us about the possible relationships between how children and youth are raised and their behavior and feelings about themselves and others. How children are reared and their family relationships depends partly on current trends in child-rearing and these have a tendency to vary to some extent with each new generation, a phenomenon to which we turn our attention first.

Changing Trends in Child-Rearing Practices

As a general rule, each new generation's attitude toward child-rearing is influenced by two primary considerations, (1) personal standards of child-rearing is influenced by each parent's life history and, (2) the current social standards and expectancies, which, if powerful enough, can change one's personal child-rearing preferences in the direction of the prevailing standards. The major emphasis during the 1800s, for example, grew out of certain assumptions about the nature of man and his innate depravity. Calvinists believed the newborn to be damned as a result of "original sin" and, as a consequence, both evil and rebellious. The child's will had to be broken so that he would submit to parents and to God's will. Religious orientations were very strong in nineteenth-century America and had a significant impact on child-rearing practices. Consider, for example, the following episodes reported by Sunley:

. . . One mother, writing in the *Mother's Magazine* in 1834, described how her sixteen-month-old girl refused to say "dear mama" upon the father's order. She was led into a room alone, where she screamed wildly for ten minutes; then she was commanded again, and again refused. She was then whipped, and asked again. This kept up for four hours until the child finally obeyed. Parents commonly reported that after one such trial the child became permanently submissive. But not all parents resorted to beatings to gain this end. One mother spoke of "constant thorough gentle drilling," which consisted partly of refusing to give the child an object just out of its reach, however much it cried. Another mother taught submission and self-denial at one and the same time by taking objects away from the child. Strictness in diet and daily routine was apparently frequently an accompaniment to obedience training.[1]

(You will recall that, in Chapter Two, we discussed how and why it is that people behave in terms of what they "believe" to be true. The above excerpt is a striking example of how a belief—in this instance, in a child's innate depravity—served as the rationale for behaving toward a child in a sadistic manner because it was "what the child needed.")

The attitude about the "evilness of the child" was around for a long time and in fact was still apparent during the early 1900s. Wolfenstein, for example, analyzed the advice given to parents in a 1914 edition of the U.S. Children's Bureau pamphlet, *Infant Care* and on the basis of that analysis made the following observations about what mothers were told at that time:

> . . . The infant appeared to be endowed with strong and dangerous impulses. These were notably auto-erotic, masturbatory, and thumb-sucking. The impulses "easily grow beyond control" and . . . "children are sometimes wrecked for life." The mother was warned that the baby may achieve the dangerous pleasures to which his nature disposes him by his own movements or he may be seduced into them by being given pacifiers to suck or having his genitals stroked by the nurse. The mother . . . is further told that masturbation "must be eradicated . . . and that the child should have his feet tied to opposite sides of the crib so that he cannot rub his thighs together." Similarly for thumb-sucking "the sleeve may be pinned or sewed down over the fingers of the offending hand for several days and nights. . ."[2]

From this point in time we may stand back and incredulously wonder how thumb-sucking and thigh-rubbing could be viewed as so much fun, but when seen in terms of impulses which "easily grow beyond control," we can begin to see why parents were concerned about behaviors of this sort.

Of course, not all parents reared their children as the 1914 pamphlet suggested, but there was, nonetheless, a general attitude about how to bring up children which made the whole process of child-rearing a bit more impersonal than is the case today. This impersonalness is probably reflected best in a 1928 book authored by the famous behavioristic psychologist, John B. Watson, titled, *Psychological Care of Infant and Child*. Consider, if you will, some typical passages from the book which eager parents, anxiously looking for guidance in how to raise their children, read back in the late 1920s:

> There is a sensible way of treating children. Treating them as though they were young adults. Dress them, bathe them with care to circumspection. Let your behavior always be objective and kindly firm. Never hug and kiss them. Never let them sit in your lap. If you must, kiss them once on the forehead when you say good-nite. Shake hands with them in the morning. Give them a pat on the head if they have made an extraordinarily good job of a difficult task. Try it out. In a week's time you will find how easy it is to

be perfectly objective with your child and at the same time kindly. You will be utterly ashamed of the mawkish, sentimental way you have been handling it.

In conclusion, won't you then remember when you are tempted to pet your child that mother love is a dangerous instrument? An instrument which may inflict a never healing wound, a wound which may make infancy unhappy, adolescence a nightmare, an instrument which may wreck your adult son or daughter's vocational future and their chances for marital happiness.[3]

The Watsonian parent, as you can see, was relatively free of the usual emotional expressions and ties which have come to be accepted as a normal part of our contemporary child-rearing ethic. Although parents of the early twentieth century were encouraged to care for their children, they had to keep an eye on how the caring was expressed. Apparently, loving your child was all right so long as the child was not too overtly aware of it.

In contrast to this coldly mechanistic view of child-rearing, the ideal home or school in the forties and early fifties was organized around greater acceptance of children's needs for gratification in order for them to experience maximum freedom of choice and self-expression. The first complete turn-about of the Watsonian trend was by Margaret Ribble in her book, *The Rights of Infants,*[4] in which she maintained that depriving a child of such basic human interactions as fondling, hugging, kissing, and other forms of body contact was as serious as denying him nourishment or sunshine. She further asserted that some of these interactions, often lumped together as ''tender loving care'' were necessary for the physical, intellectual, and emotional growth and well-being of any child. Support for Ribble's position came fast. A new ''softer,'' warmer approach grew more popular. Granting the child more freedom of choice and self-expression became the thing to do. Indeed, Dr. Benjamin Spock's very influential 1946 edition of *Baby and Child Care*[5] not only advocated the above practices during infancy, but encouraged their extension into the child's developmental years as well.

However, by the mid-fifties the pendulum was beginning to swing back again. For example, comparing the changes in child-rearing practices from 1940 to 1955 in his 1957 edition of *Baby and Child Care,*[6] Spock stated that ''Since then a great change in attitude has occurred, and nowadays there seems to be more chance of a conscientious parent's getting into trouble with permissiveness than with strictness.''

Oddly enough, each generation of parents seems to reflect a kind of reaction-formation behavior to its own parents' child-rearing standards. The intensity of that reaction is by no means uniform for all parents, but seems, rather, to be influenced by the extent to which a parent may have felt his own parents were extreme in the position they took in raising him. Spock[7], for example, made the interesting observation that his own mother, who bore five children between 1903 and 1913, rebelled very much against the stern Victorian propriety of her parents and offered her own children a more balanced diet of firmness and permissiveness. I think that is what happens in many cases. Children raised under a very firm, unbending, authoritarian hand are likely to modify that position for the same reasons as cited above, that is, they may see a greater need for direction in their children's lives precisely because they're in a position now to look back and see that they could have used more direction in their *own* lives as they were growing up.

What Are the Current Trends?

Contemporary child-rearing practices do not suggest that we have returned to firm, heavy-handed discipline, but there are indications that parents are less easy-going than was the case in the forties and early fifties. If anything, the current emphasis is on *understanding* the child rather than being too restricting or too laissez-faire. If, for example, a three-year-old is frightened by thunder, rather than saying, "There's nothing to be scared of, it's just a loud noise," or "It can't hurt you, it's just clouds banging together," a parent is encouraged to understand the *meaning* of it to the child and respond with something like "I know sounds are very scary to children—come sit in my lap," or "Almost all kids your age get frightened of thunder—it's a kind of angry sound, isn't it? But I promise it won't hurt you." Or, as another example, let's say that a five-year-old is afraid to fight back when a bully keeps attacking him on the street or playground (even though they may be matched in physical size). Rather than a parent saying "You're acting like a sissy—all you have to do is let him know you're not afraid of him," or "You're as big as he is, so learn to fight back. Here, I'll show you how," a parent is encouraged to respond with comments which recognize the child's feelings—like "I guess the best thing to do is

© 1968 United Feature Syndicate, Inc.

When it comes right down to it, most parents probably feel a little like Lucy and most kids probably feel a bit like Snoopy.

to try to play somewhere else—I know he's a bully," or "Sometimes you do have to let a mean boy know he can't push you around, but for a person like you that can be very hard. You're a strong boy, but you're also a nice boy."

The emphasis on understanding the child does not mean that we are returning to a permissive child-rearing ethic. With delinquency and adult crimes on the rise there seems to be little patience these days for philosophies that talk only about children's freedoms and rights without also emphasizing their obligations and responsibilities. Indeed, as we will note at greater length later on in this chapter, children who tend to do well in school and to have high self-esteem are more apt to have parents who are firm than parents who are permissive.

Fifty or more years ago, parents seemed to feel that the way to cure the fault was to attack the child. On the whole, I think today's parents have a better understanding of the idea that if you reproach a fault it can be reformed, but if you attack a personality it can only defend itself.

What this current psychological approach does is to remind us that, whether a child is five or fifteen, he tends to see everything as either black or white, with no shades of gray in between. He sees things as either good or bad, cowardly or courageous, nice or naughty, lovable or awful. It also reminds us that to be human is to have all kinds of feelings—love and hate, compassion and competitiveness, courage and cowardice—and that children wrestle daily with this profound fact of life, trying to reconcile themselves to accepting all of it. Understanding children's personal feelings while holding them accountable for their behavior is one way of helping them to learn that both their inner and outer worlds are real, that they can, to a large extent, comprehend and control their worlds, and that both are negotiable realities with which they can make their peace.

There seems little question that what a child becomes depends to a large extent on how he or she is raised. It also depends on who does the raising. Which leads us to ask an important question.

What Influences Parents To "Parent" the Way They Do?

We somehow assume that all parents instinctively know "how to be a parent," which is in the face of a large body of evidence suggesting that this is not true. A human mother or father cannot rely on innate, "built-in" instincts to guide their parental behaviors. To what sources, then, may we attribute parental behavior and attitudes? We have already seen how current fads and fashions in child-rearing influence parental behavior; now we will turn to two additional parent variables, generational continuity and parent personality.

Influence of Generational Continuity on Parental Behavior

It is not surprising that our own parents (or parent substitutes) have a major impact on how we behave as parents ourselves. We are not only witnesses to what they do, but recipients of it, both good reasons for being more or less like them in our parenting style.

There is a good example of how generational continuity works in Harris'[8] study of the backgrounds of a group of normal children. He observed that what had happened to the mothers as children was also happening to their own children, and that what had happened to their parents was also happening to them as parents. Four considerations influenced this continuity from one generation to the next. One was the degree to which the mothers were consciously aware of the similarities between their own childhood behavior and that of their children: "Karlene is just like I was at that age—sort of flighty and unconcerned." The second was the extent that they wished to see repeated the experiences of their own childhood: "I want Debbie to enjoy the kind of summer outings I enjoyed as a child." The third was the degree to which the mothers wanted to have the same kind of role as adults that they had in childhood: "I really need my mother's advice about what is the best thing to do." (A dependency role in this case.) The fourth consideration was in the extent that some mothers reflected about their own unfulfilled childhood expectations: "I want to be a much better mother to my children than my mother was to me."

Harris also found that the kind of connection the mother made to her own childhood affected the way she adjusted to her maternal role. For example, mothers who adhered too rigidly to the past or who had too much unresolved conflict associated with it were likely to have more problems with their own children. Three general mother "types" were described: traditional, rebellious, and dependent mothers. Each type carried over into her own maternal role attitudes which had a direct bearing on how she related to her children. The *traditional* mother was reasonably satisfied with her own mother's child-rearing practices and attitudes and used them as a frame of reference in raising her own children. The *rebellious* mother, on the other hand, made a conscious effort to be less controlling than her own mother, toward whom she had negative feelings because of excessive control, strictness, and interference. Indeed, there was some evidence to suggest that mothers of this kind sought to work out their rebellious feelings toward their own parents through their children, which usually meant going in the direction of having too few rules and being too lenient. As you might suspect, the children of rebellious mothers were inclined to fuss more about rules and boundaries which interfered with having things their way. The third type, the *dependent* mother, was disenchanted with her own mother because she felt deprived of sufficient attention, love, and interest as she was growing up. Children of such mothers seemed to search for interpersonal warmth. Not having received a great deal of warmth as they were growing up, these mothers were less able to show warmth to their own children.

There even tends to be a certain continuity of child-rearing patterns when it comes to discipline. Radke[9], for instance, found that there was a tendency for parents to use disciplinary techniques similar to those remembered from their own childhood. Along this same time, Bronson, Kalten, and Livson's[10] investigation of the patterns of authority and affection over two generations discovered that mothers were likely to wield strong authority in their homes if they remembered their own mothers as having been strong authority figures. A similar pattern was noted among fathers in the study. That is, they were apt to copy their fathers, but more so in the area of affectional relationships than of authority. Why this should be more so in one area than another is open to speculation, but one reason may be that, in our culture at least, giving or receiving affection by a man is not well-defined, certainly less specifically defined than is the case for women. We are more certain about how the American male should demonstrate his strength and stability than we are about how he should show his caring and affection. Since the rules for what constitutes appropriate or inappropriate expressions of affection for a man are more diffuse, he may rely more heavily on his father for cues in this area.

The continuity of parenting practices from one generation to the next is seldom a conscious process and is always a matter of degree. Through the very powerful and daily process of unintentional teaching, parents pass on to their children those fundamental child-rearing attitudes transmitted to them by their own parents. What happens between children and their parents during their developmental years will greatly influence—for better or for worse—their own behavior as parents later on.

A parent's personality can make a difference. The question is, how much?

Influence of Parent Personality on Children's Behavior

A parent's personality can have a great influence on the personality and self-concept development of a child. Handel's[11] review of family-related research shows rather clearly that family interaction frequently comes to be centered around "themes," which are given form and expression through the personalities of individuals within the family unit. Whether a family's theme or "personality" is active and outgoing or passive and quiet, the ultimate impact of a parent's personality on a child lies more in how a parent *feels* than in what a parent *does*. The fact that a family is active and does many things together is no guarantee that the children within the family will develop healthy, positive self-images unless there is also a positive *valuing* and *feeling* for each other. Unfortunately, this is where many parents stop. A mother values her children, a father feels love for his children, but sometimes those inner feelings are never expressed directly and openly. Love is more than just feeling; it is also a matter of communicating. How many children, I wonder, grow up surrounded by what amounts to "inferential love?" Not ever hearing that they are loved, they infer it, which means they have to do a bit of mind-reading. A nineteen-year-old male client of mine put it to me this way:

> Oh sure, my dad did a lot of things with me—even bought me most of the things I wanted—but I never had the feeling that he really *cared* for me. We would do things like fish or hunt together or go to sports events, but I sometimes feel I was included more because he may have felt he had to take me—sort of like it was his obligation as a father or something. Sometimes he'd tell me he liked the way I handled the car, or liked the fact I made the team, or liked the fact I got good grades, but he never told me, not once, that he liked *me*.

You may be interested to know that the father referred to above was actually a very personable, friendly man, who, in fact, did care for his boy a great deal. But he was also a very inward person with his feelings, particularly his loving and nurturing feelings. His idea of showing his love was to *do* things with his son or *buy* things for him, which were substitutes for *saying* how he felt. It was precisely because the boy *did* enjoy doing things with his father that the perceived absence of any kind of *caring* or feeling from his father was so painful. Like many young people who end up angry or disillusioned about their parents, this boy had to accept the idea that his father would probably never change and that if he wanted a relationship with his father to exist at all he would have to cease fretting about what his father *could* be and accept him for what he *was*. No simple task, this, because it demands that the boy be more mature, more understanding, and certainly more giving than his own father.

To no one's great surprise, the father in question here is the way he is because his own father was that way. There is a good chance that my nineteen-year-old male client will break away from that mold in his own future role as father because: (1) he is *aware* of the possibility of being different—that is, awareness frees him from being simply a conditioned reflex of his past upbringing, and (2) he is entering an era when it is more permissable for men to not only have feelings but to *express* feelings.

How a parent comes across as a *total* person can also make a difference in how a child behaves and thinks about himself. For example, Behrens[12] assessed the adjustment of a group of twenty-five preschool children with clinical problems and related their feelings about themselves to the feeding, weaning, and toilet-training methods of their mothers. Also, she rated each mother as a "total mother person," which reflected personality in a more global sense. Although there was little consistency among the three child-rearing practices and no tie between the ratings of children's behavior and their mothers' procedures, there was a close connection between child adjustment and "total mother ratings." Again, evidence to suggest that what a parent *is* bears more on child adjustments than what he or she *does*.

Probably no facet of a parent's personality is more crucial than self-esteem. As an anguished, depressed mother of four relatively young children expressed it during one of her therapy sessions: "My god, what am I to do, what am I to do? I don't even like myself—how can I love my children?" In her despair she recognized a simple, but profound psychological truth: we love others as we love ourselves. Erich Fromm[13] and Karen Horney[14] have written eloquently to this point. This is an important point because self-love is the mortar with which self-esteem and self-acceptance can be built into one's personality. When we accept ourselves we are better able to accept others. This is no less true in relationships between parents and children. For example, in a study[15] of fifty-six mothers and their nursery school children, it was found that mothers who had high self-acceptance reflected higher acceptance of their children than mothers with low self-acceptance. This conclusion is consistent with those reached by Coopersmith[16] who found that mothers of children with high self-esteem tended to be high in their own self-esteem. At the same time, mothers of children with low self-esteem were themselves low in self-esteem. In addition, they were fairly apt to be emotionally unstable. Apparently high self-esteem mothers (and fathers, as noted later) convey a certain confidence, poise, and liking for themselves that is mirrored in their general personality style, which their children, in all likelihood, eventually identify as part of themselves.

Overall, the impact of a parent's personality on a growing child's ideas and attitudes about himself are considerable. In the final analysis, what a child becomes probably depends more on what a parent *is,* than what a parent *does*.

The Role of Identification and Sex-Typing in Parent-Child Relationships

Identification is a concept derived from psychoanalytic ideas about how personality evolves and develops over time. Essentially, identification is a largely unconscious process through which a growing child comes to think, feel and behave in ways similar to the primary people in his life. In its simplest terms, identification is a process whereby one individual takes on the behavior of another individual and behaves as if he were that individual. Indeed, a child's self-concept is build upon the foundation of his earliest and most primary identification with people (or a person) most meaningful to him.

Identification is preceded by what is commonly referred to as *sex-typing,* which is more on the order of *modeling* or *imitative* behavior. Whereas identification is largely an unconscious process of incorporating an entire personality, sex-typing is a more conscious process of copying specific behaviors. Examples of identification and sex-typing would include such behaviors as the three-year-old boy mimicking his dad shaving in the morning by lathering up and going through all the shaving motions dad uses, or the little four-year-old girl with her own gob of dough going through all the motions that mom does as she bakes bread.

Sex-typing refers to the process through which a child acquires the psychological and social behavior considered appropriate to his/her own biological sex in a given society. Indeed, of all aspects of the child's self-concept, one of the most important is his discovery of and attitude toward his own sex. Part of a growing youngster's self-image is the knowledge that "I am a boy" or "I am a girl," and that knowledge carries rather specific implications for how a child feels about him/herself and how others treat him/her.

At what age does sex-typing and identification begin? It very likely begins at the moment of birth. Parents typically want to know, first of all, "Is it a boy or a girl?" The answer to this question does more than satisfy nine months of curiosity. It sets in motion a chain reaction of stabilized and stereotyped ideas about how little boys or girls, as the case may be, should be treated. American boys get blue things and girls get pink ones. Friends and relatives give the boy tiny trousers to grow into, and adorn the girl in frilly frocks. A girl baby is admired for her delicate features and a boy baby for his husky appearance. Boys get playthings labeled masculine, girls get feminine ones.

By age three, most children are able to correctly label themselves as *boy* or *girl*. By age four, most children can use the labels *boy* and *girl* correctly in more general ways. For example, they use the right pronouns to refer to people (he, she, him her), and can classify and group dolls or pictures according to sex differences—four-year-olds also begin to show more marked preferences for toys and activities associated with their own sex. Research[17] shows, however, that four-year-olds do not ordinarily realize that their sex is a permanent part of themselves, nor have they clearly associated sex with role distinctions. The idea here is nicely illustrated in a cute story told by comedian Robert King:

> My niece was about four years old and she was playing in the kitchen with the boy next door who was the same age. The boy said to my niece, "You want to wrestle?" My niece said, "I can't wrestle, I'm a girl." The boy said, "Oh, well, you wanna play football?" "I can't play football," she said, "I'm a girl." "Well, do you want to throw the baseball around?" And my niece said, "How many times do I have to tell you—I'm a girl?" The boy said, "Oh, all right. Wanna play house?" And she said, "O.K., I'll be the father."

By around age five or six, most children have figured out that gender is constant. They also have a reasonably clear idea of their own sex and of the stereotypical "female" and "male" role and characteristics. At about the same time or a little later, children begin to understand the relationship between genital differences and sexual identity. It is also at around age five that the child begins to show consistent imitation of and identification with adults of the same sex. Which brings us to our next consideration.

A Parent's Role in Sex-Typing and Identification

Parents are enormously important in helping to shape a child's sex-role preference. The most fortunate children are those who have so adequate a father (male model) and mother (female model) that they come early to prefer the sex-role dictated by their physiology, move naturally and easily into its rehearsal, and eventually identify thoroughly with it.

The girl who has made a female identification is the girl who has happily and willingly adopted femaleness as her way of life. She thinks of herself as a female, she accepts and likes her biological status, its advantages and disadvantages, and she assumes the responsibility and challenge that being female demands. In order for this to happen, she must be *identified with* (love, respect, and, in many ways, imitate) her mother or mother-figure in order to be consistently and genuinely *female-identified*.

With respect to the boy, identification is very much as it is for the girl, except, of course, that he identifies with the father or father-figure.

Research rather consistently points to three parental variables, *warmth, availability,* and *power* as the crucial ones in determining the course of a child's identification. For example, Sears[18] and Mussen[19] and Moulton[20] all found that boys of fathers who were warm, affectionate, nurturing, and available tended to be more closely identified with their fathers and to engage in more sex-role appropriate behavior than boys whose fathers were more distant and cold. Sears also noted that boys who behaved in more effeminate ways were likely to come from homes in which the *mother*, but not the father, was high in warmth. Mussen's study made particular note of the fact that highly feminine girls are more likely than girls low in femininity to perceive their mothers as significantly warmer, more nurturant, and more affectionate.

Why is parental warmth a factor in a child's identification with that parent? The reason seems to be that it allows the child to be emotionally close to the parent, a quite necessary prerequisite to becoming *like* the parent. In addition, a warm parent in very likely a *rewarding* parent—the kind of father, for example, capable of making his son feel good about being around him.

Parental power or dominance also plays a major role in the identification process. There are several possible reasons for this. One, a child may identify with the parent, not necessarily the same sex parent—with the most power (dominance, authority, strength) because it is the safer thing to do. Psychoanalysts call this "identification with the aggressor"—that is, if I'm on your side you won't hurt me. Sociologist Talcott Parsons[21] theorizes that a child identifies with the most powerful parent because he or she holds the trump cards in dispensing both punishments and rewards. It is very likely that both of these reasons play a part in influencing a child's perception of dominance and subsequent identification. Hetherington's[22] research with boys and girls between the ages of four and eleven indicates that boys who come from mother-dominant homes reflected more feminine sex-role preferences than boys from father-dominant homes. The idea is sometimes expressed that a mother-dominated boy will lose whatever feminine sex-role behavior he has as he grows older and experiences a certain amount of social pressure from his male peers to change his ways. Hetherington's research did not find this to be true. If anything, boys from mother-dominant homes showed *more* feminine sex-role preferences as they got older. Let's remember that the mother in a mother-dominant home is not neccesarily bad or doing something wrong. She may be dominat *only because the father is very passive or lazy or even absent much of the time*. Her dominance may be an extension of her personality or a consequence of circumstances. The same in reverse can be true in a father-dominant family. It would be fairer to say that it is the *combination* of dominance and passiveness that can affect the identification process.

This combination of mother-dominance and father-passiveness can be quite detrimental to boys. For example, the results of a study[23] involving upper elementary grade boys showed that boys who were consistently more fearful, anxious, dependent, and indecisive were more closely feminine identified than boys who were more decisive, independent, and less affectionate. Closeness to mother and distance from father has been clinically identified time and again as the emotional spawning ground for male homosexuality.[24, 25, 26, 27] This is not surprising. In order for a boy to develop into an independently functioning, normally aggressive man, he must be able to identify to a considerable degree with his father (or father figure). He can do this only if father has a certain amount of power, and is warm and available. If this cannot be done during childhood, it often is during adolescence when substitutes for a cold and passive father are sought out. Since adolescence is a time when sexual impulses are beginning to be felt, it is not surprising that the search for a close relationship at this age carries with it some sexual needfulness.

The importance of a father or father-figure in a boy's life is probably no better illustrated than in the work of two Australian psychiatrists[28] who, after interviewing 959 aborigines—usually through an interpreter—failed to find even a single instance of male homosexuality either in their own research or other published reports on such behavior among aborigines. The reason for this apparently has to do with the fact that the aborigine community is an extended family in which a designated or actual brother takes over for an absent father, even to taking the widow as his own wife if the brother dies. No child lacks for a father. In addition, male and female roles are so strictly defined that a youngster cannot confuse them.

As far as boys are concerned, the existing evidence supports the notion that boys identify more completely with loving fathers and powerful fathers, particularly when this "power" (size, strength, total presence, ability to make decisions, and so on) is primarily benevolent than they do with rejecting and punishing fathers. A boy *may go through the motions of identifying with a powerful, but rejecting, punishing father while young* (I'll never beat him—I'd better join him), *but grow increasingly more alienated from his father as he is able to match him in size and strength.* One seventeen-year-old, six-foot, one-inch delinquent boy serving time in a boys' training school expressed it to me this way when asked about his feelings about his father.

> That bastard used to beat me when I was small, used to beat me all the time. And I'd take it. I even remember hanging around him when I could and hugging his leg so he would think I really liked him and maybe he wouldn't beat me. Didn't really work though. Still beat me (Clenching his fist) I'd like to see him try to lay a hand on me today—just once—I'd show him.

The matter of which parent has the most power does not seem to play such an important part in the sex-role development of girls. Hetherington's[29] research, for example, showed that father-dominance made it easy for the girl to identify to some extent with the father, but did not disturb the primary process of same-sex identification with the mother. Thus the mother-daughter and father-daughter similarity in mother-dominant homes did not differ significantly. (We might note that *neither* the sons nor daughters in mother-dominant homes identified with the passive father.)

Healthy sex-role identification for girls is best encouraged by a warm and nurturing mother and a strong and caring father. Indeed, research[30, 31, 32] indicates rather clearly that when the father plays an active and competent masculine role in the family, his daughter is more likely to incorporate his non-sex-typed behaviors and be more flexibly adaptive in her own behavior than when he is unmasculine and/or aloof. Going a step further, psychiatry professor Seymour Fisher[33] has found that highly orgasmic married women are more likely to have been raised by men who were "real fathers" to their daughters—that is, men who were dependable, caring, demanding, and insistent that their daughters meet certain moral standards and expectations. Implicit in this seems to be the idea that a strong, dependable, masculine father is able to lay the sort of trust groundwork that will be necessary in his daughter's subsequent adult relationships with men. This is quite consistent with my own clinical observations of women I've worked with in therapy. When there is a problem of not being able to trust men, the genesis of that problem usually goes back to the father relationship. Clinical literature,[34, 35] for example, indicates that female homosexuals are not so much attracted to each other as they are afraid of intimate relationships with men, which frequently goes back to their early father-daughter relationships where they learned to fear and not trust men at the hands of fathers who were weak and incompetent and/or puritanical and possessive.

All in all, the evidence from both clinical and empirical research suggests that a girl does not have to be as closely identified with her mother as the boy does with his father in order to experience appropriate sex-role identification. There are probably several reasons for this. One, boys are usually more strongly pressured and, hence, motivated to behave in traditionally sex-role appropriate ways. And, two, girls experience more leeway for behaving in more different ways as they grow up. For example, young boys can wear cowboy outfits or play ball but be laughed off the block if they wore dresses or played with dolls. Little girls, on the other hand, can wear either outfit or play either game without being criticized. Girls may play with boys without censure, but boys are still made fun of if they play with girls too much. It's apparently all right for preschool boys and girls to play with each other—sex lines haven't been drawn yet—but by the time they begin elementary school this changes. (One four-year-old boy was overheard saying to his buddy: "I plan on enjoying these years before girls turn into the opposite sex.")

It seems clear that some cross-sex identification of girls with their fathers is both healthy and advisable. That is, girls *do* compete, not only academically, but, increasingly, in the world of athletics as well. Indeed, it seems to be increasingly characteristic of our child-rearing ethic to encourage girls to be aggressive and achieving as they grow up. In fact, as a girl grows up there is less pressure on her to be "girllike" in all her behaviors than there is for a boy to be manly.

In sum, let us say that in order to encourage maximum self-concept integration, boys need every opportunity possible to identify with a father figure during their developmental years and girls with a mother figure. A boy learns how to be a man and accept his sexuality *by being around a man he values and feels close to*. A girl learns how to be a woman and accept her sexuality *by being around a woman she values and feels close to*. Both boys and girls seem to profit from a certain amount of "cross-identification" with the parent of the opposite sex and this is even truer for girls.

Influence of the Women's Liberation Movement on Sex-Role Modification

My sixteen-year-old "went out" for track last spring and ran on the cross-country team this past fall. This would not be particularly remarkable or noteworthy, except for the fact that my sixteen-year-old is a girl. And this is the first time that she and her friends have had a chance to form, or join, a track team. (Now they have a softball team and basketball team as well.) My daughter's essential identification with what we ordinarily associate with femininity or "femaleness" hasn't changed, but what has changed are the opportunities she has for expressing herself in more different ways as she gets older.

Thanks to the new social consciousness which has grown from the women's liberation movement, we are beginning to learn that much of what we have thought of as "biological" differences are merely cultural distortions imposed from without, rigidly enforced, and then pointed to as examples of "male" or "female" traits. The fact is, the arts are not only for girls, nor sports only for boys. Men have an esthetic sense just as women do and women have a need for physical activity just as men do. This does not mean that there are not real differences between boys and girls and men and women. Research[36, 37] indicates that there are many differences. Sometimes, however, what we have construed as differences have been erected as barriers that have needlessly segregated the sexes according to culturally defined sex-roles that have little or no relationship to their inherent abilities and talents. For instance, girls have a lesser proportion of body weight devoted to muscle tissue than boys, but, as my daughter, Debbie, has reminded me, that doesn't mean they can't run.

Fortunately, the traditional and constricting boundaries around what constitutes "masculine" and "feminine" behavior are slowly expanding so as to include a broader range of behavioral and occupational goals for both sexes. From a purely socio-economic point of view, this seems a desirable and sensible way for a society to achieve maximum utilization of its available skills, talents, and creative thinking regardless of sex. From a purely psychological point of view, expanding sex-role boundaries may make it more possible for both sexes to more nearly realize their full potentials as total persons without fear of encroaching upon the still-existing and somewhat arbitrary parameters around what we've always thought of as "man's" work and "woman's" work. People—young and old—get unhealthy, develop poor self-concepts, and feel unfulfilled when, because of either internal or external constraints, they stop moving toward personal and/or professional goals which may otherwise fill them out as complete individuals. Sex-role modification may encourage parties of both sexes to consider more and different ways to achieve a greater variety of goals which, in the long run, cannot help but have a healthy and desirable payoff for society in general and individual boys and girls, men and women in particular.

Will modification in sex roles really occur? Consider the following letter received by the editors of *Ms* magazine:

> I had just put the kids to bed, the house was a wreck, and I still had the dinner dishes to do. But this month's *Ms.* had just arrived, and I couldn't resist sitting down with it. One article led to another before I realized that any minute the door would open on the shambles around me. What could I say? The door opened. It was time to practice what I'd been reading. "I left the dishes for you for a change," I said, cool as a revolutionary. My wife, home from her graduate-school class, was flabbergasted! I hope she doesn't cancel our subscription. (Signed) Mike T.

Three Major Child-Rearing Styles

Most parents, naturally enough, want to give their children the best they can give them. In spite of good intentions, however, children don't always turn out for the best. Some turn out to be hostile, hateful, and suspicious, others are fearful and anxious, and some turn out to be unhappy, shy adults wondering who they are and what they stand for. On the other hand, many children turn out with a positive self-concept and grow into productive, integrative, self-actualized adults. The question is: What kind of child-rearing style produces what kind of children?

There is no simple answer to this, but child-rearing research in recent years has given us a pretty fair idea about what we might reasonably expect given certain child-rearing styles. Psychologist Diana Baumrind[38, 39] has enhanced our insights considerably by identifying and researching three distinct patterns of how parents relate to their children and use the authority implicit in the parental role. Let us take a brief look at each of them.

Authoritarian Parenting This style characterizes parents who operate according to rather rigid standards of conduct, who favor punitive, forceful measures of discipline, and who value strict obedience as a high virtue. Authoritarian parents work hard to inculcate their children with such instrumental values as respect for authority, respect for work, and respect for the preservation of order for the traditional structure. There is not a whole lot of give and take in the authoritarian home. The parent is pretty much the center of things.

Authoritative Parenting This approach is best described as one that is rational and issue-oriented. Authoritative parents rely less on the power of their role, as do authoritarian parents, and more on the power of reason to accomplish their goals. There is frequently a good deal of spirited give and take between parents and children in the authoritative home. Parents of this persuasion are able to be quite firm when there is a need for firmness, but they do not box the child in with rigid restrictions.

Permissive Parenting This style is used by parents who are inclined to behave in rather easy-going, nonpunitive, and accepting manner toward most things their children do. Children are usually given a voice in family decisions and rules, but there are few demands on them for household responsibility and orderly behavior. Permissive parents tend to allow children to regulate their own activities as much as possible, but do not particularly encourage them to behave according to externally-defined standards. The child is pretty much the center of things.

Behavioral Consequences of These Three Styles

In what ways did each of these parent-child patterns influence children growing up under their influence? Consider some of the findings. Both authoritative and authoritarian parents demanded socially responsible behavior (following certain rules, controlling impulses, listening when talked to, behaving, and so on.) from their children but encouraged it in different ways. Authoritarian parents, for instance, permitted their own needs to take precedence over those of the child, assumed a stance of personal infallibility, and in other ways showed themselves to be more concerned about their own ideas being right than with the child's welfare. Thus, although they preached socially responsible behavior, they were not likely to practice it themselves. Authoritative parents, on the other hand, both preached and practiced responsible behavior and, as a consequence, their children were significantly more responsible than those of authoritarian parents.

Permissive parents were different still. They neither demanded socially responsible behavior nor were they particularly aggressive in rewarding it when it did occur. They issued few directives and those that were issued were seldom enforced by either physical means or verbal influence. Indeed, permissive parents seemed to make it a point to avoid confrontations when the child disobeyed. The children of permissive parents, particularly the boys, are found to be clearly lacking when it came to socially responsible and achievement-oriented behavior. One reason for this is that, in the absence of negative sanctions ("This is something you must not do") or positive expectations ("I expect you to listen when the teacher talks"), the child is left with the impression that either there are no rules to follow or, if there are, it is okay to go ahead and disobey them anyway. Indeed, Siegel and Kohn[41] found that when adults do not react at all to a child who disobeys or breaks an existing rule, the child is even more likely on subsequent occasions to repeat that same behavior. If, for example, a seven-year-old boy punches his four-year-old sister every time he's mad at her, his behavior is not likely to change unless someone older and, presumedly, wiser steps in and points out that hitting one's sister simply is not allowed under any circumstances. The fact is that some children misbehave not because they're necessarily "bad," but because no one has ever taught them correct or more appropriate behavior. Sometimes the most difficult thing that some children have to do is to learn good manners without seeing any.

All in all, research strongly indicates that both authoritarian control and permissive noncontrol tend to inhibit a growing child's opportunities to engage in vigorous interaction with people. Demands that cannot be met, refusals to help, and unrealistically high standards all tend to roadblock normal, healthy commerce with the environment. On the other hand, expecting little if anything from a child or establishing unchallenging low standards for behavior may understimulate him. Is there a reasonable balance between total control and no control? Apparently there is. However, it is not so easy as saying that the best kind of parents are those who combine just the right mixture of being tough and being permissive. The qualities of explicit warmth and caring are important ingredients in that mixture. What the warmth is mixed with makes a difference. Let us turn our attention to how.

Warm–Restrictive Versus Warm–Controlling Parents

It is not enough to say that sufficient amounts of parental warmth is the answer to raising healthy, balanced children. It depends on what the warmth is combined with. On the one hand there are the warm-restrictive parents, while on the other hand there are the warm-controlling parents—each having a different effect on children. In the first place, there's a difference between restrictive control and firm control. *Restrictive* control is associated with the use of extensive proscriptions and prescriptions covering practically all areas of a child's life and severely limiting his autonomy to test himself out in new ways and to learn new skills. There are many "No's," "Keep off" signs, and "Don't touch" signals in this child's life. *Firm* control is different in the sense that the emphasis is more apt to be one which says, "I *expect* you to be a good boy." There is firm and consistent enforcement of the rules, effective resistance against the child's demands, and generally more guiding and showing as opposed to the ordering and telling behavior of restrictive-controlling parents.

Influence on Children's Behavior

What kind of child behaviors are likely to be associated with each parenting style? Becker[42] reported that warm-restrictive parents tended to have passive, fearful, dependent children who were generally well-behaved. (It is difficult for a passive, fearful, dependent child *not* to behave.) Baumrind[43] found, however, that warm-controlling (by contrast with warm-restrictive) parents were likely to have responsible, assertive, self-reliant, and independent children. Parents of these children consistently enforced their directives and resisted the child's demands. Lots of times parents "give in" to their children because it's the easiest thing to do but feel guilty for having done so, and, then, to make up for this lapse get "tough" with the child the next time he asks for something. This not only confuses the child, but makes the parent look inconsistent and more restricting than ever.

Finally, we should recognize that there are both desirable and undesirable aspects to any particular child-rearing style. There is probably no one kind of home atmosphere that guarantees the "perfect" child. For example, although fearless, curious, and self-directed children are likely to come from homes in which a psychological climate of democracy and autonomy prevails, these same children are also inclined to be aggressive, rebellious, and nonconforming. On the other hand, the obedient well-behaved child of a home characterized by strict, unbending control may show signs of a constricted personality and high dependency needs.

Perhaps we can understand more deeply the relationship between self-concept and child-rearing practices if we look at some specific expressions of self-concept outcomes.

Self-Concept Outcomes Related to Specific Child-Rearing Practices

There is little question that personality expands in complexity and consistency as the years pass. It grows more complex because each person's range of experience increases, reproducing more intricate and overlapping interactions. It increases in consistency because, as one's physical growth terminates, body image becomes more stable and roles become clearer and more tightly incorporated into the self-concept.

Since child-rearing practices play such a critical part in shaping our ideas about ourselves and others, what we will do now is examine specifically three expressions of the self which have their origin in the experiences of early parent-child relationships. These are dependence-independence, aggressiveness, and conscience development.

Dependence—Independence

Dependency is a condition of the human infant and since independence grows out of dependence, the two must necessarily be considered together. What are the earmarks of independent and dependent behavior? Some of the more common dependency symptoms in children include such behavior as seeking help, seeking physical contact, seeking attention and recognition and hanging around one or both parents. Independent behaviors include such things as taking initiative, working through problems by one's self, finishing things once they are started, and trying to do routine tasks by oneself. In general, the independent children or adults are relatively detached from outside sources of appraisal and rely heavily on themselves in making judgments and appraisals. Dependent children are much more at the mercy of others and there are some sources, possibly as few as one, from whom they cannot dismiss themselves and who have the capacity to raise, lower, threaten, or stabilize their self-esteem. For example, the mother-dependent little six-year-old boy may not care what his teacher, his brothers, or sisters, or the whole neighborhood thinks about his water-color painting, but he does care about what his mother thinks. As we discuss the dependency-independency continuum of behavior, we should keep in mind that even though some children display generally more dependent behavior than others, some of both kinds of behavior can be seen in all children. The question is, to what *degree* does it exist? Another question is, when does it start?

Critical Periods for Dependency Development

Psychologist Celia Stendler[44] has made a strong case for the idea that there are two critical periods during the early years when over-dependency may result. The first of these occurs toward the end of the first year when the infant becomes aware of his dependence. Having made this discovery, Stendler reasons that the child shows his sudden recognition of the importance of his mother by making increased demands for her time and presence. It is, in effect, a kind of testing period during which time a child develops the formative beginnings of what psychiatrist Erik Erikson[45] has called an attitude of "trust and mis-trust." During this critical period from about nine to twenty-four months, it is imperative that young children have their dependency needs met in regular, predictable ways. It is in this manner that the child learns to trust (depend on, count on) the larger world around him. If, for some reason during this period, a young child is denied the consistent and regular attention of a primary caretaker—mother, father, or someone else—during his waking hours (for example, if the child is hospitalized, or mother becomes ill, or he is shifted from caretaker to caretaker), Stendler reasons that the child will experience increasing anxiety, which he will try to resolve by making excessive demands on the primary caretaker when that person is around. Thus, it is through the absence of a primary caretaker during a critical period, during a time when a child really needs a particular person, that he becomes more *dependent* on that person because of his *anxiety about losing that person*. This is consistent with research[46] that has shown a high frequency of attention-seeking behavior when the primary adult is relatively unavailable. This would suggest that dependency behavior is likely to increase when the primary adult(s) in a young child's life are either not readily available or inconsistently available. Perhaps one of the conditions of the growth of independence is that young children must first be able to trust their dependency on at least one primary caretaker during the first two years of their lives.

Notice we've been talking about a "primary caretaker" rather than limiting this person exclusively to mother. The fact is, more and more mothers work. For example, twenty-five years ago, only 1.5 million mothers were in the labor force. Today, 14 million are. Before 1969, most women with children between the ages of six and seventeen spent their days at home. Now, nearly three million have little ones aged three to five, and 2.5 million have babies under three.[47]

If a mother works, will this interrupt the course of normal dependency–independency development? Apparently not. Available research[48] suggests that it is not *whether or not* the mother works that is important for a child's well-being, but what kind of alternative care is provided. Other research[49] has shown that young children are quite capable of forming meaningful attachments to substitute caretakers so long as there aren't a lot of shifts from one person to another.

Returning to our critical periods idea, the second of these occurs during the two- to three-year-old period. In Stendler's words:

> . . . this is the time in our society when demands upon the child to change his old ways of doing things increase tremendously. Now the child must give up his control of his mother and come to accept his dependence upon her, yet at the same time learn to be independent in culturally approved ways. In normal socialization the anxiety generated (about having to be less dependent on the mother) produces the right amount of dependency. But where disturbances of a traumatic nature occur (e.g., death, separation, divorce, remarriage, both parents working, etc.) so that important habits must be suddenly and drastically changed, so much anxiety may be generated that overdependency will result.[50]

To support her critical periods theory, Stendler[51] has shown that a larger number of disturbances in personality adjustment turned up in *dependent* children than in others.

How Dependency Behavior May Be Encouraged

Why does dependent behavior persist? One obvious reason is that dependent behavior ("Help me"; "look at me": "show me"; "tell me how") is encouraged and rewarded and competence or independence behavior ("I can do it"; "no, let me"; "I'm big enough now"; "don't help") is not. In fact, some parents seem fearful that their children will become *too* competent because *then their children would not need them as much.*

Other research[52, 53] indicates that a child is apt to be overly dependent if he or she experiences too much parental rejection. The reason for this may very likely be that parental rejection may cause a child to feel excessively anxious and helpless, which do little to help a child (or anyone else for that matter) feel strong and independent. If you have ever been rejected by a loved one—someone you would like to feel close to and accepted by, then you may have a good idea of how the feeling of rejection tends to exaggerate feelings of neediness and dependency. It is difficult to feel strong and independent if we don't first feel accepted by the primary people in our lives. Persons who have been rejected by the primary people in their lives, but who claim to be emotionally strong and personally autonomous may do so, I suspect, more for the purpose of protecting a shakey self-image than as a means of enhancing an already positive one.

Other studies point strongly to the conclusion that dependent behavior is likely to grow from too much parental overconcern and over-protectiveness. Heathers,[54] for example, noted that the homes of dependent youngsters rated higher on child-centered and babying counts, and maternal protectiveness.

Toward Encouraging Independence Behavior

Using college students as his subjects, Mueller[55] found that the *most* independent boys perceived their fathers as both *strong* and *passive;* that is, the father had plenty of power (psychologically) but kept quiet about it, thus leaving the boy free to develop his own independent ways, but all the time being sure his father could rescue him if necessary. A comforting feeling—to be free and protected at the same time. Another factor encouraging the growth of independence is the parent's willingness to permit independent and exploratory behavior without becoming unduly alarmed by a growing child's natural inclinations to expand the range of his activities and experimentations. (A natural human laboratory for observing the dynamics of parent-child interactions is in supermarkets and department stores. Observe for yourself the vast differences among parents when it comes to allowing their children freedom to explore—in this case, in store settings, which we might reasonably infer would be a good index of a parent's attitude toward exploratory behavior in other places as well. Some children, you'll find, are free, within limits, to explore, roam, and touch things while other children are admonished severely if they venture too far from the parent's side. Who, in the long pull, do you think might develop a keener sense of independence?)

Another way parents can foster independence is by being careful of the duration and intensity of contact with their children. Sometimes parents fail to recognize that by monopolizing their children's time, they limit their possibilities for contact with other persons and thus make it more difficult for them to test themselves outside the protective tent of their parents' influence. Research[56, 57] shows, for example, that children who depend heavily on adults are not likely to be very popular with their peers.

Apparently, however, the *kind* of dependency a child shows makes a difference. A child who is dependent on adults for *emotional* support (seeking reassurance, clinging to the adult as a helpless child might lean on his mother) is less likely to be popular than a child who leans on an adult for "instrumental" support, that is, seeks out an adult for practical help in carrying out a specific project. In addition, it appears that the child who looks for help and support from his agemates is likely to be more popular than the one who continues, as he grows older, to depend on adults. From the point of view of children themselves it's apparently all right for one of them to seek adult help in doing something that is obviously beyond his ability to do (pound a big nail, ride a bike for the first time, lift a heavy object), but running home to mom or dad as a general solution to problems is socially frowned upon in a child's peer culture.

In sum, dependent persons have learned, since the time they were children, to place heavy reliance on others to determine their opinions, courses of action, and sense of personal worthiness. Children who are overprotected and restricted, who are overindulged and constrained, are existing in an artificial environment. Like a plant growing within a house, they can survive within its shelter, but frequently are too fragile to survive the shifting elements of the real world. Parents who seriously restrict their children's freedom and constantly worry about their private enterprise and exploration ("Will he drive carefully?" "Will she behave herself?" "Will she come home on time?" "Oh dear, where is he now—I can't see him.") seriously hinder their children's need to discover their strengths and weaknesses for themselves. They may raise children carefully tuned to the needs of their parents, but they may also turn out adults who may seek constant assurance about the significance of their own views about most anything, including themselves.

Aggressiveness

In our culture there is some ambivalence as to how aggressive behavior should be regarded. During childhood, aggression is discouraged and yet aggressiveness carries a certain premium in the adult world. Indeed, our society encourages and rewards such disguises of aggression as competitiveness, ambition, standing up for one's rights, and even getting downright angry or at least "righteously indignant" over certain personal or social issues. The whole thing must be pretty confusing for growing youth. Consider it. We tell youngsters not to fight, but we persist in either waging or supporting wars; we support—although ambivalently—capital punishment, and in the interests of producing "successful" shows, literally hundreds of persons are shot, stabbed, beaten, maimed, or murdered during any evening's prime time television hours. Keeping in mind that 97 percent of all American homes have one or more television sets (a greater percentage than has automobiles) and that the typical family watches an average of 36.5 hours of television per week, consider the following synthesis of some of the basic research findings related to television viewing.[58]

1. By the time a child finishes high school he will have probably watched 15,000 hours of television—4,000 more than he will have spent in school.
2. It is estimated that the average 18-year-old sees 18,000 television murders, and an almost uncountable number of rapes, robberies, bombings, tortures, and other forms of violent aggression.
3. Psychiatrist Michael Rothenberg has estimated that there is an average of six times more violence during one hour of children's television than in one hour of adult television.
4. Research done at the University of Pennsylvania's Annenberg Institute of Communications found that up to three-fourths of prime-time network dramatic programs and children's dramatic programs on Saturday and Sunday used violence as standard content.

In the midst of this "tranquil" setting, we try to teach children something about impulse control and regard for others.

Aggression in childhood seems to be almost universal. For example, of the 379 mothers studied by Sears, Maccoby, and Levin,[59] every mother at one time or another had been forced to cope with angry outbursts or quarreling on the part of her children and 95 percent reported instances of strong aggression directed by the child against his parents. Another study reported that some kind of conflict, ranging from fairly mild to violent, occurs during free play about every five minutes for boys to about every seven or eight minutes for girls.[60] As Sears and his co-workers have pointed out, the aggressive child is likely to be an angry child, and an angry child is not a happy child. Indeed, there is evidence to suggest that aggressive behavior is related to low self-esteem. For example, one study concluded that college students who had *low* self-esteem were more likely to react aggressively in aggression-provoking situations than students with *high* self-esteem.[61] Coopersmith's study of elementary school children, also reported the same phenomenon, namely, low self-esteem children are more destructive than high self-esteem children. He noted that low self-esteem children were more prone to vent their hostility against inanimate objects and remarked that: "It is the reaction of an individual who admits his weakness to himself, but is in no position to confront his adversary."[62]

How Aggressive Behavior Is Encouraged

The parent serves as a model for the child and sets examples for behavior. Logically, then, it would follow that the more aggressive the adult's behavior, the more aggressive the child's. This view is supported by the data from the study by Sears and others,[63] who observed that when parents punish—particularly when they use physical punishment—they are providing a living example of the use of aggression at the very moment they are trying to teach the child not to be aggressive. This "counter-attack" on the part of the parent, though it may work for a moment,

A certain amount of aggressiveness is natural during childhood, although it sometimes does get carried to extremes.

appears to generate still more hostility, anger, and resentment in the child, which eventually gets expressed. An angry, resentful child may not attack his parent's back directly, but what he frequently does is displace his anger, that is, he takes it out on someone else, his younger brother, or the boy across the street (when no one's looking), or kids on the playground. (I wonder how many bullies, who usually delight in terrorizing smaller, younger children are themselves physically abused by their bigger, stronger, parents?)

Several studies[64, 65] have shown that children's expression of aggression is strongly related to the aggression they observe in adult models, which would suggest that adults interested in tempering their children's aggressive expressions would do well to watch their own.

Aggression is more likely to occur when it is permitted, and it has been observed that highly aggressive children can also come from homes in which the parents are permissive of the child's outburst, whether or not the aggression is directed against them. It has been noted, for example, that mothers who are both permissive and physically punishing are most likely to produce highly aggressive children.[66]

Not only do children see a lot of aggression and violence on television, but there is evidence to suggest that television may cause heavy TV viewers to not only behave more aggressively, but to be less sensitive to the effects of aggression. For example, after studying the TV viewing habits of 427 male and female students from the time they were in third grade until they were through high school, the investigators of this ten-year study concluded that "there is a probably causative influence of watching television programs in the early years on later aggression.[67] Still another study concludes: "Our research shows that among both boys and girls at two grade levels (junior and senior high) the more the child watches violent television fare, the more aggressive he is likely to be.[68]

Does exposure to televised aggression make children more tolerant of the real thing? Apparently it does. Psychologists Drabman and Thomas[69] exposed one group of twenty fifth-graders to a fifteen-minute segment of a shoot-'em-up detective program and another group to a fifteen-minute segment of a baseball game. Then the experimenter said he had to leave for a while and asked each child to keep an eye on two kindergartners playing nearby. The child was told that the toddlers were being filmed by camera and could be watched on the television screen. If anything went wrong, the fifth-grader was to get help. Actually, what the fifth-grader saw was a staged sequence in which the kindergartner became more and more unruly and fought to the point of apparently knocking the camera over and the monitor went blank. The researcher wanted to see how long it would take the fifth-grader to seek help after seeing the real-life violence. The children who watched the detective show took much longer to respond than did the baseball watchers. In fact, of the twenty detective show viewers, five (two boys and three girls) never went for help at all, as opposed to only one girl in the baseball group. A similar experiment found the same results with third- and fourth-graders. Drabman and Thomas explained their results by suggesting that perhaps violence on television teaches children that aggression is a way of life, not to be taken seriously, or perhaps real-life aggression simply seems bland, in contrast to the vicious violence on TV.

It should not be surprising that television violence can so affect the behavior of growing children. As we discussed more fully in Chapter One, youth between the ages of birth and thirteen years or so do not have a completely formed concept of self. In absence of a consolidated self-image, children during those formative years are as impressionable as they ever will be. Whether it be from home or school or church or television, *growing children are inclined to believe what they hear and accept what they see*. A child is like a sponge. He will absorb all that surrounds him. Later, when he develops his capacity for critical appraisal or abstract thinking, as Piaget[70] has called it, he will sift through his knowledge, discard some, retain some: But as a child he will absorb his environment—the attitude of playmates, the wisdom of teachers, the love of parents, and the solutions he learned to frustration and anger, however he saw it in the world he grew up in.

Although the discussion here has focused on the parents as models and the influence of television, we know from our everyday observations that a child may also imitate siblings peers, and other adults. In fact, one study[71] showed that if a quiet, passive preschooler plays with a more aggressive peer, the passive child begins to behave more aggressively himself. This is, by the way, more apt to be true of boys than of girls, who are generally found to be less physically aggressive during childhood and adolescence.[72] In general, we are fairly safe in saying that the more children are exposed to aggressive behaviors in others, in real-life or television, the more likely they are to manifest similar behavior in themselves and to incorporate aggressive behavior as part of their self-concepts. Which leads us to an important question.

How Can We Cope with Aggression?

The literature concerned with aggression, as well as everyday social observation, clearly suggests that a child's aggression cannot be so thoroughly squelched that he becomes defenseless and passive. Indeed, from the natural aggression expressed in childhood is born the self-confidence it takes to express one's ideas and opinions in adulthood. On the other hand, rampant acting out of aggression through physical violence and verbal tirades can be socially and personally destructive and must be controlled.

The way for parents and teachers to cope with aggression is to make it abundantly clear that destructive, physical aggression is frowned upon and to stop this sort of aggression when it occurs with the use of some non-physical punishment technique. The best, or at least the most effective, ways of handling aggressive behavior are the use of diversion, appeal to non-hostile motives, such as friendship and rational explanations about *why* aggressive acting-out behavior is undesirable. Spanking children for being aggressive only makes them more aggressive. However, we must also remember that children easily construe adult permissiveness about aggression as approval and, when so handled, are likely to be more aggressive than the average. A growing child *wants* adults to help him control aggressive behavior and finds considerable security in growing up with someone who not only cares for him but helps him control his periodic impulse to slug someone. This is not so difficult as it may seem. Children can stand almost any amount of strictness; it is injustice that unstrings them. Unfortunately, it is many times the strictest disciplinarian who had the weakest sense of justice, which can create bigger problems than the crime itself.

A child, like anyone else, should have a right to have angry feelings. Psychologists Thomas Gordon[73] and Haim Ginott[74] have written excellent books that help explain the differences between angry feelings and angry acts and how to deal with them. Actually, the fact that any of us gets angry or is angry is not so important as what we do with it. Constructive anger, that is, finding out what is wrong, working harder to solve the problem, can lead to positive changes in one's self and others. Destructive anger, that is, losing one's head, physical violence, is usually harmful to one's self, to others, and if there is a "cause" involved, to that as well. Honest recognition and acceptance of angry and aggressive feelings are two of the most important facets of good adjustment and a healthy self-concept.

Conscience Development

Sooner or later, if all goes well, each child acquires a conscience, a system of ideas, attitudes, and inner controls that decree what is right and wrong and what his duties and responsibilities are. It is a significant aspect of a person's self-concept since it reflects one's acceptance of values concerning right and wrong behavior. Conscience is sometimes referred to tongue-in-cheek as "that which keeps us from doing what we shouldn't when no one is looking." Jersild very aptly defines the conscience as follows:

> The conscience usually does not represent a unitary, internally consistent set of principles or sanctions. It has many facets. It may be the voice of experience (better not, someone might be looking). It may be rigorous in some matters, not in others. It may prevail over temptation. Or it may be sort of a gadfly, which does not prevent a person from doing what he thinks he ought to do, but only prevents him from enjoying it.[75]

For the most part, a preschool child's behavior is pretty much governed by whatever he feels like doing at a particular moment. Early conscience development tends to be erratic, largely confined to prohibitions against specific behaviors, and based on external rather than internal sanctions. Piaget's[76] research teaches us that from ages five to twelve most children experience a dramatic shift in their concept of justice as it passes from a rigid and inflexible notion of right and wrong, learned from parents, to a sense of equity in moral judgments that takes into account the specific situation in which a moral violation has occurred. Five-year-olds, for example, are apt to view lying as bad, regardless of the situation or circumstances in which it occurs. With increasing age, children become more flexible and learn to recognize when there may be exceptions to this strict rule when lying or stretching the truth or whatever you care to call it is justifiable. An eight-year-old might fib about the whereabouts of her younger brother to the inquiring neighborhood bully, while the four-year-old might easily point her finger to the corner he was hiding in.

Signs of Healthy Conscience Development

Sears, Maccoby, and Levin[77] have observed that there are at least three signs of healthy conscience development which adults should be alerted to when assessing a child's ability to know the difference between "right" and "wrong" behavior. One sign is the extent to which a child can resist temptation, even when he knows he's not being watched by a potential punisher. If, for example, a parent can leave valuable possessions or tempting foods within reach of a child who has been asked "not to touch or get into things" and feel sure that the child will obey in the parent's absence, then this is one indication that the child is learning to control his impulses.

A second sign of healthy conscience development, which usually means accepting his parents' standards as his own, is the child's efforts to teach these standards to his friends and siblings, that is, to act the parental role. For example, a brother admonishing his sister with something like "You better get out of mom's jewelry, she wouldn't like it." or a little boy reminding his friend with "You shouldn't go to the bathroom outside—that's not nice.'' are each examples of assuming a kind of parental role in real-life interactions with siblings or friends.

A third sign of conscience development is the way a child acts *after* he has done something wrong. A child with a well-developed conscience is troubled not only by a fear of punishment, but also by a certain amount of self-blame. If, in fact, he disapproves of himself in the same way he thinks his parents will disapprove of him, he can only feel better after he has atoned for, or has been punished for, the misdeed in some way and has been forgiven. In fact, he may act so guilty and sheepish and even hang around his mother in such a way that she knows something is wrong. Sometimes a child will arrange things in such a way so his parents are bound to find out what he's done, even though he might not actually confess. (In my own case, as a young boy, I was always too anxious to do a lot of ''extra'' favors for my mother, a dead giveaway to her that I was wrong *and* guilty about something.)

In general, a child's capacity to admit that she did something ''bad'' and to apologize or make some kind of restitution, are important steps along the road to the development of a self-concept which is able to discriminate between right and wrong. It means that she is willing to risk outside punishment in order to recover her self-esteem and the esteem of her parents.

Are there ways to recognize that conscience development is not progressing as it should? Indeed there are.

Signs of Unhealthy Conscience Development

Redl and Wineman[78] have described some ingenious rationalizations which a group of delinquent children used to justify, without guilt, a wide variety of immoral behaviors. Consider them carefully. They are symptoms of conscience development gone awry and include:

1. *Repression of intent.* An inability to recall the original motive for performing the crime, though there was full recall of the details of the crime itself.
2. *''He did it first.''* Though the action was wrong, the fact that another person had done such a thing evidently served as a precedent, and this precedent made the action ''legal.''
3. *''Everybody else does such things anyway.''* If everybody does such things, then they can't be wrong, and so I need not feel any guilt for doing them.
4. *''We were all in on it.''* Since it was a group activity, the responsibility, and hence the guilt, either belongs to the leader, or the group, but not to any one person.
5. *''But somebody else did that same thing to me before.''* Because I was once the victim of such an act before, I am entitled to do the same thing to some present innocent party without having to feel guilt for it.
6. *''He had it coming to him.''* The wronged person was such a sinner himself that he deserved to be sinned against; ergo, I need not feel guilty.
7. *''I had to do it, or I would have lost face.''* Justifying one's actions on the assumption that status in a group with deviant values is more important then conformity with society's morals.

8. *"I didn't use the proceeds anyway."* An appeal to the "Robin Hood" mechanism. If I used the proceeds of illegally gotten money, and so on, for charitable or highly moral purposes, there need be no guilt.

9. *"But I made up with him afterwards."* If I befriend the victim of my immoral activity, I have thus undone the crime and need feel no guilt.

10. *"He is a no-good so-and-so himself."* Similar to No. 6.

11. *"They are all against me, nobody likes me, they are always picking on me."* Since the person is living as if he is in an enemy camp, then all activity is justifiable.

12. *"I couldn't have gotten it any other way."* Self-exculpation on the premise that what was gained immorally was somehow the person's inviolable right; he is entitled to get it by any means.

Although these rationalizations were gathered from a group of delinquent preadolescents, it is not difficult to see that they are also the prototypes of many adult rationalizations. These are unhealthy reactions and interfere with normal conscience development, because they represent efforts to run away from one's guilt or wrong-doing rather than facing it. When a person has repressed, projected, displaced, or rationalized the guilt he accumulates, his defenses usually have to become more drastic to keep the guilt from conscious awareness. Typically, reactions of this sort lead to increased alienation from the self, ease of being threatened ("What if someone finds out what I'm *really* like; I'd better be careful"), and a reduction in the capacity for free, open, honest communication with others—all unhealthy consequences. A person—no matter what age—with something to hide is a cautious, guarded, closed person.

Toward Encouraging Healthy Conscience Development

The concept used most frequently to explain a child's conscience development is that of *identification*, which we discussed earlier in this chapter. Conditions which favor strong positive identification with parents also tend to encourage conscience development. That is, as a child "becomes like" his parents, he also comes to adopt his parents' values about "right" and "wrong." For example, it has been found that kindergarten boys who were highly masculine, presumably because of identification with their fathers, were also high in conscience development.[79] There is also experimental evidence to show that in temptation situations children are inclined to imitate the adult model who yields to temptation,[80] which suggests that parents serve rather directly as models for their children with regard to moral behavior.

As you might suspect, the kind of discipline parents use is very much related to a child's conscience development. For example, Sears and his colleagues[81] observed that psychological or "love-oriented" techniques as reflected in the use of praise, isolation, and withdrawal of love produced relatively more children with high conscience than the use of more "thing-oriented" or physical methods such as those reflected in tangible rewards, deprivation, and physical punishment.

Basically there are at least three essential conditions for conscience development: (a) The child has to know what is right and wrong, what is acceptable and what isn't; (b) She has to be loved and know it; (c) She must know for sure that those who care for her do not indiscriminately accept everything she does. If a child has free reign to do pretty much what she wants, in the absence of expectations to live up to, then she seldom has to live with the guilt which usually follows from letting someone valued down. *Experiencing and working through guilt feelings is a primary prerequisite to healthy conscience development.* If a child violates an expectation and the parent tries to comfort him with either a subtle or obvious, "Well, it really doesn't matter that much anyway." response, the effect of this on the child is two-fold: (a) It deprives him of an opportunity to modify his behavior and sharpen his sensitivity to the demands of the outside world and, (b) it makes the parent look, not only inconsistent, but also like someone who doesn't really mean what he says anyway.

Birth Order: Influence on Child-Rearing Practices and Personality Outcomes

A child's place in the family by way of birth can have a powerful effect on his attitudes toward himself and others. It makes no difference to a baby—and to the roles he eventually plays—whether he comes first in a family or follows other children. Usually, the first child "breaks trail"—that is, the parents learn about child-rearing the hard way, by practicing on the first-born, who is on the receiving end not only of their fumblings and uncertainties, but also of their undivided attention and overprotective inclinations. The research related to birth order and its effects on self-control and personal-social development is voluminous, to say the least, and what follows is a sampling of that research as it relates directly to child-rearing practices and personality outcomes.

One of the most consistent findings related to birth order is that first-born children achieve eminence in higher proportion than do subsequent children within the same family. For example, it has been noted that:

> . . . marked surpluses of first-borns have been reported in samples of prominent American men of letters, of Italian university professors, of the starred men in *American Men of Science,* of the biographies in *Who's Who*, of ex-Rhodes scholars and of eminent research biologists, physicists, and social scientists.[82]

This finding is similar to the conclusion of another study which found that first-borns were overrepresented in the college population.[83] Interestingly enough, there is also evidence to suggest that college attendance decreases regularly with each later birth-order position.[84] Other research[85, 86, 87] indicates that although first-borns are no more intelligent, they are better readers as children; they tend to do better in high school and on National Merit Scholarship tests; they dominate graduate schools and account for more than their fair share (about a third) of physicians, lawyers, architects, college professors, and astronauts.

As a group, first-borns are no smarter than subsequent children in a family, but they do tend to do better academically from the beginning. One of the reasons for this is that first-borns try harder. But why should they try harder? Consider it: not only is the first-born likely to receive overdoses of parental anxiety and insecurity, but also overdoses of their love and attention, which is directed at him and him alone. As a consequence, first-borns tend to learn to speak earlier and more precisely and, as research[88] has indicated, are also likely to receive a great deal more verbal stimulation from their parents than will later-born children, who must compete for their parents' attention. Since the first-born is likely to continue to be the child to whom the parents direct their commentaries on performance and the one at whose level conversation is pitched, he is seemingly more inclined toward greater acceptance of conventional or adult-approved activities and interactions—traits that frequently lead him to be variously labeled as *adult-oriented, conscientious, studious, serious,* and so on. And then, too, parents seem to *expect* more of their first child, almost as if he or she were a kind of trail-blazer responsible for establishing the standards and establishing guidelines for subsequent children. Indeed, some parents seem to feel that, if they do a good job raising their first-born, later children will just naturally follow in his footsteps and are shocked to find that subsequent children are not at all like either the first-born or each other. In any case, although the superior school performances of the first-born and their greater frequency among high achievers is a fairly consistent finding, it is not at all clear that first-born children strive comparably or excel in other pursuits. For example, there is suggestive evidence that outstanding athletes are more likely to be *later-born* than first-born.[89] This is consistent with more recent evidence which indicates that first-borns respond with more fear to physical harm than do later-borns,[90] and also that their greater anxiety about the prospect of physical harm is likely to discourage them from participating actively in high-risk (injury-wise) sports such as football, hockey, or basketball.[91] Since new parents tend to overreact and to respond with greater fear and anxiety to anything physically wrong with their first-born, it is not difficult to adopt a cautious, conservative approach to physical activities.

It has also been suggested that the first-born, confronted by powerful adults, learns to repress his aggressive tendencies while the later-born, having an older sibling (or siblings) with whom to contend, can more readily express aggression.[92] Moveover, parents are more likely to constrain the older, stronger child who aggresses against a younger sibling, while at the same time encouraging the younger child to stand up for his rights.

A review of literature by Clausen[93] found evidence to indicate that first-born males are more readily influenced than are later-borns, more likely to yield to group pressures, and are more suggestible. First-born females, on the other hand seem, if anything, less susceptible to influence than later-born females, more responsible, aggressive, and competitive. There is no clear explanation for this, but one reason may be that a mother is more inclined to overprotect and overreact to her first-born if it is a son than if it is a daughter partly because she knows less about "what makes little boys tick" and so is more cautious with him. It may also be due partly to the fact that she responds to "the son her husband always wanted" and so takes extra precautions to see that nothing happens to him.

In a study involving interviews with 3050 adolescents, Douvan and Adelson[94] produced a number of interesting findings. For example, they found that first-borns of both sexes were highly ambitious and achievement oriented, while middle children tended to have lower aspirations. While the oldest child showed close identification with parents, the youngest was more closely identified with the peer group and relied less on the family. This difference may well reflect changes in parental needs and concerns. For example, it is conceivable that the younger child is given greater freedom of social interaction because the parents do not need to form the close emotional attachment with him that they had with the older child. Other research[95] indicates that later-born children are more identified and more popular with their peer group because they may feel less powerful at home and, as a consequence, may be more motivated to develop their interpersonal skills along more egalitarian lines.

You may be interested to know that the only child is somewhat like the first-born in a family. Although some parents feel they must have a second child so the first won't end up as an overindulged ego-maniac, research[96] suggests that many only children actually enjoy striking advantages both as children and as adults. As with first-borns, a disproportionately high number of only children appear as National Merit scholars, science prize winners, astronauts, doctors, and persons listed in *Who's Who in America*. There is no evidence that I am aware of to suggest that the only child is destined to grow into a maladjusted, egocentric adult. If a child—only child or not—does grow up to be that way, birth-order has little to do with it.

Let us remember that the general conclusions we have discussed in regard to birth order and behavior may hold statistically, but there are many, many individual exceptions. For example, Count Leo Tolstoy, the famous Russian author, was the youngest of five children. And Benjamin Franklin was the fifteenth of seventeen children. In the long pull, a child's order in the family is far less important than are the attitudes and interaction patterns of his parents toward him.

Not only may birth-order be an important variable in self-concept development, but the number of brothers and sisters we have and where we stand in relation to them may also have an impact.

Sibling Position and Interpersonal Relationships: Some Speculations

Psychologist Walter Toman[97] has a fascinating theory which suggests that the kind of person we choose for a spouse, friend, or working partner may be determined by the kinds of siblings we lived with while growing up. Our adult relationships may duplicate the ones we had with our brothers and sisters. A boy raised with sisters, for example, gets used to interacting with girls, and females lose that "strange" or "different" quality to him. A boy raised with brothers, however, may feel uncomfortable around women and prefer the company of men. Sibling position is particularly important in Toman's theory. By virtue of their position, Toman theorizes that older children are more likely to learn to be leaders, while younger children get used to the idea of being followers. Thus, first-borns are likely to look for relationships they can dominate, which is not so apt to be as strong a need for younger children.

Toman also uses his theory to predict how marriages will work:

> Suppose that the older brother of a sister marries the younger sister of a brother. They are getting in marriage precisely the peer relation that they had at home. He is used to a girl his junior, and she to a boy her senior. Hence there should be no conflict over their dominance rights. And both of them are used to the other sex, so they should have no great sex conflicts either. If this fellow had married an oldest sister of sisters, however, he could have expected some problems. Both partners would expect to have seniority rights and each one would try to rule the other. In addition, the wife would have had little experience in getting along with men.[98]

Toman reasons that you may have trouble in marriage if you are an only child because you have had only your parents to learn from, which means you may have a more difficult time getting along with peers. Only children may be looking for a father or mother rather than a peer when they marry, and they may not want or have children of their own since they want to remain a child themselves.

You may find some interesting insights into your own personality style and self-concept feelings by looking at yourself using Toman's system. Here are some examples:

Oldest sister of sister(s): (OSS) She tends to be dominant, assertive, and bossy. When she cannot take charge, she's inclined to be angry, unhappy, or sullen. She is competent, responsible, and does things efficiently. The youngest brother of sisters would be her best marriage choice.

Youngest sister of sister(s): (YSS) She likes adventure, change, and entertainment, and may seek them spontaneously, even haphazardly. She has a bouncy enthusiasm and a certain charm about her, but she is also pretentious, gullible, and emotional—and a brat. She may have problems in marriage, since she's not used to living with a male. Her best partner might be a dominant and indulgent man—an oldest brother of sisters, perhaps.

Oldest sister of brother(s): (OSB) She tends to be independent, strong, practical, and concrete. She likes men, and they like her. She will enjoy taking care not only of her husband but also of any number of children. The youngest brother of sisters might be her best marriage choice.

Youngest sister of brother(s): (YSB) The YSB is everything a traditional man would like a woman to be: feminine, friendly, kind, tactful, submissive to some extent, and a good companion and good sport. Women don't always like her, but she gets along well with males.

Oldest brother of brothers(s): (OBB) The OBB is a man's man: aggressive, assertive, and in control at most times. Whether by force or by cunning, he tends to be a leader. He gets along well with other males, especially when they are not older. His best marriage choice is probably the youngest sister of brothers.

Youngest brother of brothers(s): (YBB) He can be daring and imaginative, but also annoying and irritating. He tends to have unpredictable work habits—sometimes productive, sometimes not—and is at his best in scientific or artistic endeavors. He tends to squander money freely. The YBB loves whatever attention he gets and works hard to get it. The oldest sister of brothers might be a good marriage bet for him.

Oldest brother of sister(s): (OBS) The true ladies' man is apt to come from this category. He is not inclined to be one of the boys or a man's man. He likes being around women and functions best with them as friends and colleagues. Women tend to be equally attracted to him. The youngest sister of brothers might suit him best as a wife.

Youngest brother of sister(s): (YBS) No matter where he is or what he is doing, there is usually a female around to tend to his needs. He tends to be somewhat passive and more inclined to be a follower than a leader. The YBS relates more easily to women than to men and may feel easily threatened when around male peers. The oldest sister of brothers might be the ideal wife for him.

Toman offers an interesting approach to the problem of birth order and one which easily fits existing theories of personality development in terms of how people learn certain behaviors through experience, exposure, imitation, identification, and reinforcement. Nonetheless, we need to remember that these are broad descriptive categories, not rigid truisms. Like all theories that put people into neat categories, it fits everyone a little, some a lot, and others not at all. Birth order and sibling position are simply two additional variables we can use in our total understanding of personality and self-concept.

So far, our discussion of how child-rearing and family influences relate to personality and self-concept development has assumed that children will experience *both* a male and female model when they grow up. What happens when this is *not* the case?

Self-Concept Development as Related to Broken Family Units

The number of children under eighteen living with only one of their parents—now one out of six—has almost doubled in the past twenty-five years. And the change has been most rapid for children under six. For example, currently 13 percent of all infants under three—nearly one million babies—live with only one parent.[99] population surveys in urban centers suggest that by age eighteen between 30 and 40 percent of all children have experienced a broken home.

That the loss of a parent through divorce, separation, desertion, or death hampers a child's adjustment cannot be denied. On the other hand, the evidence does not allow us to assume that *because* only one parent lives at home the child or children in that home will be maladjusted or emotionally damaged. What seems to make a difference to a child is not so much that a separation, or divorce, or death has occurred, but rather *how it is handled by the adults involved.*

An intact family is no guarantee that the children within it will grow up to be happy, productive, high self-esteem adults. For example, in his investigation of family disorganization, Goode observed:

> . . . that a family in which there is continued marital conflict, or separation, is more likely to produce children with problems of personal adjustment than a family in which there is divorce or death. . . . (The) choice usually has to be between a continuing conflict or divorce. And the evidence suggests that it is the *conflict of divorce,* not the divorce itself, that has an impact on the children.[100]

Consistent with this observation, Nye[101] found that adolescents from *broken homes* showed *less* psychosomatic illness, *less* delinquent behavior, and better adjustment to parents than those from *unhappy, unbroken* homes, which would suggest that in some cases separation and disruption of the home is desirable. Perhaps this might follow an additional finding of Nye's that indicated that the adjustment of parents individually and to their spouses was superior in broken homes than in unhappy homes that remained intact.

Burchinal,[102] in a study involving over 1000 adolescents, found that youth in homes broken by divorce do not fall into a class by themselves, with common characteristics that distinguish them from other children. In fact, they are as heterogeneous, with their share of good adjustment and poor adjustment, as young people who do not come from broken families. There are indications from other research,[103] however, that adolescents who formerly perceived their home as a happy place are more disturbed by divorce than youth who viewed their home as unhappily torn by dissension.

Evidence related to the long-range impact of broken homes and rearing by a single parent is extremely meager. One of the most thorough studies of adult mental health—the Midtown Manhattan Project—found that people who had experienced a broken home in childhood had only slightly higher risk of psychological difficulties later in life than those from intact homes.[104] There was, however, a marked increase in the number of emotional problems among those whose remaining parent remarried, especially in those instances when the same sex parent remarried.

Since remarriage is a frequent sequence to divorce, many children must adapt themselves to stepparents. Studies of children reared by a remarried parent suggest that ambivalence toward the stepparent and interpersonal friction are extremely common, especially when the child is nearing or has entered adolescence. This point was apparent in a study by Bowerman and Irish[105] who compared information obtained from 2000 seventh- to twelfth-grade stepchildren with similar information drawn from several thousand children of unseparated parents. Children with stepparents reported more stress, ambivalence, and less cohesivness in the home than children living with their natural parents. As a group, daughters reacted more strongly than sons to the presence of a stepparent.

Since in divorce or separation the mother is given legal custody of the children roughly nine times out of ten (this trend is changing slowly), the mother in these circumstances carries an enormous responsibility for the self-concept and personality development of the children. This is particularly critical for boys raised in father-absent homes. Recent research literature in this area clearly indicates that the lack of a masculine relationship during childhood has the effect of feminizing the young boy, creating eventual difficulties in his peer relationships, and producing more passiveness and greater dependency on the mother.

Perhaps even more important than the absence of a male model for the boy reared by his mother will be her expressed attitudes about the boy's father and other men. Children form attitudes about their parents not only through their own observations of their parents, but also from hearing their parents talk about each other. When a growing boy and girl hear, for example, their mother talk about the absent father in angry, reducing, put-down ways, this only serves to undercut their trust in not only the father, but in their own judgments about him as well. An unmarried thirty-three-year-old female client of mine, reflecting over her childhood years and her parents' divorce, expressed the idea here in the following way:

> My parents were divorced when I was eight. I knew they were unhappy and fought a lot and so I wasn't really surprised, I guess. My mother was really mad at my dad. Sometimes she would cry; other times she would say what an S.O.B. he was. At first I didn't know what to think, but, you know, pretty soon I started to think he was an S.O.B., too. I didn't see him very often, but when I did I had a hard time trusting him. I think I thought he might do to me what he did to my mother (a long pause here)—whatever that was. I'm not sure exactly why, but I just have always had the feeling that I wouldn't want to trust *any* man too much. And that's what I want to change. It gets so damn lonely at times.

From the time she was eight years old this woman had learned from her mother that her dad was rotten. An eight-year-old is in those impressionable years—she tends to believe what she hears and accept what she sees. Although she loved her father, her mother's persistence eventually nurtured the deep-seated attitude that her father could not be trusted and from this grew the more general and pervasive attitude that *men in general should not be trusted.* A little girl grows up being able to trust a man in a close, intimate relationship by first of all being able to trust her father or father figure. The same is true for a boy—he learns to trust a woman in a close, intimate relationship by first of all being able to trust his mother or mother figure. Among other reasons, this is why children who experience broken homes need to be free to love both of their parents, unencumbered by negative editorial remarks from either of the parents judging the character of the other. Wise parents—married or unmarried—will look for the positive aspects in each other and pass those on. Kids have always been pretty good at picking up on parental flaws all by themselves.

Tensions, insecurities, lack of proper and available models for identification, hostilities, guilt feelings—all of these can follow in the wake of broken family units. To understand and identify the precise impact of death, separation, or divorce on any child, one needs to know how much love and understanding will continue after the action and how much real concern and affection remains for the youngster. In other words, does the child see the "brokenness" of the home as punishment and rejection or has the situation been handled with the sort of maturity and understanding that allows the child to retain his love and confidence in the parents? A basic condition for healthy self-concept development for children from broken homes lies in the fact that they are loved and *know* it—not the overindulging, overprotecting love of guilty parents trying to undo what they've done, but rather a love which allows them to grow up without feeling responsible for something they had no control over in the first place. One thing is for certain: *Ceasing to be a wife or a husband through separation or divorce does not mean that one has to stop being a parent.*

Toward Raising Children with High Self-Esteem

As we discussed in Chapter One, when we talk about self-esteem, we are referring to an individual's *personal* judgment of worthiness or unworthiness, approval or disapproval that are expressed in the attitudes he has about himself. Essentially, *high* self-esteem persons see themselves as valuable and important, as persons worthy of respect and consideration, who have a pretty definite idea of what they think is right. In addition, they are not afraid of a little risk-taking now and then in terms of doing something new and different, and they don't go to pieces when things don't go well right off the bat.

Low self-esteem persons are quite different. They usually don't see themselves as important or likeable, and, furthermore, don't see much reason for others to like them either. They do not view themselves as the sort who can do what they really want to do, nor do they believe they could do it very well even if they did try. Low self-esteem people prefer to stick to what's known and safe inasmuch as they don't believe they have much control over their lives anyway.

To be sure, there are plenty of people—young and old—who fall somewhere between these two descriptions. They don't exalt themselves, but they don't denigrate themselves either. The question is, how can we encourage children in the direction of high self-esteem?

Research[106, 107, 108] is rather clear in showing that the adult qualities most clearly associated with high self-esteem in children include warmth and caring, encouragement, some freedom for exploration, high expectations, and *firm* discipline. Coopersmith's[109] monumental investigation of the antecedents of self-esteem among 1700 fifth- and sixth-grade children also support these research findings. For example, he found that most notable antecedents of high self-esteem were directly related to parental behavior and the consequences of the rules and regulations that parents establish for their children. As an illustration, he noted that definite and consistently enforced limits on behavior were associated with high self-esteem; that families which maintained clear limits utilized less drastic forms of punishment; and that families producing high self-esteem children exerted greater demands for academic performance and excellence.

Sometimes parents have to be firm, which helps children to know where the limits
are and what is expected of them.

It should also be noted that parents of high self-esteem children had attitudes
of total or near total *acceptance* of their children and also allowed considerable
flexibility for individual behavior *within* the established limits.

Why firmness and clearly defined limits are associated with high self-esteem
can be explained in several ways. One, establishing a limit: "Yes, you can ride your
bike up to Tom's, but stay off the street," or "Yes, you can go out tonight, but
remember to be home by 10 o'clock," is an expression of *caring*, particularly if the
parent is viewed as warm, understanding, and autonomy-granting. If, on the other
hand, the parent is cold, distant, inconsistent, rejecting or some combination of
these behaviors, his limits are more likely to be seen as unfair ("All the other kids
are going."), or arbitrary ("Well, you let me do it yesterday."), or punitive ("You
never let me do anything!"). Indeed, research[110] indicates that when parents are
hostile *and* restrictive, they are apt to have children whose behavior is marked by
passivity, dependence, social withdrawal, and passive aggressiveness. When children are loved and accepted and know it, they are much more likely to interpret the
limits and discipline they are subjected to as expressions of caring. On the other
hand, children who are *not* accepted, usually interpret parental restrictions exactly
for what they are, namely, expressions of rejection and hostility. This is significant,
since high self-esteem is deeply rooted in the experience of *being* esteemed (valued,
prized) by others.

Secondly, clearly defined limits not only provide children with a basis for evaluating how well or poorly they're doing, but they also serve to define their social world in terms of what is safe and what is hazardous, what they can and cannot do. For example, if a child is supposed to stay off the street and does it, he *knows* he did right. If he's supposed to be in by ten o'clock and makes it, he *knows* he lived up successfully to an expectation. In other words, the existence of limits can leave the child with the feeling that a definition of his social environment is possible and that the world does impose restrictions and make demands and that he can learn to handle in everyday living. Parents who are less certain and more permissive about their standards are likely to have children who are not only more dependent on their parents (not knowing exactly what's expected, they may linger around longer waiting to be told), but more compliant with their peers. Another consideration is that if children have no limits to live up to, they are apt to be left with the feeling that everything they do is all right, which, in the long run, robs them of important practice opportunities in dealing with situations and circumstances when everything is *not* all right.

Coopersmith also found that parents who *expect* their children to live up to the standards they established were more likely to facilitate healthy growth than parents who do *not* have these expectancies. Expectations perform an important function. They not only represent a belief in a child's adequacy, but they also relay the message that he has the ability to do what is required of him. When set at reasonable levels, expectations represent the strongest vote of confidence possible. Self-esteem grows out of successfully doing those things we weren't too sure of being able to do in the first place, and if we have someone who believes in us, "expects that we can," then taking that first step is at least a bit easier.

Another important observation growing out of the Coopersmith study was that, although all parents wanted their children to be self-confident, some behaved as if they wanted this characteristic to exist only *after the children grew up and left home*. In the meantime they preferred to keep their children meek, submissive, and dependent. For example, how often have you heard parents make remarks such as these to their children: "Here, let me do that. You're so clumsy, you'll probably drop it." "No, no! Put the fork on the left side—can't you tell right from left?"

Such remarks reveal quite clearly a parent's desire, conscious or unconscious, to lower a child's self-esteem—at least for the present. Unfortunately, children who are thus belittled while they are small are all too likely to carry a crippling self-distrust with them into the adult world. Sometimes we adults fail to appreciate the idea that our initial and seemingly innocent *perceptions* ("You're so clumsy!"), when repeated enough times and in enough different ways, get converted in the child's mind to more powerful *conceptions* (I am clumsy.), which become part of a child's self-concept.

All in all, Coopersmith's study shows that self-esteem is a pervasive characteristic. Children and adolescents with a higher levels of self-esteem are apt to have parents who give them not only lots of attention and affection, but they also provide them with clear expectations, firm rules, and just punishments. This is exactly the sort of atmosphere that enables the youth in such homes to work hard and aspire to do their best, both necessary prerequisites for maintaining a healthy level of personal self-esteem.

A reasonable question at this point is whether there is a *pattern* of conditions necessary to produce high self-esteem, or whether there is any single condition or set of conditions which play a greater role than others. In answer to this question, Coopersmith observes:

> First and foremost, we should note that there are virtually no parental patterns of behavior or parental attitudes that are common to all parents of children with high self-esteem. Examinations of the major indices and scales of *acceptance, limit definition, respect, and parental self-esteem* provides explicit support for the view that not all of these conditions are essential for the formation of high self-esteem. . . . (The data) suggest that *combinations* of (these) conditions are required—more than one but less than the four established for this study. . . . In addition it is likely that a minimum of devaluating conditions—that is, rejection, ambiguity, and disrespect—is required if high self-esteem is to be attained.[111] [italics added.]

In Perspective

How a child behaves and what he becomes depend, in large measure, on how he was reared and the nature of his relationship to the adults who were primarily responsible for raising him. Indeed, how any of us feel about ourselves and others is linked to the relationships we had with our own mothers and fathers. The influence that parents can have on the lives of their children over a period of fifteen to eighteen years is incredible. Through the subtle, but powerful process of identification we are like our parents in ways which are beyond conscious recognition. No single day, or hour, or experience with our parents made a difference in our lives. Rather, it is the total of many days, and hours, and experiences strung together over many years that has shaped and formed the essence of our self-other attitudes. Whether parents are aware of it or not, through their daily life styles and the *consistency* of their behavior they teach their children how to blend, for better or worse, the basic ingredients for living—how to deal with anxiety, failure, how to handle money, make friends, *be* a friend, how to resolve conflicts and make decision, how to love and how to be loved.

Some parents—the wise ones—recognize that they begin to lose their children almost as soon as they get them. They have what you might call a "readiness to be forgotten" and are willing participants in their children's growth toward independence. They recognize that it is their task to help develop their children into the best kind of human beings they are capable of becoming; they also know that this will be their whole reward. Wise parents know that a child, as he matures, must first of all fall *out* of love with his own parents—and feel free to do so—before he can fall *in* love with another person and become, of all things, a parent himself.

Some parents—the not-so-wise ones—assume that a child "belongs" to them, like a thing. But a child is not a thing and can never be a possession. A child treated like a possession you do things to is robbed of many experiences, not the least of which is the experience of being valued for his humanness, for his capacity to feel and have emotions. Children raised as possessions by cold, detached, uninvolved parents may learn to *think* feelings, but they may be hard-pressed to know what it is to *have* feelings.

Research is telling us that healthy, balanced children who value themselves and others are likely to come from homes in which the parents respect and care for the children, each other, and themselves; where there are firm rules which are consistently enforced; and where there are high standards for behavior and performance which children are *expected* to live up to.

Raising children is a delicate process, but fortunately children are resilient enough to survive many foolish adult mistakes. Child-rearing involves many things, among which include the proper blend of encouraging growing youth to do those things they *can* do and pushing them in the direction of doing those things they *should* do. And perhaps, as adults, who supposedly know about such things, we ought to remember to encourage a growing child to *be* something in whatever route he chooses to *accomplish* something.

If I am interpreting the research and my own clinical experiences correctly, it would appear that the most deprived youth are those who have to do nothing to get what they want, while the most fortunate are those who are expected to work hard for what they want and in so doing, end up with a greater respect for both themselves and their efforts.

Notes

1. R. Sunley, "Early Nineteenth Century American Literature on Child Rearing," in M. Mead and M. Wolfenstein (Eds.), *Childhood in Contemporary Cultures*. Chicago: University of Chicago Press, 1955, pp. 150–167.
2. M. Wolfenstein, "The Emergence of Fun Morality," *Journal of Social Issues*. 1951, 7: 15–25.
3. J. B. Watson, *Psychological Care of Infant and Child*. New York: W. W. Norton & Company, Inc.) 1925, pp. 81–82, 87.
4. M. A. Ribble, *The Rights of Infants*. New York: Columbia University Press, 1943.
5. B. M. Spock, *Baby and Child Care*. New York: Pocket Books, 1947.
6. B. M. Spock, *Baby and Child Care: Revised and Enlarged*. New York: Pocket Books, 1957, p. 2.
7. B. Spock, "Don't Blame Me!" *Look Magazine*. January 26, 1971.

8. I. D. Harris, *Normal Children and Their Mothers*. New York: The Free Press, 1959.
9. M. J. Radke, *The Relation of Parental Authority to Children's Behavior and Attitudes*. Minneapolis: University of Minnesota Press, 1946.
10. W. C. Bronson, E. S. Kelton, and N. Livson, "Patterns of Authority and Affection in Two Generations," *Journal of Abnormal and Social Psychology*. 1959, 58: 143–152.
11. G. Handel, "Psychological Study of Whole Families," *Psychological Bulletin*. 1965, 63: 19–41.
12. M. L. Behrens, "Child Rearing and the Character Structure of the Mother," *Child Development*. 1954, 251: 225–238.
13. E. Fromm, "Selfishness and Self-Love," *Psychiatry*. 1939, 2: 507–523.
14. K. Horney, *Neurosis and Human Growth*. New York: W. W. Norton & Company, Inc. 1955.
15. G. R. Medinnus and F. J. Curtis, "The Relation between Maternal Self-Acceptance and Child Acceptance," *Journal of Consulting Psychology*. 1963, 27: 542–544.
16. S. Coopersmith, *The Antecedents of Self-Esteem*. San Francisco: W. H. Freeman and Co., Publishers, 1967, 96–117.
17. H. L. Bee, "Sex Differences: An Overview," in H. L. Bee (Ed.) *Social Issues in Development Psychology*. New York: Harper & Row, Publishers, 1974.
18. P. S. Sears, "Child-Rearing Factors Related to Playing of Sex-Typed Roles," *American Psychologist*. 1953, 8: 431 (abstract).
19. P. Mussen and E. Rutherford, "Parent-Child Relations and Parental Personality in Relation to Young Children's Sex-Role Preferences," *Child Development*. 1963, 34: 589–607.
20. R. W. Moulton, P. G. Liberty, Jr., E. Burnstein, and N. Altacher, "Patterning of Parental Affection and Disciplinary Dominance as a Determinant of Guilt and Sex-Typing," *Journal of Personality and Social Psychology*. 1966, 4: 456–463.
21. T. Parsons, "Family Structure and the Socialization of the Child," in T. Parsons and R. F. Bales (Eds.), *Family, Socialization, and Interaction Process*. New York: The Free Press, 1953, 35–131.
22. E. M. Hetherington, "A Developmental Study of the Effects of Sex of the Dominant Parent on Sex-Role Preference, Identification, and Imitation in Children," *Journal of Personality and Social Psychology*. 1965, 2: 188–194.
23. B. Sutton-Smith and B. G. Rosenberg, "Development of Sex Differences in Play Choices during Preadolescence," *Child Development*. 1960, 31: 307–311.
24. J. Chang and J. Block, "A Study of Identification in Male Homosexuals," *Journal of Consulting Psychology*. 1960, 24: 307–310.
25. D. J. West, "Parental Figures in the Genesis of Male Homosexuality," *International Journal of Social Psychiatry*. 1959, 5: 85–97.
26. D. G. Brown, "Homosexuality and Family Dynamics," *Bulletin of the Menninger Clinic*, 1963, 27: 227–232.
27. R. Green, "Children's Quest for Sexual Identity," *Psychology Today*. February 1974.
28. H. J. Jones and D. J. De L. Horne, "Psychiatric Disorders among Aborigines in the Australian Western Desert," *Social Science and Medicine*. 1973, 7: 219–227.
29. E. M. Hetherington, p. 188–194.
30. H. B. Biller and S. D. Weiss, "The Father-Daughter Relationship and the Personality Development of the Female," *Journal of Genetic Psychology*. 1970, 116: 79–93.
31. E. M. Hetherington and G. Franks, "Effects of Parental Dominance, Warmth, and

Conflict on Imitation in Children," *Journal of Personality and Social Psychology*. 1967, 6: 119–125.

32. E. M. Hetherington, "Girls without Fathers," *Psychology Today*. February, 1973: 47–52.

33. S. Fisher, *The Female Orgasm: Psychology, Physiology, Fantasy*. New York: Basic Books Inc., 1972.

34. E. Bene, "On the Genesis of Female Homosexuality," *British Journal of Psychiatry*. 1965, 3: 815–821.

35. H. E. Kaye, "Homosexuality in Women," *Archives of General Psychiatry*. 1967, 17: 626–634.

36. B. Lloyd and J. Archer (Eds.), *Exploring Sex Differences*. New York: Academic Press Inc., 1976.

37. C. Hutt, "Sex Differences in Human Development," *Human Development*. 1972, 15: 153–170.

38. D. Baumrind, "Authoritarian vs. Authoritative Parental Control," *Adolescence*. 1968, 3: 256–261.

39. D. Baumrind, "Current Patterns of Parental Authority," *Developmental Psychology Monographs*. 1971, 1: 1–103.

40. D. Baumrind, "Socialization and Instrumental Competence in Young Children," in W. W. Hartup (Ed.), *The Young Child*, vol. II. Washington, D.C.: National Association for the Education of Young Children, 1972, pp. 202–205.

41. A. E. Siegel and L. G. Kohn, "Permissiveness, Permission, and Aggression: The Effects of Adult Presence or Absence on Aggression in Children's Play," *Child Development*. 1959, 36: 131–141.

42. W. C. Becker, "Consequences of Different Kinds of Parental Discipline," in M. L. Hoffman and L. W. Hoffman (Eds.), *Review of Child Development Research*, vol. I. New York: Russell Sage Foundation, 1964, pp. 239–271.

43. D. Baumrind, "Child Care Practice Anteceding Three Patterns of Preschool Behavior," *Genetic Psychology Monographs*. 1967, 75: 43–88.

44. C. B. Stendler, "Critical Periods in Socialization and Overdependency," *Child Development*. 1952, 23: 3–17.

45. E. H. Erikson, *Childhood and Society*, 2nd ed., New York: W. W. Norton & Company, Inc. 1963.

46. F. L. Gewirtz, "A Factor Analysis of Some Attention-Seeking Behavior of Young Children," *Child Development*. 1956, 27: 17–36.

47. S. W. Olds, "When Mommy Goes to Work," *Family Health*. February, 1977: 38–40.

48. H. Bee, *The Developing Child*. New York: Harper & Row, Publishers, 1975: 247–248.

49. T. Moore, "Children of Part-Time and Full-Time Mothers," *International Journal of Social Psychiatry*. 1964, 2: 1–10.

50. Stendler, p. 8.

51. C. B. Stendler, "Possible Causes of Over-dependency in Young Children," *Child Development*. 1954, 25: 125–146.

52. R. R. Sears, E. E. Maccoby, and H. Levin, *Patterns of Child Rearing*. Evanston, Ill.: Row, Peterson & Company, 1957.

53. W. McCord, J. McCord, and P. Verden, "Familial and and Behavioral Correlates of Dependency in Male Children," *Child Development*. 1962, 33: 313–326.

54. G. Heathers, "Emotional Dependence and Independence in a Physical Threat Situation," *Child Development*. 1953, 24: 169–179.

55. W. J. Mueller, "Need Structure and the Projection of Traits Onto Parents," *Journal of Personality and Social Psychology*. 1966, 3: 63–72.

56. B. R. McCandless, C. B. Bilous, and H. L. Bennett, "Peer Popularity and Dependence on Adults in Preschool Age Socialization," *Child Development*. 1961, 32: 511–518.

57. S. Moore and R. Updegraff, "Sociometric Status of Preschool Children Related to Age, Sex, Nurturance-Giving, and Dependency," *Child Development*. 1964, 35: 519–524.

58. D. Katz, "TV Helps To Spread Epidemic of Violence," *Detroit Free Press*. May 2, 1976.

59. Sears, Maccoby, and Levin, pp. 218–269.

60. B. R. McCandless, and C. Balsbaugh, and H. L. Bennett, "Preschool-Age Socialization and Maternal Control Techniques," *American Psychologist*. 1958, 13: 320 (abstract).

61. M. E. Rosenbaum and R. F. Stanners, "Self-Esteem, Manifest Hostility, and Expression of Hostility," *Journal of Abnormal and Social Psychology*. 1961, 63: 646–649.

62. Coopersmith, p. 137.

63. Sears, Maccoby, and Levin, pp. 218–269.

64. C. L. Winder, and L. Rau, "Parental Attitudes Associated with Social Deviance in Preadolescent Boys," *Journal of Abnormal and Social Psychology*. 1962, 64: 418–424.

65. A. Bandura, "The Role of the Modeling Process in Personality Development," in W. W. Hartup and N. L. Smothergill (Eds.), *The Young Child*. Washington, D.C.: National Association for the Education of Young Children, 1967, pp. 42–58.

66. Sears, Maccoby, and Levin, pp. 218–269.

67. L. D. Eron, L. R. Huesmann, M. M. Lefkowitz, and L. O. Walder, "Does Television Violence Cause Aggression?" *American Psychologist*. April, 1972: 263.

68. R. M. Liebert and J. M. Neale, "TV Violence and Child Ag. ssion: Show on the Screen," *Psychology Today*. April 1972: 39.

69. R. S. Drabman and M. H. Thomas, "Does TV Violence Breed Indifference?" *Journal of Communication*. Autumn, 1975: 86–89.

70. J. Piaget, *The Psychology of Intelligence*. London: Routledge & Kegan Paul Ltd., 1950.

71. D. Hicks, "Imitation and Retention of Film-mediated Aggressive Peer and Ault Models," *Journal of Personality and Social Psychology*. 1965. 2: 97–100.

72. J. Kagen and H. A. Moss, *Birth to Maturity: A Study in Psychological Development*. New York: John Wiley & Sons, Inc., 1962.

73. T. Gordon, *Parent-Effectiveness Training*. New York: Wyden, 1970.

74. H. Ginott, *Teacher and Child*. New York: The Macmillan Company, 1972.

75. A. T. Jersild, *Child Psychology* (6th ed.). Englewood Cliffs, New Jersey: Prentice-Hall Inc., 1968, p. 512.

76. J. Piaget, *The Moral Judgment of the Child*. London: Routledge & Kegan Paul Ltd., 1932.

77. Sears, Maccoby, and Levin, pp. 376–381.

78. F. Redl and D. Wineman, *Children Who Hate*. New York: The Free Press, 1951, pp. 145–156.

79. P. Mussen and L. Distler, "Child-Rearing Antecedents of Masculine Identification in

Kindergarten Boys," *Child Development.* 1960, 31: 89–100.

80. A. Stein, "Imitation of Resistance to Temptation," *Child Development.* 1967, 38: 157–169.

81. Sears, Maccoby, and Levine, pp. 376–381.

82. S. Schacter, "Birth-Order, Eminence, and Higher Education," *American Sociological Review.* 1963, 28: 757–767.

83. W. Altus, "Birth Order and Academic Primogeniture," *Journal of Personality and Social Psychology.* 1965, 2: 872–876.

84. S. R. Warren, "Birth Order and Social Behavior," *Psychological Bulletin.* 1966, 65: 38–49.

85. L. Forer, *The Birth Order Factor.* New York: David McKay Co., Inc., 1976.

86. R. L. Adams and B. N. Phillips, "Motivational and Achievement Differences among Children of Various Ordinal Birth Positions," *Child Development.* 1972, 43: 155–164.

87. P. S. Very and R. W. Prull, "Birth Order, Personality Development, and Choice of Law as a Profession," *The Journal of Genetic Psychology.* 1970, 116: 219–221.

88. J. K. Lasko, "Parent Behavior toward First and Second Children," *Genetic Psychology and Monographs.* 1954, 49: 96–137.

89. E. Chen and S. Cobb, "Family Structure in Relation to Health and Disease: A Review of the Literature." *Journal of Chronic Diseases.* 1960, 12: 544–567.

90. R. E. Nisbett and S. Schachter, "Cognitive Manipulation of Pain," *Journal of Experimental Social Psychology.* 1966, 2: 227–236.

91. R. E. Nisbett, "Birth Order and Participation in Dangerous Sports,: *Journal of Personality and Social Psychology.* 1968, 8: 351–353.

92. R. Zimbardo and R. Formica, "Emotional Comparison and Self-Esteem as Determinents of Affiliation," *Journal of Personality.* 1963, 31: 141–162.

93. J. A. Clausen, "Family Structure Socialization and Personality," in H. W. Hoffman and M. L. Hoffman (Eds.), *Review of Child Development Research,* vol. 2. New York: Russell Sage Foundation, 1966, pp. 1–53.

94. E. Douvan and J. Adelson, *The Adolescent Experience.* New York: John Wiley & Sons, Inc., 1966.

95. N. Miller and G. Maruyama, "Ordinal Position and Peer Popularity," *Journal of Personality and Social Psychology.* 1976, 33: 123–131.

96. R. Kramer, "A Fresh Look at the Only Child," *New York Times Magazine.* October 13, 1972.

97. W. Toman, "Birth Order Rules All," *Psychology Today.* December 1970.

98. Toman, p. 45.

99. *Congressional Record,* January 4, 1977, E4.

100. William J. Goode, "Family Disorganization," in R. K Merton and R. A. Nisbet (Eds.), *Contemporary Social Problems.* Harcourt, Brace and World, Inc., 1966, pp. 425–426.

101. F. I. Nye, "Child Adjustment in Broken and in Unhappy Homes," *Marriage and Family Living.* 1957, 19: 356–361.

102. L. G. Burchinal, "Characteristics of Adolescents from Unbroken, Broken, and Reconstituted Families," *Journal of Marriage and the Family.* February 1964: 44–51.

103. J. T. Landis, "The Trauma of Children When Parents Divorce," *Marriage and Family Living.* 1960, 22: 7–13.

104. T. S. Langner and S. T. Michael, *Life Stress and Mental Health*. New York: The Free Press, 1963.

105. C. E. Bowerman and D. P. Irish, "Some Relationships of Step-Children to Their Parents," *Marriage and Family Living*. 1962, 24: 113–121.

106. D. Baumrind, "Parental Control and Parental Love," *Children*. 1965, 12: 230–234.

107. R. R. Sears, "Relationships of Early Socialization Experiences to Self-Concepts and Gender Role in Middle Childhood," *Child Development*. 1970, 41: 267–286.

108. B. L. White and J. C. Watts. *Experience and Environment: Major Influences on the Development of the Young Child*, vol. I. Englewood Cliffs, N.J.: Prentice-Hall Inc., 1973.

109. Coopersmith, pp. 235–264.

110. W. C. Becker, D. R. Peterson, Z. Luria, D. J. Shoemaker, and L. A. Hellmer, "Relations of Factors Derived from Parent-Interview Ratings to Behavior Problems of Five-Year-Olds," *Child Development*. 1962, vol. 33, pp. 631–648.

111. Coopersmith, pp. 239–240.

References of Related Interest

Biller, H., and D. Meredith, *Father Power*. New York: David McKay Co., Inc. 1975.

Clarke-Steward, K. A., "Interactions between Mothers and Their Young Children: Characteristics and Consequences," *Monographs of the Society for Research in Child Development*. 1973, vol. 38.

Corsini, R. J., and G. Painter, *The Practical Parent*. New York: Harper & Row, Publishers, 1975.

Ginott, Haim, *Between Parent and Child*. New York: The Macmillan Company, 1965.

Ginott, Haim, *Between Parent and Teenager*. New York: The Macmillan Company, 1965.

Henderson, R. W., and J. R. Bergan, *The Cultural Context of Childhood*. Columbus, Ohio: Charles E. Merrill Publishing Co., 1976, Chapters 11, 12.

Horowitz, F. D. (Eds.), *Child Development Research*, Vol. 4. Chicago: University of Chicago Press, 1975.

Johnson, R. C., and G. R. Medinnus, *Child Psychology: Behavior and Development* (3rd Ed.). New York: John Wiley & Sons, Inc., 1974, Section III.

Lamb, E. M., *The Role of the Father in Child Development*. New York: John Wiley & Sons, Inc., 1976.

Robertiello, R., *Hold Them Very Close, then Let Them Go*. New York: The Dial Press, 1976.

Rosenberg, B. G., and B. Sutton-Smith, *Sex and Identity*. New York: Holt, Rinehart and Winston, 1972.

Salk, L., *What Every Child Would Like His Parents To Know*. New York: David McKay Co., Inc., 1972.

Stone, L. S., and J. Church, *Childhood and Adolescence* (3rd ed.). New York: Random House, Inc., 1973.

Turner, R. H., *Family Interaction*. New York: John Wiley & Sons, Inc., 1970.

Self-Concept, School Achievement, Academic Adjustment, and Implications for Teaching Practices

PROLOGUE

The way we think about ourselves is closely related to our ability to learn and to achieve academically. Some persons, for example, have trouble with school work or their life's work, not necessarily because of low intelligence or poor hearing or even poor motivation, but because they have learned to consider themselves as unable or inadequate. For instance, if a student says," I'll *never* pass that test, I just know it," he is telling us something rather important about his inner feelings of powerlessness and intellectual impotency. All things being equal, chances are fairly good that a student with this attitude probably *will not* do well on the test. We are beginning to understand that how people perform in school—or anyplace else for that matter—depends not only on how capable they actually *are,* but also on how capable they *feel* they are.

Basically, the self has two aspects—concept and feeling. That is, we know ourselves to have particular qualities, but, more importantly, we have certain feelings about those qualities. For example, a student may "know" that her measured IQ is, say, 115, but unless she has sufficient self-confidence and belief in herself to act on her intelligence, her 115 IQ is a practically useless possession. What we *have* by way of personal qualities is far less important than how we *feel* about those qualities.

What is the impact of school failure on the development of self-concept and self-esteem? Is there a relationship between self-concept and academic achievement? How much of an influence do child-rearing practices have on a youngster's academic self-concept? Do teacher expectations really influence achievement outcomes? What teaching practices are most conducive to healthy self-concept development? It is to these and related questions that we will address ourselves in this chapter.

Let us begin by looking at a school experience that can have absolutely devastating consequences for millions of school-age youth.

Effect of Early School Failure on Self-Image Development

In a land where education is so highly valued and so much the key to one's personal advancement and society's total growth, it is a curious and sad paradox to note that approximately one-third of those students who start first grade will drop out before reaching the eleventh grade.[1] If history repeats itself, as it has a knack for doing, these students will drop out not because of a sudden whim or capricious impulse, but because of more or less continuous exposure to failure experiences that reinforce feelings of worthlessness and inadequacy. On the average, almost one million young people leave school each year. One of the first explanations for this staggering number is that those who drop out are ones who cannot benefit from educational experiences anyway. Were it that simple. The fact is that well over half those who drop out have average mental ability. For example, in a U.S. Department of Labor study of seven widely dispersed, middle-sized cities, 6 percent of the dropouts were found to have IQs (intelligence quotients) over 110 and 55 percent had IQs over 90.[2] This means that the majority of those who dropped out had the necessary intellectual equipment to complete high school.

Too Much Failure Leads to Low Self-Esteem and Possible Dropping Out

The question is: Why do so many young people drop out of school? Some, we know, leave because they're bored. Others leave because they're angry or emotion-

© 1974 United Feature Syndicate, Inc.

Attitudes like Patty's frequently precede a student's eventual decision to drop out of school.

ally disturbed or both, and it is doubtful whether any school program—no matter how good—could hold them. The great majority, however, drop out because they simply cannot tolerate more failure and the commensurate feelings of low self-worth and self-esteem. This being the case, it should come as no surprise to note that one of the major findings of a four-year study of dropouts was that dropouts' self-esteem got *higher* once they were out of school.[3] In fact, measures of self-esteem of those who graduated were not much higher than those who dropped out. What a sorry commentary it is to think that students must leave school in order to feel better about themselves. And what a tragedy it is to find, as several studies have, that almost half of those who drop out cite adverse school experiences and negative feelings about themselves as their reasons for leaving the educational fold.[4,5]

How extensive is the experience of school failure? Consider some of the evidence:

a. Of those students dropping out between grades eight and nine in a Kentucky school system, all had experienced failing a grade at least once and over four-fifths had experienced failing two grades.[6]

b. Out of 2,000 children who began first grade at the same time in the same school system, 643 dropped out before completing high school. All but five of these dropouts, 638, or 99 percent, had been retained in the first grade. As a combined total, these 643 students failed a total of more than 1,800 grades during their first six years of school. This averages out for each dropout failing every other year for six years![7]

c. Over 74 percent of the dropouts in one school system repeated at least one grade as compared to only 18 percent among students who graduated from high school.[8]

d. More than 1,200 students in grades 6 and 7 from 14 representative schools in a North Carolina study were investigated to differentiate between repeaters and nonrepeaters. Results showed that those who had not been retained were reading at 6.8 grade level; those repeating one grade scored a 5.2 level, and those who had repeated two or more grades dropped to a 4.5 grade level. On mathematics achievement, nonrepeaters averaged in the 27th percentile; those repeating one grade in the 10th percentile; and those repeating two or more grades dropped to the 5th percentile. All in all, the data do not indicate that retention helps a student "catch up" academically—the usual justification for having students repeat. Failing was also found to have a strong influence on a student's feeling of self-worth. For example, on all the subscales of the *Tennessee Self-Concept Scale,* students who repeated grades scored lower than those who had not. Students repeating two or more grades scored far below the mean on each subscale.[9]

Not All Drop Out—Some Stay, but Suffer

I have stressed the dropout problem to this point because it is one very explicit and dramatic consequence of failure experiences that occur too early and too frequently among those who leave school. What we haven't mentioned are those hundreds of thousands of children who are victimized by excessive early school failure experiences but who do not choose so dramatic an exit as dropping out. Rather, they persist on through school, suffering quietly and inwardly, and eventually graduate into a competitive society that demands not only a reasonable level of competence in some kind of work, but also a certain degree of confidence in one's ability to do the work. Unfortunately, thousands of young people graduate after thirteen years of school feeling somewhat helpless, hopeless, and defeated. Feelings like these, whether among those who drop out because they can't tolerate more failure or among those who stay in and suffer through it, start during the elementary school years.

For example, although studies indicate that approximately 70 percent of all dropouts complete at least a ninth-grade education, there is increasing evidence to show that the negative attitudes about school and thoughts about leaving it begin early in a child's school experiences. Wolfbein concluded from a series of dropout studies that

> . . . the problems which finally result in a dropout begin, and are quite overt, way back in elementary grades. In fact, it is quite early in grade school that many of the potential dropouts begin to fall behind in their scholastic achievements. . . .[10]

In an intensive study of forty-five girls and sixty boys who were about to drop out of school, Lichter[11] found that the reason was not the result of any specific learning failure, but rather a broad educational disability that, for boys in particular, started in elementary school. Why is elementary school so crucial? Let's turn our attention to this.

Why Is Elementary School Success so Crucial?

Success experiences for elementary school youngsters are important because they can be numbered among those positive early happenings upon which an increasingly more complex psychological superstructure can be built. In order to build a firm house, we give it a firm foundation that rests squarely on solid ground. The same is true for the human psyche. In order for it to be strong, it must begin with a firm foundation. Some adults, as we all know, have very shaky foundations, and these must be repaired before further growth is possible. The point I'm trying to make is that what happens to children during their elementary school years is critical because these are their foundation laying years. Everything that happens to them is incorporated as part of the basic personality formation that occurs, as far as school is concerned at least, during the years from five to twelve, or grades one through six. These are the years when the roots of a child's personality are either firmly established in experiences of success, accomplishment, and pride in himself or flimsily planted in shifting sands of self-doubt, failure, and feelings of worthlessness. There are at least three reasons why the elementary years are so crucial for a growing child.

1. *The elementary child's self-system is incomplete and impressionable.* Elementary age children are in the early phases of forming a concept of self. This is not to say that they have no sense of identity whatsoever, but it is to suggest that the sense of who they are and what they can do is incompletely formed. Characteristically, elementary age youngsters are malleable and impressionable. They are not only ready to please adults, but to *believe* them as well. Indeed, what adults say about them or how they evaluate either their person or performance is incorporated more readily, more easily, and more uncritically than at any other stage during their developmental years. This means that the feedback a child receives from peers and adults—particularly significant adults like parents and teachers—is more likely to have a greater impact because it is more readily absorbed into a developing self-system, which, precisely because it is still developing and incomplete, is more open to input and more available to change.

2. *Elementary age children have immature defenses—they are vulnerable.* Elementary school age children are not well defended psychologically. In the absence of a consolidated and reasonably well-integrated self-image, they are less likely to use active and assertive mechanisms such as denial or projection in order to protect themselves from ego-damaging experiences and more likely to use the passive and more primitive mechanism of regression, which allows them to stay at a safer and more dependent level of development. (Indeed, whether in children or

adults, regressive behavior is not an uncommon phenomenon following failure experiences.) In order for defense mechanisms to be effective, first of all one has to have a reasonably well-defined self to begin with. This is not to suggest that the elementary age child is totally incapable of compensating for his failure or displacing his anger or projecting blame for poor work on the teacher. It is a matter of degree. If a second grader fails a spelling test, he is more likely to "believe" that mark (this is, incorporate it, internalize it) than a twelfth-grade girl with a positive view of herself and a history of doing well in school, who fails a geometry test. The twelfth grader can blame her performance on a fluke, deny its importance, rationalize her lack of study, or project it on her teacher. As long as her performance is inconsistent with her concept of self, she can defend herself against the loss of self-esteem. The second grader, on the other hand, does not yet have a well-defined self with which he can or has to be consistent. Hence, whether it is a failure or success experience, the elementary age children are less resistant to its impact and more susceptible to its consequences.

Simply put, elementary age children do not yet have a consolidated self-system to serve as the framework within which they can evaluate another person's evaluations of them. For example, if you say something negative about me, I must first of all have some idea of who I am (a consolidated self-system) in order to evaluate what the meaning of your comment is for me.

3. *The elementary child is still in the "industry versus inferiority" stage.* The six to twelve-year-old age group represents a growth phase that psychiatrist Erik Erikson[12] refers to as the "industry versus inferiority" stage. In other words, this is a natural time in children's growth and development when they learn to be either industrious, productive, and autonomous, or inferior-feeling, withdrawn, and dependent. The major danger of this period, as Erikson sees it, is the development of a sense of inadequacy and inferiority in children who do not receive recognition for their efforts. The kind of feedback that children receive from adults who are important to them at this point in their lives—parents and teachers particularly—can have an incredible impact, for better or for worse.

Stabilization of School Achievement Begins Early

Sometimes those children who have many failure experiences in elementary school are difficult not to fail precisely because of their general slowness or recalcitrant behavior. On the other hand, they are precisely the children who should not fail, particularly at a time in their lives when they are most susceptible to its effects. Longitudinal research findings indicate that there is something like a critical period for the formation of abilities and attitudes for school learning that occurs, or is set or stabilized, sometime between the ages of five and nine. For example, Bloom's[13] surveys of longitudinal research suggest that adolescent or adult intelligence is about 50 percent stabilized or predictable by the first grade, whereas adolescent school *achievement* is predictable to the same extent only at age nine or about the end of grade three. This means that factors that contribute to school achievement other than intelligence are to a considerable extent stabilized during the first three grades. In large measure, these factors are sheer skill factors, which are cumulative in nature. That is, if a child has more skills in the first grade, he accumulates further skills in the second, and more in the third, and so on. Again, Kolberg makes an observation that needs to be stressed at this juncture:

> In large part, however, this stabilization of school achievement is based on the stabilization of factors of interest in learning, attention, and *sense of competence*.[14] (italics added)

What all this points to is the establishment during the early school years of an attitudinal set that can have either a positive or negative valence and that can influence, for good or evil, subsequent school achievement. Apparently, a child's feelings about his ability to do school work are rooted in his early school experiences and these determine, to a great extent, both the intensity and direction of his emerging self-image as a student.

When it comes to assessing the importance of early success experiences for later adult behavior, Bower has observed:

> . . . there is an increasing clinical research and empirical evidence to support the hypothesis that children who find healthful satisfactions in relationships with family, neighborhood, and school will as adults find these same satisfactions; and that the children who find frustration and defeat in these primary institutions also tend to be defeated as adults.[15]

There is, in other words, a certain consistency in behavior that persists over time, an idea worth our brief consideration.

Self-Consistency as Related to School Achievement

Whether we are conscious of it or not, we each have a certain mental blueprint that we carry about with us. It may be vague and ill-defined, but it is there, complete down to the last detail. The blueprint is composed of a system of interrelated ideas, attitudes, values, and commitments that are influenced by our past experiences, our successes and failures, our humiliations, our triumphs, and the way other people reacted to us, especially during our formative years. Eventually, we each arrive at a more or less stable framework of beliefs about ourselves and proceed to live in as consistent a manner as possible within that framework. In short, we "act like" the sort of person we conceive ourselves to be. Indeed, it is extremely difficult to act otherwise, in spite of a strong conscious effort and exercise of will power. The girl, for example, who conceives herself to be a "failure-type student" can find all sorts of excuses to avoid studying, doing homework, or participating in class. Frequently, she ends up with the low grade she predicted she would get in the first place. Her report card bears her out. Now she has "proof" that she's less able! Or, as another example, the socially isolated boy who has an image of himself as the sort of person nobody likes may find that he is indeed avoided by others. What he does not understand is that he may behave in a style that literally invites rejection. His dour expression, his hangdog manner, his own overzestfulness to please, or perhaps this unconscious hostility towards those he anticipates will affront him may all act to drive away those who might otherwise be friendly.

Because of this objective "proof," it seldom occurs to a person that his trouble lies in his own evaluation of himself. If you tell a student that he only "thinks" he cannot grasp algebra, or English, or reading, or whatever, he may very well give you that "Who are you trying to kid?" look. In his own way, he may have tried again and again, but still his report card tells the story. A request (more often a demand or admonishment) destined to fall on deaf ears is the one parents and teachers frequently make of some students to "study harder." This is fine if the student already has a high self-concept and high need for achievement, because he is likely to respond to the challenge in order to produce at a level consistent with his self-image. However, for a student whose self-picture is that of being a poor student, the impact is lost. As a low-concept, low-achieving ninth-grader girl once told me, "Study? Ha! Why should I study to fail?"

Although we may not like this girl's flip answer, it is important to understand that from her point of view it was a perfectly logical conclusion. She saw herself as fairly dumb and of course dumb people don't do well. So why study? She was expressing a need that all of us have, namely the need to maintain an intact self-structure so that the person we are today can be counted on as being pretty much the same person tomorrow. Again, we should remind ourselves that *this consistency is not voluntary or deliberate, but compulsive, and generally unconsciously motivated.*

It is important to keep the self-consistency idea in mind because it will help us to understand better the relationship between school performance and self-concept. *Once a student "locks in" on a perception of what he is and is not able to do, it is difficult to shake him from it, particularly if the perception has time to root itself into a firmly established belief.*

A pioneer in the area of relating self-consistency to school performance was Prescott Lecky,[16] who was one of the first to point out that low academic achievement may be related to a student's conception of himself as being unable to learn academic material. He observed, for example, that some students made the same number of errors in spelling per page no matter how difficult or easy the material. These students spelled as though they were responding to a built-in upper limit beyond which they could not go. It occurred to Lecky that they were responding more in terms of how they *thought* they could spell than in terms of their actual spelling abilities. He arranged to have a group of these students spend some time with the counselor who helped them explore their feelings about their spelling abilities. As a consequence of these discussions and despite the fact that these students had no additional work in spelling whatever, there was a notable improvement in their spelling! There was less improvement for some children than for others, but the general trend was in the direction of better spelling. One can only speculate about the dynamics at work here, but it does not seem unreasonable to suggest that as spelling *confidence increased, so, too, did spelling skills.* In other words, as they acquired new perceptions of their spelling abilities, they also acquired new consistencies, which is to say that, as a student moves from believing he is a poor speller to believing he is at least a better speller than he thought he was, his performance changes in the direction of being consistent with his new perception. Discussion of this sort inevitably leads people to ask. . . . .

The Chicken or The Egg Question

Which comes first, a positive self-concept or high achievement? It is not possible to give a definitive answer to this question because the fact is that we just don't know for sure. Although one could argue that a student would first have to have a positive self-image in order to do well in school, the flip side of that argument is that doing well must precede a positive self-concept rather than follow it. In fact, there's some evidence to support the argument's flip side from research done by Shore, Massimo,

© 1973 United Feature Syndicate, Inc.

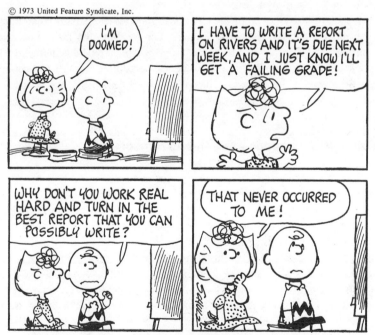

Charlie Brown not only has a good point, but it is probably the best thing that one can do to turn a low academic self-image into a more positive one.

and Ricks,[17] who found that, among delinquents at least, changes in competence preceded changes in self-concept. They further noted that this change was then followed by improvement in social behavior and adjustment.

Even though it is not possible to specify exactly which came first, good school work or high self-regard, *it does not seem unreasonable to suggest that each is mutually reinforcing to the other to the extent that a positive change in one facilitates a positive change in the other.* That is, if a child begins school with a low level of self-confidence and self-regard but experiences success almost in spite of himself, we could reasonably expect that his concept of self as far as school ability is concerned will be elevated. In fact, there is research evidence to suggest that persons who initially are the least confident in their ability to do well or to even complete a particular task end up feeling the most satisfied upon completing something they didn't think they could do in the first place.[18] In other words, unexpected success can do great things for a student's ego, whether he is in first grade, high school or college, and this in turn makes him feel more confident, which then gets translated into higher self-imposed expectations that he strives harder to live up to. On the other hand, an equally plausible possibility is that if a student begins school with high confidence in his ability to do school work and experiences excessive failure his concept of self may be lowered. When this happens, he will either have to shift his attention to other areas, usually nonacademic, to maintain his self-esteem, or continue to lose self-confidence and self-esteem.

Fortunately, the chicken or the egg question is more academic than practical. If we get too caught up in deciding which comes first, we may miss the real issue—namely, the student, who he or she is and where he or she is in development.

There seems little doubt but that students' perceptions of self and school can influence achievement for better or for worse. The question is, how much and in what ways? Let's turn our attention to this.

Students' Perceptions of Self and School

Students—all ages—not only learn about things and ideas in school, but they also learn about themselves. Unfortunately, thousands upon thousands learn an "I can't" rather than an "I can" attitude as they progress through school. In 1971, for example, 800,000 students[19] did not even finish high school—many because of the "I can't, so why try?" attitude.

As we have seen earlier in this chapter, the negative effects of a poor self-image on academic performance begin their toll early in the elementary years. Even though a student's self-perceptions start out on a positive note, this is no guarantee that they will end up that way. For example, Morse[20] found that to a statement like "I feel pretty sure of myself," 12 percent of the third-graders say "unlike me," while 34 percent of the eleventh-graders make that response. Morse further reported that 84 percent of the third-graders were proud of their school work, while this was true for only 53 percent of the eleventh-graders. In the elementary grades, 93 percent feel they are doing the best they can, but only 37 percent of the seniors can say the same thing. Morse concluded with the observation that "the general impression one gets is that for the young child, school is a secure place with regard to mental health, but as they grow older this confidence diminishes."

Another study, designed to assess over 1200 students' perceptions of school, teachers' skills, self, and student-teacher relations in grades six through twelve, found some interesting differences in perception when students' sex and grades received were taken into account.[21] The major conclusions were as follows: (1) Girls have generally more positive attitudes about school than boys; (2) Girls' perceptions about school and themselves become increasingly more positive as they progress from grade six to grade twelve, while boys' attitudes become more negative; (3) Girls consistently report receiving higher grades than boys from grade six through grade twelve. Understandably, things get brighter and better for those who get mostly A's and B's as they progress through school.

The finding that A–B students have more positive perceptions about school is not surprising, particularly in light of the preferential treatment they usually receive from teachers. For example, DeGroot and Thompson[22] found that teachers give more praise to the youngsters who are brighter, better adjusted, and higher achievers. Less capable students were observed by these investigators to receive more disapproval from their teachers.

The finding that female students have more positive perceptions is also not surprising in view of what other studies have uncovered. Carter[23] for instance, reported that girls are more likely to get higher grades than boys of *equal ability and achievement*. In addition, the results of another investigation found that boys received reliably more disapproval from their teachers than the girls.[24]

In sum, research related to students' perceptions of school indicate that, in general, perceptions become more negative as students move into the upper grades. On the other hand, if the student is a girl and bright to boot, then the total school experience is likely to be fairly positive. If, however, the student is a boy, and not so bright, then the total school experience is more likely to include negative perceptions about self, school, and teachers. Which leads us to an important consideration.

Self-Concept and Relationship
to Academic Achievement

There is a mounting body of evidence to suggest that how a student performs in school is influenced in both subtle and obvious ways by his concept of self. In his investigation of the role of self-concept in achievement, Roth concluded: ". . . in terms of their conception of self, individuals have a definite investment to perform as they do. With all things being equal, those who do not achieve, *choose* to do so."[25] The "choice" Roth is talking about is not necessarily a conscious choice, but rather a choice which is unconsciously motivated by a need to achieve at a level which is consistent with one's current self-perceptions. For example, some students—and adults, too, for that matter—choose not to read very much in favor of watching television because they view themselves as poor readers or at least as slow ones. Now the fact is, they may be poor or slow readers, as the case may be, but when they watch television over reading a paper or a good book *they are making a choice*. The reasons behind the choice may be unconscious, but it is a choice. Each time a poor or slow reader makes a choice in favor of watching television over reading a book, that person reaffirms a belief he or she started out with in the first place—I can't read very well.'' In little ways like this, a negative self-image can be self-perpetuating.

Speaking of reading, this is one school activity that is very much related to self-concept.

Reading Skills Adversely Affected by a Low Self-Image

There is evidence to suggest that a low or negative self-concept can adversely affect a child's reading skills beginning at a very young age. For example, Wattenberg and Clifford[26] found that an unfavorable view of self and poor achievement is already established in many children before they even enter first grade. In a study that included 128 kindergarten students in two schools, they measured intelligence, self-concept, ego-strength, and reading ability of all the students when they were in kindergarten and then again when these same students finished second grade. What they found was that measures of self-concept and ego-strength made at the beginning of kindergarten were more predictive of reading ability two and one-half years later than were measures of intelligence. In other words, the self-attitudes of kindergarten students were a more accurate indication of their potential reading skills than intelligence test scores. We cannot, however, assume from this finding that there is no relationship between mental ability and reading achievement. All we can safely conclude is that a measure of kindergarten students' self-concept and ego-strength is a better predictor of how they might fare in their reading skills by the third grade than is a measure of their intelligence. In addition, we should also keep in mind that a five-year-old's verbal skills are usually not sufficiently developed to be measured with great accuracy, which may be one reason why Wattenberg found a low relationship between intelligence and later reading achievement.

Wattenberg and Clifford are by no means alone in their conclusions. In a later study by Lamy,[27] which investigated the relationship between kindergarten children's perceptions of themselves and their subsequent reading in the first grade, it was found that self-perceptions gave as good a prediction of later reading achievement as intelligence test scores. Lamy went on to suggest that the perceptions children have about themselves are not only related to, but may in fact be causal factors in, their subsequent reading achievement.

In another investigation, the personality characteristics and attitudes toward achievement of two groups of fourth- and fifth-grade children differentiated in reading ability were analyzed. Subjects in this study consisted of seventy-one "poor" readers and eighty-two "good" readers equated as nearly as possible for age, sex, ethnic composition, and intelligence. As compared to the poor reader, the good reader was found to be more apt to describe himself as "well adjusted and motivated by internalized drives which result in effortful and persistent striving for success." This is in contrast to the picture presented by poor readers, who, according to the investigators, ". . . willingly admit to feelings of discouragement, inadequacy, and nervousness, and whose proclaimed goals are often emphermeral or immediate—especially in avoiding achievement."[28] The results of this study are consistent with Bodwin's,[29] who found a significant positive relationship between immature, low self-concepts and reading disabilities among students in the third and sixth grades.

The relationship between reading ability and self-concept is a tricky issue— one of those true chicken or egg questions. Each cannot help but influence the other. We would probably be well-advised to not worry unduly about which comes first, but to concern outselves with helping any person with a reading problem to improve *both* his reading skills *and* self-concept.

Underachievement as Related to Self-Concept

In an investigation to explore possible relationships between academic under-achievement and self-concept, Fink[30] studied a group of ninth-grade students, which included twenty pairs of boys and twenty-four pairs of girls. They were matched for IQs (all in the 90 to 110 range), and each individual student was judged as under-achiever or achiever depending on whether his grade point average fell below or above the class median. One achiever and one under-achiever made up each pair. The self-image of each student was rated as adequate or inadequate by three separate psychologists, based on data from three personality tests, a personal data sheet, and a student essay: "What I will be in twenty years." The combined ratings of the three psychologists showed significant differences between achievers and under-achievers, with achievers being rated as far more adequate in their concepts of self. Fink concluded that there was a strong significant negative relationship between self-concept and academic under-achievement, and further, that this relationship was stronger for boys than for girls. In view of the fact that boys are more likely than girls to acquire negative perceptions of themselves and school, Fink's conclusion does not seem surprising.

Later research by Campbell[31] supports the conclusions reached in the study cited above, but this time with fourth-, fifth-, and sixth-grade children. Among other things, the author found a direct relationship between self-concept and academic achievement and also noted that girls were more inclined to have a higher self-concept than boys.

Walsh[32] conducted a study involving twenty elementary school boys with IQs over 120 who were "under-achievers" and who were matched with twenty other boys who had similar IQs but who were high-achievers. She found that bright boys who were low-achievers had more negative feelings about themselves than did high-achievers. In addition, she noted that low-achievers differed reliably from high-achievers in (1) feelings of being criticized, rejected, or isolated; (2) acting defensively through compliance, evasion, or negativism; and (3) being unable to express themselves appropriately in actions and feelings.

In a study involving junior high students, Nash[33] developed a set of 100 items which included three dimensions of self-perceptions assumed to be important: (1) the importance of peer relationships, (2) nonconformity and (3) satisfaction with self. Interestingly, the items which were found to be best in differentiating between high- and low-achievers were those concerned with the student's perception of the quality of his performance in school work, such as, "My grades are good," and "I am accurate in my school work."

It's True—Nothing Succeeds Like Success

In a significant investigation by Dyson dealing with the relationships between self-concept and ability grouping among seventh graders, it was found that high-achieving students reported significantly higher self-concepts than did low-achieving students and that this was true regardless of the type of grouping procedures utilized in the academic program. Noteworthy is the author's final observation in which he states:

© 1971 United Feature Syndicate, Inc.

Sometimes students do poorly in school because of too much inner tension.

If there is one particularly significant result growing out of this research, it is that "nothing succeeds like success." This is not a new understanding, as the old cliché indicates. The work reported here does, however, re-emphasize the importance of success in the learning situation as a contribution to positive psychological growth and it indicates that this feeling of success is probably more crucial in its effect on the student's self-concept than how an individual is grouped for instruction.[34]

The results of the above study are consistent with one of the conclusions reached by Borislow[35] in his investigation of relationships between self-evaluation and academic achievement among 197 college freshmen. He observed that students who underachieve scholastically have a poorer concept of themselves as learners than do achievers subsequent to their scholastic performance, *regardless of initial intention to strive for scholastic achievement as a goal.* In other words, though an under-achiever may say something like "I don't care if I do well or not," indicating that he isn't motivated anyway, doing poorly still leaves a mark on him. Just as success is likely to breed a "success feeling," so, too, does failure, in spite of the assertion "I don't care whether or not I fail," breed a "failure feeling." Indeed, it would not be unreasonable to speculate that low academic performance may make a student even more defensive and willing to claim "I don't care whether I fail or pass." Funny thing about people—sometimes those who holler loudest about *not* caring, care the most.

When looking at relationships between self-concept and achievement, we need to keep an important principle in mind.

A Positive Self-Concept Is Necessary, but not Enough

In a monumental search effort designed to study the relationship between self-concept of ability and academic performance of over one-thousand students from the time they had started seventh grade and completed tenth grade, Brookover[36] and his associates found that self-concept was a significant factor in achievement at each grade level studied. In the final phase of this project the following important observation was made:

> The correlation between self-concept of ability and grade point average ranges from .48 to .63 over the six years. It falls below .50 only among boys in the 12th grade. . . . In addition, the higher correlation between perceived evaluations and self-concepts tends to support the theory that perceived evaluations are a necessary and sufficient condition for (the growth of a positive or high) self-concept of ability, but (a positive) self-concept of ability is only a necessary, but *not* a sufficient condition for achievement. The latter is further supported by the analysis of the achievement of students with high and low self-concept of ability. This revealed that although a significant proportion of students with high self-concepts of ability achieved at a relatively lower level, practically none of the students with lower (less positive) self-concepts of ability achieved at a high level.[37]

The research reported by Brookover and his colleagues is important for several reasons. One, it pointed out the critical impact which "significant" people (persons who are valued, prized, important) can have on the self-concept of a growing child.

As we discussed in Chapter One, development of the self begins early in life and is nurtured in a framework of social interaction. A substantial dimension of any person's feelings about himself is derived from his incorporation of the attributes he perceives other people assigning to him. It is through our long immersion in an interpersonal stream of reflected appraisals from people important to us that we gradually develop a view of ourselves which we strive to maintain. And number two, the Brookover research serves to remind us that it takes more than a positive self-concept in order for there to be high academic achievement. Why should this be? Why do some students with high, positive self-concepts fail to achieve at commensurately high levels?

We have to understand that the possession of a high, positive self-concept does not *cause* high academic achievement. It appears to be a necessary and vital personal quality for one to have *prior to* achievement, but it is no guarantee that high achievement will naturally follow. A person could have a positive self-concept that is sustained and nurtured by success in nonacademic pursuits—athletics, extra-curricular participation, popularity with the opposite sex, creative expression in the various arts, and so on. If a student is motivated to do well in some nonacademic area and *does* well, he is less likely to be deflated by failure experiences encountered in the scholastic arena. Indeed, some students work very hard and diligently in nonacademic areas so as to be certain to compensate for any deficits tallied in their academic work. For example, an artist friend of mine in graduate school always tried to save as much face as possible in the wake of his sometimes mediocre academic work by reminding his friends of the "long hours he had to spend on his best paintings, and, after all, one can't be good in all things at once." The fact was, he couldn't care less about his academic performance. He did, however, care considerably about his painting skills and it was on canvas, and not in the classroom, that he was motivated "to be somebody" and to enhance and maintain his positive concept of self.

Parental Variables Related to Self-Concept and Achievement

The effect that certain parental practices have on a student's self-concept and motivation for achievement are considerable. These include the emotional relationship between parent and child, the attitudes of the parent toward school and school achievement, and parental concern for the interest in the child's performance. In addition, there is the consideration of the importance which students assign to their parent's evaluations of their (the students') ability to do schoolwork. For example, Brookover[38] found that practically all students in grades seven through twelve identified their parents as persons who were "significant" or "important" to them. Furthermore, when asked to indicate who was concerned about how well they did in school, parents were again named by over 90 percent of all the students. The perception of parental evaluations by students are, therefore, likely to have an impact on the self-perceptions of most students. The question is, how are these self-perceptions related to their feelings about their ability to do schoolwork and how are these feelings picked up from their parents?

Consider the following interview examples. This first one is from an interview I had with a low-achieving, low self-concept, ninth-grade girl. As we enter the conversation, it has just moved into schoolwork and the girl's parents' attitudes toward her performance. Listen carefully for the implicit and explicit ways in which her parents convinced her that she wasn't very good in math.

Counselor:	How does your mom feel about your school work?
Girl:	It could be better, I guess, I don't know exactly—we don't discuss it much.
Counselor:	Do your parents say anything to you about your report card?
Girl:	Sometimes they do.
Counselor:	I noticed you did about C work last year.
Girl:	Yeah, mostly I do that and sometimes not that good. I used to do better.
Counselor:	Could you tell me more about that?
Girl:	Well, last year I got a B in social studies, and that's pretty good. Math got me though. I guess if I really tried—but I don't think I can because I've tried all I can. I'm telling you; it really gets me. My mother wasn't good in math either, but she's better in it now.
Counselor:	How do you know your mother used to be poor in it?
Girl:	She told me. *She says it's no wonder I'm not very good at it.*
Counselor:	What does she mean by that?
Girl:	Well, she says, well, I'm dumb—"I guess I've handed it to you" or something like that. I mean I'm real slow in math—it takes hours to get something in my head. One time my father and I were working on a problem, and he lost his patience. He said I was so stupid that I should be in a special school. He was really mad.
Counselor:	How did that make you feel:
Girl:	Well, it hurt me, I was a little bit mad, but I got over it, *Maybe I am stupid. . . .*

What follows in an excerpt of another interview I had with a different ninth-grade, fourteen-year-old girl, who was also a low-achieving, low-self-concept student. The conversation was about school, grades, and feelings about ability to succeed in different subjects. As it happens, the subject area here, as in the above illustration, is math. Once again, listen carefully to the parental feedback that is gnawing away at this girl's self-confidence.

Counselor:	I see you've been having some trouble with math.
Girl:	Well, I don't know. My mother wasn't too good at it; my dad wasn't—I don't know, I'm just not very good at it.
Counselor:	How do you know that your mom and dad had trouble with math?
Girl:	Well, my mom told me the first time I got a D, and I brought it home, and I said, "I got a D in math," and she says, *"I'm not surprised because I wasn't exactly great in it."* And my dad, he isn't the best in it either. He said he didn't always do the best in the subject.
Counselor:	How did that make you feel when you found they didn't do well in math?
Girl:	Well, I don't know. My brother, he must be pretty good at it because he's an engineer. He's pretty good; *I guess I was the one that got it.*

Anyway, boys are better than girls in math anyway. I don't know why.
Counselor: "You were the one that got it." What does that mean?
Girl: I don't know, I guess my mom and dad passed it on to me. Maybe not, but *they aren't surprised that I do poorly in it.*

It's not difficult to see how a parent can negatively influence a youngster's feelings about his ability to do schoolwork by telling him he's stupid or by inferring that he inherited bad genes which make it impossible for him to do well. How students feel about their ability to do schoolwork depends, in part, on how they perceive those who are important to them, evaluating their ability. Helper,[39] for example, found a positive relationship between the way parents saw their children and the way the children saw themselves. Children who evaluated themselves highly were likely to have parents who evaluated them highly.

Whether a parent is basically rejecting or accepting is apparently a very important aspect of how students view themselves and their ability to do school-work. One study, involving achieving and under-achieving high school juniors and seniors, found that mothers of achievers were more accepting of their children than were mothers of under-achievers.[40] Intensive case studies by Kimball[41] have demonstrated how lack of sufficient acceptance is a basic antecedent condition for the development of a low concept of self, low self-esteem, and a low-level feeling of personal security. Lack of acceptance usually leads to low security and high dependency, both of which stand in the way of a person's realizing his potential.

In terms of the actual rejection expressed by the parents of underachievers, it may help us understand the phenomenon better if we look at the etiology of under-achievement, as it is described by Roth and Meyersburg.

> The psychogenesis involves a series of very subtle devaluations of the child, stemming from the parent-child relationship. In our experience, the most frequent pattern is that of the parent who pays no attention at all to the accomplishments or failures of the child. (These students frequently exclaim, "What's the use; nobody gives a damn," in reference to their current college failure.) The life space of the child and the life space of the parent are in different realms, a state of affairs which constitutes a parental rejection. The only way a child can bring the life spaces together, albeit momentarily, is through the production of a crisis, occasionally necessitating outsiders such as police, teacher, principal, or a counselor.
>
> Next in frequency is the parent who attends only to the child's failures and rarely to his successes. The latter are taken for granted, but the failures are punished. Thus, the contact between parent and child is through failure. If the child succeeds, he is alone, but if he fails, he is part of the concern of his parents.
>
> Both of these early experiences lead to three devastating, incipient pathological processes: The first of these is a process of self-denigration. In order for the child to maintain some kind of identity with the parent he must learn to see himself as a failure. He must hold back his productivity and blame himself for his lacks. Hostility, he is taught, is received by him and never expressed toward others. When he does experience resentments he directs them against himself and thus supports his own constructs about himself as being worth little.[42]

Clinical studies of learning difficulties have noted that under-achievement may reflect not only a low self-concept, but a rebellion against parents as well. What seems to happen in instances of this sort is that excessive pressure for achievement *in the absence of a satisfactory relationship with parents* leads to a high level of anxiety and resentment in the child or adolescent. The anxiety interferes with the ability to concentrate on schoolwork and the resentment motivates some students to disappoint their parents by not meeting their expectations. As a high-ability but low-achieving eleventh-grade boy expressed it to me (referring to his parents): "They're always bugging me to do well in school, get good grades, make the honor roll. Hell, that's practically the only time they talk to me, when it has something to do with school or grades. If there was no school, they probably wouldn't talk to me at all." What this boy wanted, which is no different than what any of us wants, was to be treated and cared for as a person, not as an achievement machine. Sometimes the only way a child or adolescent can get back at parents is to *withhold* his success. After all, what more does any growing youngster have to offer his parents *except* his success? Withholding success can be a powerful punishment and one has to wonder how many school failures are traceable to that conscious or unconscious motivation. (Child psychiatrist Bruno Bettelheim[43] has written a deeply insightful article on why some youth *decide to fail,* which you may find helpful for more understanding on this issue.)

Rather than examining parental factors related to general school achievement, several recent areas of research have sought to specify more exactly the particular kinds of parental influence which affect specific aspects of the youngster's achievement.

Bing,[44] for example, investigated a group of elementary-school children who showed marked discrepancy between verbal and mathematic ability. He found that high verbal children experienced much more verbal stimulation in the preschool years, as evidenced by such variables as amount of play time the mother had with the infant, verbal stimulation of the infant, mother's responsiveness to the child's early, questions, and interest shown in the child's good speech habits. Although the *mothers of high verbal children were rather controlling and pressuring, the mothers of those children high in mathematical ability were less interfering and permitted greater independence.* Bing concluded that high verbal ability is encouraged by intensive interaction between parent and child, while number and spatial abilities, on the other hand, develop from interaction with the physical rather than the interpersonal environment. The development of these latter abilities apparently requires greater independence to investigate and explore one's surroundings.

Although, in general, parents who value intellectual achievement for themselves stress intellectual achievement for their children, some areas of achievement are emphasized more than others. In a study of parental values for achievement in the intellectual, physical, artistic, and mechanical areas, parents who valued achievement in the artistic and mechanical areas tended also to value such achievement for their children.[45]

Before children begin their formal schooling they are in the custody of their parents or parent-surrogates, whatever the case may be, for five or six years. In that period of time, the beginnings of a self-system are molded and predispose them to view themselves and school in certain ways. As you have seen, parent variables such as parental feedback and evaluation, parental caring or lack of it, and parental acceptance or rejection can have a striking effect on how children view their general intellectual ability and their ability in specific subject areas. Research suggests that parents who combine caring acceptance, along with firmness, and high expectations are likely to raise children who think well of themselves and who strive to do as well as they can in school.

The next question is—what are the implications of self-concept research for teaching and teachers?

Teacher Variables Related to Self-Concept and Achievement

Teachers—at all levels—can have an enormous influence on a student's self-attitudes, particularly as these attitudes are related to his feelings about being able to think, answer questions, and solve problems. Teachers are quickly established as "significant" persons in the lives of most students. Sometimes a teacher becomes significant to a student because he or she may be the only person in the whole wide world who makes that student feel like an individual of worth and value. Other teachers are significant because they are perceived as having the ultimate responsibility of evaluating a student's ability to do schoolwork and to compete with other students. Even more important, as far as the student is concerned, a teacher has the ultimate responsibility for *recording* these evaluations for both parents and posterity. Teachers can either help students recognize their strengths and possibilities or they can remind students again and again of their weaknesses and shortcomings. No matter how you look at it, the teacher is an important factor in the inter-personal field of forces which influence a student's developing self. Even if a student's self has been nurtured in a healthy home atmosphere, a teacher who is cold, rejecting, and emotionally distant may interfere with the process of otherwise healthy development. With this kind of teacher students can no longer be their natural selves, free to inquire and develop. Instead, they become defensive and reactive, concerned more with survival than with learning.

Let us turn now to a more specific examination of teacher variables which are most directly related to a student's academic performance and self-concept development.

Teacher Personality

A teacher may know a great deal and be extremely competent in what he or she does, but in the final analysis, it will be that teacher's personality and manner of relating that ultimately turn students on or off, as the case may be. What is it that students respond positively and negatively to in teachers? Your own feelings about different teachers you've had are one good source for an answer to that question. Consider what some of the research says about the effects of teacher personality.

No one has ever disconfirmed Jersild's[46] early research with elementary school children, who mentioned the following qualities as typical of the teachers they liked best: *human qualities as a person*—sympathetic, cheerful, good tempered; *physical appearance, grooming, voice*—attractive, neat, nice manner of talking; *traits as a disciplinarian or director of the class*—fair, consistent, did not scold or shout; *participation in activities*—joined in or permitted games or play; *performance as a teacher*—enthusiastic, resourceful, explained well, permitted expression of opinion. The age trend in the descriptions is worth noting; high school students more frequently picked characteristics bearing on teaching ability, whereas younger children singled out interesting projects introduced by the teacher. At all ages children valued highly the teacher who was enthusiastic, sensitive, and understanding. Witty's[47] later research with high school students came up with essentially the same results.

Even at the college level there is strong evidence[48] to suggest that students still rank first the professor's interest in students and their problems and a willingness to give attention to them. Indeed, more recent research[49] is showing that personality and teacher effectiveness is highly correlated. For example, an analysis of 1500 student evaluations of 108 men and women faculty showed that dynamic, pragmatic, amicable, and highly intellectually competent faculty received higher competency ratings than did professors low on those traits. The effect of teacher personality on student achievement and attitudes is a complex phenomenon. Other research,[50, 51] for example, indicates that the impact of a teacher's personality depends not only on the sex of the teacher, but also of the student. These are, however, only subtle shadings. None of the research suggests that there are such gross differences between male and female teachers as far as their teaching styles or impact on students is concerned as to warrant the development of something akin to "an ideal personality profile" for teachers of each sex.

So far, we have been examining desirable personal characteristics of teachers as these characteristics are identified by students. For the most part, these characteristics group themselves under the general heading of capacity for warmth, understanding, interest in students, and dynamic. What happens when these personal qualities are related to the more rigid test of whether having them or not makes any difference in the actual performance of students? Let's consider some of the evidence.

Sears,[52] for example, found that there are positive relationships between the extent to which a teacher reflects a personal interest in and willingness to listen to students' ideas and the creativity shown by students. As a further example, Cogan[53] observed that warm and considerate teachers got an unusual amount of original poetry and art from their high-school students. Reed[54] and Wright[55] found that teachers higher in capacity for warmth and responsiveness to students' questions favorably affected pupils' interests and achievement in science. Van Horn[56] found that when teachers combine information-giving with positive and rewarding feedback to students, that students who get this kind of feedback are more likely to have higher self-concept of ability scores in particular subjects than those who receive negative feedback. It is apparent from this research that not only does *who* a teacher is make a difference in how students perform and feel about themselves and their work, but so, too, does *what* a teacher says and *how* it is said.

Heil, Powell, and Feifer[57] went a step further and related student achievement to interaction between different teacher and student personalities. They compared the various teacher-pupil personality combinations in terms of pupil achievement, teacher knowledge, and classroom settings. Using scores from achievement tests as their criterion measure, they found that the well integrated (healthy, well-rounded, flexible) teachers were most effective with *all* types of students. Two other identified teacher personality "types" (fearful and turbulent) were successful with only certain types of students. Subsequent research[58, 59] has shown that different types of teachers do, indeed, have different effects on students. Not only can a teacher's personality influence, for better or for worse, the behavior and performance of students, but, to further complicate the issue, Klein's[60] research indicates that students can influence teachers in similar ways.

Spaulding[61] found that the self-concepts of elementary school children were apt to be higher and more positive in classrooms in which the teacher was "socially integrative" and "learner supportive." What this and other research cited here seems to suggest is that through the psychological principles of imitation and identification the teacher becomes a model for appropriate behavior and that students take on, assume, and ultimately reflect (probably unconsciously) those personal characteristics most dominant in the teacher.

All in all, the evidence seems quite clear when it comes to describing good or effective teachers on the basis of personal characteristics. Effective teachers appear to be those who are, shall we say, "human" in the fullest sense of the word. They have a sense of humor, are fair, empathetic, more democratic than autocratic, and apparently can relate easily and naturally to students on either a one-to-one or group basis. Their classrooms seem to reflect miniature enterprise operations in the sense that they are open, spontaneous, and adaptable to change.

Self-Perceptions of Teachers

We do not have to go any further than our own personal experiences to know that the way we see, regard, and feel about ourselves has enormous impact on both our private and public lives. How about "good" versus "poor" teachers? How do they see themselves?

Ryans,[62] in a monumental study of teachers' characteristics involving some 6000 teachers in 1700 schools and 450 school systems, found that there were, indeed, differences between the self-related expressions of high emotional stability teachers versus low emotional stability teachers. For example, the more emotionally stable teachers were more apt to have the following kinds of self-reports: (1) frequently named self-confidence and cheerfulness as dominant traits in themselves;

(2) said they liked active contact with other people; (3) expressed interests in hobbies and handicrafts; and (4) reported their childhoods to be happy experiences.

On the other hand, teachers with lower emotional maturity scores (1) had unhappy memories of childhood; (2) seemed *not* to prefer contact with others; (3) were more directive and authoritarian; and (4) expressed less self-confidence.

We can be even more specific. For example, Arthur Combs in his book, *The Professional Education of Teachers,*[63] cites several studies which reached similar conclusions about the way good teachers typically see themselves.

1. Good teachers see themselves as identified with people rather than withdrawn, removed, apart from, or alienated from others.
2. Good teachers feel basically adequate rather than inadequate. They do not see themselves as generally unable to cope with problems.
3. Good teachers feel trustworthy rather than untrustworthy. They see themselves as reliable, dependable individuals with the potential for coping with events as they happen.
4. Good teachers see themselves as wanted rather than unwanted. They see themselves as likable and attractive (in personal, not physical sense) as opposed to feeling ignored and rejected.
5. Good teachers see themselves as worthy rather than unworthy. They see themselves as people of consequence, dignity, and integrity as opposed to feeling they matter little, can be overlooked and discounted.

In the broadest sense of the word, good teachers see themselves as good people. Their self-conceptions are, for the most part, positive, tinged with an air of optimism and colored with tones of healthy self-acceptance. I dare say that self-perceptions of good teachers are not unlike the self-perceptions of any basically healthy person, whether he be a good brick-layer, a good manager, a good doctor, a good lawyer, a good experimental psychologist, or you name it. Clinical evidence has told us time and again that *any* person is apt to be happier, more productive, and more effective when he is able to see himself as fundamentally and basically OK.

Teacher's Perceptions of Others

Research is showing us that not only do effective and ineffective teachers view themselves differently, but they also reflect characteristic differences in the way they perceive others. For example, Ryans[64] reported several studies which have produced findings that are quite similar and in agreement when it comes to sorting out the differences between how good and poor teachers view others. He noted, among other things, that outstandingly "good" teachers rated significantly higher than notably "poor" teachers in at least five different ways with respect to how they viewed others. The good teachers had (1) more favorable opinions of students; (2) more favorable opinions of democratic classroom behavior; (3) more favorable opinions of administrators and colleagues; (4) a greater expressed liking for personal contacts with other people; and (5) more favorable estimates of other people generally. In addition, good teachers expressed the belief that very few students are difficult behavior problems, that very few people are influenced in their opinions and attitudes toward others by feelings of jealousy, and that most teachers are willing to assume their full share of extra duties outside of school.

Interestingly, the characteristics that distinguish the "lowly assessed" teacher group suggested that the relatively "ineffective" teachers are self-centered, anxious, and restricted.

Before going further, it might be well for us to bear in mind Ryans' cautionary note:

> Certainly the research (referring to his own) has not settled the question, who is the good teacher? However, there are some interesting suggestions here—some clues that may help to identify "good" and "poor" teachers if one is willing to accept the kind of definition employed in this research. Such a definition indicates that teachers are "good" if they rank very high among their colleagues, with respect to such observable classroom behaviors as warmth and kindliness, systematic and businesslike manner, and stimulating and original teacher behavior. [65]

Combs has investigated the perceptual differences between good and poor teachers, and he suggests that good teachers can be clearly distinguished from poor ones with respect to the following perceptions about people: [66]

1. The good teacher is more likely to have an internal rather than external frame of reference. That is, he seeks to understand how things seem to others and then uses this as a guide for his own behavior.
2. The good teacher is more concerned with people and their reactions than with things and events.
3. The good teacher is more concerned with the subjective-perceptual experience of people than with objective events. He is, again, more concerned with how things *seem* to people than just the so-called or alleged "facts."
4. The good teacher seeks to understand the causes of people's behavior in terms of their *current* thinking, feeling, beliefs, and understandings rather than in terms of forces exerted on them now or in the past.
5. The good teacher generally trusts other people and perceives them as having the capacity to solve their own problems.
6. The good teacher sees others as being friendly and enhancing rather than hostile or threatening.
7. The good teacher tends to see other people as being of worth rather than unworthy. That is, he sees all people as possessing a certain dignity and integrity.
8. The good teacher sees people and their behavior as essentially developing from within rather than as a product of external events to be molded or directed. In other words, he sees people as creative and dynamic rather than passive or inert.

I am sure it comes as no surprise to any of us that how we perceive others is highly dependent on how we perceive ourselves. If a potential teacher (or anyone else for that matter) likes himself, trusts himself, and has confidence in himself, he will likely see others in this same light. Research is beginning to tell us what common sense has always told us, namely, students grow, flourish, and develop much more easily when in relationship with someone who projects an inherent trust and belief in their capacity to become what they have the potential to become.

There is little doubt about it, students can be dramatically influenced for the better
when they know their teachers think well of them.

It is easy to say that good teachers have a generally more positive view of
others, but does this have anything to do with how students achieve and behave?
There is evidence to suggest that it does. For example, Davidson and Lang[67] found
that among the boys and girls in grades four through six those children with positive
self-images were more likely to be among those who perceived their teachers as
having positive feelings toward them. They also found that the more positive the
perception of their teacher's feelings, *the better was their academic achievement.*

In summary, we can sketch at least five interrelated generalizations from what
research is telling us about how effective teachers differ from less effective teachers
when it comes to perceptions of others. In relation to this, effective teachers can be
characterized in the following ways:

1. They seem to have a generally more positive view of others—students, colleagues,
   and administrators.
2. They are not as prone to view others as critical, attacking people with ulterior
   motives, but rather see them as potentially friendly and worthy in their own right.
3. They have a more favorable view of democratic classroom procedures.
4. They have the ability and capacity to see things as they seem to others, that is, the
   ability to see things from the other person's point of view.
5. They do not see students as persons "you do things to" but rather as individuals
   capable of doing for themselves once they feel trusted, respected, and valued.

Now, then, let us turn our attention to some important student variables which have implications for self-concept, academic adjustment, and teaching practices.

Student Variables Related to Self-Concept and Achievement

A student's total academic adjustment, which includes his performance and behavior, is influenced by personality factors, individual reactions to praise and blame, personal experiences with success and failure, and differences in learning style. Let's look at each of these variables one at a time.

Student Personality

Three separate experiments[68, 69, 70] have reported findings which indicate that teaching methods do, indeed, interact with student personality characteristics to affect academic adjustment. In all of these experiments some students were placed in discussion or lecture sessions where expectations were clearly defined, while other students were placed in more open-ended sections where they were free to establish objectives and course procedures. In one experiment, the more highly structured sections were conducted in a warm, supportive, and permissive way. In all three studies, a certain kind of student emerged who appeared to require a high degree of structure to make optimum progress. These students were described as being personally insecure and dependent. In addition, they tend to become rigid and vindictive in their evaluations of instructors. To this student, the permissive section meetings were "absolutely worthless," a place where one finds only intellectual confusion and anxiety.

On the other hand, there were the more personally secure students who found the permissive, open-ended class very much to their liking and who flourished under its conditions. In any case, whether a student is secure or insecure, dependent or independent, these personality dimensions do make a difference when it comes to determining whether one teacher method or another will be successful as a motivating technique.

Compulsivity and anxiety are two other student personality characteristics which apparently influence academic adjustment. For example, Grimes and Allinsmith[71] found that when teaching is structured, compulsive students do substantially better than less compulsive students. Highly anxious students do poorly in unstructured classrooms. Students who are both highly anxious and highly compulsive do their best work in structured classes.

Other evidence also points to individual differences in nonintellectual factors. Della-Piana and Gage,[72] for example, found that some pupils are more concerned about feelings and personal relationships, while others are mainly achievement-oriented. Feeling oriented students tend to accept the teacher whom they like and reject the teacher whom they dislike on personal grounds. Achievement oriented students pay less attention to teacher warmth and more attention to teacher competency.

If you are one of thousands of persons suffering from mathophobia (fear of math—Lazarus[73] has written an excellent article about this), it may come as no surprise to you to learn, as Aikan[74] did in his monumental review of research, that personality factors are very much related to the ability or inability to comprehend mathematical concepts. Persons who tend to have a low sense of personal worth, high anxiety, low self-confidence, and who are more introverted than extroverted usually have more problems with math than persons on the other end of these scales. Mathematics surely does not *cause* those personality characteristics, but what it may do is leave a student with an exaggerated sense of their presence. Wise teachers and parents would do well to take personality variables such as these into account when trying to figure out ways to get students to learn math. Highly anxious, low self-confident students are hardly made less anxious or more self-confident by forcing today's math lesson down their throats before they're through digesting yesterday's math teachings. Personality variables can, indeed, influence how and what a student learns. How students respond to praise and criticism makes a difference, too.

© 1970 United Feature Syndicate, Inc.

Some students have mathophobia, while other students seem to have no trouble with math at all.

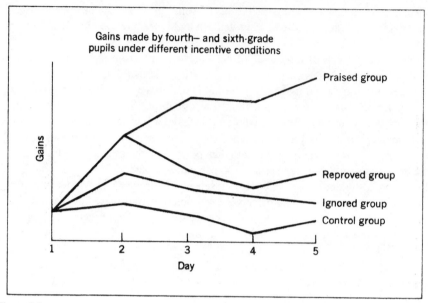

Figure 6.1

(From E. Hurlock. "An Evaluation of Certain Incentives Used in School Work." *Journal of Educational Psychology,* 1925, 16, 145–159.)

Student Reactions to Praise and Criticism

Generally speaking, praise is a more powerful motivator than either blame or criticism. In one study,[75] 106 fourth- and sixth-grade children of both sexes were divided into four groups matched on the basis of intelligence and arithmetic skill. A fifteen-minute daily practice period in addition was given to the groups for five consecutive days. One of the four groups served as the control group and received its test separately without any comment as to performance. Irrespective of the score obtained, one of the three remaining groups received consistent praise; one received reproof; and one was ignored. The children in the praised group were called by name, told of their excellent results, and encouraged to improve. The reproved group was called out and criticized for poor work, careless mistakes, and lack of improvement. The ignored group received no recognition but merely heard what occurred to the other two groups. Figure 6.1 provides a diagram of the results.

As you can see, the praised group made the greatest gains and the reproved group made greater gains than the ignored group. Apparently, even reproof is a sign of recognition and is better than no recognition at all!

However, the effects of praise and criticism on motivation and learning are not so simple as the above study indicates. Psychologist Richard Farson[76] has noted that praise does not always motivate people to thrust forward with renewed confidence. Rather, some people react to it with discomfort, uneasiness, and defensiveness. You may recognize yourself in some of the following common replies to praise:

> "Well, I really can't take credit for it."
> "Oh, you're just saying that."
> "I was just lucky, that's all."
> "Gosh, yours is nice, too."
> "Well, I do the best I can."

What these statements have in common is that they are all defensive reactions—efforts to cope with a difficult situation. If the praise is inconsistent with one's self-concept, then it triggers a stress reaction, which causes some people—young and old—to feel quite uncomfortable, almost to the point of imitating the toe-digging reactions of small children. For some, praise is something to be coped with, to be handled. Another possible reason for feeling uncomfortable with praise may be related to the fact that praise is, after all, an evaluation, and to be evaluated usually makes us feel uncomfortable. If we are weighed, we *may* be found wanting.

Several research efforts[77, 78] have indicated that the effects of praise or blame were related to personality differences as well. The major conclusions reached by these studies indicate that:

1. When introverts and extroverts are grouped together (as is the case in most classrooms), either praise or blame is more effective in increasing the work output than no external incentives.
2. If repeated often enough, praise increases the work output of introverts until it is significantly higher than that of introverts who are blamed or extroverts who are praised.
3. If repeated often enough, blame increases the work output of extroverts until it is significantly higher than that of extroverts who are praised or introverts who are blamed.

It is apparent that the use of praise or blame has different effects on children with different self-concepts. It seems altogether possible that indiscriminate praise may be as detrimental to students' motivation and learning as indiscriminate blame or criticism. Praise which is won too easily or which is indiscriminately given to students, no matter what their effort or performance, quickly loses its effect. Praise, like success, means little if it is too easily won. However, if praise is honest: "You've done a fine job," or "You've done a good job, but I think you could have done better," and proportionate to the task accomplished, then it can be a sincere form of acknowledging another person's efforts.

Student Reactions to Success and Failure

We probably do not have to go much further than our own life experiences in order to understand the differential effects of success and failure. As we discussed earlier, what is a success experience for one student is a failure experience for another.

Look at it this way: each of us, like each of our students or children, has what we could call a "psychological bank account." Just as we deposit money in our savings account, we deposit successes in our psychological account. Some people have less money, therefore can deposit less and, in fact, have less to draw on in time of need. Somewhat the same is true of success. Some adults and children simply have fewer successes to deposit in their psychological accounts, and just as is it possible to go financially bankrupt, it is possible to experience psychological bankruptcy. The difference is that when we are financially bankrupt, there is always the possibility of starting over again. Not so with psychological bankruptcy; one's failures are not so easily wiped away. If we take this analogy into the school world, we can think of students we know who pay their way through school (if they make it) on what amounts to a "psychological deficit financing plan." For the most part, they are students for whom school success is neither easily won nor easily available. Just as having enough money encourages some to invest to make more, so having enough success encourages some to invest in greater success, such as studying harder, taking more difficult courses, and the like. But there has to be an "account" to begin with.

Research has shown that our success experiences contribute to our setting realistic levels of aspiration.[79,80] For example, people who have little money will sometimes engage in wild, risk-taking ventures to get more or become uncommonly conservative in order to reduce the risk of losing what they have. Students with histories of academic failure do somewhat the same thing. They set goals either so low that no hazard is involved or so high that success is impossible. As demonstrated by the work of Atkinson[81] and Moulton,[82] what seems to happen is that persons with a history of failure tend to raise their level of aspiration following failure and lower it after success. On the face of it, it would appear the individuals who have a history of failure take greater risks by raising their level of aspiration. Not so. What they actually do is to *lower* the risks by creating the possibility of blaming their poor performance on the exceptional difficulty of the task. For example, if failure-oriented students choose goals that are clearly beyond their reach (a tough course, a vocational possibility far over their heads, and so on), they can always say to themselves, "The task was so hard that anybody might have failed." It can happen the other way, too. For instance, when students who have experienced a lot of failure find success at their doorstep, there is a tendency for them to lower their level of aspiration as a way of protecting themselves if they don't do as well again. If, for example, you get an A on a test you didn't expect to do so well on, then the way to avoid being too disappointed if you don't get an A on the next one is to hope for at least a C.

People with a history of success, on the other hand, tend to choose experiences in which the chances for success are in the middle range of those ordinarily encountered, and they avoid either very high- or low-risk situations. Middle range experiences provide them with sufficient challenge to satisfy their needs for achievement while at the same time offering them reasonable chance for success. In a very real sense, risk-taking is greater for the student choosing middle-range experiences because it would be more difficult to excuse away or rationalize poor performance if that should happen. He cannot say, for example, "The task was so hard that anyone might have failed."

If we are to help students—particularly those who have difficulty in school—to be more consistent and realistic about goal-setting, we ought to remind ourselves that not all students will be motivated in the same way or interested in the same things. If we can remain aware of this, perhaps we can work harder at making success more available in more different ways and at more different levels. One way of doing this is to recognize that different students learn in different ways.

Student Differences in Learning Styles

Although little formal research on this subject has been conducted, we are beginning to understand that there are, indeed, different "styles" for learning.[83] There is no evidence that any one style is better or worse than another but if we are not careful, we may get caught in the trap of judging a learning style wrong just because it doesn't match our own. Most learning styles may be categorized as principally visual (reading), aural (listening), or physical (doing things), although it is possible that any one person may use more than one.

In the interests of effective motivation, it is important to identify each student's learning style as quickly as possible. If, for example, some students seem to learn best by reading, it may be wise not only to suggest books to them, but also to call on them more often in class to encourage them to experience more physical or verbal learning encounters. (Some students even *hope* to be called on because they lack the confidence to raise their hands.) On the other hand, it may be beneficial to encourage the more physical and aural students to read more. The point is that once a student's particular "style" for learning is identified, a teacher can encourage his best use of that style and help him experience other modes of learning as well.

In sum, what is important for one student may not be important to another; this is one reason why cookbook formulas for good teaching are of so little value and why teaching is inevitably something of an art when it comes to motivating students and helping them learn. The choice of instructional methods makes a big difference for certain kinds of pupils, and a search for the "best" way to motivate can succeed only when student variables such as intellectual *and* self-concept differences are taken into account. What are some of the behavioral differences between high and low self-concept students? A good question—it deserves our attention.

Behavioral Differences between High and Low Self-Concept Students

Self-concept is not some mystical abstract construct that can only be discerned by people with the right kind of eyesight, but a psychological reality that is helpful for distinguishing behavioral similarities and differences among people. If we are to be as effective as we can be with youth we work with, then it would be useful to know what to look for in differentiating between possible high self-concept and low self-concept behavior. Table 6.1 may help you do this.

TABLE 6.1

Behaviors Associated with High and Low Self-Concept Students

Behaviors Commonly Seen in Students with High, Positive Self-Concepts	Behaviors Commonly Seen in Students with Low, Negative Self-Concepts
1. Active, curious about surroundings, makes wide variety of contacts.	Somewhat passive, tends to avoid new experiences, has limited contacts.
2. Makes friends easily, talks, laughs, gets into trouble now and then.	Shy, bashful, often called a "good" child by parents and teachers.
3. Has a sense of humor, is a good sport, can take a joke on himself.	Tends to be over-serious, over-sensitive, afraid to be laughed at.
4. Asks questions, defines problems, willingly does his part in planning for solutions and carrying out plans.	Avoids getting to the problem, grumbles that what is wanted isn't clear, plans in terms of wishful thinking.
5. Willing to take risks in class, contributes to discussions, able to stand up for what she thinks is right.	Unsure, backs down easily, frequently asks others: "Do you think this is right?" "What do you think?"
6. Takes modest pride in own contributions, is not overbearing, does not cheat.	Over-asserts own ability and contributions, bullies, cheats, belittles others
7. Works and plays with others, cooperates easily and naturally, helps others.	Overly competitive, finds it difficult to share, undermines others when possible.
8. Usually happy, confident, doesn't whine for what cannot be had, doesn't worry needlessly.	Usually gloomy and fearful, worries as a matter of course, complains a lot.

Strategies for Enhancing Self-Concept and Achievement

Recognizing the differences between low and high self-concept students is an important first step. The question remains: Are there specific things a teacher can do to enhance a student's self-image as part of an overall effort to raise achievement? Let's turn our attention now to some possibilities for answering that question.

What a Teacher Says Makes a Difference

A psychologist by the name of Staines[84] got interested in the question of what teachers do and say in a classroom that influences students to feel either good or badly about themselves and did some interesting research to find out more about this. He began by asking the following questions:

1. What part do teachers play in the development of the child's self?
2. Can teachers change a student's self-picture if they try to do so?
3. If they can, what methods of teaching produce what kinds of self-picture?
4. Is it possible to distinguish between teachers in the frequency and kind of comment that they make about a student's self?

The basic assumption of the study was that since a teacher is an important aspect of a student's emotional world, it is likely that he can have an important influence on a student's self-concept.

In order to test this assumption, two elementary classes were matched for age, intelligence, and socioeconomic class. In one class, Teacher A deliberately set out to actively assist students to view themselves as planning, purposing, choosing, responsible, and accountable individuals. It was considered important that students should test their purposes by carrying them through, see themselves as adequate and causal, (that is), persons who can *make* things happen) and, at the same time, differentiate between strengths and weaknesses. In order to facilitate these goals, Teacher A made it a point to get to know each student and also to familiarize himself with the general area of self-concept dynamics and how these dynamics were related to behavior. In class, the teacher was likely to make comments such as the following, all designed to help students toward a more positive view of themselves, while at the same time assisting them to be realistic about their abilities:

1. "Randy, you're tall. Help me with this."
2. "Barbara, you know, you're very good at solving addition problems."
3. "Good boy! Look at this, everyone!"
4. "Sally, you seem to do better in arithmetic than English."
5. "You're a fine one, you are."

Note the emphasis on highlighting specific strengths, assets, and skills; on helping students sort out their strengths and weaknesses; and, as in the last statement, on commenting on the student's value as a total or "whole" person.

Teacher B was judged to be an equally effective teacher, but his techniques were more along the lines of traditional teaching and not adapted to fit within a framework that explicitly considered self-concept enhancement variables.

When the twelve-week experimental period was concluded, data from Teacher B's class indicated that traditional high pressure teaching, with vigorous personal emphasis, with great stress on correctness and on the serious consequences of failure, and with the *constant emphasis* on passing examinations, leads to greater insecurity. As far as achievement was concerned, the students of Teacher A reflected slightly higher average improvement than the students of Teacher B in standardized reading and number tests. If there are objections that a teacher cannot spend time assisting students toward a more positive, healthy attitude for fear of shortchanging them in the way of content, here is some evidence to suggest that at least equally good academic results may be obtained while helping students to see themselves in a more positive light.

When it comes to what a teacher can say to students and how to say it in order to enhance students' self-concept, I would like to bring to your attention an excellent book by clinical psychologist Thomas Gordon titled, *T.E.T.: Teacher Effectiveness Training.*[85] The whole focus of the book is on how to communicate in constructive and facilitating ways in order to maximize healthy teacher-student relationships. A book well worth reading.

Teacher Feedback Is Important

The kind of feedback that students get regarding how they're doing in their school work can have an important impact not only on how they feel about their academic efforts but on how they feel about themselves as well. I remember to this day a comment a psychology professor wrote on one of my papers in my freshman year: "A good paper, but I have the feeling you have the ability to have explored this topic more fully." He gave me a B on the paper, but more importantly, he gave me encouragement to believe more fully in myself. The grade he gave me didn't mean all that much, but the feedback mattered a great deal.

Does the nature of a teacher's feedback influence actual achievement? There is evidence that it does. For example, Page[86] conducted an experiment with high

Actually, the sort of feedback that Sally wants is probably the kind that would do some students the most good.

school and junior high school students and teachers in which the teachers graded objective tests of their pupils and then randomly assigned each paper to one of three groups. The group-one students were given back their papers with no comment except a mark. The group-two students were given back their papers with no comment except a stereotyped, standard comment from "excellent" if their scores were high to "let's raise this grade." Every C student, for example, received his mark with the notation, "perhaps try to do still better." For those in group three, teachers wrote a personal comment on every paper saying whatever they thought might encourage that particular student. On the next objective test, groups two and three outperformed group one. This suggests that the personalized comments had a greater effect than standardized comments and that even a very short standard comment written on the paper produced measureable achievement gains. The greatest improvement was made by the failing students in group three, who received encouraging personal notes on their papers. This study points up the motivational implications of evaluative practices that go far beyond the simple indication of right or wrong answers. It certainly does seem to be true that teachers who reflect an active personal interest in their students' progress and *who show it* are more likely to be successful in enhancing students' confidence in themselves than teachers who are more distant and impersonal.

As pointed out by Coopersmith and Feldman,[87] feedback serves another important function. It gives students some external criteria from which to guage how well they are doing and what needs to be improved. Perhaps the best kind of feedback is the kind that gives not only information but a bit of inspiration, direction, and perhaps offers some hope as well.

Teacher Expectations Can Influence Achievement

Predicting rain or sunny skies doesn't affect tomorrow's weather, but a Harris poll predicting victory or defeat for a certain political candidate can have a definite effect on the outcome. Betting on the flip of a coin doesn't change the odds, but letting an athlete know you've bet on him can considerably affect his performance. When Roger Bannister began training for the four-minute mile, hardly anybody believed it could be done. Bannister himself wasn't sure, but he is quoted to have said many times, "I knew my trainer believed in me and I couldn't let him down." Charles E. Wilson, former General Motors president, was fond of saying that one of the differences between good bosses and poor bosses is that "good bosses make their workers feel that they have more ability than they think they have so that they consistently do better work than they thought they could." Hundreds of years ago Goethe observed: "Treat people as if they were what they ought to be, and you help them to become what they are capable of being."

The essence of this is that one person's expectancy of another person's behavior somehow comes to be realized—not always, but enough so that increasing attention is being given these days to the idea of how self-fulfilling prophecies work in the classroom. In George Bernard Shaw's famous play, *Pygmalion,* Eliza Doolittle, who changed from an awkward Cockney flower girl into an elegant lady, describes the process involved quite simply: ". . . the difference between a lady and a flower girl is not how she behaves, but how she is treated." Although it does not work quite so simply in the classroom, there is increasing evidence to suggest that perhaps one difference between poor students and good students is not how they behave, but how they are treated. Like Eliza, students in school—whether in first grade or twelfth—have a tendency to perform as they are expected to perform. What does research have to say about this?

Rosenthal and Jacobson's[88] pioneering research was among the first to show that a teacher's expectations can indeed influence students' performance and behavior in school. For example, within each of the six grades in a particular school were three classrooms, one each of children performing at above average, average, and below average levels of scholastic achievement. In each of these classes, an average of 20 percent of the children were identified to the teachers as having scores on the *Test for Intellectual Blooming* which suggested that they would show unusual academic gains during the academic year. Actually, the children had been picked at random from the total population of children taking the same test. Eight months after the experimental conditions were instituted, all children were retested with the same test. What were the results?

For the school as a whole, those children from whom the teachers had been led to expect greater intellectual gain showed significantly greater gain in IQ scores than did other children in the school! In fact, the lower the grade level, the greater the IQ gain. Apparently teachers interacted with the "brighter" children more positively and more favorably, and the children responded in kind by showing greater gains in IQ. Why should there be more change in the lower grades? One reason is that younger children are generally more malleable, less fixed, and more capable of change. A second possibility is that younger elementary school children do not have firmly established reputations which can be passed on from one teacher to the next. It might not be a too far-out speculation to suggest that as a student gets older, a teacher's interactions with that student are determined to some extent by a kind of "reputation" (good student or poor, delinquent or well-behaved, "Better watch him—he can't be trusted" or "He's a good student—he'll work hard for you") he has established.

Rosenthal's research is somewhat unique in that it involves an outside person who in some way manipulates teachers to have certain expectations. Other studies[89, 90] have included the same process. What happens, however, when teachers form their *own* expectations based upon their *own* experiences?

Seaver[91] studied teachers' "natural expectancies" by analyzing the performance of twenty-seven elementary age students who had had older siblings precede them in school by no more than three grade levels and who, in addition, had the same teachers the younger siblings were having. Seaver reasoned that teachers who had taught a student's older brother or sister have a built-in expectancy for the younger child, high if the older child did well and low if he or she did poorly. In addition, the school environment provided a natural control group of students whose older siblings had different teachers. Seaver found that teacher expectancies did, indeed, make a difference. When the older sibling's performance had been high, the performance of children in the high-expectancy group was higher than that of the control group on eight different measures of academic achievement. When the older sibling's performance had been low, the expectancy group scored lower than the controls on seven of the eight tests. Research shows us what we may always have suspected: the reputation that older siblings in a family establish in school gets passed on to their brothers and sisters, and teachers tend to expect—and therefore get—from the younger members of the family what they had learned to expect from the older ones.

Additional support for the power of naturally induced teacher expectations comes from an investigation by Palardy[92] who found that if first-grade teachers believed boys would achieve as well as girls in reading, the boys did, in fact, perform better than boys with teachers who believed girls were better readers. Another study[93] along this vein found that elementary level teachers have a tendency to overestimate the IQs of girls and underestimate the IQs of boys. The revealing aspect of this is that even though there was no *actual* IQ difference between boys and girls, the girls showed higher reading achievement. Not only that, *but within both sexes, the children whose IQs had been overestimated by teachers showed higher reading achievement.* Remember, actual IQ is not the important factor here. What seems to make a difference is the teacher's *perceptions or beliefs* about a particular student's IQ, which, in turn, sets in motion certain expectancies. Which leads us to ask an important question.

How Do Teacher Expectations Work?

How do expectations work, and how do they influence another person's behavior? Specifically, how and why do a teacher's expectations influence a student's behavior and performance? In the first place, expectations make it clear to students that they cannot, willy-nilly, do what they want just because they want to do it. Having the opportunity to do what they want just because that is what they want to do is an important right that all students should be able to exercise. However, if that's all there is, they may seldom be stretched beyond the *safety* of their own choices.

I say ''safety'' of their own choices because there is evidence to indicate that when people do only what they choose to do, they feel less successful and competent, even if they succeed at what they choose to do, than those who accomplish a task that they did not choose and that represents another person's expectations. Luginbuhl[94] has noted, for example, that if a person succeeds at a problem that he chose from a number of problems, his feelings of success may be blunted by the knowledge that *he influenced the situation to make success more possible.* This suggests that it may not be wise for a teacher to permit students to have their own way (for example, choose the number or kind of books to read or the kind of paper to write, and so on.) *all the time.* Living up to a teacher's expectations (for example, writing a report on an assigned topic, getting it done and in on time) can be another way students can feel successful and thereby add to their feelings of competence and self-esteem.

Clearly defined teacher expectations can serve as an important framework for student self-evaluation. For instance, if an elementary school child is supposed to keep quiet when someone else is talking and does it, he *knows* he's successful. If a high school student knows she's expected to participate in class discussion and she does it, she *knows* she tried her best. If she's supposed to have a book report in by Friday noon and she does it, she knows she successfully lived up to an expectation. In other words, the existence of teacher expectations can leave students with the feeling that a definition of their school environment *is* possible and that the world does impose restrictions and make demands that they can learn to handle on an everyday basis.

Expectations perform another important function. They not only represent a belief in a student's adequacy, but they also relay the message that he has the ability to do what is required of him. When set at reasonable levels, expectations represent the strongest vote of confidence possible.

In an effort to explain why teacher expectations work the way they do, Rosenthal[95] has proposed a "four-factor theory" of the influences that are likely to encourage students to do well when teachers encourage them to do well. As Rosenthal sees it, people who have been led to expect good things about their students, children, clients, or what-have-you appear to:

1. Create a warmer social–emotional mood around their "special students" (climate factor).
2. Give more positive feedback to those students about their performance (feedback factor).
3. Teach more material and more difficult material to their special students (input factor).
4. Give their special students more opportunities to respond to questions (output factor).

Each of these factors interact together in such a way as to create a more positive and facilitating learning environment for students for whom teachers have high, positive expectations. It is easy to see why some students may flourish and others may not. The next question is, what is it that teachers may do that communicates low expectations? Before we look at some of the ways for doing this, it may be important to underscore an insight highlighted by educational psychologists Good and Brophy,[96] namely, teachers are usually *unaware* of their behaviors that communicate high or low expectancies for their students. It is largely an unconscious process, one that can be made more conscious by being aware of what different behaviors may mean. For example, consider the following summary of teacher behaviors documented by Brophy and Good[97] that say to students, in so many words, "I don't expect much from you:"

1. Waiting less time for low achievers to answer questions.
2. Responding to lows (more so than highs) incorrect answers by giving them the answer or calling on someone else to answer the question.

3. Criticizing lows more frequently than highs.
4. Praising lows less frequently than highs.
5. Not giving feedback to public responses of the lows.
6. Paying less attention to lows.
7. Calling on lows less often.
8. Seating lows further from the teacher.
9. Demanding (expecting) less from the lows.

If you look carefully at figure 6.2, you can get a good conceptual idea of the behavioral cycle that exists between teacher input and student output. Notice the many variables that contribute to a student's total person, which in turn influence a teacher's expectations, which in turn have an impact on how a teacher behaves toward that student. You can quickly see why being a good teacher is such a demanding and complex professional activity.

Do Teacher Expectations Make That Much Difference?

Although Rosenthal's original expectancy research has been roundly criticized[98, 99, 100] for shortcomings in design and methodology, none of those criticisms denied the possibility that teacher expectation may be a crucial variable in students' learning. Since the first trickle of studies related to teacher expectations came out in the mid-sixties, a plethora of expectancy research has been done and, for that matter, is still going on. Not all research supports the expectancy phenomenon. But much of it does. For example, Rosenthal[101] reviewed 242 studies and found 84 of them reported that the experimenter's or teacher's expectations made a significant difference in how subjects performed in various situations. Eighty-four may not seem like a large number of supporting studies. However, if we apply the rules of statistical significance to the number, we could expect that only about five percent of those 242 studies (about 12) to have come out as predicted just by chance. The fact that we have 84, seven times more than chance would dictate, suggests that expectations do indeed affect performance in certain circumstances. Several large-scale reviews[102, 103, 104] of expectancy research tend to confirm this conclusion.

Do teacher expectations make a difference? On the basis of the evidence, I think they definitely do. There is no magic in this. Students will not do better or work as hard as they are able just because the teacher "expects" or "believes" that they can do good work. A teacher's expectations or beliefs in a student's adequacy probably wouldn't make a whit of difference unless those beliefs were explicitly expressed in teacher behavior that was supportive, encouraging, and functionally helpful. All in all, it appears that teachers see what they expect to see, and the pupil sees what the teacher sees.

A Note of Caution about Expectations

There is nothing mystical about how a teacher's expectations work and the influence these expectations can have on student behavior and performance. If students strive

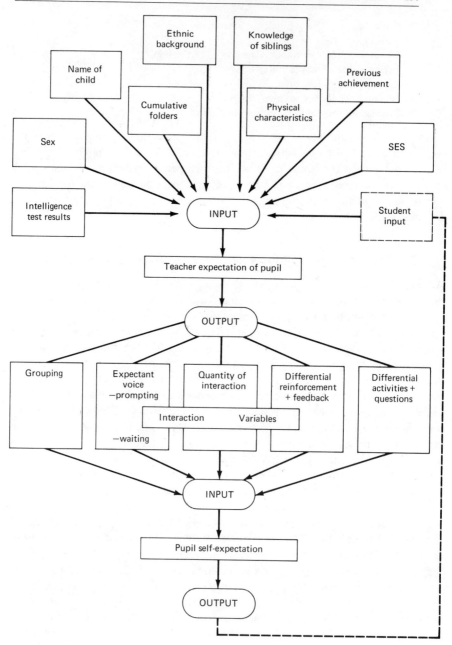

Figure 6.2

The behavioral cycle between teacher input and student output that influences teacher expectations and student achievement. (From C. Braun, "Teacher Expectation: Sociopsychological Dynamics," *Review of Educational Research*. Spring 1976, vol. 46, p. 206, by permission.)

to live up to teachers' expectations, it will not only be because the expectations are reasonable, but also because of the existence of an interpersonal relationship in which teachers are viewed as persons who are basically trustworthy, friendly, warm, and sure of themselves. (It is difficult for an uncertain person to have expectations for another person if for no other reason than that he is doubtful about what his expectations are for *himself.*)

It is entirely possible that one teacher's reasonable expectations can become another teacher's unfair demands. If a teacher is viewed as harsh, authoritarian, and competitive, it may become a matter of face-saving principle and personal strength not to do what the teacher expects. We do not easily live up to the expectations of a dictator whose primary aim is to control us or hurt us. We do, however, strive harder to cooperate with a person we see as having our best interests at heart.

There is one final note of caution. No matter how benign, trustworthy, or friendly a teacher is, that teacher's expectations will still have different effects on different students. The teacher is not the only variable; the student is also. For example, students who are adult-oriented, who have a high need for approval from adults, or who are "other-directed" will probably be more affected by teacher expectations than will students who are peer-oriented, independent, or "inner-directed." A wise teacher will take these student differences into account by encouraging adult-oriented students to be less dependent and by working a bit harder with peer-oriented students to help them see that adult values aren't so bad after all.

Self-Involvement in the Curriculum: Implications for Teaching

Nearly everything in a curriculum is charged with psychological and motivational possibilities when looked at in terms of what it might do to help students find themselves, realize their potentialities, use their resources in productive ways, and enter into relationships which have a bearing on their ideas about school and attitudes toward themselves.

Sometimes, in the quest for "the right answers," teachers fall into the trap of asking only one kind of question: the convergent kind. Of course, there can be only one kind of answer to this sort of question, and it is usually a response which sorts through, synthesizes, and integrates answers from existing data. Divergent questions, however, invite a quite different type of thinking and responding. They demand answers which are original, novel and creative. To ask a divergent question is to ask not only "What do you *know* about this?" but also "What do you *think* about this?"

Examples of both types of questions can be drawn from the classroom. If while teaching *Macbeth,* the teacher asks, "Who killed Duncan?" then clearly only convergent thinking is involved: students either know the answer (from reading the play or *Dan's Notes*) or they do not know. When the teacher asks, "Why did Macbeth kill Duncan?" the student's task is to gather appropriate data from the play and come up with a cogent answer. When the teacher asks, "What would you have done if you were Lady Macbeth?" students are invited to think divergently, to make up alternative plots for the play based on their own feelings. Finally, if the teacher asks, "Should Macbeth have gotten away with all the murders?" he is attempting to get some sort of moral judgment, which is an open invitation to all sorts of divergent, "way-out" thinking.

Convergent, memory-type questions do have a place in the classroom, but we may seriously hinder motivation and learning if we encourage only convergent thinking. To take another example from English, divergent questions and composition assignments about literature invite students to participate in the book, to become a character in it, to shape its plot to fit their own experience. The convergent question about the same book forces students to come to terms with the book as it is given, a collection of information to be analyzed in some logical way. If we remain aware of these distinctions between kinds of thinking, then we can plan more purposefully, and we can also plan to make deliberate shifts from one kind of thinking to another.

Sometimes, in a teacher's anxiety to cover a certain unit of material in a given amount of time, to give his students what he considers to be crucial information and knowledge, he ends up teaching in a non-self-related manner. Many times students dislike English, or history, or social studies, or some other subject because it seems to have no personal meaning or relevance to their own lives. Indeed, many students see little relationship between what happens in school and what goes on outside of school. Can we make school more personally meaningful? Very probably so if we exploit the psychological as well as the academic content of a curriculum. Let's take some examples.

In social studies, we could encourage more inquiries into human values, needs, aspirations, and the competitive tendencies involved in economic affairs. In civics, for example, rather than simply talk about the different forms of city government, the class could actually set them up in the classroom. Students could run for office, conduct campaigns, debate issues—in short, *live* the government, the election, the victory, and the defeat. Take history as another case in point. Wouldn't it be better to teach history in terms of people and their experiences rather than just in terms of events, institutions, and movements? We all know something about significant historical dates, but what do we know about the motivations of the men behind them? Or, as another example, isn't it possible that high school students might get more out of Shakespeare's works by reading them not only as great literary masterpieces, but as unfolding dramas of human greed, love, and hate? How many students actually "see" *Julius Caesar* as an example of what untamed, selfish ambition can do to a person? Think a moment. How many contemporary people can you think of who reflect the personal qualities which led to Caesar's downfall? Could they be used as examples in class? I know of a class of slow-learning ninth-graders who not only read *Romeo and Juliet,* but enjoyed it! A wise sensitive teacher, Leah Graham, first exposed them to something they already knew about—*West Side Story,* the book of which was based on *Romeo and Juliet.* They listened to the music in class, and since the movie was playing at a local theater, most of the students saw the film, too. True, the characters were Tony and Maria, not Romeo and Juliet; the scene was a fire escape, not a balcony; but they were in love; there were two feuding families; and it did end tragically. Thus through the simple process of exposing students to something they already knew about and liked, the teacher made the study of *Romeo and Juliet* not only possible, but of all things, fun! What could easily have been a laborious, nonmeaningful English assignment was converted into an exciting adventure as the students puzzled through the similarities and differences between the two stories. This, in the best sense of the word, is exploiting the psychological potential of a curriculum while, at the same time, enhancing its motivational possibilities.

Biographies and autobiographies offer mirrors in which students can study, among other things, their own self-reflections. Drama and fiction are filled with conflicts such as occur in our daily lives; it only remains for the teacher to point these things out, to help students see the similarities to their lives, to utilize the feelings that exist in all of us.

Physical education abounds in psychological possibilities. It can be more than basketball, swimming, and push-ups. It can be that part of a curriculum where students can learn to discover and accept their own bodies. They can be introduced to a human laboratory in which they can see acts of meanness, cruelty, and hostility on the one hand, or behavior which reflects good sportsmanship and greatness in defeat on the other. More than that, they can learn to recognize the healthy as well as the morbid features of competition. Some students may discover that winning is not so impossible after all. Others may find that to do anything well, whether in the classroom or on the game field, takes persistence, effort, hard work, and discipline. They may even discover that you don't have to win to be a winner. As Vince Lombardi used to put it: ''Winning isn't everything, but *wanting* to win is.'' Indeed, if physical education is more than basketball, swimming, push-ups, and the like, then more students may carry over into life itself the sort of constructive, positive attitude about the use and care of the body which could make possible a more healthy, vigorous, physical, as well as mental, existence.

Exploiting the psychological possibilities of a curriculum offers exciting new avenues for enhancing motivation and learning. This doesn't mean that we negate the importance of content, not at all. In fact, our concern about how to motivate students may be less of a problem if we can teach in a more self-related manner. In the final analysis, none of us is highly motivated to learn about those things which appear to be disengaged from and unconnected to our own personal lives.

Students are always motivated, but they may be motivated in different ways and toward different ends. Some students are motivated to cut up in class, skip school, and even drop out. Others are motivated to listen quietly, study diligently, and set long-term goals. This does not mean that a teacher's job is a hopeless task. Not at all. It does mean that he must be constantly aware of himself and his students as unique individuals with different ways of responding to and interpreting the world. When we consider the multiplicity of teacher, student, and self-concept variables, it is plain that there is *no one best* way of teaching any more than there is one best way of learning. Rather, there seems to be *many best* ways of both teaching and learning. It depends on the teacher, the student, and indeed, the moment. Available evidence would not support any position which suggested that successful teaching is possible only through the use of some specific methodology. A reasonable inference from existing data is that methods which are more democratic than authoritarian, which provide for adaptation to individual differences, encourage student initiative, urge individual and group participation—and stimulate "self" involvement are likely to achieve positive results in both student attitude and achievement. To encourage methods of this sort, perhaps what we need first of all are flexible, "total" teachers who are as capable of planning around people as around ideas.

In Perspective

There is substantial evidence to link both students' school behavior and achievement to their feelings about themselves. As a general statement, high self-concept students do better in school than low self-concept students, although this is not always so. The possession of a high positive self-concept does not *cause* good or high academic achievement, but it does seem to be related to it. The attitudes students have about themselves and their ability to do school work depends partly on how they were treated by people significant to them, their experiences with success and failure, and their perceptions of school and teachers.

Each student brings to school a certain attitude about his or her ability to compete and succeed, whether the school is grade school or college. A student's self-attitudes either motivate him to participate vigorously with his classmates or to sit quietly in hopes of not being called on. If the self-concept is learned as a function of experience—and evidence from all quarters suggests it is—then, whether students are aware of it or not, part of their accumulation of knowledge about themselves is acquired in the classroom. A child ridiculed at the blackboard by an insensitive teacher in front of all her peers may learn that it's better not to raise her hand, that maybe she's not as smart as the other kids. Or a shy, uncertain child appropriately praised in the presence of his classmates for doing a good job on something may learn that speaking out, that taking a risk now and then is not so dangerous after all.

Many different experiences ultimately influence how an individual feels about himself. What happens to youngsters as they go through school must certainly rank as one of the most important experiences in their lives. Depending upon what occurs in school, children and adolescents learn that they are able or unable, adequate or inadequate. The "self" is learned and what is learned can be taught. The question is not whether we approve of teaching for a positive sense of self in school settings, but whether the effects of schooling are positive or negative. For young students particularly, school is not so much a vestibule to society as we adults picture it. For them, it *is* society. As such, its effects are enormously far-reaching. How children and adolescents do is related to how they think they can do, and schools play a considerable part in shaping the direction of that attitude.

Notes

1. D. E. Hamachek, "Effects of School Failure Experiences on Self-Image Development," *Thresholds in Secondary Education.* Spring 1977.
2. D. Schreiber, "The School Dropout—A Profile," *Guidance and the School Dropout.* Washington, D.C.: National Education Association and the American Personnel and Guidance Association, 1964, pp. 1–16.
3. J. Bachman, S. Green, and I. Wirtanen, *Dropping Out—Problem or Sympton?* Youth in Transition Series, Vol. III. Ann Arbor, Mich.: Institute for Social Research, 1972, pp. 169–183.
4. S. L. Wolfbein, "Transition from School to Work: A Study of the School Leaver," *The Personnel and Guidance Journal.* October 1959: 98–105.
5. K. L. Harding, "A Comparative Study of Caucasian Male High-School Students Who Stay in School and Those Who Drop Out." Unpublished Ph.D. dissertation. Michigan State University, 1966.
6. A. M. Livingston, "Key to the Dropout Problem: The Elementary School," *Elementary School Journal.* 1959, 59: 267–270.
7. H. A. Dillon, *A Major Educational Problem.* New York: National Child Labor Committee, 1949, pp. 35–40.
8. J. Hall, *A Study of Dropouts.* Miami, Fla.: Dade County Schools, Dept. of Research and Information, 1964, p. 21.
9. E. Godfrey, *North Carolina Education.* October 1971, 2: 10–11, 29.
10. Wolfbein, p. 103.
11. S. O. Lichter, *The Drop-Outs.* New York: The Free Press, 1962.
12. E. Erikson, *Childhood and Society* (2nd ed.). New York: W. W. Norton & Company, Inc., 1963.
13. B. S. Bloom, *Stability and Change in Human Characteristics.* New York: John Wiley & Sons, Inc., 1964.
14. L. Kolberg, J. LaCrosse, and D. Ricks, "The Predictability of Adult Mental Health from Childhood Behavior," in B. B. Wolman (Ed.), *Manual of Child Psychopathology.* New York: McGraw-Hill, Inc., 1972, p. 1240.
15. E. M. Bower, "Primary Prevention of Mental and Emotional Disorders: A Frame of Reference," *The Protection and Promotion of Mental Health in the Schools.* Bethesda, Md.: U.S. Dept. of Health, Education and Welfare, 1965, p. 3.
16. P. Lecky, *Self-Consistency—A Theory of Personality.* New York: Island Press, 1945.

17. M. F. Shore, J. L. Massimo, and D. F. Ricks, "A Factor Analytic Study of Psychotherapeutic Change in Delinquent Boys," *Journal of Clinical Psychology.* 1965, 21: 208–212.

18. N. T. Feather, "Attribution of Responsibility and Valence of Success and Failure in Relation to Initial Confidence and Task Performance," *Journal of Personality and Social Psychology.* 1969, 13: 129–144.

19. P. M. Mussen, J. J. Conger, and J. Kagen, *Child Development and Personality* (4th ed.). New York: Harper & Row, Publishers, 1974, p. 511.

20. William C. Morse, "Self-Concept Data in the University School Project," *The University of Michigan School of Education Bulletin.* 1963, 34: 49–52.

21. D. E. Hamachek and J. Conley, *An Exploratory Study of Students' Perceptions of School, Teachers' Skills, Self and Student-Teacher Relations in Grades Six Through Twelve.* A paper presented at the American Educational Research Association Convention, Chicago: February 1968.

22. A. F. DeGroot and G. G. Thompson, "A Study of the Distribution of Teacher Approval and Disapproval among Sixth-Grade Pupils," *Journal of Experimental Education.* 1949, 18: 51–75.

23. R. S. Carter, "How Invalid Are Marks Assigned by Teachers?" *Journal of Educational Psychology.* 1952, 43: 218–228.

24. W. J. Meyer and G. G. Thompson, "Sex Differences in the Distribution of Teacher Approval and Disapproval among Sixth Grade Children," *Journal of Educational Psychology.* 1956, 47: 385–396.

25. R. M. Roth, "Role of Self-Concept in Achievement," *Journal of Experimental Education.* 1959, 27: 265–281.

26. W. W. Wattenberg and C. Clifford, "Relation of Self-Concepts to Beginning Achievement in Reading," *Child Development.* 1964, 35: 461–467.

27. M. W. Lamy, "Relationship of Self-Perceptions of Early Primary Children to Achievement in Reading," in I. J. Gordon (Ed.), *Human Development: Readings in Research.* Glenview, Ill.: Scott, Foresman and Company, 1965.

28. I. L. Zimmerman and G. N. Allebrand, "Personality Characteristics and Attitudes Toward Achievement of Good and Poor Readers," *Journal of Educational Research.* 1965, 59: 28–30.

29. F. B. Bodwin, "The Relationship of Immature Self-Concept and Certain Educational Disabilities." Unpublished doctoral dissertation. Michigan State University, 1957.

30. M. B. Fink, "Self-Concept as it Relates to Academic Achievement," *California Journal of Educational Research.* 1962, 13: 57–62.

31. P. B. Campbell, "Self-Concept and Academic Achievement in Middle Grade Public School Children," *Dissertation Abstracts.* 1966, 27: 1535–1536.

32. A. M. Walsh, *Self-Concepts of Bright Boys with Learning Difficulties.* New York: Teachers College Press, Columbia University, 1956.

33. R. J. Nash, "A Study of Particular Self-Perceptions as Related to High School Age Pupils in a Middle Class Community," *Dissertation Abstracts.* 1964, 14: 3837–3838.

34. E. Dyson, "A Study of Ability Grouping and Self-Concept," *Journal of Educational Research.* 1967, 60: 403–405.

35. B. Borislow, "Self-Evaluation and Academic Achievement," *Journal of Counseling Psychology.* 1962, 9: 246–254.

36. W. B. Brookover, J. M. LePere, D. E. Hamachek, S. Thomas, and E. Erickson, "Self-Concept of Ability and School Achievement, II," *Final Report of U.S. Office of Education Cooperative Research Project #1636.* Lansing: Bureau of Educational Research Services, Michigan State University, 1965.

37. W. B. Brookover, E. L. Erickson, and L. M. Joiner, "Self-Concept of Ability and School Achievement, III," *U.S. Office of Education Final Report of Cooperative Research Project #2831.* E. Lansing: Human Learning Research Institute, Michigan State University, 1967, pp. 142–143.

38. W. B. Brookover, et al., "Self-Concept of Ability and School Achievement, III," pp. 140–141.

39. M. M. Helper, "Parental Evaluation of Children and Children's Self-Evaluations," *Journal of Abnormal and Social Psychology.* 1958, 56: 190–194.

40. T. Hilliard and R. M. Roth, "Maternal Attitudes and the Non-Achievement Syndrome," *The Personnel and Guidance Journal.* 1969, 47: 424–428.

41. B. Kimball, "Case Studies in Educational Failure During Adolescence," *American Journal of Orthopsychiatry.* 1953, 23: 406–415.

42. R. M. Roth and H. Meyersburg, "The Non-Achievement Syndrome," *The Personnel and Guidance Journal.* 1963, 41: 531–538.

43. B. Bettelheim, "The Decision To Fail," *School Review.* 1961, 69: 398–412.

44. E. Bing, "The Effect of Child Rearing Practices on Development of Differential Cognitive Abilities," *Child Development.* 1963, 34: 631–648.

45. W. Katkovsky, A. Preston, and V. Crandall, "Parents' Attitudes toward Their Personal Achievements and toward the Achievement Behaviors of Their Children," *Journal of Genetic Psychology.* 1964, 104: 67–82.

46. A. T. Jersild, "Characteristics of Teachers Who Are Liked Best and 'Disliked Most'," *Journal of Experimental Education.* 1940, 9: 139–151.

47. P. Witty, "An Analysis of the Personality Traits of the Effective Teacher," *Journal of Educational Research.* 1947, 40: 662–671.

48. W. A. Bousfield, "Student's Ratings on Qualities Considered Desirable in College Professors," *School and Society.* February 24, 1940: 253–256.

49. B. R. Sherman and R. T. Blackburn, "Personal Characteristics of Teaching Effectiveness of College Faculty," *Journal of Educational Psychology.* 1975, 67: 124–131.

50. W. J. McKeachie, Yi-Guang Lin, and W. Mann, "Student Ratings of Teacher Effectiveness: Validity Studies," *American Educational Research Journal.* 1971, 8: 435–445.

51. W. J. McKeachie, and Yi-Guang Lin, "Sex Differences in Student Response to College Teachers: Teacher Warmth and Teacher Sex," *American Educational Research Journal.* 1971, 8: 221–226.

52. P. S. Sears and E. R. Hilgard, "The Effect of Classroom Conditions on Strength of Achievement Motive and Work Output of Elementary School Children," in E. Hilgard (Ed.) *Theories of Learning and Instruction,* 63rd year book of the National Society for the study of Education. Chicago,: University of Chicago Press, 1964, p. 195.

53. M. L. Cogan, "The Behavior of Teachers and the Productive Behavior of Their Pupils," *Journal of Experimental Education.* 1958, 27: 89–124.

52. P. S. Sears and E. R. Hilgard, "The Effect of Classroom Conditions on Strength of *Science Education.* 1962, 46: 473–486.

55. C. J. Wright and G. Nuthall, "Relationships between Teacher Behavior and Pupil Achievement in Three Experimental Elementary Science Lessons," *American Educational Research Journal.* 1970, 7: 471–491.

56. R. W. VanHorn, "Effects of the Use of Four Types of Teaching Models on Student Self-Concept of Academic Ability and Attitude Toward the Teacher," *American Educational Research Journal.* 1976, 13: 285–291.

57. L. M. Heil, M. Powell, and I. Feifer," Characteristics of Teacher Behavior Related to the Achievement of Different Kinds of Children in Several Elementary Grades," *U. S. Office of Education Cooperative Research Project #352.* New York: Brooklyn College, 1960.

58. W. Cunningham, "The Impact of Student-Teacher Pairings on Teacher Effectiveness," *American Educational Research Journal.* 1975, 12: 169–189.

59. D. Hunt, B. Joyce, J. Greenwood, J. Noy, R. Reid, and M. Weil, "Student Conceptual Level and Models of Teaching: Theoretical and Empirical Coordination of Two Models," *Interchange.* 1974, 5: 19–30.

60. S. Klein, "Student Influence on Teacher Behavior," *American Educational Research Journal.* 1971, 8: 403–421.

61. R. Spaulding, "Achievement, Creativity, and Self-Concept Correlates of Teacher-Pupil Transactions in Elementary Schools," *U.S. Office of Education Cooperative Research Project #1352.* Urbana, Ill.: University of Illinois, 1963.

62. D. G. Ryans, "Research on Teacher Behavior in the Context of the Teacher Characteristics Study," in B. J. Biddle and W. J. Ellena (Eds.), *Contemporary Research on Teacher Effectiveness.* New York: Holt, Rinehart and Winston, 1964, pp. 67–101.

63. A. W. Combs, *The Professional Education of Teachers.* Boston: Allyn and Bacon, Inc., 1965, pp. 70–71.

64. Ryans, p. 88.

65. Ryans, p. 84.

66. Combs, p. 55.

67. H. H. Davidson and G. Lang, "Children's Perceptions of Their Teachers' Feelings toward Them Related to Self-Perception, School Achievement and Behavior," *Journal of Experimental Education.* 1960, 29: 107–118.

68. W. J. McKeachie, "Students, Groups, and Teaching Methods," *American Psychologist.* 1958, 13: 580–584.

69. D. E. Smith, "Reading Improvement as a Function of Student Personality and Teaching Method," *Journal of Educational Psychology.* 1956, 47: 47–59.

70. L. G. Wispe, "Evaluating Section Teaching Methods in the Introductory Course," *Journal of Educational Research.* 1951, 45: 161–186.

71. J. W. Grimes and W. Allinsmith, "Compulsivity, Anxiety, and School Achievement," *Merrill-Palmer Quarterly.* 1961, 7: 247–271.

72. D. M. Della-Piana and N. L. Gage, "Pupils' Values and the Validity of the Minnesota Teacher Attitude Inventory," *Journal of Educational Psychology.* 1955, 46: 167–168.

73. M. Lazarus, "Mathophobia: Some Personal Speculations," *National Elementary Principal.* 1974, 53: 16–22.

74. L. R. Aiken, Jr., "Update on Attitudes and Other Affective Variables in Learning Mathematics," *Review of Educational Research.* 1976, 46: 293–311.

75. E. Hurlock, "An Evaluation of Certain Incentives Used in School Work," *Journal of Educational Psychology.* 1925, 16: 145–159.

76. R. E. Farson, "Praise Reappraised," *Harvard Business Review.* September–October 1963.
77. G. Farlano and H. C. Axelrod, "The Effect of Repeated Praise or Blame on the Performance of Introverts and Extroverts," *Journal of Educational Psychology.* 1937, 28: 92–100.
78. G. G. Thompson and C. W. Hunnicutt, "The Effect of Repeated Praise or Blame on the Work Achievement of Introverts and Extroverts," *Journal of Educational Psychology.* 1944, 35: 257–266.
79. P. S. Sears, "Levels of Aspiration in Academically Successful and Unsuccessful School Children," *Journal of Abnormal and Social Psychology.* 1940, 35: 498–536.
80. R. R. Sears, "Initiation of the Repression Sequence by Experienced Failure," *Journal of Experimental Psychology.* 1937, 20: 570–580.
81. J. W. Atkinson, "Motivational Determinants of Risk-Taking Behavior," *Psychological Review.* 1937, 54: 359–372.
82. R. W. Moulton, "Effects of Success and Failure on Level of Aspiration as Related to Achievement Motives," *Journal of Personality and Social Psychology.* 1965, 1: 399–406.
83. F. Riessman, "Styles of Learning," *NEA Journal.* 1960, 55: 15–17.
84. J. W. Staines, "The Self-Picture as a Factor in the Classroom," *British Journal of Educational Psychology.* 1958, 28: 97–111.
85. T. Gordon, *T.E.T.: Teacher Effectiveness Training.* New York: Wyden, 1974.
86. E. E. Page, "Teacher Comments and Student Performance," *Journal of Educational Psychology.* 1958, 46: 173–181.
87. S. Coopersmith and R. Feldman, "Fostering a Positive Self-Concept and High Self-Esteem in the Classroom," in R. H. Coop and K. White (Eds.) *Psychological Concepts in the Classroom.* New York: Harper & Row, Publishers, 1974, pp. 193–225.
88. R. Rosenthal and L. Jacobson, *Pygmalion in the Classroom.* New York: Holt, Rinehart and Winston, 1968.
89. R. Rosenthal, S. S. Baratz, and C. M. Hall, "Teacher Behavior, Teacher Expectations, and Gains in Pupil Related Creativity," *The Journal of Genetic Psychology.* 1974, 124: 115–121.
90. D. Meichenbaum, K. Bowers, and R. A. Ross, "A Behavioral Analysis of Teacher Expectancy Effect," *Journal of Personality and Social Psychology.* 1969, 13: 306–316.
91. W. B. Seaver, "Effects of Naturally Induced Teacher Expectancies," *Journal of Personality and Social Psychology.* 1973, 28: 333–342.
92. M. J. Palardy, "What Teachers Believe, What Children Achieve," *Elementary School Journal.* 1969, 69: 370–374.
93. W. Doyle, G. Hancock, and E. Kifer, "Teachers' Perceptions: Do They Make a Difference?" Paper presented at the annual meeting of the American Educational Research Association, Chicago, 1971.
94. J. E. R. Luginbuhl, "Role of Choice and Outcome on Feelings of Success and Estimates of Ability," *Journal of Personality and Social Psychology.* 1972, 22: 121–127.
95. R. Rosenthal, *On the Social Psychology of the Self-Fulfilling Prophecy: Further Evidence for Pygmalion Effects and Their Mediating Mechanisms.* New York: MSS Modular Publications, Inc. 1973.

96. T. L. Good and J. E. Brophy, *Looking in Classrooms*. New York: Harper & Row, Publishers, 1973, pp. 22–38.

97. J. E. Brophy and T. L. Good, *Teacher-Student Relationships: Causes and Consequences*. New York: Holt, Rinehart and Winston, 1974, pp. 330–333.

98. J. D. Elashoff and R. E. Snow, *A Case Study in Statistical Inference: Reconsideration of the Rosenthal-Jacobson Data on Teacher Expectancy* (Tech. Rep. No. 15). Stanford, Calif.: Stanford Center for Research and Development in Teaching, Stanford University, 1970.

99. W. J. Gephart, "Will the Real Pygmalion Please Stand Up?" *American Educational Research Journal*. 1970, 7: 473–475.

100. R. L. Thorndike, "Review of Pygmalion in the Classroom," *American Educational Research Journal*. 1968, 5: 708–711.

101. R. Rosenthal, "The Pygmalion Effect Lives," *Psychology Today*. September 1973: 59.

102. C. Braun, "Teacher Expectation: Sociopsychological Dynamics," *Review of Educational Research*. 1976, 46: 185–212.

103. J. B. Dusek, "Do Teachers Bias Children's Learning?" *Review of Educational Research*. 1975, 45: 661–684.

104. J. D. Finn, "Expectations and the Educational Environment," *Review of Educational Research*. 1972, 42: 387–410.

References of Related Interest

Bloom, B. S., *Human Characteristics and School Learning*. New York: McGraw-Hill, Inc. 1976.

Boy, A. V., and G. J. Pine, *Expanding the Self: Personal Growth for Teachers*, Dubuque, Iowa: William C. Brown Company, Publishers, 1971.

Briggs, D. C., *Your Child's Self-Esteem: The Key to Life*. Garden City, N.Y.: Doubleday & Company, 1975.

Canfield, J., and M. C. Wells, *100 Ways To Enhance Self-Concept in the Classroom: A Handbook for Parents and Teachers*. Englewood Cliffs, N.J.: Prentice-Hall, Inc., 1976.

Combs, A. W., "The Human Side of Learning," *The National Elementary Principal*. January, 1973: 38–42.

Covington, M. V., and R. G. Beery, *Self-Worth and School Learning*. New York: Holt, Rinehart and Winston, 1976.

Felker, D. W., *Building Positive Self-Concepts*. Minneapolis, Minn.: Burgess, 1974.

Ginott, H., *Teacher and Child*. New York: The Macmillan Company, 1972.

Glasser, W., *Schools without Failure*. New York: Harper & Row, Publishers, 1969.

Hamachek, Don E., (Ed.) *Human Dynamics in Psychology and Education* (3rd ed.). Boston: Allyn and Bacon, Inc., 1977, Chapters 2, 3, 4, and 6.

Insel, P. M., and L. F. Jacobson (Eds.), *What Do You Expect? An Inquiry into Self-Fulfilling Prophecies*. Menlo Park, Calif.: Cummings, 1975.

LaBenne, W. D., and B. I. Greene, *Educational Implications of Self-Concept Theory*. Pacific Palisades, Calif.: Goodyear, 1969.

Purkey, William W., *The Self and Academic Achievement*. Englewood Cliffs, N.J. Prentice-Hall, Inc., 1970.

Rogers, Carl R., *Freedom To Learn*. Columbus, Ohio: Charles E. Merrill Books, Inc., 1969.

Rosenberg, M., *Society and the Adolescent Self-Image*. Princeton, N.J.: Princeton University Press, 1965.

Silberman, C. E., *Crisis in the Classroom: The Remaking in American Education*. New York: Random House, Inc., 1970.

Wells, H., and J. T. Canfield, *About Me: A Curriculum for a Developing Self*. Chicago: Encyclopedia Britannica Education Corp., 1975.

Wells, L. E., and G. Marwell, *Self-Esteem: Its Conceptualization and Measurement*. Beverly Hills, Sage Publications, Inc., Sage Library of Social Research, Vol. 20, 1976.

Toward Developing
a Healthy Self-Image

PROLOGUE

To achieve the good life, said Socrates, there is one paramount rule: *Know thyself.* This is not an easy thing to do. Knowing oneself, deeply and fully, also means *facing* oneself, squarely and honestly. This means looking beyond and through the emotional costuming, the sham, and the pretense in order to more clearly see ourselves as we actually are and not just the image of what we want to be. It means reconciling in a realistic way the discrepancies between our hopes and our accomplishments and making our peace with the differences that may exist between our ambitions and our talents. It means accepting, in a deep and final way, a simple psychological truth: The self is not something we find, but something we create. Becoming an emotionally healthy, happy person, or a self-actualized, fully

functioning individual, or whatever you care to call your version of someone who has it all together, is not something found by accident or coded in
the genes. Rather, it is an emotional position built over time and constructed by blending reasonable, reachable goals with hard work, some sac-
rifice, and a willingness to take some risks now and then.

The voluminous literature related to the idea of the self and self-
concept leaves little doubt that mental health and personal adjustment depends deeply on each individual's basic feelings of personal adequacy. Just
as it is possible to learn a healthy orientation to objective reality so, too, is
it possible to learn to think of ourselves in healthy ways. Feelings of personal inadequacy, inferiority, and worthlessness tend to erode and weaken,
sometimes to the point of collapse, the main pillars of one's self-structure.
The growth of an adequate self-concept, free of neurotic pride and unrealistic fears is a critically important first step toward creating a healthy self-
image. In order to cope successfully with the reality of everyday living, we
must have a firm grip on our own identity. Indeed, Socrates' admonition to
"Know thyself" has been passed down through the ages as the criterion of
wisdom and peace of mind until our present day where it has emerged
from a religious-philosophical notion into a slogan for better mental health.

Attaining a healthy self-image with its concommitant feelings of adequacy, ableness, personal worth, and confidence is not some lofty goal beyond mortal reach, standing as a kind of poetic ideal. It is an attitude or
cluster of attitudes that are learned and acquired, which means that sometimes "bad" (negative, destructive, self-defeating) attitudes must be re-
placed by healthier attitudes. Most people seem to want to move forward
toward higher levels of physical and psychological health, although we
would have to admit that there are those odd personalities who seem to get
a perverse pleasure out of *un*health and suffering because it is the chief
way of knowing they're alive. Sometimes we hear people say they would
like to change their neurotic ways and have healthier attitudes about themselves and others, but then say they can't change because, after all, their
unfortunate childhood experiences made them the way they are. So busy
are they blaming the past, contriving new defenses, inventing new excuses,
and enjoying their own self-pity that they seldom have any energy left over
for considering more constructive avenues for living and looking ahead to
better days. Along these lines, Maslow has suggested that:

> From Freud we learned that the past exists *now* in the person. Now we must
> learn, from growth theory and self-actualization theory, that the future also
> *now* exists in the person in the form of ideals, hopes, goals, unrealized po-
> tentials, mission, fate, destiny, etc. One for whom no future exists is reduced
> to the concrete, to helplessness, to emptiness. For him, time must be end-
> lessly "filled." Striving, the usual organizer of most activity, when lost,
> leaves the person unorganized and unintegrated.[1]

There is little doubt but that past experiences can have a vast influence on current behavior. However, even though we cannot change what happened yesterday, we can change how we feel about it today. We cannot change past experiences, but we can change our feelings *about* those experiences, which is one step in moving toward a healthy self-image. There is another thing we can do.

Make Self–Other Understanding a Personal Goal

Sometimes it is assumed that we get to know ourselves by learning about human-kind in the abstract, that is, humans as psychological, social, biological, economic, and religious beings. Necessarily, then, the "knowledgeable person" winds up knowing about a fictional being fabricated from theories, research, and other people's experiences, not the individual who lives and breathes, nor the one to whom the personal pronouns "I" and "me" apply. Indeed, it is possible to major in psychology and to end up knowing a very great deal about psychology, but very little about one's self. For instance, a man may have no idea whatsoever that his fear, let's say, of getting too "involved" with a woman is related to a basically bad relationship with his mother, even though he may be very well versed in the field of psychology and able to discuss at length other men's problems and hangups with women. Clearly, such information is not wisdom, nor does it bring peace of mind, nor does positive mental health commence and prevail because of it. Self–other understanding appears to be specific knowledge about how one's unique individuality grows in an interpersonal social context. How can we arrive at a deeper understanding of ourselves and others as unique individuals?

A maxim of Goethe may help here. "If you want to know yourself, observe what your neighbors are doing," he said. "If you want to understand others, probe within yourself." Most of us are inclined to do exactly the opposite. We observe the other person in order to understand him, and we probe within ourselves in order to understand ourselves better. Seems obvious enough, but it doesn't often work quite that simply. Why? Normally we look at the other person objectively, but look at ourselves subjectively. We see others with the 20–20 vision of sanity and realism—no myopia here—we behold their flaws, weaknesses, self-deceptions, and even recognize their prejudices masquerading as principles.

However, when we probe within ourselves, we are not inclined to see the same personal distortions. Actually, it is difficult to see the picture when we're inside the frame. Indeed, from an inside-the-frame point of view, most of us "see" only our good intentions, our fondest dreams and hopes, our secret fears and deepest needs, and our unremitting calls for love and recognition. When we persist in distorting our self-perceptions, then of course we are in a poor position to change those things about us that may, in the interests of a healthier and more accurate self-image, need correcting. There are, however, ways to see ourselves more accurately and to know ourselves, as Goethe suggested, through "observing what our neighbors are doing." Let's turn our attention to three possible ways for doing this.

Practice Social Feeling or Empathy

Adler's[2] concept of social feeling provides us with a useful conceptual tool for developing a healthy self-image. What does social feeling mean? Basically, it is a notion which refers to a person's ability to empathize with another: to see, hear, and feel with him. The usefulness of this concept lies in the fact that it combines the idea of social, which is an objective reference to common experiences, with the idea of feeling, which is a subjective reference to private experiences. The synthesis of the objective "social" with the subjective "feeling" is one way of bridging the gap between "you" and "me."

Self–other understanding involves, strangely enough, self-transcendence, which calls for one to go beyond his own private motives and thoughts in order to better understand and share another person's needs and goals. Social feeling is an attempt to understand one's self through the understanding of others. It is becoming less involved with one's own hopes, fears, shame, and doubt in order to become more in tune to how the other person thinks and feels. Erich Fromm,[3] for example, has observed: "I discover that I am everybody, and that I discover myself in discovering my fellow man, and vice versa." Self–other understanding through the process of social feeling means to see one's self (insight) by participating and sharing mutual concerns with another, or more succinctly, being an "I" for a "thou" as Buber[4] would say.

The fact is, we have a great deal in common, you and I. When I understand myself better, either because I see myself reflected clearly in the similarities of our behavior or because your behavior is so different from mine that I am able to see my own more clearly by contrast. Personal insights via this route are a common occurrence among people in growth groups or therapy groups, which is one very important reason why a positive group experience can assist in facilitating self–other understanding. An example from one of my group sessions may help make this idea clearer:

> During a particular group session, an eighteen-year-old girl, the youngest of the nine people in the group, began to talk about her feelings toward her father. At one point she said: "I love him so much. And that's the part that hurts. I don't know whether he loves me or even really cares about me in any way. I think he loves me, but (she stopped here and cried quietly for a moment) you know, he has never said those words to me. Not ever. (And again she sobbed quietly.) I looked at the man sitting next to her, a gentleman in his mid-forties, and tears were streaming down his cheeks. He reached for her hand (the first time he had ever touched anyone in the group) and said to her in a gentle voice, "Your father could be me. My daughter could be you. I just

never realized how important it could be until this moment to actually tell my daughter how I feel about her. Thank you for helping me to understand that.'' In an eighteen-year-old girl's story, this man saw a buried part of himself clearly and for the first time. He resolved to change and to be more open with his feelings. As time went on the girl grew to understand her father better through understanding this man who was like him, and she was able to use that understanding to feel closer to her father.

Practice Honesty and Self-Disclosure

This does not mean being brutally and indiscriminately frank, but it does mean showing some of yourself to another person, exhibiting some of your own feelings and attitudes. This is not an easy thing to do. Self-disclosure and honesty requires courage. Not merely the courage to *be*, as the theologian Paul Tillich[5] eloquently described it, but the courage to *be known,* to be perceived by others as we know ourselves to be. Psychologist Sidney Jourard,[6] whose self-disclosure research opened new doors to understanding interpersonal relationships, was among the first to admit that self-disclosure could be risky business ''. . . you expose yourself not only to a lover's balm, but also to a hater's bombs! When he knows you, he knows just where to plant them for maximum effect.''

It frequently happens that honesty is a one-way street. When a person says to us, ''I want to be perfectly honest with you,'' this often means that he wants to be perfectly honest about us, rather than about himself. Honesty and self-disclosure go hand in hand. You can more easily accept in a nondefensive way my honest feedback—particularly if it is along more critical lines—if I am able to be self-disclosing about my own faults and shortcomings. Not only that, but if I am willing to disclose facets of myself to you, it is very likely that you will feel more open to revealing aspects of yourself to me. Research[7, 8, 9, 10] has rather consistently shown the validity of this phenomenon. We might add, too, that research[11] has shown that timing of one person's self-disclosure can influence how they are accepted by another person. An individual, for example, who jumps in with great self-revelations very early in a new relationship is apt to be viewed as immature, insecure, and seen as somewhat of a phony. If an individual makes a highly personal remark to us early in a conversation, we may conclude that this remark has little to do with his feelings toward us and more to do, perhaps, with his insecurities or needs for attention. On the other hand, if someone makes a personally disclosing comment after talking to us for a while, we are more likely to take the remark personally and infer that it has possible implications for a developing relationship.

A major thesis in Jourard's work was the idea that maladjusted people are individuals who have not made themselves known to other human beings and, in consequence, do not know themselves. In Jourard's words:

> When I say that self-disclosure is a means by which one achieves personality health, I mean something like the following: It is not until I am my real self and I act my real self that my real self is in a position to grow . . . People's selves stop growing when they repress them. . . . Alienation from one's real self not only arrests one's growth as a person; it tends also to make a farce out of one's relationship with people.[12]

What this means is that when we repress our inner feelings, we are not only withholding awareness of these feelings from someone else, but we are also withholding from ourselves. We might note here what students of psychosomatic medicine have known for a long time, namely, that those individuals who chronically hold their inner feelings in check are likely candidates for ulcers, asthma attacks, colitis, migraine problems, and even heart trouble.[13,14]

A positive outcome of exposing and sharing feelings is usually greater interpersonal closeness. (Which, in fact, may help explain why some people do not easily expose and share themselves at a feeling level—they are fearful of being too close to another person.) If I am self-disclosing and honest with you and about myself, this encourages you to be more self-disclosing and honest with me about yourself. If you are honest with me, I am freer to be more honest with you. And so the cycle goes. Consider an example.

Suppose a teacher has put in a relatively sleepless night and goes to class irritable, cranky, and short-tempered. (And what teacher doesn't from time to time?) She has two alternatives for handling her feelings. One, she can say nothing to the class and end up snapping at innocent students all day as if they were the cause of her sleepless night. Or, two, she could frankly admit to her irritable feelings, why they exist, and thereby give her students a chance to respond to her honesty. Once they know that her lack of patience and irritability is for a reason, then they will have less need to be defensive and irritable themselves. Furthermore, once the students learn that their teacher has *feelings,* not all of which are pleasant or good, then they are more apt to face up to and *admit feelings within themselves* which might otherwise have remained buried. If teachers are honest with their students and share with them some of their own personal inner feelings, they can be much more assured of their students giving them honest feedback about the conduct of the course, its content, and them as teachers. Carl Rogers, discussing his way of facilitating or "teaching" a class, puts it this way:

> For me, trust is *the* important ingredient which the facilitator provides. . . . He will, I hope, participate with his own feelings (owned as *his* feelings, not projected on another person). He may risk himself in expressing his problems and weaknesses. . . . The trust is something which cannot be faked. It is not a technique. . . if it is real and complete, even in a narrow area, it will have a facilitating effect upon the process of the group.[15]

In sum, honesty and self-disclosure are ways of facilitating social feeling and healthy self–other understanding because they encourage greater freedom and openness of interpersonal exchange, the medium in which self-knowledge begins.

Practice Being a "Total" Listener

Another response which may be useful in developing a healthy self–other attitude is to listen. This doesn't merely mean to wait for a person to finish talking (and to spend our listening time preparing what we are going to say), but to try to see how the world is viewed by this person and to communicate this understanding to him. The sort of "total" listening we're talking about here is the kind that responds to the person's *feelings* as well as his *words*. It implies no evaluation, no judgment, no agreement (or disagreement). It simply conveys an effort to understand what the person is feeling and trying to communicate. It is the sort of listening that psychoanalyst Theodore Reik[16] referred to as "listening with the third ear" in a now famous book of the same title. It is an effort to communicate to another person that we can accept, without judging or criticizing, that his feelings and ideas are valid for *him*, if not for us.

One reason behind being a poor listener lies in the fact that it is difficult to do. You can test this out. For example, try establishing in any group discussion the ground rule that none of the members may present their own view until they have first satisfied the one who has just spoken that they fully comprehend what this person meant to communicate. That is, they must rephrase in their own words the total meaning of the other person's message and obtain this person's agreement that this was indeed what he said. In doing this you may find out that: (1) it is extremely difficult to get agreement between what was said and what was heard ("listened" to); (2) we frequently are remiss in our good intentions to listen; (3) when we do listen carefully, we have a hard time remembering what it was that we were going to say, and when we do remember, we find it is a little off the subject; (4) much argument and irrational emotionality is absent from such a discussion because we spend less time responding to what we *thought* we heard or *wanted* to hear and more time responding to what was actually said, particularly when our misconceptions, if any, are cleared away.

Poor listeners are sometimes so preoccupied with their own sense of self-importance that they leave little room for expanding the range of their self-other knowledge. A person, whether a parent, a teacher, or a friend who talks a lot *could* have much that was meaningful to say, or he could be protecting himself from running the risk of having to change if he listened too carefully to another person's point of view.

Self-understanding is enhanced through understanding others. Understanding others is a function of one's capacity for social feeling. This capacity is both developed and encouraged by honest communication and good listening. Indeed, most of us know from personal experience that some of our most significant self–other discoveries have resulted from being in the company of persons characterized not only by their total honesty but also by their lack of preconceptions about how they expect us to behave, which has the effect of freeing us to be the person we really are.

Self–other understanding, then, can be one step toward developing a healthy and accurate self-picture. As we move toward a more positive and accurate self-picture, we are also able to move toward greater self-acceptance, an idea we turn to next.

When we don't listen carefully to what the other person is saying, we may misinterpret what he or she really means.

Self-Acceptance: Its Meaning and Expression

While no single definition of self-acceptance is likely to be accepted by all who use the term, it generally has reference to the extent to which a person's self-concept is congruent with his description of his "ideal" self. Many self-concept studies, for example, in addition to asking subjects for *self-perceptions* also ask the subjects to go through the same set of items again and indicate how he would like to be *ideally*. Since most of us would like to be "better" than we are, the *ideal* self is usually judged to be at least as good and almost always better than the perceived or "actual" self. The difference between the scores for the perceived self and ideal self is the *discrepancy* score, which is obtained by subtracting the score of the perceived real self from the score representing the perceived ideal self. The larger this discrepancy score the more dissatisfied with himself and less accepting the person is presumed to be.

McCandless reviewed twelve studies designed to investigate the psychological consequences of discrepancies between the perceived self and the ideal self and concluded with the following:

In summary, most research evidence indicates that people who are highly self-critical—that is, who show a large discrepancy between the way they actually see themselves and the way they would ideally like to be—are less well adjusted than those who are at least moderately satisfied with themselves. Evidence indicates that highly self-critical children and adults are more anxious, more insecure, and possibly more cynical and depressed than self-accepting people. They *may* be more ambitious and driving, however. At least some evidence indicates that people experience conflict about the traits on which they have the greatest self-ideal discrepancy, and that this conflict is sharp enough to interfere with learning involving such areas. . . . There is some question whether the topic of self-ideal discrepancy is really different from the topic of positive and negative self-concepts.[17]

As you can see, research suggests that self-accepting persons are likely to have smaller self-ideal discrepancies than less self-accepting persons. You might wonder at this point if it is ever appropriate to be *dissatisfied* with oneself. We might begin looking at this by considering a brief case excerpt.

In one of our early therapy sessions, a client of mine—a man in his mid-twenties—asked what I have since come to discover is a kind of universal question shared by many people who are searching for a self-concept that "fits" and best expresses the inner person they would like to be. As he expressed it:

It seems that all my life I've heard two different kinds of messages—from my parents, friends, the church, even—but the messages seem to conflict. On the one hand, I've been told that I should accept myself as I am. That's fine, I would like to do that. But on the other hand, the advice I've heard seems to be that I should be dissatisfied with myself, almost as if who I am isn't quite good enough and that I should strive to be different. Which is right?

The trouble with what surely appears to be conflicting advice to this man is not that either side of it is untrue but, rather, that each side stresses one part of the truth at the expense of the other part. Probably no reasonable person would advise that we accept the way we are if that acceptance meant persisting in self-defeating behaviors or if it appeared to be leading us to smugness and complacency. And we would probably not be advised to be satisfied with ourselves if we were behaving in a manner that short-circuited our best talents and fondest hopes.

"Becoming what you are" implies two things at once: accepting our basic strengths and limitations, while at the same time struggling to realize our outer limits and full potentialities. A creative and developing life open to new possibilities usually results in a continued "tension" between these two.

The kind of self-acceptance that is probably the healthiest is the kind that says, in so many words: "This is what I was born with, this is how I look, and this is what I have. I will change what I can, accept that which I cannot, and do what I have to do to be the best that is within me."

The kind of "self-dissatisfaction" that likely will get us the furthest is the kind that is aimed at the proper targets—not at the inner self or those parts of us we cannot change, but, rather, at those modes of thinking, feeling, and behaving that interfere with our potential to become what we could be.

Each of us stands as the final judge of what should be accepted or rejected within ourselves. No person can do this for us—unless, of course, we allow this to happen. Martin Luther King, Albert Schweitzer, and Eleanor Roosevelt, for example, probably changed some people directly by what they said or wrote, but they had a far greater impact as persons who had come to terms with themselves by accepting who they were and rejecting all that was alien to their nature.

The Differences between Direct and Indirect Self-Acceptance

The idea of self-acceptance is a complex issue because, as it turns out, there are at least two ways to go about it. It is something we all need and want, which is probably why there is more than one route to its ego-enhancing effects. The route we choose, however, can make a big difference in how we behave and feel about ourselves.

Sociologists Snell and Gail Putney have written a timely, and in many ways, disturbing book titled: *The Adjusted American*[18]. Among other things insightfully discussed is the idea that many persons are so hungry for the approval of others that they become what Riesman[19] called "other-directed." When a person lacks *self*-approval, this usually means that he has not developed a self-concept that he can believe is both accurate and workable. When this happens, people learn to seek self-acceptance indirectly, which is basically a process of substituting the good opinion of others for self-approval. In this way, people become "other-directed."

Ultimately, the search for indirect self-acceptance is self-defeating. Why? Consider it this way. If our motivation is to present ourselves to others in an appealing way primarily as a means of commandeering their acceptance and gaining their good will, then we might have to give up who we are in order to become what we think *they want us to be*. In this way, some people become quite chameleon-like in their relationships with other people. A young woman I once worked with in therapy, who had a problem along this line, expressed the idea this way:

> I am so tired of waiting to see what others want and what others are thinking and how others will behave before I can ever do anything myself. I sometimes feel like I'm carrying a portable wardrobe around with emotional changes I can hop into depending upon who my audience is. Damn, I'm so sick of it. There are times when it seems that I make so many changes in a day that I can't even recognize myself in the mirror. And the worst of it is that even when others do seem to accept me and like me, *I can't believe it.*

You may recognize the self-defeating aspects of this woman's behavior, which are vividly reflected in her comments. *We can believe what others say about us— particularly if it is positive—only when we believe that others see us for what we really are.* Ironically enough, the more successful we are in our quest for indirect self-acceptance, the more difficult it becomes to take credit for any favorable image we may reflect. Inside we know that the applause we received was simply the outcome of a clever one-person production: the role we assumed, but only acted; the lines we recited, but didn't mean; the agreements we nodded, but without conviction; the friendship we volunteered, but without commitment; the smile we flashed, but without sincerity; or the hand we offered, but without feeling. It makes no difference that some of our audience may see through the plot to the inner person we seek to conceal. What makes a difference is how we feel about our own performance. Ultimately, our own inner critic will wield far more powerful stings and arrows than all of those on the outside amassed together.

Paradoxically, other people may be quite aware and tolerant of certain characteristics which an individual has been trying to conceal. For example, a man bent on concealing from others the fact that he has little in the way of a formal education may never realize that others know he is largely self-educated, admire and respect him for it, and make allowances for whatever gaps there may be in his academic background. However, so long as he is afraid of being himself and accepting his limited academic training himself, he will never be in a position to believe that he is acceptable to others. As eloquently expressed by the Putneys:

> Inevitably, the pursuit of indirect self-acceptance produces an exaggerated concern with outward appearance. It leads a man to feign a friendliness he does not feel, rather than to develop a capacity for warmth. It leads a woman to feel that her grooming, but not her self, is acceptable. It leads to anxious conformity and a tense struggle for recognition. . . . It leads to the fake, to a mode of existence that, like a Hollywood set, is only an elaborate front with nothing but a few props to shore it up.[20]

The behavior associated with *direct* self-acceptance grows from a quite different motivational base. The intent is not to win approval "out there" through deception, but to gain acceptance "in here" through genuine give-and-take, honest self-disclosure, and sincere attempts to make what appears to others on the outside congruent with what is felt on the inside. People who seek self-acceptance directly do not seem paralyzed by a fear of failure, which, of course, has the effect of freeing them to test their upper limits, to explore untapped potentials, and to develop their capacities as much as possible. I think the Putneys were quite right when they observed that "Self-acceptance comes only to those who have the courage to investigate the areas where their self-doubts reside."[21]

In the final analysis, direct self-acceptance seems to reflect the ability to accept ourselves, within the limits we've defined, for what we are without either apology or braggadocio. I can't help but be reminded here of an anecdote I read involving the great former world's heavyweight champion, Joe Louis. On this particular occasion, he was with a small group of people waiting to be seated in a large, but crowded restaurant. The head waiter came by and said that he might be able to get them a table near the back, but away from the floorshow. One of the men in Louis' party said: "Joe, why don't you tell this guy who are?" To which Joe unabashedly replied: "If you have to tell 'em who you are, you ain't." Joe Louis was champion of the best world of all—his own. And that's what self-acceptance is all about.

Self-Acceptance and Acceptance of Others

Self-acceptance and acceptance of others seem to go hand in hand. Research[22, 23, 24, 25] has rather consistently shown that what we see in others is pretty much what we feel about ourselves. Moreover, there is evidence[26] to suggest that a high regard for oneself is reflected by healthy personal adjustment. There is good reason for this. If I think highly of myself, then I'm more likely to think highly of you. And if I think well of you, you are more apt to think well of me in return, which has the pleasing effect of reinforcing my good feelings about myself. It is a cyclical process.

Self-acceptance is the other side of self-alienation. Alienation results when we fail to acknowledge or accept aspects of the self, which are then seen as foreign or alien. People usually remain aware of their disowned capacities—they do not cease to exist—but they tend to rationalize their awareness of them by contending that they belong to someone else. When a person does this, he quite literally *projects* his alienated characteristics onto some convenient bystander, where he can view them with indignation and even contempt. For example, people who carry around a store of suppressed anger are more likely to feel hostile toward other people (whose behavior, in their eyes, represents their own suppressed feelings) than people who are more open to their anger and willing to admit that their anger does exist. Or as another example, it frequently happens that people who are most threatened by their own sexual stirrings are the first to criticize, moralize, and even feel self-righteously indignant when they perceive other persons behaving in sexual ways. On the other hand, persons who accept their *own* sexual feelings are usually more tolerant of sexual expression by others. It seems to be generally true that we tend to hate in others those things—and usually only those things—that we despise in ourselves. The man who gives the appearance of being strong and self-sufficient, all the while denying (and despising) his needs to be dependent and weak now and then, may feel a strong loathing for men who can be dependent when necessary or who allow themselves to be taken care of when they are weak. By loathing men who behave like this, he reaffirms his belief that he is above that sort of thing. The avid women's liberationist, who denies (and despises) her need to be emotionally close to a man (perhaps because of an unconscious fear of losing her identity), may look contemptuously at women who choose to be ''only housewives and mothers.'' In this way she is able to avoid confronting her own longing for closeness by concentrating her energies on what she views as other women's misguided choices.

All in all, self-acceptance, which we could say is a lack of cynicism about the self, appears to be associated with accepting other people. This indicates that self-accepting people are inclined to view the world as a generally more congenial place than the self-rejectors and are less defensive toward others and about themselves because of it. From his many years as a psychotherapist, Rogers[27] has observed that ''when the individual perceives and accepts into one consistent and integrated system all his sensory and visceral experiences, then he is necessarily more understanding of others and more accepting of others as separate individuals.''

Self-acceptance, then, is an important step in a healthy self-image. What happens, though, if one does *not* feel as adequate as others? Let's examine this question in greater detail.

The Inferiority Complex: Its Meaning and Expression

Allport[28] has defined an inferiority complex as a "strong and persistent tension arising from a somewhat morbid emotional attitude toward one's felt deficiency in his personal equipment." What this refers to is an attitude which a person may have about feeling less able than others. Closely allied to, but not to be confused with inferiority, is the feeling or conviction of inadequacy. However, where inferiority, whether conscious or unconscious, implies unfavorable comparison with others, inadequacy suggests personal inability to meet the demands of the situation.

The feeling of inferiority is no stranger to most people. For example, one study[29] found that 88 percent of a group of college students felt inferior to others in one way or another. Consider the data presented in Table 7-1.

As you can see, inferiority feelings are organized into four major categories. On the surface of it, women appear to have more inferiority feelings than do men. I think, however, that this is more an artifact of the socialization differences experienced by men and women as they grew up than it is an expression of any sort of innate differences between the two sexes. The fact is, it is still more permissible for both girls and women to openly express their inner feelings than it is for boys and men. A woman may learn to be more sensitive to her inner feelings and more open about them because she has learned that it is all right to do so. It is not surprising, then, that she may be more likely to spot qualities ("inferiorities") in herself that may be less well developed than those she may see in other people. It has not been my impression that men, as a group, have fewer feelings of inferiority or inadequacy than women, but they do seem less free to admit to those feelings and less

TABLE 7.1
College Men and Women Reporting Inferiority Feelings

Type of Inferiority Feeling	Percentage Reporting Persistent Inferiority Feelings	
	MEN	WOMEN
Physical	39	50
Social	52	57
Intellectual	29	61
Moral	16	15
None at all	12	10

able to recognize their inner feelings for what they are when they do have them. Psychiatrist Lawrence Green,[30] for example, found in his sampling of almost 1000 adult males that the majority of them choose to handle stress problems in their lives by either thinking the problem through, or trying to forget about it by having sex, drinking alcohol, or smoking. Today's equality movement notwithstanding, most men rejected emotional stress relievers, such as crying. Without access to their inner feelings, men, it seems, are more likely to let their tensions build until "the inevitable explosion" occurs. In contrast, Green found that the almost 1000 randomly selected women he sampled were availing themselves to almost every kind of coping mechanism—crying, talking it through, reading, getting professional help. Eating sweets and consuming soft drinks ranked high for the women. Unlike men, making love and drinking alcohol ranked low as coping mechanisms for them.

Inferiority feelings, then, are probably no different for men than they are for women. If anything, women, as a group, are more honest about their deficiencies because they are more able to recognize and discuss their inner feelings. Men seem to have a way to go in this regard. As a man in one of my personal growth groups expressed it:

> You know, I think I have as many feelings as anyone else—feelings about a lot of things—but, dammit, I don't seem to know what my feelings are when I do have them. My wife is so good at being able to say to me, for example, that she loves me. And I really like hearing that. But I have so much trouble just expressing a simple feeling like that. My dad always told me to "act like a man." I think I've had the funny idea that I can't be a man and have feelings at the same time. That's crazy.

Yes, it probably is a little crazy. However, until such a time when boys and men can more freely admit to their private doubts and secret fears, we will probably continue to see them display more bravado and strength than may actually be there.

We might make note of the fact that *feelings* of inferiority cannot be taken as an index of *actual* inferiority. A feeling of inferiority is a purely subjective affect related to the self, and is roughly equal to the felt difference between one's successes and failures. Objective facts seem to make little difference in determining whether a person feels inferior or not. The highest ranking student, or the best athlete, or the beauty contest winner may each suffer from a deep-seated sense of inferiority. On the other hand, the lowest student, the poorest athlete, or the plainest girl may not feel inferior at all. What we do, what we have, or how we look is far less important than how we feel about those things and what we aspire to be. For example, if a pretty girl aspires to be an excellent student, but falls short of that goal, being pretty is not likely to compensate for failing to achieve her academic goals.

Important for us to understand is the fact that a sense of *inferiority is developmental or learned, rather than organic or innate*. This means that inferiority is in no sense necessary, and with insight into causes and consequences, it can be handled, coped with, and in many instances, dispelled. Inferiority feelings are the result of too many failure experiences and frustrations; they are learned reactions that, if not corrected early, may eventually lead to the growth of deeply rooted attitudes of inferiority. Attitudes of this sort can dominate and condition a person to the point where he is left with a general feeling of not being able to do anything very well.

The next question is, how can we recognize inferiority feelings when they exist?

Symptoms of Inferiority

There are at least nine symptoms of inferiority feelings that we can be sensitive to in spotting existence in others or, for that matter, in ourselves.

1. *Sensitivity to criticism:* An inferiority-ridden person does not like his weakness pointed out to him. Criticism, as viewed by him, is further proof of his inferiority and serves only to accentuate the pain associated with it. Research[31, 32] is quite clear in showing that persons with inferiority feelings want very much to avoid the negative implications of failure.

2. *Overresponse to flattery:* Persons with inferiority feelings have a tendency to grab at straws, particularly those constructed from praise and flattery because they help them stand more secure against feelings of uncertainty and insecurity. The other response to flattery or praise, of course, is to stand in red-skinned embarrassment wondering, "How could anyone say anything good about me? Me, of all people!"

© 1965 United Feature Syndicate, Inc.

Feelings of inferiority can seriously interfere with doing things that might otherwise be challenging and fun.

3. *Hypercritical attitude:* This is a frequent defense and serves the purpose of redirecting attention away from one's own limitations. Whereas overresponse to flattery is defensive in character, hypercriticism takes the offensive and is used as a way of actively warding off the implications of inferiority. For example, if I feel inferior about the quality of something I've done in relation to what you have done and aggressively criticize your effort, you may become so busy defending what you've done that you won't notice the flaws in *my* effort. In other words, hypercriticalness creates the illusion of superiority and relies on this illusion to belie inferiority.

4. *Tendency toward blaming:* Whenever personal weaknesses and failures are projected into others, it is relatively easy to find in them the cause of one's own failures, leading directly to the response of blaming. Indeed, some persons operate a kind of psychological "pulley system" in the sense of being able to feel normal or adequate only if they are pulling other people down and themselves up in the process. Unless others are made to appear inferior, some persons cannot feel even normal.

5. *Feelings of being persecuted:* It is only a short step away from blaming others for our personal misfortune to the position that they are actively seeking our downfall. For example, if you fail me in a course and I can believe that you failed me because you don't like me or are against me, then I am spared the pain of having to consider that I alone am responsible. In this way, not only do I blame you for my failure but I assign you a motive for doing it—you're out to get me.

6. *Negative feelings about competition:* An inferiority-ridden person is as anxious to win in competition as anyone else, but far less optimistic about winning. He is inclined to react to competition as would a person who knows that he lacks the skills or knowledge for successful competition. People who feel inferior are usually among the first to complain about the breaks, their opponents' good luck, or favoritism. In some instances, the attitude toward competition is so extreme that they refuse to participate in any competitive situation and tend to shy away in a fearful and hesitant manner. I'm reminded of a sign that my high school football coach used to have tacked on the bulletin board in his office: "If you're afraid of competition, then learn to do something difficult."

7. *Tendency to be easily persuaded and influenced:* Research[33, 34] rather consistently shows that people who feel inferior and who have low self-esteem tend to be more conforming and more easily influenced than people with higher self-esteem. And why not? If I am not sure of my own opinions, then one way to reduce the ambiguity of my indecisiveness and the anxiety of my not being able to make a decision is to rely on what I should do from your point of view. Not only will you tell me what to do but I am absolved of responsibility if it is the *wrong* thing to do.

8. *A neurotic need for perfectionism:* I think the dynamics involved here are well illustrated by a student in one of my graduate classes who once asked me, "When I finish my term paper, will you like it?" On another occasion, a client, working through a marital difficulty, wondered, "What if I try my very best and the marriage still doesn't work out? How do you think you'll feel about me?"

Built into these two simple and direct questions is one of the most important inner workings of the neurotic perfectionist—the overwhelming need for approval from other persons because their own self-approval system is short-circuited by low self-esteem and commensurate feelings of inferiority.

Most of us have a certain perfectionistic strain in us, but we may not be neurotically driven. "Normal" perfectionists (whom we could just as easily refer to as skilled artists or careful workers or masters of their craft) are those who derive a very real sense of pleasure from the labors of painstaking effort and *who feel free to be less precise as the situation permits*. Psychiatrist W. H. Missildine[35] has noted that one of the most important differences between normal and neurotic perfectionists is that the striving of the first group brings them a deep sense of satisfaction. This is not, however, apt to be true for neurotic perfectionists. Here we have persons whose efforts—even their best ones—never seem quite good enough, at least in their own eyes. It always seems to people like this that they could—and should—do better. What this does, of course, is to rob them of the satisfaction that might ordinarily accompany a superior achievement or at least a well-done job. As a consequence, no effort is ever quite good enough. And this is what keeps the neurotic perfectionist neurotic—always reaching, but never attaining. It is an endless cycle of self-perpetuating and self-defeating behavior of trying, frustration, and failure because there is no conclusion to the trying because there is no such thing as perfection.

9. *Tendency toward seclusiveness, shyness, and timidity:* Inferiority feelings are usually accompanied by a certain degree of fear, particularly in situations involving other people.[36] Inferior-feeling persons prefer the cloak of anonymity, feeling that if they are neither seen nor heard their shortcomings (real or imagined) will less likely be seen. Not infrequently, students who feel less able than their peers sit near the back of the classroom because of the protection this offers. (If I'm not so easily seen, perhaps I will not so easily be called upon.)

These are not mutually exclusive symptoms; they overlap in expression and character. For example, timidity leads to avoidance of competition and also to greater sensitivity to criticism. At the same time, sensitivity to criticism can lead to blaming others or overresponding to flattery or to a neurotic need to be perfect. All of these symptoms spring from a basic sense of inferiority and any one of them can serve as the catalytic agent, triggering a chain-reaction of defensive and generally self-defeating behavior.

There is still another, albeit distorted, expression of a sense of inferiority worth our consideration.

Self-Contempt as a Substitute for Self-Worth

People on the verge of losing their feelings of personal worth sometimes feel a strong need to condemn themselves. ("I'm no good." "I can't do anything."

"Others are better than me." "Look how stupid I am," and so on.) Rollo May,[37] a practicing psychoanalyst, has noted that self-condemnation may not be so much an expression of self-punishment as it is a technique to get a quick substitute for a sense of self-worth. It is as though the person were saying to himself, "I must be important that I am so worth condemning." or "Look how good I am—I have such high ideals that I am ashamed of myself for falling so short of them." Along this line, Allport[38] has observed that "[When a person] is over-scrupulous and self-critical, he may be endeavoring to show how praiseworthy he really is."

Self-condemnation, then, may not be so much an honest statement of one's shortcomings as it is a cloak for arrogant self-deception. There are many ways in which this strategy may work. The student, for example, who does poorly on a test can always say to himself, "If I had studied more, if I had really wanted to do well on this test, I could have." Or the child who feels she is not loved by her parents can always say to herself something like, "If I were different, If I were not bad, they would love me." In the case of both the student and the child, self-condemnation is a means of avoiding a head-on confrontation with the possibility that he is not intellectually capable, in the first instance, or not loved in the other.

The dynamics of self-condemnation usually work in such a way as to protect a person from the pain of feeling worthless. For we can always say, "If it were not for such and such a defeat, or bad habit, or lack of motivation, I would be as good as anyone else." The student who says, "I could've passed that test if I had studied harder," may really be saying, "I'm really not that inadequate, and furthermore it hurts to consider the possibility that I might be." An observation by Rollo May may help us to understand better the hidden meaning behind self-condemnation:

> . . . the emphasis upon self-condemnation is like whipping a dead horse: it achieves a temporary life, but it hastens the eventual collapse of the dignity of a person. The self-condemning substitute for self-worth provides the individual with a method of avoiding an open and honest confronting of his problems of isolation and worthlessness, and makes for a pseudo-humility rather than the honest humility of one who seeks to face his situation realistically and do what he can constructively. Furthermore, the self-condemning sutstitute provides the individual with a rationalization for his self-hate, and thus reinforces the tendencies toward hating himself.[39]

Strategies for Maintaining and Enhancing a Positive Self-Image

What can one do with inferiority feelings besides feel bad? Feelings of inferiority are usually deeply rooted and not easily eradicated. Projection ("It's not really my fault I did this poorly on the exam—The teacher was unfair.") and rationalization ("I could have done better on the exam if I had really wanted to and studied harder.") are two frequently used defense mechanisms to defend against feeling inferior. There is still another, and it has a variety of forms and expressions.

Compensation as Related to Positive Self-Esteem

Several types of compensation can be distinguished. *Direct action* is one kind and occurs when a person persistently attacks the *source* of an actual inferiority and attempts to remove it. When the original weakness or shortcoming is not only removed but turned into a source of strength, we think of this as *over-compensation*. For example, Demosthenes, so the story goes, not only overcame his stammer to become a normal speaker, but a great orator. Theodore Roosevelt built up his small physique, conquered his early childhood frailty, and went on to become a daredevil Rough Rider and a rugged outdoorsman.

We speak of *substitute* compensation when a person cannot remove his handicap or shortcoming but develops other satisfactions. A Helen Keller may compensate for lack of sight and hearing through extraordinary development of tactile and intellectual ability. A physically small boy may work very hard to become a swift and elusive halfback or perhaps he excels in his studies. A somewhat plain-looking woman may seek to become an outstanding leader in social movements. The point is, in every walk of life, there are personal opportunities which do not involve setting up unreachable goals, unwisely selected activities, or the cessation of effort and hope. There are legitimate, wholesome, and necessary compensations that can add zest and meaning to any person's life.

Most of us can stand low points in any one aspect of our personal lives. A man may be wretched in his job, but still manages to get along. A woman may be unhappy in her marriage, but she is able to function in a more or less productive way. Still another person may have poor health, but he copes for years without collapsing.

The fact is, those who keep afloat despite one shortcoming or catastrophe or other are invariably those who attain some major gratification in another area of life. The man with the dull job may find his satisfactions in a good family life; the woman in the unfortunate marriage may find her entrancements doing the work she loves; the sickly person may be sustained by work or love, or both.

Our capacity to survive a crushing blow in almost any aspect of our lives is practically limitless—so long as some compensation exists elsewhere, so long as the sun can be glimpsed, if only now and then, above the cloud cover of our emotional lives.

The personal values we choose can also serve to enhance a positive self-image.

Selection of Personal Values as Related to Positive Self-Esteem

To know if someone considers himself inferior with respect to some particular quality is insufficient information to tell us what he thinks of himself. We must also have some idea of how much he *values* this quality. What is the mechanism whch determines what a person will *value* in his life? Let's see if we can understand this better.

Some years ago, Allport and Odbert[40] gathered a list of over 17,000 adjectives by which objects could be characterized. Not all of them were applicable to individuals, but an enormous number were. There is practically no end to the types of qualities people may consider important in evaluating themselves. For example, different people may consider it important to be good-looking, or nonconforming, or daring, or ruthless, or imaginative, or thoughtful, and so on and on.

Given this number of choices, which does a person choose? Why? On the whole, people are inclined to value those things they consider themselves good at and to devalue those qualities at which they consider themselves poor. As an illustration of this, the quality of "good at working with your hands" was chosen by 68 percent among those who felt they possessed this skill and by only 6 percent of those who felt they lacked this quality. Self-values, we see, tend to be selected in a way that enables an individual to maintain a congenial self-picture. Research[41] in this area indicates that we are inclined to value (prize, esteem) those qualities of personal living and aspects of life that enhance our belief systems, bolster our egos, and support the course we have chosen for our daily behavior.

As noted by one psychologist:

> If people are reasonably free to choose their own values, we are led to an interesting paradox of social life: almost everyone can consider himself superior to almost everyone else, as long as he can choose *his own* basis for judgment. Take four boys. One is a good scholar, the second a good athlete, the third very handsome, and the fourth a good musician. As long as each focuses upon the quality at which he excels, each is superior to the rest. At the same time, each person may blithely acknowledge the superiority of the others with regard to qualities to which he himself is relatively indifferent.[42]

One of the outcomes of a healthy, integrated self-concept is the evidence of a wise sense of values. When a problem arises, a careful, thoughtful person considers various possible avenues of action, considers the consequences of each, and then chooses the course most likely to lead to results which are most probable and most important. Psychologically healthy people will usually evaluate an issue in terms of degrees rather than absolutes and will recognize that some values, for them at least, are more important than others.

The way we interpret "facts" can also contribute to a positive self-concept.

Selective Interpretations of the "Facts" as Related to Positive Self-Esteem

In judging oneself, one must take account of the "facts." However, "facts" are highly susceptible to the personal meanings we assign to them. Take a stranger who, in the face of a roaring fire, rushes into a burning house and leads to safety two previously trapped people. What he has done is certainly an objective fact. But how shall we interpret it? Does it mean that he is a fearless, courageous man so unselfish as to take little note of his own welfare? Or does it mean that he is simply too stupid and blind to recognize obvious danger when it stares him in the face? The act was clear, but whether it reflects "courage" or "foolhardiness" is a matter of interpretation.

Whenever there is sufficient lack of clarity about what a "fact" or "set of facts" mean, there is always room for a person to salvage a certain amount of self-esteem. Consider, for example, the matter of grades. One study found that although most people agree that grades are a good indication of whether they are good students, they are by no means convinced that grades indicate much about whether they are "clear-thinking and clever" or "imaginative and original."[43] In fact, it was found that nearly three-fourths of the students with D and F averages considered themselves very likely or fairly likely to be imaginative and original and to have good sense and sound judgment.

This is not a denial of reality. "D" or "F" students *know* that they have poor grades. There are, however, many expressions of intelligence and there is nothing in their "objective" grades to compel them to believe that they are less "clear-thinking" or "clever" than students with higher grades.

Another factor which makes it easy (or at least easier) to interpret the "facts" to fit our personal needs and thereby maintain and enhance our self-esteem is the nature of the language used to describe personal traits. For example, if one person says we are sensitive observers about human behavior and another says we are a nosy busybody, are they really describing anything different? If someone says we are ingenious and resourceful and another observes that we are cunning and cagey, is there really any difference between the two? Indeed, both you and your critic may agree that you are "too tough and aggressive," terms he engages to condemn qualities in which you may take the utmost pride. Even though you and your critic may agree on the evidence, you do not necessarily agree on the meaning.

The point is, there is scarcely any behavior which we cannot interpret as admirable in some way. In the seclusion of our mind's eye, generally free of the intrusion of alternative interpretations, we are free to review and weigh the evidence (the "facts") as our biases dictate, to shift our personal perceptions until a congenial one emerges, and to eventually settle for one which is self-enhancing.

Most of us, for example, become quite adept at describing the "facts" surrounding our motives and behavior in such a way as to make ourselves seem virtuous and even noble. On the other hand, the "facts" associated with the behavior and motives of those with whom we take exception are painted with a verbal hue of somewhat darker color. Some examples you may recognize:

> I am frank; you are outspoken; he is rude.
>
> I have a large frame; you are heavy; she is fat.
>
> I am appropriately cautious; you are fearful; he is paranoid.
>
> I am discriminating; you are prejudiced; she is bigoted.
>
> I merely assert my point of view; you push yourself on others; he walks all over people.
>
> I change my mind because I am flexible; you change yours because you are wishy-washy; she changes hers because she has no convictions.

Well, I think you get the idea.

Just as selectivity of the "facts" influences the interpretation of the meaning of evidence pertaining to the self so, too, does it influence the *choice* of evidence. The type of evidence relevant to a given characteristic is widely varied. For example, by what criteria shall a person judge whether or not he is a sociable person—did he speak to a stranger? Has he gone to a party with friends? Is he among the first to speak in a crowd? Does he have many close friends but few casual acquaintances? Does he have one close friend but many casual acquaintances? Does he smile when passing someone on the street? He is not obliged to consider *all* these criteria: he can choose one, any one he wants, any one that *fits*. And he is right—the quality, in this instance, of being sociable is so ambiguous that there is no way to prove him wrong. By his choice of criteria, he may be a very friendly person. By your choice, he may fall short. And the same is true of the vast range of personal characteristics that reflect a person's behavior.

Selective interpretation of the "facts," then, is one way of maintaining and enhancing a positive self-image.

Selection of Personal Standards as Related to Positive Self-Esteem

It is not simply how good we *think* we are with regard to some quality, but how good we *want to be* that counts. When you think about it, we have a wide range of options in setting standards for ourselves. For example, we can aspire to the very pinnacle of achievement, to a high level of performance, to a good level of performance, to moderate accomplishment, or even to modest success. We may aspire to be the superintendent of a school system or to be a competent teacher within that system. The principle is all the more true of nonoccupational goals. Some of us may aspire to love and care for "all mankind," whereas others of us are satisfied to love and care for just a few individuals we know well. There is obviously a wide choice available in the setting of personal standards of performance in the immense sweep of areas pertaining to the self.

Given these alternatives, what personal standards do people select for themselves? We have already seen from our discussion in Chapter One that, as a general rule, people are apt to set higher standards in those areas in which they back themselves to be good, or competent, or above average. In Chapter Six we noted that persons who experienced more failures than successes were unpredictable in setting personal standards; that is, they established standards for performance which were either too high or too low. On the whole, however, research evidence suggests that most people tend to set goals that they interpret as falling within reasonable range of their potential accomplishments.

Surveys of occupational aspirations tend to confirm laboratory findings related to the selection of personal standards. For example, in a study by Rosenberg[44] of college students' values, a sample of respondents was asked: "What business or profession would you *most like* to go into?" and "What business or profession do you realistically think you are *most apt* to go into?" It was found that most students had scaled down their aspirations to correspond to what they considered within their ability to fulfill. In general, we tend to select goals (standards, levels of performance, aspirations) in accord with our assessment of our abilities. This selectivity enables us to achieve our personal goals, to consider ourselves "good enough" and to maintain a favorable self-image.

It is a sociological fact that the occupational attainments of people of working-class origins are usually lower than those raised in the middle-class environment. Does lower occupational "attainment" or "achievement" result in lower self-esteem? Not necessarily, because level of personal standards is a relative matter. For example, if a boy aspires to be a master plumber and makes it, this can be as self-enhancing for him as the boy who aspires to be a lawyer and makes it. What is important is not so much the *kind* of goal one sets, but its achievement. Accomplishment of a personal goal, whether in a physical, or intellectual, or social realm, can be a self-enhancing experience to the extent that it is personally meaningful and not too easily won.

Interpersonal Selectivity as Related to Positive Self-Esteem

One of the most consistent findings in mass communications research is that *people tend to relate to other people with whom they agree.*[45] A fundamental principle of social interaction is the idea that people, when given the choice, will tend to associate with those who think well of them and to avoid those who dislike them, thereby biasing the communications about themselves in a favorable direction.

The outstanding case in point is *friendship,* which is, perhaps, the purest example of selectively choosing one's propaganda. Characteristically, not only do we like our friend, but he likes us. Indeed, it is possible that we may like him *because* he likes us. And of course friends are inclined to say friendly things, which increases the likelihood of hearing more of what we like to hear about ourselves. Friendship is at least to some extent a "mutual admiration unit," whereby each party helps to sustain the desired self-image of the other.

Indeed, one of the most important props of romantic love is the remarkable intensity of the mutual admiration. To discover that someone considers us the most wonderful girl in the world or the most talented boy is the kind of communication we very much like to hear.

What is true for friends and lovers is equally true of groups. The persistent search for social acceptance is a major enterprise of both young and old and is apparent in our active involvement in groups that accept and approve of us, thereby enhancing our self-esteem.

It is important to note, however, that interpersonal selectivity which is too cautious, too careful, and too defensive may serve to stunt personal growth. For example, the loner who has no friends, or the suspicious soul who avoids friends who might be "too honest" about him both limit the possibility of feedback which might, in fact, spur them to greater insights into themselves and their behavior. Inasmuch as the self grows best in an interpersonal stream of reflected appraisals, the opportunity for this kind of nurturance is severely curtailed when the selectivity is too guarded. *The point is, if we interact only with those who agree with us and seldom challenge us, then we are seldom forced into the position of having to*

Being reminded of our shortcomings is not always easy to hear.

re-evaluate ourselves and our positions on different issues. Perhaps the best kind of friend is one who can, when it seems appropriate, challenge our most cherished beliefs without being threatened by the possibility of being rejected if he does.

Taking into consideration one's selective interpretation of the "facts," one's selective interpretation of personal standards, and one's selection of interpersonal relationships, Rosenberg has observed from his research that:

> The communications about ourselves are thus either biased in a generally favorable direction or are so ambiguous that our own biases are free to operate. That this is the case is suggested by the responses of our adolescent subjects to the question: "What do most people think of you?" Nearly 97 percent said that most people thought well or fairly well of them, and only 3 percent said fairly poorly or very poorly. Even two-thirds of those with low self-esteem attributed such benevolent attitudes toward others. They may, of course, be right. It is possible that a vast wave of mutual love and good will engulfs the world. One cannot, however, evade the suspicion that, with the ambiguity inherent in determining another's attitudes, a great many people are giving themselves the benefit of the doubt.[46]

Situational Selectivity as Related to Positive Self-Esteem

In a society as complex as ours, we are not always able to *create* our environment, but we are often able to *select* our environment. A primary motivation in this selectivity is an ever-present desire to maintain a congenial self-image. For the most part, we tend to expose ourselves to experiences in which we have a fair chance of success rather than those in which we may be found wanting. Occupational selectivity is a good illustration of situational selectivity. For example, research[47] shows that, given a choice, most people naturally gravitate toward occupational situations in which their skills are likely to find expression and their talents appreciated.

Situational selectivity is reflected in many areas of everyday life. For example, if we are witty rather than deep, we may be inclined to go to parties or social gatherings rather than to lectures or discussions. If we are close-minded rather than open-minded, we may prefer to press our own point of view rather than consider someone else's. If we are insecure rather than secure, we may choose friends who are more nurturant than challenging. If we are good at bowling, but poor at bridge, we will usually prefer to socialize in a bowling alley where our skill is more obvious. We tend to take courses and to elect subjects in which we are strong and avoid those in which we are weak. This is an effective way to avoid failure, to be sure, but it can also be detrimental to the development of a healthy self-concept. The psychology of success is such that it means little if the possibility of failure is virtually absent. Winning which is guaranteed or an ''A'' grade with no effort contributes little to an individual's sense of personal accomplishment and self-esteem. The willingness to gamble, to ''take a risk'' now and then can be a healthy activity for anyone. For it is in the accomplishment of those things we were not sure we could do in the first place that the foundation for a healthy, positive self-image is laid.

And so it goes—selections of standards, friends, a spouse, an occupation and so on are a pervasive and central outgrowth of our need to maintain and enhance a positive self-image. The maintenance of a positive self-image is thus a highly constant and ubiquitous aspect of determination of our longer-range goals and aspirations. There are, however, certain restrictions on selectivity which we should take into account.

Restrictions on Selectivity

The mechanism of selectivity is such that it operates to help shape our self-attitudes in accord with our desires and in line with our strengths. A reasonable question, then, is why all people do not have favorable self-attitudes. Some people have mild doubts about themselves, others more serious doubts, and still others have doubts so serious as to be convinced beyond question that they are worthless.

This does not mean that the principle of selectivity is wrong, but it does suggest that there are given conditions of human experience which are characterized by a narrow range of alternatives. It is in the interpersonal realm that the range of options is most severely limited. For example, while we are relatively free to choose who our friends will be, the same is not true of our parents, teachers, or classmates. If our parents reject us, or our teachers berate us, or our classmates laugh at us, we

Breaking out of whatever rut we're in is a good way to enhance self-esteem.

are largely deprived of our option of avoiding their company or their criticism. When looked at from the point of view of interpersonal selectivity, it is not difficult to see why it is that some children run away from home, or drop out of school, or become social isolates.

Psychological research clearly shows that the self-attitudes that are the easiest to change, modify, or form are those which are least structured.[48] And it is precisely in childhood that the self-image is most unstructured and unformed. Until children reach the age of about sixteen or so, their range of interpersonal alternatives is somewhat restricted by virtue of being the offspring of a particular set of parents. They must abide by *their* rules, listen to *their* appraisals, and relate as they can to such friends as there are in *their* neighborhood. These are their parents' choices, not theirs. Of course, with no options there can be no selectivity. Hence, with parents holding a virtual monopoly on the options, the selections parents make have a particularly powerful influence on a youngster's self-esteem. For better or for worse, a child is stuck with his parents. If they choose wise options, if they love him, then he may have a substantial foundation for thinking well of himself. If they do not make wise selections: if they, say, live in a neighborhood where there are few children for their child to play with, he may be slow in developing social con-fidence; if they indulge and overprotect him, he may grow anxious and insecure; if they disparage or reject him, he may feel insignificant and unworthy.

Rosenberg[49] has noted that the relative absence of interpersonal options for a growing child is no less serious than the restrictions on his situational selectivity. That is, a child's environment is largely fixed and there is not much he can do about it. For example, a bright child with intellectual potential, in a family which values things and not ideas, cannot choose to move into a family happy to answer her questions and encourage her curiosities. Similarly, there is no guarantee that one's personal whims and interests will meet the norms of the neighborhood peer group. If a child gains no recognition and applause for talents disdained by the group, he is powerless to select a different school or neighborhood.

Once again we can see the enormous impact that childhood experiences and parents can have on children's later feelings about themselves. Despite the generality and power of the principle of selectivity, it is easy to see why many people *do* have low or moderate self-esteem. All in all, the evidence is consistent in suggesting that people *want* to have favorable opinions of themselves and that compensation (not to mention the other defense mechanisms described and discussed in Chapter One) and the various mechanisms of psychological selectivity are some of the strategies we use, consciously and unconsciously, to maintain and enhance positive self-attitudes.

Signs of a Healthy, Positive Self-Image

Since this chapter is devoted to a discussion of ways and means for moving toward a healthy self-image, it seems altogether fitting that we end it on a positive note.

Increasing literature and research devoted to understanding the expression of self-concept in everyday behavior leave little doubt that mental health depends deeply on the quality of our feelings about ourselves. Psychologically healthy people are able to view both themselves and the world around them in essentially positive ways. A person who has a strong, self-accepting attitude presents a behavioral picture very much the opposite of one who feels inadequate and inferior. Although there are certainly variations from one individual to another and for the same individual between situations, generally speaking, psychologically healthy people can be characterized in the following ways:

1. They have certain values and principles they believe in strongly and are willing to defend them even in the face of strong group opinion; however, they feel personally secure enough to modify them if new experience and evidence suggest that they are in error. (Insecure people find it difficult to change their position for fear that it may be interpreted as weakness, or lack of ability, or incompetency. "You may be right, but I'm not wrong.")

2. They are capable of acting on their own best judgment without feeling excessively guilty or regretting their actions if others disapprove of what they're doing. When they do feel guilty, they are not overwhelmed by the guilt. These are people who can say, "I made a mistake—I'll have to improve," rather than "I made a mistake—how terrible I am."

3. They do not spend undue time worrying about what is coming tomorrow, or being upset by today's experiences, or fussing over yesterday's mistakes. I remember a

little poem which used to hang on the wall in my grandparents' living room. It goes like this:

> It's easy enough to be pleasant
> When life flows along like a song,
> But the person worthwhile
> Is the one who can smile
> When everything goes dead wrong.

4. They retain confidence in their ability to deal with problems, even in the face of failures and setbacks. They do not conclude, "Because I failed, I am a failure," but are more likely to say, "I failed; I'll have to work harder."
5. They feel equal to others *as a person*—not superior or inferior—irrespective of the differences in specific abilities, family backgrounds, or attitudes of others toward them. They are able to say, "You are more skilled than I in a specific endeavor, but I am as much a person as you," which is different from thinking, "You are more skilled than I, therefore you are a better person." They are able to see that another individual's skills or abilities neither devalue nor elevate their own status as individuals.
6. They are able to take it more or less for granted that they are persons of interest and value to others—at least to those with whom they choose to associate. Another way of saying this is that they are not paralyzed by self-consciousness when in the company of other people. They seem able to conclude, "I'm OK and you are, too."

Resisting domination is not always easy.

7. They can accept praise without the pretense of false modesty ("Well, gosh, *anyone* could have done it.") and compliments without feeling guilty ("Thanks, but I *really* don't deserve it.").

8. They are inclined to resist the efforts of others to dominate them, especially those who are their peers. The resistance, in effect, is a way of saying, "I am as good as you—therefore there is no reason why I should be dominated by you."

9. They are able to accept the idea (and admit to others) that they are capable of feeling a wide range of impulses and desires, ranging all the way from being very angry to being very loving, from being very sad to being very happy, from feeling deep resentment to feeling great acceptance. It does not follow, however, that they *act* on all their feelings and desires.

10. They are able to genuinely enjoy themselves in a wide variety of activities involving work, play, creative self-expression, companionship, or, of all things, just plain loafing. An unknown author—a very wise person, no doubt—has expressed this idea in the following manner:

A master in the art of living draws no sharp distinction between his work and his play, his labour and his leisure, his mind and his body, his education and his recreation. He hardly knows which is which. He simply pursues his vision of excellence through whatever he is doing and leaves others to determine whether he is working or playing. To himself he always seems to be doing both.

11. They are sensitive to the needs of others, to accepted social customs and particularly to the idea that they cannot, willy-nilly, go about "self-actualizing" themselves at the expense of everyone around them.

13. Samuel Johnson once observed: "It is not within our power to be fond, but it is within our power to be kind." Psychologically healthy people make good use of this "power." It seems a natural by-product of liking themselves, looking for the best in others, and feeling that this world and this life, whatever their shortcomings, are really pretty good things after all.

Perhaps we would do well to keep in mind that these are not destinations that only a fortunate few have passage to, or end states arrived at by a select number but, rather, possibilities which any person desiring to better himself can hold as goals within his reach. Usually, motivation is more effective, and happiness more attainable, if we concentrate on improvement rather than perfection.

In Perspective

Healthy people see themselves as liked, wanted, acceptable, able, and worthy. Not only do they feel that they are people of dignity and worth, but they behave as though they were. Indeed, it is in this factor of how people see themselves that we are likely to find the most outstanding differences between high and low self-image people. It is not the people who feel that they are liked and wanted and acceptable and able who fill our prisons and mental hospitals. Rather, it is those who feel deeply inadequate,

Whether we're the receivers or the givers, it may be one of the best
ways of all for developing and maintaining a healthy self-image.

unliked, unwanted, unacceptable, and unable. Research[50] is showing that
self-acceptance and personal happiness has a lot to do with accepting
others and enjoying what one is and what one has, maintaining a balance
between expectations and achievements.

Self and self-other understanding are not mystical ideals standing
someplace ''out there'' as unreachable goals. Social feeling, empathic listening, honesty, and an understanding of how we use our defense mechanisms are all ways to assist in the development of greater self-awareness
and self-understanding.

Our feelings about ourselves are *learned* responses. Sometimes bad
feelings have to be unlearned and new feelings acquired. This is not always easy, but it is possible. Sometimes this means ''taking stock'' of
oneself—a kind of personal inventory. Or it may mean baring one's self to
another person—a friend or therapist—so that the possibility for honest
evaluation and feedback is more probable. And for certain, it means changing those things which one can and accepting those which one cannot.

For most persons, a positive, healthy self-image is quite within reach
if they are willing to accept the risks and responsibilities for mature living
and if they know how to go about it.

If, as parents or as professional persons, we have a basic understanding of how a healthy self is developed and the conditions and interper-

sonal relations which nurture it, then we are in a position to move actively in the directon of *creating* those conditions and interpersonal relationships most conducive to positive mental health.

Perhaps the best place to begin is with ourselves.

Notes

1. A. H. Maslow, "Some Basic Propositions of a Growth and Self-Actualization Psychology," in A. W. Combs (Ed.), *Perceiving, Behaving, Becoming,* Association for Supervision and Curriculum Development Yearbook. Washington, D.C.: National Education Association, 1962, p. 48.
2. H. Adler, *The Individual Psychology of Alfred Adler.* New York: Basic Books, Inc., Publishers, 1956, pp. 135–136.
3. E. Fromm, *Beyond the Chains of Illusion.* New York: Pocket Books, 1962, p. 186.
4. M. Buber, *I and Thou.* New York: Charles Scribner's Sons, 1958.
5. P. Tillich, *The Courage To Be.* New Haven: Yale University Press, 1952.
6. S. M. Jourard, *The Transparent Self* (Rev.). New York: Van Nostrand Reinhold Company, 1971, p. 5.
7. S. M. Jourard, *Self-Disclosure: An Experimental Analysis of the Transparent Self.* New York: John Wiley & Sons, Inc., 1971.
8. S. L. Tubbs and J. W. Baird, *The Open Person: Self-Disclosure and Personal Growth.* Columbus, Ohio: Charles E. Merrill Publishing Co., 1976.
9. I. Altman, "Reprocity of Interpersonal Exchange," *Journal for the Theory of Social Behavior.* 1973, 3: 249–261.
10. G. Egan, *Interpersonal Living.* Monterey, Calif.: Brooks/Cole, 1976, pp. 38–63.
11. C. B. Wortman, P. Adosman, E. Herman, and R. Greenberg, "Self-Disclosure: An Attributional Perspective," *Journal of Personality and Social Psychology.* 1976, 33: 184–191.
12. S. M. Jourard, "Healthy Personality and Self-Disclosure," *Mental Hygiene.* 1963, 43: 499–507.
13. J. C. Coleman and C. L. Hammen, *Contemporary Psychology and Effective Behavior.* Glenview, Ill.: Scott, Foresman and Company, 1974, pp. 188–189.
14. G. C. Davison and J. N. Neale, *Abnormal Psychology: An Experimental Clinical Approach.* New York: John Wiley & Sons, Inc., 1974, pp. 155–172.
15. C. R. Rogers, *Freedom To Learn.* Columbus, Ohio: Charles E. Merrill Publishing Co., 1969, p. 75.
16. T. Reik, *Listening with the Third Ear.* New York: Grove Press Inc., 1948.
17. B. R. McCandless, *Children: Behavior and Development* (2nd ed.). New York: Holt, Rinehart and Winston, 1967, p. 280.
18. S. Putney and G. J. Putney, *The Adjusted American: Normal Neuroses in the Individual and Society.* New York: Harper & Row, Publishers, 1964.
19. D. Riesman, *The Lonely Crowd.* New Haven, Conn.: Yale University Press, 1950.
20. Putney and Putney, p. 74.
21. Putney and Putney, p. 71.
22. P. H. Baron, "Self-Esteem, Ingratiation, and Evaluation of Unknown Others," *Journal of Personality and Social Psychology.* 1974, 30:104–109.

23. C. W. Ellison and I. J. Firestone, "Development of Interpersonal Trust as a Function of Self-Esteem, Target Status, and Target Style," *Journal of Personality and Social Psychology*. 1974, 29: 655–663.

24. S. Morse and K. J. Gergen, "Social Comparison, Self-Consistency, and the Concept of Self," *Journal of Personality and Social Psychology*. 1970, 16: 148–156.

25. E. L. Phillips, "Attitudes toward Self and Others: A Brief Questionnaire Report," *Journal of Consulting Psychology*. 1951, 15: 79–81.

26. R. Wylie, *The Self-Concept*, Vol. I (Rev.). Lincoln, Neb.: University of Nebraska Press, 1974, pp. 126–144.

27. C. R. Rogers, *Client-Centered Therapy: Its Current Practice, Implications, and Theory*. Boston: Houghton Mifflin Company, 1951, p. 520.

28. G. W. Allport, *Patterns and Growth in Personalities*. New York: Holt, Rinehart and Winston, 1961, p. 130.

29. Allport, pp. 130–131.

30. L. W. Green, "Stress Patterns," *Family Health*. April 1977: 18–19.

31. P. Brickman, J. A. W. Linsenmeier, and A. G. McCareins, "Performance Enhancement by Relevant Success and Irrelevant Failure," *Journal of Personality and Social Psychology*. 1976, 33: 149–160.

32. M. Sigall and R. Goulel, "The Effects of Self-Esteem and Evaluator Demandingness on Effort Expenditure," *Journal of Personality and Social Psychology*. 1977, 35: 12–20.

33. C. I. Hovland and I. L. Janis (Eds.), *Personality and Persuasibility*. New Haven: Yale University Press, 1959.

34. K. J. Gergen, *The Concept of Self*. New York: Holt, Rinehart and Winston, 1971, 65–91.

35. W. H. Missildine, *Your Inner Child of the Past*. New York: Simon & Schuster, Inc., 1963.

36. J. S. Shrauger, "Self-Esteem and Reactions To Be Observed by Others," *Journal of Personality and Social Psychology*. 1972, 23: 192–200.

37. R. May, *Man's Search for Himself*. New York: W. W. Norton & Company, Inc., 1953, pp. 98–101.

38. G. W. Allport, *The Individual and His Religion*. New York: The MacMillan Company, 1950, p. 95.

39. May, p. 100.

40. G. W. Allport and H. S. Odbert, "Trait-Names: A Psycho-Lexical Study," *Psychological Monographs*. 1936, No. 211.

41. M. Rokeach, *The Nature of Human Values*. New York: The Free Press, 1973.

42. M. Rosenberg, "Psychological Selectivity in Self-Esteem Formation," in C. W. Sherif and M. Sherif, (Eds.), *Attitude, Ego-Involvement and Change*. New York: John Wiley & Sons, Inc., 1967, pp. 28–29

43. Rosenberg, pp. 26–50.

44. M. Rosenberg, *Occupations and Values*. New York: The Free Press, 1957.

45. S. L. Tubbs and S. Moss, *Human Communication* (2nd ed.). New York: Random House, Inc., 1977, pp. 369–394.

46. M. Rosenberg, "Psychological Selectivity in Self-Esteem Formation," p. 47.

47. D. E. Super, "The Present Status of Vocational Choice," in J. M. Whitely and A. Resnekoff (Eds.), *Perspectives on Vocational Development*. Washington D. C.: American Personnel and Guidance Association, 1973.

48. A. W. Combs, A. C. Richards, and F. Richards, *Perceptual Psychology*. New York: Harper & Row, Publishers, 1976, pp. 179–196.
49. M. Rosenberg, "Psychological Selectivity in Self-Esteem Formation," p. 48.
50. P. Shaver and J. Freedman, "Your Pursuit of Happiness," *Psychology Today*. August 1976: 26–32, 75.

References of Related Interest

Dyer, W. W., *Your Erroneous Zones*. Funk & Wagnalls, Inc., 1976.

Fensterheim, H., and J. Baer, *Don't Say Yes When You Want To Say NO*. New York: Dell Publishing Co., 1975.

Flach, F. F., *The Secret Strength of Depression*. New York: Bantam Books, Inc., 1975.

Ford, E. E., and R. L. Zorn, *Why Be Lonely?* Niles, Ill.: Argus Communications, 1975.

Lakein, A., *How To Get Control of Your Time and Your Life*. New York: Wyden, 1973.

James, D., and M. Jongeward, *Born To Win*. Reading, Mass.: Addison-Wesley, 1971.

Kalish, R. A., *The Psychology of Human Behavior* (4th ed.). Monterey, Calif.: Brooks/Cole, 1977.

Narcisco, J., and D. Burkett, *Declare Yourself: Discovering Me In Relationships*. Englewood Cliffs, N.J.: Prentice-Hall, Inc., 1975.

Newman, M., and B. Berkowitz, *How To Be Your Own Best Friend*. New York: Random House, Inc., 1971.

Selye, H., *Stress without Distress*. New York: Signet Books, 1975.

Smith, N. J., *When I Say No, I Feel Guilty*. New York: *The Dial Press,* 1975.

Steiner, C. M., *Scripts People Live*. New York: Grove Press, Inc., 1974.

Young, P. T., *Understanding Your Feelings and Emotions*. Englewood Cliffs, N.J.: Prentice-Hall, Inc., 1975.

Index